D1250831

4 6

JANUA LINGUARUM

STUDIA MEMORIAE
NICOLAI VAN WIJK DEDICATA

edenda curat

C. H. VAN SCHOONEVELD

Indiana University

Series Maior, 51

THE GRAMMATICAL FOUNDATIONS OF RHETORIC

Discourse Analysis

by

BENNISON GRAY

P 302
.G68

Mouton Publishers
The Hague - New York - Paris

ISBN 90-279-7915-4

© Copyright 1977
Mouton Publishers, The Hague, The Netherlands

No part of this book may be translated or reproduced in any form, by print, photoprint, microfilm, or any other means, without written permission from the publishers

Printed in the Netherlands

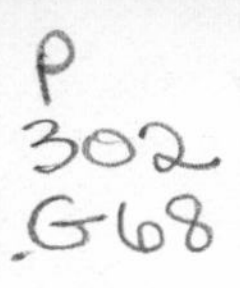
P
302
.G68

TEXAS WOMAN'S UNIVERSITY LIBRARY

CONTENTS

Introduction: Dialog and Discourse VII

Part I Semantic Grammar

1. The Sentence as Dialog 3
   A. The Nature of the Sentence – Semantic and Formal 4
   B. The Nature of Dialog – Question and Answer 12

2. The Meaning of Assertions 17
   A. Describe Subject by Function 29
      (1) Agent by Function 34
      (2) Object by Function 44
   B. Describe Subject by Nature 50
      (1) Subject by Characteristic 51
      (2) Subject by Identity 69
   C. Describe Subject by Class 77
      (1) Individual by Class 81
      (2) Subclass by Class 86

3. The Structure of Assertions 92
   A. Independent 94
   B. Parallel 99
   C. Modificational 109

4. The Uses of Modification 122
   A. Non-restrictive 122
      (1) Additive 123
      (2) Redundant 135
   B. Restrictive 138
      (1) Limiting 138
      (2) Conditional 155
      (3) Inclusive/Exclusive 159

74-90521

2-05403

5. The Problem of Implication 168
A. Necessarily Implied 169
B. Not Necessarily Implied 178

6. Inter-assertional Relations 190
A. Descriptive – Continue and Contrast 193
B. Explanatory – Conclude and Support 201
C. Rhetorical – Question and Answer 205

Part II Generative Rhetoric

7. Generating a Composition 213

8. Integrating a Composition 230

9. The Framework of Dialog 287
A. The Subdivisions of a Composition 290
B. A Composition as a Subdivision 298

10. Dialog as a Tool of Analysis 312

Appendix

A. Inflection 345
B. Key to the Diagraming Symbols 347

Bibliography 349

Index 355

INTRODUCTION: DIALOG AND DISCOURSE

The distinction between dialog and discourse – or dialog and monolog – is, on the surface, one of the most obvious that can be made in the study of language. And, hardly less obvious, is the equating of dialog with speaking and discourse with writing. To be sure, some speaking is monolog rather than dialog (for example, an oration), and some writing is in dialog form (for example, a Platonic dialog). But on the whole, speaking occurs naturally as dialog, and writing occurs naturally as discourse.

Another traditionally obvious distinction has been between grammar and rhetoric. Grammar is the analysis of the elements of language, the study that seeks to break down language into its ultimate units. Its data is not extended discourse, indeed, usually not even extended sentences, but the combinations of elements that are found within sentences. Rhetoric, on the other hand, has been the study of extended discourse, and not so much the breaking down of extended discourse as the building up. But like grammar, rhetoric has tended to take for granted the sentence, although it has looked for its data in more extended, complex discourse rather than within sentences.

Attempts to correlate grammar and rhetoric can be found scattered through the history of linguistic pedagogy right up to the present. Despite their superficial variety, such attempts have proceeded on only two alternatives. The first alternative is to derive a grammar of inter-sentence relations directly from one's grammar of intra-sentence constituents, to reduce rhetoric to grammar. "The second alternative involves," to quote Nils Erik Enkvist's recent programmatic statement,

> building a special discourse grammar which explicitly describes or generates units beyond the sentence – say, paragraphs consisting of many sentences. The latter solution is, of course, enormously ambitious. It at once begs the question whether generating units larger than one sentence is the business of grammar proper or of some other area of linguistics such as semantics or a new linguistic logic or rhetoric. The latter might be free to use types of rules different from those of grammar . . . [1]

Neither alternative has come close to success, but certainly there is already a separate area of "discourse grammar": rhetoric. Rhetoric has always attempted to be generative, to discern patterns from which extended discourse could be created. Thus rhetoric has always been concerned with "units beyond the sentence". The ambitiousness of the enterprise derives not, however, from the question of what discipline would have its jurisdiction but from the more basic one of what exactly would be generated.

Perhaps a clearer notion of what is to be generated would indicate that the difference between the two alternatives has been overdrawn. The need is not a *choice* between the two but a *rapprochement* between them. Indeed, the desire for rapprochement is strong, especially among those who carry the burden of teaching linguistic proficiency. But the promise of generativeness being the common factor of grammar and rhetoric has not yet been fulfilled, because the indispensable notion of the sentence is still as undefined as it was when the first textbook of Greek grammar was completed.

The thesis of the present work is that there is indeed a common factor in speaking and writing, and in breaking down language and in building it up – a factor that can bring about a rapprochement between grammar and rhetoric and facilitate the teaching and acquiring of linguistic proficiency. This key factor is the notion of dialog, and what it unlocks is the problem of the sentence. Instead of side-stepping the defining of the sentence, we go at once to the heart of the matter. Whatever the various kinds of discourse and whatever the variety of audiences, the sentence is fundamental. Once the sentence is understood – understood in terms of assertions linked together in an implied dialog – then further refinements can follow as a matter of course.

If it can be said that the primary goal of modern linguistic study has been to discover or establish the *smallest* linguistic unit, then it can be said that the primary goal of this study is the *largest* such unit. There is, of course, no limit on the size and complexity of linguistic constructs, but what we need to know is the largest *unit* that is a basic constituent of all such constructs – large or small, oral or written. This largest unit is the question and answer pair of dialog.

The questions in an implied dialog are not, however, 'transformations' of the sentences, nor do they in any way modify the nature of the sentences that provide the answers. Sentences as they actually appear rather than as they are assumed to be in the realm of 'deep structure' must be the primary concern of linguistic analysis. A grammar that is forced to resort to wholesale 'transformations' admits its inability to analyze the data *qua* data. There is nothing new in the grammarian's temptation to rewrite his data to make it easier to explain, and there will never be a complete grammar that can avoid one degree or another of transforming in order to account for some kinds of forms. But the goal of discerning the grammar of a natural language can not be achieved by transforming this nature into something else. In this respect, at least, the model of a logical calculus is more hindrance than help to the grammarian.

Yet, while the true *grammatical goal* is to avoid as much as possible the need to resort to transformations, the true *rhetorical goal* is actual (and not merely metaphorical mathematical) generativeness. A rhetoric that really functions as the principles of composition must provide nothing less than a usable means of actually *creating* new assertions to follow reasonably upon previous assertions. For rhetoric, such a designation is more true than metaphorical. But the model of biological generation, of like springing from like, is neither true nor appropriately metaphorical for grammar. Grammar can be generative in only a very limited sense because the units that go to make up assertions are not themselves assertions. But rhetoric, with the common unit of the assertion, can hope to develop principles for creating and joining assertions to form extended discourse because succeeding assertions in a very important sense grow out of previous assertions. Assertions and sentences cannot be adequately explained as the linking of individual words or morphemes; the principles of grammar are much more complex. However, extended discourse can be adequately (if not completely) explained as the linking of individual assertions.

To what extent the present study is properly within the field of linguistics is difficult to say. If, as Göran Hammarström emphasizes, "units and relations between units are the basic linguistic facts to be described",[2] then discourse analysis is squarely in linguistics as long as it is able to focus consistently on objectively delimitable units. Of course linguists can then differ among themselves as to what constitute the most important units and what are the kinds of relationships possible between them. But they cannot legitimately lay down in advance what kind of units or relationships these must be in order to qualify as linguistic. What is linguistically new in the present study is the consistent use of assertions as the basic units and a thoroughgoing examination of the kinds of inter-assertional relations. This is a larger unit than heretofore employed for any consistent linguistic analysis, but its use allows us to see various relations heretofore ignored in other kinds of linguistic studies. Obviously, an assertional – or discourse – grammar cannot pass for a complete linguistic theory, because there are various sub-assertional units and relations that cannot be accounted for in assertional terms. But just as obvious is the fact that no past or present candidates for a complete linguistic theory are able to account for the inter-assertional features of language.

One of the rare attempts to extend linguistic analysis to discourse is William Labov's claim to have discovered "Some Invariant Rules of Discourse Analysis".[3] However, his failure to formulate any precise conception of a basic unit of discourse (such as the assertion) and his dedication to transformational, rule-oriented theory render his brief attempt not only a failure but also well-nigh incomprehensible. This failure is accounted for in two ways: Labov eschews transformational orthodoxy when he should take advantage of it, and he adheres to transformational orthodoxy when it would be to his advantage to deviate from it.

The advantage of transformational grammar that Labov does not make use of in his discourse analysis but that the present study relies on completely is "well-formed" data. The place to begin, at least, is not with irregular, fragmentary, inconsistent speech collected on the street corner but with language in its most regularized, complete, consistent form – that is, with the written prose of skillful writers when they have something precise to communicate. Not until discourse analysis has proven itself capable of handling such data can it aspire to the infinitely more difficult task of handling spontaneous speech. The disadvantage of transformational grammar that Labov does make use of is the concept of "rule". As is often the case, Labov is admirably lucid in stating the problem: "The fundamental problem of discourse analysis is to show how one utterance follows another in a rational, rule-governed manner – in other words, how we understand coherent discourse" (p. 252). Unfortunately, the seed of incomprehensible jargon and distorted interpretations is already present in this lucid summary. "Rule-governed" could mean simply that a number of patterns or types of relationships can be abstracted from coherent discourse and are useful in explicating and criticizing what is said. But, as Labov uses it, this is a technical transformational-generative term for invariant, quasi-mathematical relationships that can be reduced to formulas. If this is what linguistic analysis must be, then there is no difficulty in understanding why most linguists assiduously avoid discourse analysis. It would multiply beyond even their comprehension the complexities of the already complex 'rules' that transformational grammar has deduced for the smallest segments of language.

The dilemma of all language study is where and for what reasons to draw the line against seemingly insignificant variation. A Bloomfieldian empiricist tolerates a great deal of (but by no means all) such variation. A Chomskyan rationalist tolerates very little of it (but some, nonetheless). Labov attempts to combine the two – to find in the actual details of largely unretouched data the neat rules of a self-contained system. Yet different as these three kinds of linguist may appear, they have a common goal – to gain knowledge.

The primary goal of a pedagogical grammar, however, is not knowledge but skill. A pedagogical grammar is not a 'scientific' grammar watered-down for classroom use; rather it is a grammar that reflects a fundamentally pedagogical conception of language study. It does not pretend that linguistic communication – conscious and deliberate and subject to frequent criticism as it is – can be treated as raw data. If there is anything in this world that is unequivocally normative, it is language. The study of language cannot legitimately ignore the fact that its data is always – for better or worse – the product of conscious and deliberate prescription. Skill in the use of language is a major goal of every society. Skill is of course impossible without a certain amount of knowledge, and skill is a notion that different individuals and different communities can disagree about. But just as a lawyer who cannot win cases cannot claim to really understand his subject, so a grammarian who cannot increase the linguistic proficiency of students cannot claim to really understand his subject. Because a certain amount of abstract knowledge is quite possible in the absence of skill, the test of any theory of linguistic analysis must include pedagogical success. Language is nothing if not use: if theoretical distinctions are not easily correlated with the agreed-upon interpretations of actual communication, then there is no proof of their *linguistic* validity.

However, those who think of linguistic pedagogy primarily in terms of introducing the rudiments of a second language and in terms of comparative phonological analysis find much less difficulty with the model of the human brain as a computer than do those who think of linguistic pedagogy primarily in terms of refining the advanced skills of precise articulation. Yet it makes no sense to think that the second is any the less linguistic than the first. The term "rhetoric" for this emphasis on advanced linguistic proficiency is hardly necessary, but some distinguishing term is needed in the face of recent success by linguists in appropriating such traditional terms as "grammar", "syntax", "linguistic" for exclusive use in designating formal, or would-be formal, conceptions. "Rhetoric" by no means implies a rejection of formal linguistic principles, but it does clearly imply a concern with semantic principles as well.[4]

Indeed, though not the primary goal of the present work, one of its secondary purposes is to explore the significant area of discontinuity between the formal features of language and the semantic interpretations that can vary from one syntactic context to another. This is not to deny the significant area of conformity, but simply to point out the futility of that academic endeavor that claims to be free of 'unscientific' semantic interpretations.

The linguistic point at which the semantic and the formal are most nearly coextensive lies on the border between the traditional areas of grammar and rhetoric: the independent assertion. The unfortunate result of reducing rhetoric to grammar has been the failure to develop a consistent system of linguistic analysis applicable to extended discourse. In one sense there is nothing new in taking the assertion/sentence as the fundamental linguistic concern, yet it is also reasonable to claim that what has never been precisely delimited has never been clearly understood. The current intellectual fashion espousing intuition as the foundation of knowledge (following Husserl's phenomenology) is no substitute for definition and classification. The justification for developing a generative rhetoric is to bring clearly into focus the assertion – its primary components and the characteristic ways that multiple assertions combine to form extended discourse. To publish the bans for a marriage between grammar and rhetoric is not, however, to acquiesce in the easy characterizing of grammar as formal and rhetoric as semantic. If grammar and rhetoric are to be treated as one flesh, then grammar will have to be *both* formal and semantic.

The great need is to bring to the teaching of rhetoric the rigor of grammatical analysis. To meet this need, generative rhetoric must avoid on the one hand the vacuous generalities about different kinds of discourse and varieties of style that have characterized so much rhetorical teaching and on the other hand the atomistic reductionism that has prevented grammatical study from ever coming to practical grips with extended discourse. Generative rhetoric is not primarily concerned with different kinds of discourse and different kinds of meaning but with what all extended discourse has semantically in common. We will obviously not be content with a conception of meaning as simply the other side of the formal coin; yet we will be too prosaic to equate linguistic or assertional meaning with all the implications that can be drawn from a discourse. Semantics is not hermeneutics.

Thus at the foundation of our generative rhetoric is what can only be termed a "semantic grammar". It is semantic because it seeks to establish the most adequate interpretation of assertions as they can or do follow one upon the other in extended discourse; it is a grammar because these interpretations are based on systematic distinctions manifested within each individual assertion. What precisely these systematic distinctions are is partly a matter of necessary agreement among the various grammatical theories that have flourished over the millenia, but partly it is still a matter of legitimate debate. For example, this semantic grammar, like transformational-generative grammar, is a return to the traditional subject-predicate conception, which has been in eclipse during the first half of this century as a result of the rebellion against the unrealistic dictates of proponents of Aristotelian logic and Latin grammar. But unlike Chomsky and his followers, we view this bipartite distinction not as primary but as merely preparatory to the more crucial distinction of subject and attribute, which is not necessarily bipartite. The importance of assertion modifiers, which include among other things traditional 'direct objects', is thereby emphasized. And, correspondingly, the grab-bag concept or category of 'adverb' is much reduced and the precision of semantic distinctions thereby enhanced. As part of this de-emphasis of the subject-predicate distinction, semantic grammar de-emphasizes 'immediate constituent' analysis. Instead of a 'cutting away' or 'peeling off' of modifiers, with little regard for their semantic relationship to the core assertion, we give primacy to distinctions of kind (restrictive and non-restrictive) and function (sub-assertional and assertional) and treat different modifiers differently.

Because the field of grammar is still as much a matter of arguments about adequacy as it is a matter of evidence for truth, there is much to be said for eschewing the handbook or encyclopedic approach to organization. To the extent that the 'facts' (a much over-used term in recent work) in this field are still in important respects matters of hypotheses and selective emphases for different purposes, one presents a grammar most responsibly by arguing for it step-by-step – presenting it discursively as well as schematically. At this stage in the development of 'modern grammar' the grammarian cannot avoid presenting his case. He can only choose to do it overtly (and attempt to be as readable as possible so as to facilitate legitimate disagreement) or to do it covertly (and attempt to obscure the hypothetical nature of his position by means of jargon and arbitrary symbols). No system of linguistic analysis will become established that is not comprehensible to those whose task it is to teach it, at the elementary as well as the advanced levels.

To minimize as much as possible, however, the factionalism that has always been a feature of language study, whether as philology or linguistics, we will reserve our analysis of Chomsky's theory for another volume. Fortunately for the field, the common subject matter guarantees a significant core of agreement, whether the latest 'discovery' is Jespersen, or Sanctius, or Dionysius Thrax. It is both disconcerting and reassuring to recognize the great amount of repetition from one generation of linguists to the next. The grammar of a language is not an arbitrary collection of information about miscellaneous patterns of usage. Behind all the various grammar books for a given language is a discernible, systematic phenomenon.

Every language is *systematic*, but none constitutes *a system* – a consistent, coherent, and unchanging body of rules for making or recognizing utterances. Despite their familiarity with the fact that all languages are in a constant state of change, linguists have tended to think that it must be possible to isolate at a given moment in space and time *the* system of rules that is responsible for a given language. Yet even at a given moment in space and time a language consists of a cross-hatching of two principal systems as well as of dozens of minor, only partially realized, patterns.

Languages are commonly divided into two grammatical types: (1) the inflectional, or synthetic – which makes basic distinctions by incorporating information into root words – and (2) the positional, or analytic – which makes basic distinctions by arranging separate words in different sequences. This division does not mean that there is or can be a language that is entirely one or the other. As contemporary linguistics has emphasized, English, unlike

Latin – which was traditionally used as the model for constructing English grammars – has a predominantly positional grammar. So fragmentary and inconsistent have English inflections become, study of them is more a matter of lexicology than of grammar. Nevertheless, it is important to remember that English does have inflectional features, and while these are not numerous as to kind, they are as to occurrence and play a role in practically every utterance. A person could never use English idiomatically without an extensive familiarity with its patterns (and pitfalls) of inflection. But while familiarity is essential, rules are practically worthless – so extensive are the exceptions. Separate words and varying word order is in English the basic means for making distinctions.[5]

Just the opposite point can be made in regard to a predominantly inflectional language such as Classical Latin or Old English. Though here the chief means of showing what words went together was by matching their forms, word order also played a role in practically every utterance, even if the distinctions it made were not numerous and thus were more or less taken for granted.

Whether a language is predominantly inflectional or positional clearly makes a difference in how best to lay out its grammar graphically. But no such *systematic presentation* can in any case give a *complete account* of any language because to make explicit the one system is necessarily to distort and reduce the other. An inflectional system must be presented paradigmatically, as in the conjugations and declensions of Latin; a positional system must be presented diagrammatically, as in many contemporary analyses of English and in the semantic grammar of English that follows here.[6] What shows up clearly in a paradigm is lost in a diagram and vice versa. A grammar, like the transformational-generative kind, that tries to incorporate the two systems succeeds in elucidating neither.

Making a grammar is like making a map. The first thing the cartographer has to do in making a map is to be clear on the kind of task he wishes to perform. Then he must determine what kind of projection best fulfills this task. One projection will give a highly accurate and useful map of area but vastly distort proportion. In order to make an accurate projection of proportion on a particular map the cartographer will have to sacrifice the accuracy of area representation. The distortion of proportion and area simply cannot be overcome together through any single projection. Yet cartography is not any less a responsible, systematic, and valuable endeavor for all that it is unable to provide principles for producing one perfect, all-purpose map. Like a map, a grammar is an abstraction. This does not mean it abstracts form from meaning for the general purpose of study, for this makes no sense and cannot really be done. What grammar does do is abstract certain matters of the relationship between form and meaning in a particular language for some particular purpose, the formulation of which will then be the fullest and most systematic formulation of those patterns for that purpose. In the formulation of a grammar, complete explicitness would be neither useful nor possible, any more than it would be in the formulation of a particular instance of language.

Once we have understood just what grammar can not do, we are in a better position to appreciate the importance of what it can do. The capacity of a semantic grammar to identify – and clarify the relationships among – all the assertions of any piece of continuous discourse is surely as significant as and must be more useful than pursuing the will o' the wisp of completeness, of 'things as they really are'. If a semantic grammar is not an all-encompassing system, it nevertheless is and must be systematic. The system-making excesses of contemporary linguistics have been salutary insofar as they have focussed attention on the need for introducing order into the interminable enumerations of data that characterized the work of their predecessors. Though a grammar cannot be a system, it cannot be a grammar unless it is systematic.

Because the pie of language can be cut in many different ways but in only one way at a time, whenever we find ourselves confronted by an incongruity between form and meaning, we will maintain our consistency by emphasizing the meaning and minimizing the form. This emphasis is not, however, a panacea; the analysis of meaning always involves varying degrees of disagreement. And arguments about meaning cannot fail to be manifested in arguments about grammar. This is especially conspicuous in attempting to decide what do and do not constitute the individual assertions, between which are to be found the inter-assertional questions. The distinction between stated and implied assertions is crucial, but it is not thereby always an easy one to make. (Certainly it is more crucial and more difficult than the superficial notion of 'deep structure' can account for.) The traditional grammatical distinction between restrictive and non-restrictive modification is a place to begin; but traditional grammar has had nothing *per se* to offer about implication, which at best has been the province of traditional rhetoric and thus tied to distinctions of different kinds of discourse, style, audience, occasion.

Another conspicuous problem in the relationship of meaning and grammar is the preliminary question of what, if any, are the basic cognitive categories that correlate with ordinary usage. But strange as it may seem, such a question has hardly even been broached yet. This is freely admitted by transformationalists (e. g. Chomsky), anti-transformationalists (e. g. Sigurd and Derwing), and neo-transformationalists (e. g. Labov) alike:

> We are still at a rudimentary stage in our understanding of the syntactic component, and we have practically no understanding of the semantic component.[7]

How do we determine what the semantic relationships 'in a language' really are? In more general terms, Sigurd asks: "Which units should be grouped as variants of one invariant? How great a formal and semantic variation should we allow? Should passive be grouped with active in spite of formal and semantic . . . differences? Should *the green book* be grouped with *the book that is green*? Should *That he came was nice* be grouped with *It was nice that he came*? Should *Eliot refused the offer* be grouped with *Eliot's refusal of the offer*?" (1970, p. 17). These questions are fundamental, and we need answers to them *before* such issues as the evaluation of alternative linguistic descriptions can be taken seriously.[8]

Our knowledge of the cognitive correlates of grammatical differences is certainly in its infancy . . . . At the moment we do not know how to construct any kind of experiment which would lead to an answer; we do not even know what type of cognitive correlate we would be looking for.[9]

In the last quotation Labov is pointing out the futility of trying to test the logical grammatical proficiency of children when we do not even know what the children should be expected to know. To refer to the present work as an "experiment" constructed to discover the answer would smack of the scientistic. It is by no means clear that such problems are really amenable to experimentation. But certainly the hypothetical possibilities need to be consistently outlined and exemplified in detail. *The Grammatical Foundations of Rhetoric* is thus a determined effort to outline and exemplify a set of basic cognitive categories that do in fact correlate with English grammar as it is actually employed in the making of precise intellectual distinctions in sustained discourse.

Yet, a word of caution is needed here. The general semantic categories employed in this book are offered as useful devices for interpreting the meaning of various sorts of utterances. They are not offered as a significant new discovery but simply as a refinement of very old and widely used concepts whose usefulness has been proven by time. Whether we are translating from language to language or composing in one language, we must come to terms both with specific meaning and with general kinds of meaning. What, as a bare minimum, are these general kinds of meaning? One answer is the distinction between fact and fiction.[10] Another answer is the distinction between question and answer. Another is the six semantic kinds of assertions outlined in Chapter 2. Another is the four kinds of inter-assertional relations outlined in Chapter 6. These will certainly not solve all the problems of translation and composition, but they will certainly prove more useful than the futile search for a non-existent mathematical deep structure.

What claim to originality the present work may have is in minimizing the traditional distinction between grammar and rhetoric without thereby reducing rhetoric to grammar. Rather, it cuts off at one end the study of atomistic units such as phonemes and morphemes, and at the other end it cuts off the study of different kinds of discourse. What is left, however, is the very large and fundamental area of different kinds, structures, and relationships of assertions. The scope of the present work thus extends from restrictive and non-restrictive modifiers within sentences to complete compositions that function as rejoinders to other complete compositions. But at every level, from the modifier on up, it is possible to discern – either explicitly or implicitly – the eliciting and answering of questions.

By keeping to this middle ground, we may of course simply fail to gain the goals at either end. It goes without saying that a middle-of-the-road position will not, on the one hand, solve the mind-body problem for philosophy or lay the foundation of a formal science of language; nor will it, on the other hand, reveal the mysteries of effective communication. We can hope, however, to lift the teaching of linguistic proficiency out of the realm of fads and intuition, where it continues to be as deeply entrenched in the post-Chomsky era as it was in the pre-Chomsky era.

NOTES

1 "On the Place of Style in Some Linguistic Theories", in *Literary Style: A Symposium*, ed. Seymour Chatman (London and New York, 1971), p. 58.
2 *Linguistic Units and Items* (Berlin, 1976), p. v.
3 In his *Sociolinguistic Patterns* (Philadelphia, 1972), pp. 252-58.
4 For a detailed analysis of the basic inadequacy of transformational-generative grammar in particular and formal grammar in general see my *The Limits of Grammar: A Primer for Linguists* (forthcoming).
5 The problems and patterns of inflection in English are treated in detail in my *Introduction to Semantic Grammar* (forthcoming), a textbook that attempts to bridge the gap between traditional, Latinate grammar and assertional or rhetorical grammar.
6 The diagraming system employed in this book resembles in some superficial respects the much maligned and contemptuously dismissed Reed-Kellogg system. Without wishing to defend the details of that system, we predict that with greater historical perspective, linguists will come to see in the development and pedagogical implementation of that first thoroughgoing diagrammatic grammar one of the major achievements of modern linguistics. For a relatively unbiased discussion of the Reed-Kellogg system and its fate at the hands of contemporary linguists see H. A. Gleason, Jr. , *Linguistics and English Grammar* (New York, 1965), pp. 142-51.
7 Noam Chomsky in his interview with Ved Mehta, originally published in the *New Yorker* and collected with other interviews as *John is Easy to Please* (Penguin, 1974), p. 164.
8 Bruce L. Derwing, *Transformational Grammar as a Theory of Language Acquisition* (Cambridge, 1973), p. 167.
9 William Labov, "The Logic of Nonstandard English", *Report of the Twentieth Annual Round Table Meeting on Linguistics and Language Studies*, ed. James E. Alatis (Georgetown University, Washington, D. C. , 1970), p. 24.
10 For this distinction, which is not treated in the present work, see my *The Phenomenon of Literature* (The Hague, 1975), esp. Chaps. II and III.

PART I

SEMANTIC GRAMMAR

1. THE SENTENCE AS DIALOG

From time to time the special skill that written composition requires – the ability to convey meaning without the aid of responsive listeners – strikes some people as constituting an excessive demand and limitation upon their desire to communicate. At such a time, consequently, writing comes under attack as being too impersonal and rational; the hope is expressed, even the prediction made, that the future will see the supplanting of written discourse by more intimate verbal and non-verbal forms of communication. This age of attempted universal literacy is just such a time when there exists vociferous discontent with the written word and all its consequences.

Those who find writing a definite aid to their intellectual endeavors, however, may be comforted by the fact that this discontent manifests itself at just those times and places where the rudimentary skills of literacy have come to be taken for granted as a birthright. It is only then that the intellectual responsibility that accompanies the privilege of being able to 'publish' one's thoughts may begin to chafe. It is only then that the frustration that grows out of trying to be understood may end in a refusal to be understandable.

The Greek world of the fifth century B. C. was another such age. The alphabet had been invented by the Greeks some time between the eleventh and eighth centuries. And since it was much simpler than any other system of writing that had ever been developed, the advantages of literacy were soon enjoyed by a substantial portion of Greek society. By the fifth century written discourse had become sufficiently commonplace for even contemporary speeches to be frequently drafted in writing. As a consequence, however, the disadvantages of literacy also were felt, and a great deal of dispute occurred about the comparative merits of speaking and writing. Such disputes naturally involved the usual paradoxes. Just as today English professors write books against reading and in print advocate the disappearance of print, so in fifth-century Athens public speakers wrote speeches against writing speeches and in published pamphlets advocated extempore speaking.

The most well-known of these criticisms of written discourse are to be found in the writings of Plato. Plato's spokesman, Socrates, is portrayed as claiming that the only proper mode of discourse among free, intelligent human beings is dialog by means of mutual question and answer, which he refers to as dialectic. Dialectic is said to provide the only genuine method of finding out what the participants really think and actually know. "The trouble with writing", Plato has Socrates declare in the *Phaedrus* (275d),

> is that it is like painting. The creations of the painter have the appearance of life, and yet if you ask them a question, they preserve a solemn silence. So it is with written discourses. They indeed seem to talk to you, as though they were intelligent. But if, in order to understand what they say, you ask them a question about it, they just go on telling you the same thing forever.

Taken literally this criticism is scarcely disputable. One cannot ask of a composition what it means in any way that will elicit an answer different from what the composition already says. Yet Socrates' objection is well-taken only so long as the unique character of written discourse is not fully understood and exploited by those who engage in it. For a written discourse, if properly composed, *can* tell you what it means and in much the same way that dialog, or dialectic, conveys meaning – by raising questions and giving answers to them.

Formally, of course, there is scarcely any resemblance whatever between a dialog and a composition. The majority of compositions contain few explicit questions and scarcely any of the so-called 'sentence fragments' that constitute the typical direct answer in a dialog. On the other hand, a live dialog, of even the most prosaic kind rarely contains anything *but* explicit questions and their 'fragmentary' direct answers. If composition is dialectical in method, it is nevertheless not dialogal in form.

This difference in form derives from the fact that in a live dialog the burden of exposition or argument by means of question and answer is distributed between the participants, whereas in a composition the burden of this discourse rests upon one person alone – the composer. This means that, while the basic semantically complete unit of discourse in a dialog will be an explicit question *plus* a direct answer, in a composition the basic semantically complete unit of discourse will be an answer that contains its question – that is, an assertion. Composition is 'composition' by virtue of the fact that it 'puts together' in subject-attribute assertions what in conversation is separated by the speakers – the raising of the questions and the rendering of the answers to them.

A. THE NATURE OF THE SENTENCE – SEMANTIC AND FORMAL

A specific understanding of how compositions convey meaning dialectically may best be acquired by looking into that ancient preoccupation of grammatical study – the definition of the sentence. At the beginning of his own attempt to delineate the nature of the English sentence, C. C. Fries pointed out that the grammarian finds himself already confronting more than two hundred different definitions.[1] Such a plethora has forced many to wonder whether, since it seems impossible to conclusively identify, there exists such an entity as the sentence. Yet the reason that grammarians felt obliged to persist in trying to define the sentence in spite of their lack of success is that without some idea of a basic syntactic unit of discourse the study of grammar can scarcely exist.

A grammarian may formally proceed in his analysis of a given language by starting out with specifying the smallest meaningful units in that language, such as phonemes, morphemes, words. But these units are recognizable and characterizable as such only because they appear arranged and combined in discourse. The grammatical study of the arrangement and combination of these meaningful units is often distinguished as a branch of grammar called syntax. All grammar, however, is really syntax because all subdividing of these arrangements and combinations derives from some implicit, if not expressed, conception of what delimits them. Neither the parts of speech nor the parts of the parts of speech can be isolated without identification of the 'speech' unit that they are part of. Grammar, like any responsible study of phenomena, can analyze – break down into parts – only what has been built up. And if this holds for grammar, it also holds for developing principles of composition. In order to write we have to be able to discern what is put together, so that we can understand and, if necessary, improve and clarify the arrangement and combination.

So essential is some concept of a basic syntactic unit of discourse to the study of grammar that, in the absence of a satisfactory definition of such a unit, the contemporary transformational-generative grammarian tries to get around the problem by claiming that the entire grammar of a language constitutes a definition of the sentence in that language. This question-begging notion of definition, which has been borrowed from logico-mathematical theory, should not recommend itself to anyone hoping to develop principles of composition, because it assumes as given precisely what the teacher knows is lacking and wishes he knew how to impart. According to Chomsky,

> A grammar of a language . . . attempts to account for the native speaker's ability to understand any sentence of his language and to produce sentences, appropriate to the occasion, that are immediately comprehensible to other speakers although they may never have been spoken or written before.[2]

While the positing of such a speaker may be convenient to the hypotheses of linguistics, he doesn't sound like a person any of the rest of us knows. For the teacher of grammar and rhetoric "sentences, appropriate to the occasion, that are immediately comprehensible" are not an object of study but a goal of effort. In the ideal world of the linguist we are all immediately comprehensible, but in the real world we have not only to learn how to make such sentences but also to recognize when we are not making them.

Moreover, as is also apparent from Chomsky's remark, the transformational-generative grammarian *does* start out with a concept of the sentence; he simply wishes to avoid taking responsibility for it because he is not able – at least within his narrow conception of grammar as "autonomous and independent of meaning"[3] – to justify his concept and his use of it as opposed to any alternative one. Other contemporary grammarians, such as H. A. Gleason, Jr. , even when not totally committed to transformational-generative grammar, are inclined to agree that, "The sentence is probably undefinable, short of a very extensive set of statements – a whole grammar, in fact . . . . It would seem best to abandon the attempt . . . ."[4] One has to go back to Fries for the last genuine attempt at definition. Nevertheless, grammarians of every persuasion go on and talk about "the sentence" although not even one "whole grammar" has yet been constructed. In sum, they all know what a sentence is, they just can't explain it.

There is no dearth of definitions, however, as we have seen, and some of the ones still current have been around for a very long time. The definition found in school grammars today – "A sentence is a group of words that expresses a complete thought" – goes back at least to Dionysius Thrax, who in his brief grammatical sketch of Greek, written about the end of the second century B. C. , was merely summarizing the commonplaces of previous centuries. And despite the great variety of definitions put forward since, the majority are only variations on this theme by Dionysius Thrax. That is, they derive from the attempt to specify "completeness", to determine what makes for the unity of the unit. Furthermore, there is, after all, a finite number of possibilities as to what constitutes the completeness of an instance of language. It can be considered complete by virtue of its content or meaning *or* by virtue of its structure or form.

The traditional conception of the sentence most prevalent among grammarians was summed up by Fries:

> For centuries it has been insisted that, for completeness, every sentence must have a word representing a person, place, or thing, and also a word 'asserting' or 'saying something' about that person, place, or thing. There must be a 'subject' and a 'predicate'. (p. 14)

The criteria of subject and predicate are obviously semantic criteria since they are to be identified in terms of their meaning or content, of their making an assertion *about* someone or something.

Difficulties arise, however, because the grammarians who apply this definition do not want nevertheless to recognize as sentences some groups of words that fully satisfy these criteria. Consider the example, "My hard-working father is tired". It contains a word representing a person, "father", but two words that assert something about the person, "hard-working" and "tired". No traditional grammarian would be willing to identify the phrase "my hard-working father", however, as a sentence, although he would identify "My father is tired" as one. Yet the one is obviously as *semantically* complete as the other: the transposition of the subject and attribute and the addition of "is" to make "My father is hard-working" adds absolutely no *information* whatsoever to "my hard-working father". On the other hand, "who the man saw" contains both a subject, "the man", and a full predicate, "saw", and yet it too would be denied sentence status. Clearly, in identifying sentences the traditional grammarian is using some additional criteria not included in his definition.

To compound the difficulties of defining, the grammarian does treat as sentences one kind of word group that is obviously semantically incomplete because it contains no subject – the imperative. The traditional way of regulating this inconsistency is to declare the subject understood. Thus "Wait a minute" is to be understood as "You wait a minute", with "you" as the subject and "wait a minute" as the predicate. Fries takes issue with this traditional account on the grounds that "Nothing in the criteria furnished in these definitions gives us any indication of a limit to the number or the kind of words that may be 'understood' " (p. 16). But this objection is quite beside the point and misleads Fries in his own search for the defining features of the sentence. For even in the full expression, "You wait a minute", "you" is not functioning as the subject – not in the way that the subject functions in all other kinds of assertions, whether sentences or not. This becomes evident if we try to substitute a noun or proper name for "you": "Boy/Mother/Sam wait a minute". In each of these examples the first term is functioning as a direct address, just as "Mother" does in "Mother, Father said to wait a minute", and is not the subject of the verb at all. It must be concluded that imperatives do not assert anything about anything. They express a desire for certain behavior just as questions express a desire to know something, but neither imperatives nor questions make a claim, true, false, or hypothetical, about the world.

To Fries, and other descriptive (or non-semantic) grammarians, the source of these difficulties seemed to reside in the very nature of trying to define the sentence as a grammatical unit "*by way of the meaning or thought content*".

> Most of those who have sought to define the sentence . . . have tried to find universal characteristics of meaning content for this speech unit – characteristics that could not only be identified in the utterances of all languages, but would serve also as defining criteria of the sentence in any language. (p. 18)

Since this approach has never succeeded in coming up with a definition that is either analytically applicable or even theoretically acceptable, Fries and his colleagues concluded that a semantic definition of the sentence is impossible. They took therefore an intentionally opposite approach. They abandoned the effort to define the sentence in terms of semantic completeness and in a way that would be valid for all languages. For semantic completeness as the characteristic of the sentence in every language they substituted formal independence in each language. "The more one works with the records of the actual speech of people", Fries concluded,

> the more impossible it appears to describe the requirements of English sentences in terms of meaning content. It is true that whenever any relationship is grasped we have the material or content with which a sentence can be made. But this same content can be put into a variety of linguistic forms, some of which can occur alone as separate utterances and some of which always occur as parts of larger expressions. (pp. 18-19)

A sentence according to this conception then will be simply whatever forms can occur alone as separate utterances.

This conception also, like its semantic counterpart, led at once of course to grave inconsistencies. Statements, imperatives, greetings, calls, questions, and answers to questions were all identified as sentences because they do occur as separate utterances. Yet no distinguishing feature could emerge from this grouping if for no other reason than that "Answers to questions may consist of practically any linguistic form of the language" (p. 165). Therefore it is untrue to say that some linguistic forms can occur alone as separate utterances and some always occur as parts of larger expressions and therefore that we can distinguish as sentences those that occur alone. Answers to questions occur alone and yet may take practically any linguistic form. This means that practically no linguistic form can be identified as occurring only as part of a larger expression, for few cannot occur alone as the answer to some question.

In sum, according to this conception practically every linguistic form can be a sentence. This rendered a distinction of the sentence on a formal basis impossible. At best the structuralist (the descriptive grammarian) has a vast inventory of the forms that can or do appear as lone utterances. He is in the position of a cook who has a list of ingredients but no recipe. What is he supposed to make of all these items? The formalist approach leads to a proliferation of grammars as each man tries to find out what kind of recipe can be worked up with all these ingredients. Individuality being what it is of course, none can agree, for indeed, given the size of the inventory and the absence of any conception of a delimitable unit of which the forms would be constituents, the possibilities are almost endless.

In an attempt to salvage the concept of formal independence we might ask if occurring as the answer to some question is really occurring alone. Can an answer to a question actually be said to be formally independent? Of course the answer to this question is both yes and no. If by independence is meant being uttered by a single speaker, then most answers to questions *are* formally independent. If by independence is meant being formally identifiable, then most answers to questions *are not* formally independent. As Fries himself admitted, although answers to questions

> are independent in the sense that they are not included in a larger structure by means of any grammatical device, their own structural arrangements have significance with reference to the questions that elicited them. In other words, the question itself is part of the frame in which the answer as an utterance operates. (p. 165)

The criterion of formal independence as the defining feature of sentences turns out to be as ambiguous and indefinite as that of semantic completeness.

Despite their inability to find a formula for the sentence, modern grammarians of every persuasion have nevertheless continued to insist that the sentence cannot be defined semantically. Granted. But then neither can it be characterized formally. Would it not be reasonable to suppose at this stage that grammarians are putting a false dilemma? Why should it have seemed reasonable to Fries and his colleagues that since a purely semantic definition did not work, a purely formal one would? It should be just as reasonable, if not more reasonable, to conclude that a sentence is a formal semantic (or semantic formal) unit rather than either one or the other.

Such a conclusion would require, however, abandoning the attempt to identify the notion of sentence with that of utterance. An utterance, or instance of language, is simply an instance of language. One can imagine a situation in which almost any expression in the language can be uttered by a single speaker. A request for a clarification of a mumbled syllable may elicit in reply nothing but a more distinct enunciation of that syllable. Identification of sentence with utterance can never lead to the systematic distinguishing of a basic unit of discourse. When Fries decided to take recorded telephone conversations as the source material for his analysis of English, he was already guaranteeing the occurrence of more formal and semantic explicitness than would have been the case if those conversing had been face to face.

As it turns out, furthermore, when sentence is identified with utterance, no means can be found to consistently classify the independent forms – the greetings, statements, calls, answers, commands, requests – that are all covered by this identification. Fries purported to establish these subclasses of utterance on the basis of the kind of response each elicits. But answers already form an exception to this grouping because they of course are themselves responses. Less superficially apparent but more important is the fact that the subdivision, "statement", is not really identified this way either. Statements are described as

> Utterances regularly eliciting conventional signals of attention to continuous discourse (sometimes oral signals, but of a limited list, unpredictable in place, and not interrupting the span of talk or utterance unit). (p. 53)

That is, the kind of response that a statement evokes is no response at all; the listener merely refrains from interrupting. Thus, what a statement or series thereof amounts to is nothing more specific than an uninterrupted flow of discourse. Fries never determined what a statement is but only what it is not: it is not a response and it does not elicit one. Yet, of those parts of the recorded conversations supposed to be distinguishable according to response, statements are said to constitute more than sixty percent (p. 51). Therefore more than half the material distinguished this way – and thus a sizable proportion of utterances occurring in the English language – is never clearly delimited and described by Fries' principles.

Must not this mass of negatively defined, unclassified instances of language be just what the grammarians have been seeking to define all along – the sentence? A sentence, whether it occurs in writing or in speech, is recognizable as *an utterance that is both semantically and formally complete*. It is identifiable neither as a 'quest' (or 'request') nor as a response to one. The reason that a sentence cannot be identified either as question or as response is because it is at the same time both. That is what makes it complete.

In order to see what enables sentences to function this way let us examine briefly a few examples of language that might be considered sentences and see how they differ.

(1) "Could you have left at eight? "
(2) "Yes".
(3) "I want to know if you could have left at eight".
(4) "I could have left at eight".

Neither of the first two examples is a sentence. One asks a question: the other answers it. But though they are both independent, neither asserts anything. "Could you have left at eight? " is formally independent in that it is uttered by a single speaker and is formally identifiable in English as a question, but it is not semantically complete. For although it contains a word construable as referring to a person, "you", it contains none that asserts something about that person. Although it does contain the phrase, "you left", and though *this* expression does contain a formally possible subject and predicate, the utterance as a whole does not assert it. The utterance as a whole, indeed, implies quite the contrary to "you have left": the person addressed neither left at the time specified nor at the time of the utterance. The second example, "Yes", obviously lacks even the elements with which an assertion could be made and does not make one, despite the fact that *in its conversational context* it could mean exactly what example (4) asserts.

The next two examples, on the other hand, are both sentences, even though example (3) could be used to ask a question and example (4) to answer it. "I want to know if you could have left at eight" is not basically a question – though it could give rise to an answer – but is a formally independent and semantically complete assertion. It does not assert anything, however, about anyone's ability to have left at eight; it only asserts that someone ("I") "wants" something – in this case information – and only answers the question "What do I (you) want? ", which may have been explicitly raised by someone else or implicitly raised by the speaker alone. Similarly, "I could have left at eight" answers the question "Could you have left at eight? " but it need not follow and be a response to such an explicit question because, unlike "Yes", it makes both the question raised and the answer given manifest by asserting something, "could have left", about a subject, "I".

All four examples are formally independent, but each of the second two, unlike the first two, answers at least one question that they implicitly raised and is thus semantically complete. That is, neither example (1) nor (2) makes an assertion; both examples (3) and (4) do. Thus we can say that a sentence – as differentiated from a question, an answer, a call, etc. – is *a unit of discourse that makes at least one formally independent assertion*.

This conception of the nature of the sentence enables us to see both why the traditional definition of the sentence as expressing a complete thought has persisted so long and why it is inadequate. It has persisted because it does define a recognizable, basic unit of language. But it is inadequate because it is not a definition of the sentence. What makes for semantic completeness is an assertion. It is the assertion that is the basic unit of meaningfulness in discourse. But assertions can not exist independent of some form, and the forms they appear in are sentences. Thus the sentence does have universal characteristics of meaning content, as earlier grammarians thought; it makes assertions. But it is also true, as Fries and his contemporaries thought, that it is impossible to describe the requirements of English sentences or those of any language in terms of meaning alone.

Assertion and sentence then are not to be identified. A sentence is a sentence by virtue of making at least one assertion that is formally independent in a particular language. But, on the one hand, other assertions may in addition occur in the sentence, and these need not be formally independent. On the other hand, a sentence need not but usually does contain more than assertions. It may, for example, include inter-assertional connectives ("and", "but", "therefore", etc.). The syntactical conventions by means of which assertions are integrated into complex sentences will vary from language to language, but what is common to all languages is the existence of conventions for doing this.

Since asking, commanding, asserting are fundamental semantic uses of language, it stands to reason that every language has specific forms for serving these functions. These uses constitute the commonality of language. The enormous diversity of languages stems from the vast range of formal possibilities available for performing these common functions. Every language by virtue of being a language enables its speakers to use all the fundamental kinds of statements, but the ways these are made will differ arbitrarily and unpredictably from language to language, however consistent and systematic they should prove to be within each language.

One way to make this distinction between semantic commonality and formal uniqueness is to say that grammar is the study of the uniqueness of individual languages. If this is so, then rhetoric – conceived as implied question and answer discourse – is the study of what all writing, irrespective of the different languages used, has in common. A rhetoric will, of course, necessarily be laid out in one language rather than another, because rhetorical analysis presupposes the ability to do syntactical analysis – to discern subjects and attributes within assertions and different assertions within complex sentences. But insofar as implied dialog is our primary concern we might use Basque just as well as English.

B. THE NATURE OF DIALOG – QUESTION AND ANSWER

If dialog used sentences to ask questions and sentences to answer them, it would be impossibly redundant and long-winded. And not only would such explicitness be superfluous, it would also be difficult to understand. In actual dialog question and answer fit like hand and glove and are thus easy to keep track of as the discourse shifts back and forth from speaker to speaker. In a live, oral situation, the listening participants might forget what the question or the answer was by the time it was paid out in sentence form. When, however, the dialog becomes a monolog – the conversation, a composition – the explicitness of assertions and the sentences that make them is exactly what is needed; it is in fact what makes 'one-sided' communication possible.

At the same time, neither explicitness nor concision can be independent virtues but exist in proportion to each other. Both monologs and compositions must also have means of achieving some economy of expression along with the necessary explicitness. If every assertion were made in an independent form, neither monolog nor composition would be possible to follow even when written. Continuous discourse, therefore, possesses the means of making assertions that are not sentences, that are formally dependent on an independent assertion and yet are semantically complete.

An example of a formally dependent assertion in an English sentence was actually given earlier. We saw that, although the phrase, "my hard-working father", in the sentence, "My hard-working father is tired", satisfies the definition of the sentence as expressing a complete thought, traditional grammarians did not in practice identify it as a sentence. The reason that they did not is that, although not part of their definition, they were in practice using the criterion of formal independence – in addition to semantic completeness – to identify sentences. "My hard-working father" in the sample sentence does express a complete thought and is thus an assertion, but it is not formally independent of the assertion "My father is tired" and is thus not a sentence. This particular means of presenting a dependent assertion in addition to an independent assertion in a single sentence is just one of several ways of presenting assertions precisely and yet concisely in continuous discourse.

Not only are there other ways of integrating multiple assertions into a single sentence – such as compounding and apposition – but also, it is important to realize, not every instance of pre-positional modification is an instance of a dependent assertion. "Younger" in "My younger [as opposed to my older] brother is tired" is restrictive and therefore is not making an additional assertion. Acknowledgment of this difference among pre-positional modifiers constitutes a recognition that not even grammar can be made up of formal distinctions alone. And when we step almost inevitably into the realm of rhetoric – of extended discourse – then even the semantic interpretation of individual assertions is not enough. In the sentence, "My hard-working father is tired", there clearly exists an implied semantic relationship between "hard-working" and "tired" that is not indicated by the grammatical form. This semantic relationship is obviously different from that between "hard-working" and "never has any money", in the sentence, "My hard-working father never has any money", and may be indicated by turning each sentence into a dialog:

Q. How's your father?	*Q*. Can't you get the money from your father?
A. Tired.	*A*. My father never has any money.
Q. How come? /Why?	*Q*. Doesn't he work?
A. He's hard-working.	*A*. He's hard-working.

The first expresses a simple causal relationship: "My father is tired because he is hard-working"; the second expresses a disclaimer that leaves the way open for another question: "My father never has any money, even though he works hard (because my mother spends it all)".

Because, then, form and meaning are two distinct aspects of the composition of sentences, it is necessary to be able to identify each assertion, whether dependently or independently expressed, in order to see what questions are raised and how they are answered. The grammatical, or better, syntactical, basis of rhetoric is the principles of sentence structure – conceived as the rules for the integrating of multiple assertions into single sentences.

Here is a brief example of a composition:

Not every legitimate problem is properly understood in scientific terms. The problem of teaching composition, like the problem of establishing national languages, is frequently misrepresented as essentially scientific. Scientific problems, ones that can be solved by discovery, are primarily matters of research; however, problems like composition are primarily matters of competing value judgments. These are often swept under the rug with the broom of "more research" but can never be solved this way. Only when agreement is reached on the goal of composition teaching will it be possible to study fruitfully different means to the end.

Here are the sentence patterns by means of which we discern multiple assertions integrated into single sentences – with simple structure in the first and last sentences, non-restrictive modification in the second and third sentences, parallel structure in the fourth sentence, and both compound structure and appositive parallelism in the third sentence.

1. Not every legitimate problem is properly understood in scientific terms.

2. The problem of teaching composition, [like the problem of establishing national languages,] is frequently misrepresented as essentially scientific.[5]

3. Scientific problems,
   [ones that can be solved by discovery,] are primarily matters of research;

   however,

   problems like composition are primarily matters of competing value judgments.

4. These are often swept under the rug with the broom of "more research"
   but
   can never be solved this way.

5. Only when agreement is reached on the goal of composition teaching will it be possible to study fruitfully different means to the end.

And here are the nine assertions that 'compose' the composition, together with the questions that are implied by them:

Not every legitimate problem is properly understood in scientific terms.

What, for example, is thus misunderstood?
The problem of teaching compositions is frequently misrepresented as essentially scientific.

Is this the only such pseudo-scientific problem in the area of language?
The problem of teaching composition [is] like the problem of establishing national languages.

What characterizes true scientific problems?
Scientific problems [are] ones that can be solved by discovery.

What characterizes non-scientific problems?
Problems like composition are primarily matters of competing value judgments.

Aren't these often treated scientifically?
These are often swept under the rug with the broom of "more research".

Are they never solved?
These can never be solved this way.

What, then, is required?
Only when agreement is reached on the goal of composition teaching will it be possible to study fruitfully different means to the end.

Notice that the questions are not 'transformations' of the assertions. Rather, each question is determined as much by the succeeding assertion as by the preceding one. The question, just as in the dialog depicted above, indicates the relationship *between* two assertions. Among the possible questions reasonably raised by an assertion, the composer who knows what he is doing chooses the one question whose answer will most directly lead to the point of his composition. Of course the example presented here is an oversimplification. The composer may wish to take up more than one question raised by a particular assertion. But he can present only one answer at a time. Therefore, some matter in such a case will have to be deferred to a later point in the sequence of assertions. Or a composer may decide to ask an explicit – rhetorical – question, for which he may or may not provide an explicit answer. No matter what complexities or subtleties are developed, however, the basic process remains the same. The meaning of a composition is the sum of its individual assertions as linked together by the inter-assertional relationships, and these inter-assertional relationships are the sum of the implicit questions and the explicit answers. To be able to discern these questions is to be able to read comprehendingly and to write so as to be comprehensible.

Individuals can, if they like, take it upon themselves to discourse. Instead of waiting to be asked about our opinions or knowledge or behavior, we can speak right out. But if we do, we take it upon ourselves also to make perfectly clear what questions our utterances answer and what ones they do not, even as we are keeping them concise enough to be grasped as a whole. If the reader or listener thinks the writer or speaker is speaking to a different point or cannot tell for certain what point he is speaking to, meaning will of course not be conveyed and communication will not occur. Speaking to the point means both putting the questions that would be raised by others and answering them. With such discourse as this, whether written or spoken, even Socrates would be satisfied.

NOTES

1 *The Structure of English: An Introduction to the Construction of English Sentences* (New York, 1952), p. 9.

2 Introduction to Paul Roberts, *English Syntax: A Programmed Introduction to Transformational Grammar* (New York, 1964), p. ix.

3 Noam Chomsky, *Syntactic Structures* (The Hague, 1957), p. 17.

4 *Linguistics and English Grammar* (New York, 1965), p. 330.

5 The basis of our system of diagraming is the sentence written in an unbroken line from beginning to end. Exceptions to this linear arrangement indicate different grammatical features. However, limits imposed by page size require compromises (as with this sentence, which should be just one line with an internal bracketed clause).

2. THE MEANING OF ASSERTIONS

The basic rule of thumb in constructing both sentences and paragraphs is that these are organizational units made up of two or more subordinate units. The basic unit of the paragraph is the sentence, and only exceptionally do we find in sophisticated expository and argumentative compositions single-sentence paragraphs. (The indenting of individual sentences in newspaper stories is a special case resulting from the need to compensate for the problems created by the narrow column format; it is not primarily a matter of organization, and these single-sentence units are not strictly speaking paragraphs because they do not differ from the sentences that constitute them.)

Similarly, the basic subordinate unit of the sentence is the assertion, and only exceptionally do we find in sustained non-fiction compositions single-assertion sentences. When used infrequently, single-sentence paragraphs and single-assertion sentences are a means of emphasis; they stand out in contrast to what is expected. But the basic function of the sentence and the paragraph is organizational, and what is organized is individual assertions. The first step in organizing a string of assertions is to incorporate them into sentences; the second step is to incorporate the sentences into paragraphs. One is not, however, in a position to do any structural organizing until he has first understood the semantic nature of the assertion.

Unlike predominantly inflected languages (e. g. Latin), where a single word may function as an assertion, predominantly positional languages (e. g. English) distinguish between basic semantic units and basic syntactic units. An English word, and even morpheme, is meaningful and thus a semantic unit, but it does not 'say' anything: it can make no claim. It is therefore not the basic rhetorical unit. An assertion may consist of one word (a combined subject and predicate), as it can in Latin, or it may consist of at least two (separating subject and predicate), as it does in English; but nothing smaller than an assertion is meaningful by virtue of saying something.

Assertions are not *composed of* subassertional units in the way that paragraphs and complex sentences are composed of assertions; they are the indivisible molecular unit Assertions can, however, be *analyzed into* subassertional units – as molecules can be analyzed into atoms and subatomic particles. But just as the assertion is not the smallest semantic unit, neither are the basic subassertional units (subject and predicate) the smallest semantic units. The smallest analyzable units of meaning (morphemes) are not in and of themselves of assertional significance – which is not, of course, to deprecate in any way the study of them. If it is correct to say that the nature and function of molecules can not be determined or explained merely by analyzing subatomic particles, then we can say that the smallest units of sound (phonemes) and sense (morphemes) are the subatomic particles of linguistic phenomena. But to be an essential ingredient of a phenomenon is not to be a miniature of it. And to possess a complete inventory of the ingredients is neither to have nor to understand the finished product.

The systematicness of semantic grammar is dependent on more than the traditional distinction between subject and predicate. The concept of subject can be taken as sufficiently self-evident for the moment, but the concept of predicate, derived from predication, is little more than a redundant indication that we are dealing with an assertion: to predicate is to assert, and to assert is to predicate. A more useful distinction, at least for the purpose of semantic grammar, is between subject and attribute. The subject/predicate distinction is useful because it is exhaustive: there is nothing left over after the subject and predicate of an assertion have been removed. But the subject/attribute distinction, though not exhaustive, is useful because it allows us to discern more readily the different *kinds of meaning* that assertions can have.

Semantic grammar, unlike for example transformational grammar, has a *core* conception of assertions rather than a *bipartite* conception. Parts of many assertions are neither subjects nor attributes but assertion modifiers. The core of an assertion is the headword (or phrase) of the subject and the headword (or phrase) of the attribute, and (if present) the intra-assertional link. This much is the core because it is sufficient to reveal – quite independently of any subject, attribute, or assertion modifiers – the membership in one of the semantic classes. All assertions have two primary components, subject and attribute, and in the great majority of English assertions these two components occur in this order. But in addition, some kinds of assertions have a separate, intra-assertional link between the two. The core of an assertion is the unmodified attribution of a *function*, a *nature*, or a *class* membership to a thing. The subject is the thing that is described or classified; the attribute is the description or the class. To assert is to attribute, to claim (correctly or incorrectly, reasonably or unreasonably, with or without qualification) that a thing *does* something, that it *is* something, or that it *is classified as* something.

All subjects are things; an attribute may be a function, a nature, or a thing (but always only a class). In one sense there are only two categories of attribution: *thing/description* and *thing/thing*. But in another, and perhaps more precise, sense all attribution is best considered as description, and descriptions then are seen to be of three types: *thing/function*, *thing/nature*, *thing/class*. To fully understand this, however, we must make a complete inventory of the semantic possibilities for assertions. What are all the possible kinds of attribution that can be claimed of a thing?

Below are the six semantic classes of assertions and the six different diagrams into which all assertions can be fitted. When we discuss the types of formal structure, in the next chapter, there will be a second set of diagrammatic distinctions, and when we discuss modification, there will be a third. Thus the diagram of a complex sentence will show three kinds of things: the assertions, the ways of formally constituting these assertions, and the modification by which the assertions are elaborated. And, finally, the analysis of modification will be expanded by means of dialog to include the ways that assertions modify each other – within a single sentence and between sentences. This will enable us to diagram not only sentences but paragraphs as well. But in introducing the basic semantic distinctions among assertions, we shall ignore structural complexity and minimize as much as possible the complexities of modification.

Assertions can be analyzed both semantically and structurally – in terms of the kinds of meaning and in terms of the ways that the meaning is presented in relation to other assertions. The one ought reasonably to precede the other, however, because the concept of structure is a dependent one. Language is by its very nature semantic; structural elements are simply those linguistic elements that are explicable apart from the meaning of particular assertions – although not apart from the knowledge that they constitute assertions. Meaning cannot exist without structure, but how an assertion is structured has no bearing on the kind of meaning it has.

Of the three types of assertional structure (*independent*, *parallel*, and *modificational*) only the first will be used in this chapter to exemplify the six semantic classes. And of the two types of independent structure (simple sentences and complex sentences) only the first will be used. A simple independent sentence is a single subject and a single attribute constituting one and only one assertion. Such an assertion is not part of a parallel construction creating another assertion, is not subordinate to or dependent on another assertion, and does not include as part of itself any modification that creates additional subordinate or dependent assertions. There are actual two- and three-word sentences that are as simple as these diagrams, and furthermore every complex sentence is at the core (or when reduced to the bare bones) one of these same six simple assertions.

A. DESCRIBE SUBJECT BY FUNCTION

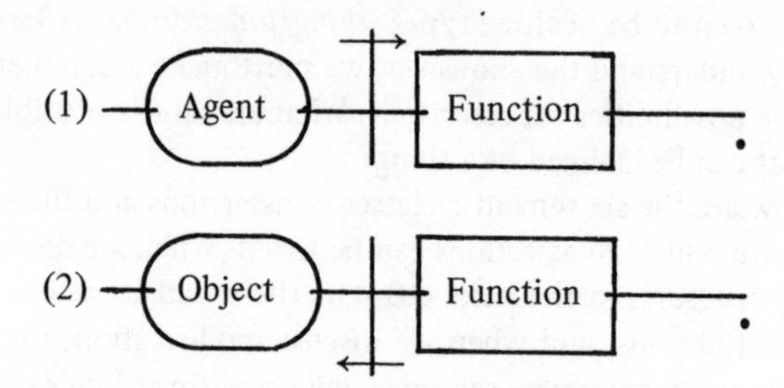

B. DESCRIBE SUBJECT BY NATURE

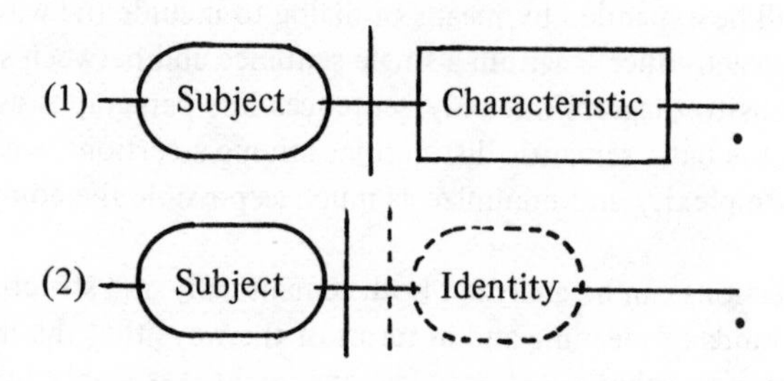

C. DESCRIBE SUBJECT BY CLASS

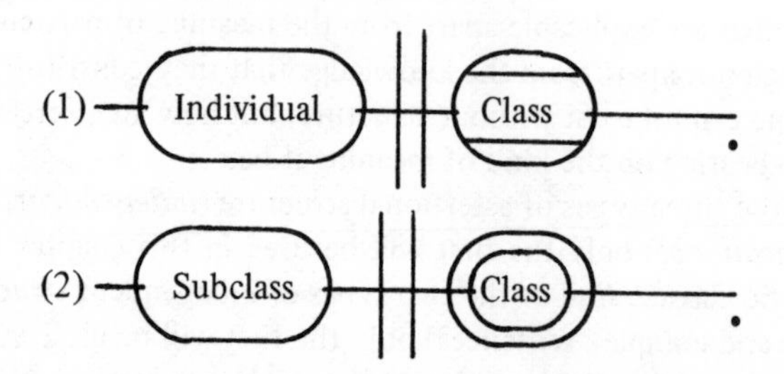

As the diagrams reveal, our semantic distinction of subject/attribute cannot be equated with the traditional bipartite distinction of subject/predicate. For function and nature assertions the two may (in the absence of assertion modifiers) be coextensive, but for classifying assertions they can not be. Quite apart from the problems created by assertion modifiers, it is as misleading to reduce all assertions to a two-part subject/predicate pattern as it is to expand them all to a three-part thing/relation/thing pattern. The core of function and characteristic assertions is always bipartite:

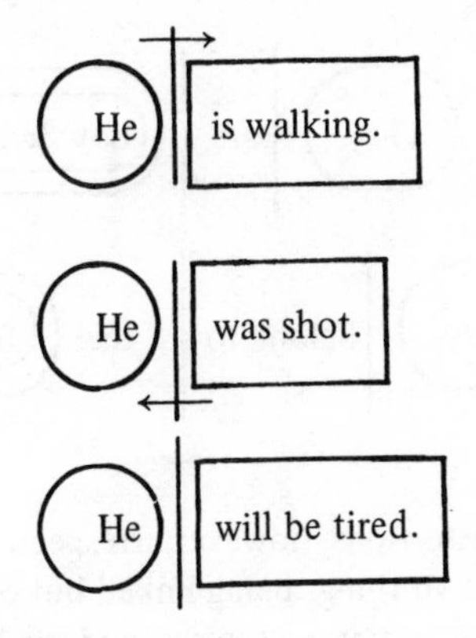

The core of identity and classifying assertions is always tripartite:

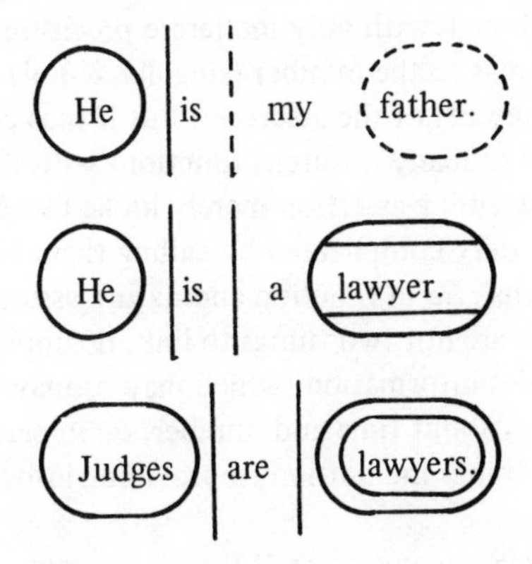

One complicating factor here is the *identity* assertion (i. e. "He is my father"). These will be analyzed below in detail, but for the moment let it suffice to call them an anomaly, for structurally such an assertion is about two things, but semantically it is about only one.

When attributing a class to a thing, there is always, in addition to the stating of the two things, a stating of the link or relationship between them. This intra-assertional link may be as vague as *is* or as precise as *belong to*, but in neither case does the link constitute one of the two subassertional components or a modification thereof.

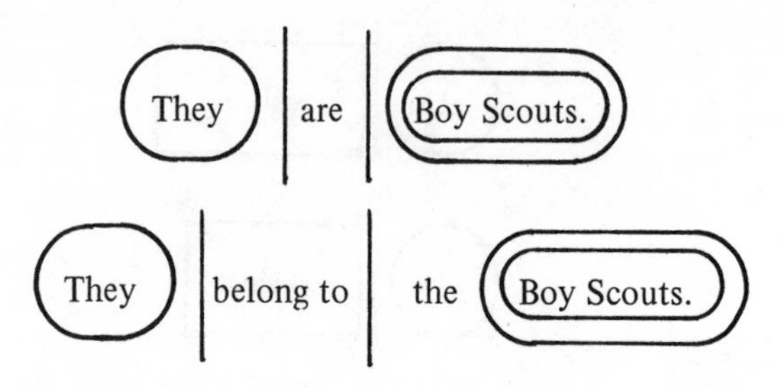

In function and nature assertions, however, irrespective of whether a form of *be* occurs, there are not two things being linked but one thing being described.

The ubiquitous *be* (*am*, *are*, *is*, *was*, *were*, and the 'participle' forms *been* and *being*) is an anomaly in English, a remnant of the older inflected language.[1] It still provides (although with only moderate precision, considering its complexity) information as to the number (singular/plural) of the subject and as to the time (past/present) of the assertion. But it is as confusing as it is helpful because it serves so many different functions with the same forms. For example, *be* in a describing assertion merely looks like *be* in a relating assertion. And the problem is only complicated by calling them both 'verbs', and even more so 'linking verbs'. *Be* in function and nature assertions does not link two things because there are not two things to link; it simply constitutes part of an attribute and provides information (which may or may not be provided elsewhere in other ways) about time and number. *Be* in classifying assertions, however, does link two things in addition to providing information as to time and number.

Similarly with *have*: in and of itself the word is almost devoid of meaning. And thus it is always diagramed as part of the attribute. Indeed, some uses of *have* in a characteristic attribute may be semantically indistinguishable from uses of *be*:

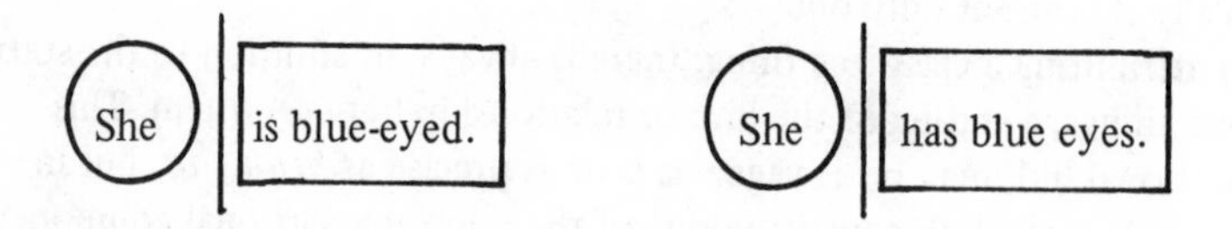

However, such synonymous usage is rare. These six kinds of assertions are termed semantic because in the most precise sense the specific meaning of an assertion correlates with the kind of assertion it is. To say, for example, that a person *is fighting* (function) is not necessarily to say that he *is a fighter*

(classification). And to say that he *is a fighter* is not necessarily to say that he *is fighting*. Similarily, if a person *is feminine* (characteristic) this is not to say that he/she *is a female* (classification). And to say that she *is a female* is not to say that she *is feminine*.

A further difference between two-part and three-part assertions is the semantic reversability of classifying and identity assertions – the converting of the attribute into the subject and the subject into the attribute, with only a change in the kind of relationship indicated by the link in the middle. But more of this later. A more important point for the moment is to forestall possible confusion on what would seem to qualify as thing/relation/thing structure. Neither the presence of an 'object' in a function assertion nor the presence of a standard in a comparative characterizing assertion qualifies as the second 'thing':

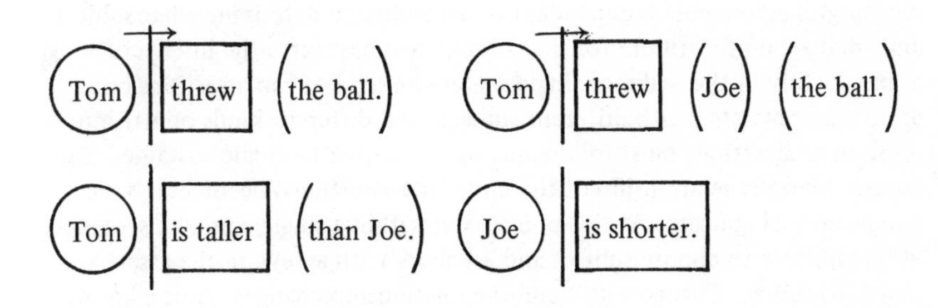

"Tom threw" provides all that is necessary for determining the core and the semantic kind of the assertion. The point is not whether the function attribute is 'transitive' or 'intransitive' (irrelevant concepts in semantic grammar) but whether the additional sentence elements do or do not change the fundamental meaning. Direct and indirect 'objects' ("the ball" and "Joe") are answers to second-level questions elicited by an understanding of a core assertion: What did he throw? Who did he throw it to or at? And this by no means exhausts the kinds of reasonable assertion modifiers that can be attached to the core assertion. For example, we can ask when this was done and why it was done, and the result would be something like this:

Tom threw (Joe) (the ball) (at once) (to catch the runner off base.)

An assertion is not thing/relation/thing unless the basic meaning requires and always requires the three elements. "She pushed" and "She pushed me" are not fruitfully analyzed as two different kinds of assertions.

For the same reason we do not distinguish among characteristic assertions between those that include the thing that makes the subject taller or shorter, older or younger. The standard may or may not be stated without changing the basic meaning of the core assertion. But why a standard is diagramed separately as an assertion modifier rather than as an attribute modifier is best explained later after we have analyzed simpler manifestations of function and characteristic assertions.

For the present let it suffice to emphasize the general principle that the rigorous interpretation of meaning is dependent on an ability to recognize the different kinds of assertions and the ways that these correlate with different intellectual categories. And by the same token, the rigorous composition of meaningful statements is dependent on an ability to determine what subject and what kind of attribute for that subject will best serve the intellectual task at hand. Only in the realm of single-sentence exercises can assertions be arbitrarily rewritten with different subjects and different kinds of attributes. As soon as assertions must follow one upon another to create sustained discourse, then the relationship of the units (the assertions) becomes a basic compositional concern. At this point, even within a single complex sentence, we are obliged to choose subject and attribute with an eye to the assertion that is to follow. Change a unit and the relationship changes. Thus a knowledge of the different kinds of units is as much a compositional necessity as a knowledge of the different kinds of relationships.

This is not, of course, to deny that some communication situations are so vague as to be adequately handled by a variety of linguistic approximations. But the more complex an intellectual task is, the more rigorous must be the thought that accomplishes it. And the more rigorous the thought, the more precise must be its expression, and alternative expressions will present themselves as differences of meaning rather than of the same thing said differently.

The most convincing demonstration of this fundamental axiom is to analyze *in context* a series of assertions that form part of a complex and precisely reasoned composition. This is the task of the final chapters. But to make certain that the six semantic distinctions are at least understood at this point, the traditional logic (or Venn) diagrams can be put to good service.[2] These will have to be modified to distinguish between assertions that describe and assertions that classify, and they will be limited to only those configurations that show no more than two things. At this stage in our discussion we need to see everything that a single assertion can do but uncomplicated by what requires *more* than one to do. Thus, there will be no diagram here for a syllogism (with its minimum of three concentric circles) because no elementary assertion can relate three things. Even if we disregard the traditional form of syllogistic deduction, a minimum of two assertions is required to refer to three things: "Judges are lawyers". "Lawyers are professionals". And for the same reason, though less obvious, there will be no over-lapping circle diagram – the kind sometimes said to represent sentences like "Some women are lawyers". To fit such a diagram, this single assertion must be taken to mean not just "Some women are lawyers", but "Some women are not lawyers", and "Some lawyers are not women". Not what sentences may or may not imply but what they do assert is the primary subject of language analysis.

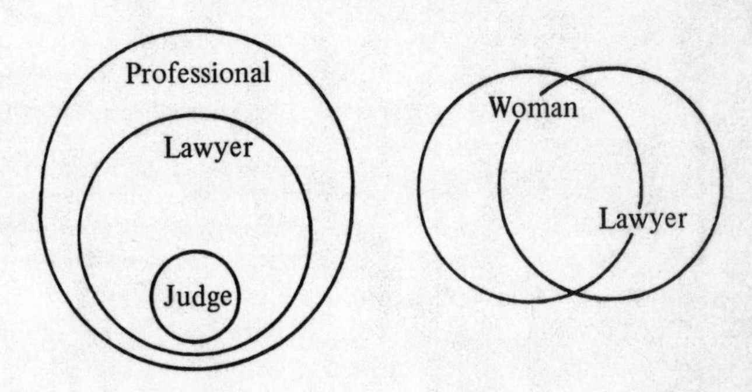

Similarly, not how sentences are modified but what they are in their most elementary state is the first concern. However, modification is important for explaining the difference between the subject/predicate distinction and our subject/attribute distinction. The final point to be made in introducing our distinction is about the different modificational relationships. This is not a difference in kind (restrictive and non-restrictive) but a difference in what is modified. And this brings us back to the question of how many things are referred to in the core assertion. Function and characteristic assertions can of course contain references to more than one thing if assertion modifiers (e. g. 'objects') are included:

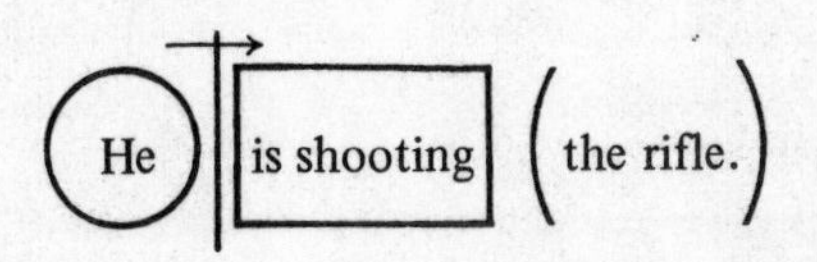

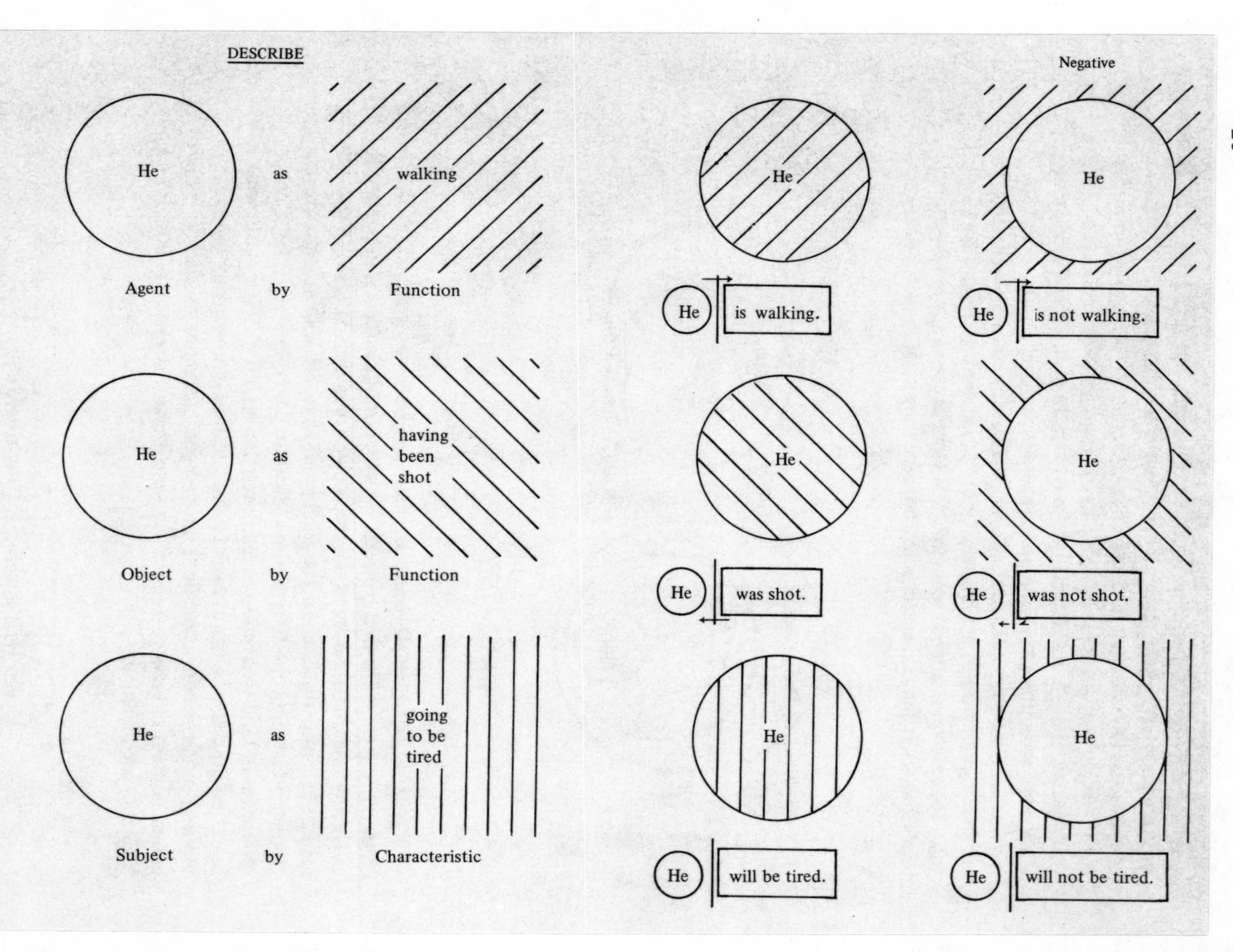
DESCRIBE
He
as
walking
Agent
by
Function
He
as
having
been
shot
Object
by
Function
He
as
going
to be
tired
Subject
by
Characteristic
He
He
is walking.
He
He
was shot.
He
He
will be tired.
Negative
He
He
is not walking.
He
He
was not shot.
He
He
will not be tired.

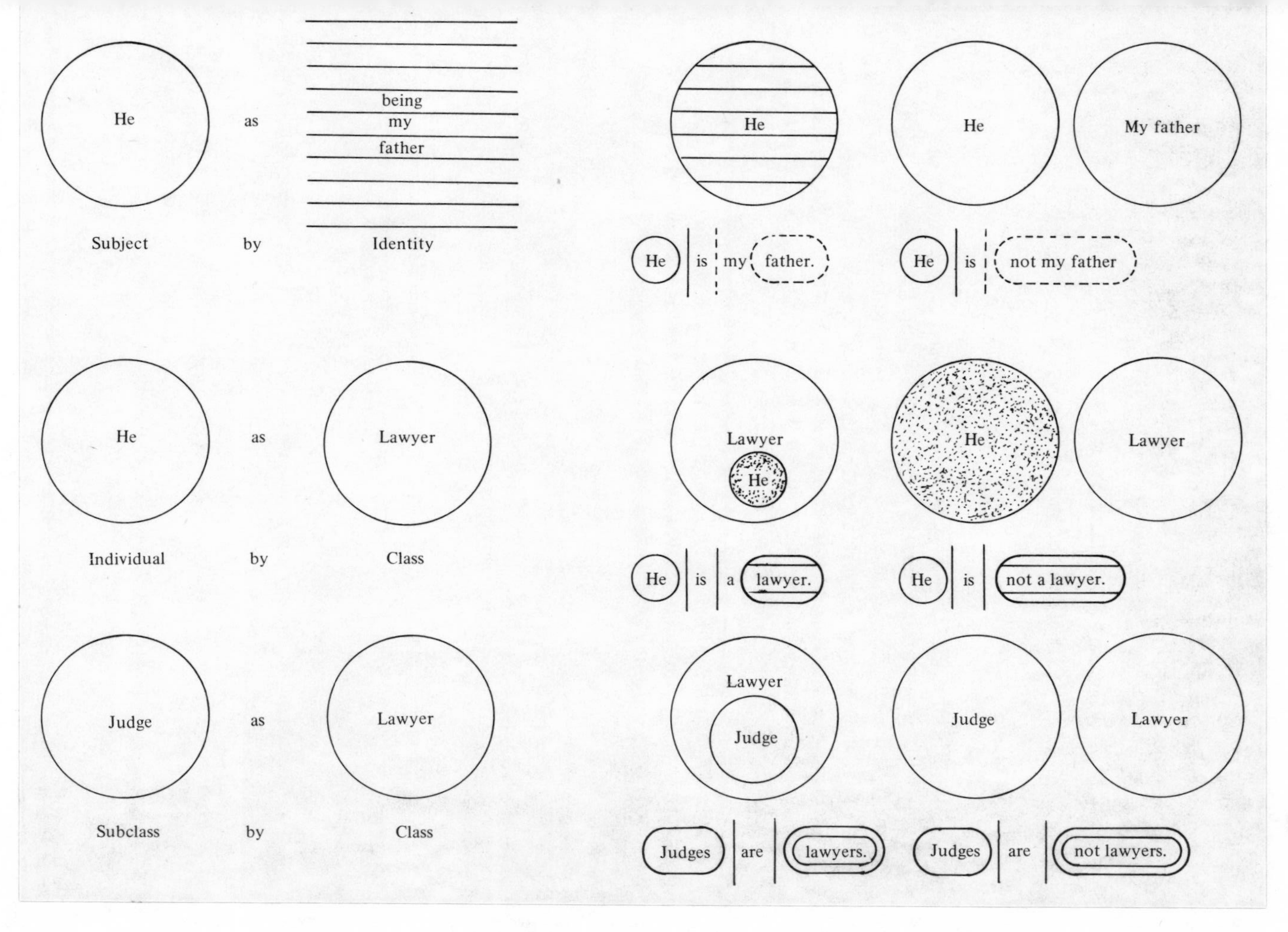
He
as
being
my
father
He
He
My father
Subject
by
Identity
He is my father.
He is not my father
He
as
Lawyer
Lawyer
He
He
Lawyer
Individual
by
Class
He is a lawyer.
He is not a lawyer.
Judge
as
Lawyer
Lawyer
Judge
Judge
Lawyer
Subclass
by
Class
Judges are lawyers.
Judges are not lawyers.

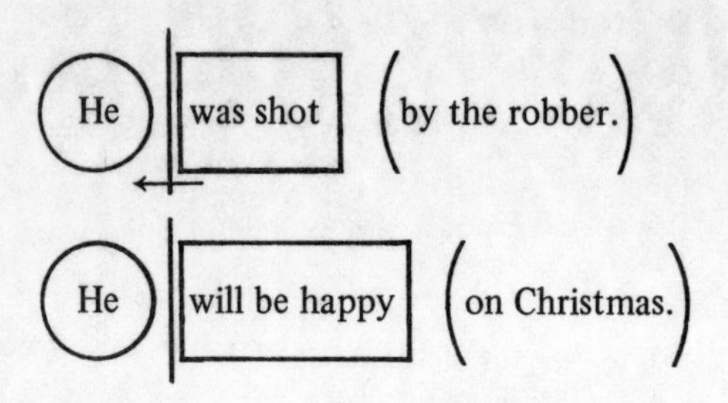

"Is shooting the rifle", "was shot by the robber", and "will be happy on Christmas" are *predicates*. But the *attributes* are simply "is shooting", "was shot", and "will be happy".

Semantic grammar acknowledges the existence of a much wider range of assertion modifiers than do most other grammars. Modifiers that do not clearly – that is, semantically – provide a clarification of the subject in and of itself or of the attribute in and of itself are best interpreted as modifiers of the assertion as a whole. Thus, it is possible for quite ordinary sentences to have several assertion modifiers (which we inclose in parentheses). But, of course, extensive modification can just as well be attached to the subjects and attributes independently (in which case we leave them unmarked):

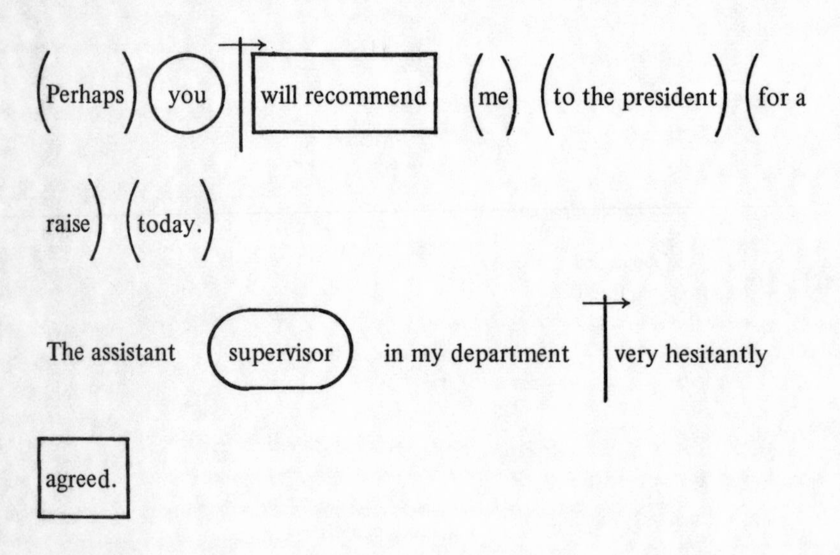

The explanation of the principles involved in these modificational distinctions must wait until we have first clarified the more basic principles that distinguish the different kinds of core assertions. It is thus to the first of these that we now turn.

A. DESCRIBE SUBJECT BY FUNCTION

It is important to bear in mind that the linguistic conception of a thing – and thus of a subject – is more inclusive than the ordinary conception of an object. Whatever is ordinarily referred to in the broadest sense as a thing can have an attribute asserted of it and is thus also a linguistic thing. A linguistic thing and what is usually thought of as a thing are the same. But linguistically, function and characteristic are restricted to those parts of assertions that serve as attributes and not as subjects. In function and characteristic assertions there is only one thing; the attribute is not a thing but a description of a thing.

All objects then can serve as subjects, but so also can what are often more precisely termed concepts, classes, characteristics, functions. Subjects can be designated not only by what are traditionally called 'nouns' – names of things – but also by words that designate functions, if these functions can have attributes asserted of them:

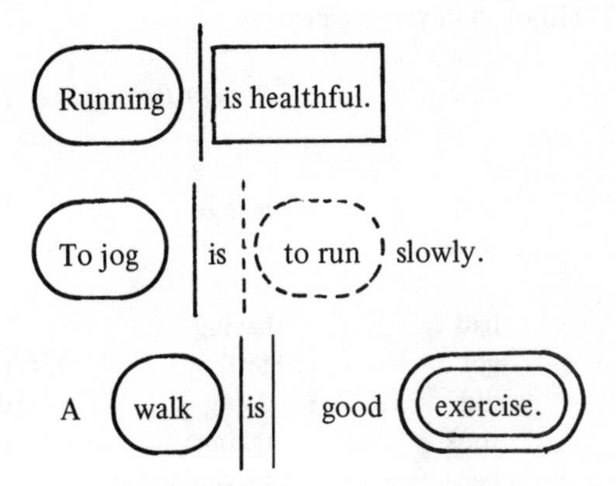

And just as some linguistic elements usually thought of as functions serve as things, other linguistic elements usually thought of as things serve as functions. As we shall see in the next section, function can be designated not only by the usual activity 'verbs' but also by special constructions such as *have* as a 'pro-verb' (on the analogy with 'pronouns') followed by an activity 'noun' from which it derives its meaning:

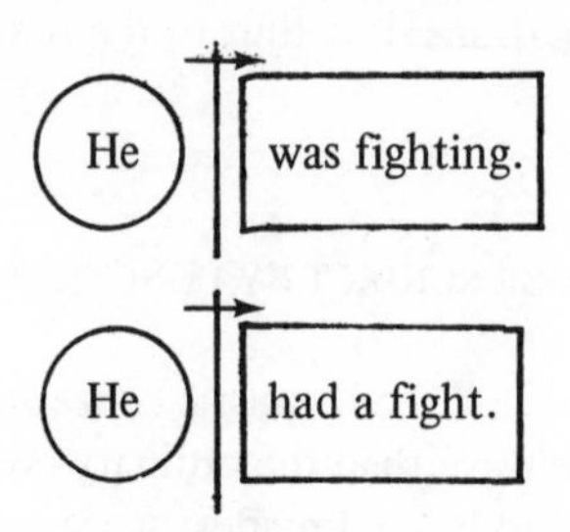

This very common kind of construction is best explained (as we shall do in more detail later) by seeing it as being essentially "He fought a fight". There are almost as many different uses of *have* as of *be*, and to group all of them together can be done only on the basis of some kind of formal principle. But in a semantic grammar, semantic considerations always take precedence over non-semantic. If to have a fight is to engage in an activity, then the assertion of which this is the attribute is a function assertion. And to round out the list of the major all-purpose 'verbs', we will mention here, in addition to *be* and *have*, *get*, *do*, *take*, and *become*. Examples of their use are given later in this section, but we will take notice here of the fact that all six of these are 'strong' or inflected – although in varying degrees:

Present	*Past*	*Present Participle*	*Past Participle*
am			
are	was	being	been
is	were		
have	had	having	
get	got	getting	gotten
do	did	doing	done
take	took	taking	taken
become	became	becoming	

These remnants of the inflectional ancestors of English are both very common in occurrence and very ambiguous in meaning. Thus they derive their meaning primarily from the different contexts in which they appear, and thus they are not diagramed alone as attributes. On the one hand, semantic grammar admittedly slights the inflectional complexity of English, but on the other hand, it can thereby reveal the semantic complexity hidden behind the inflectional facade.

This same kind of reasoning obliges us to recognize that not everything traditionally thought to be a 'verb', even excluding these six special cases, expresses function. The test is to apply modification appropriate to activity or change. If there can be a reasonable answer to the question "How done? " (in the sense of "in what manner" rather than "by what means"), then a construction is properly designated as function.

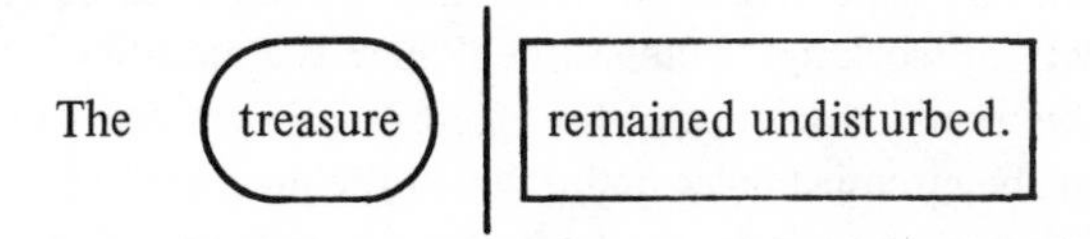

Since no such answer can be given to *remained* here, the treasure cannot be said to be doing anything. Therefore, this is a characterizing assertion rather than one that indicates function. Fighting, on the other hand, is a function because it can be done in various ways:

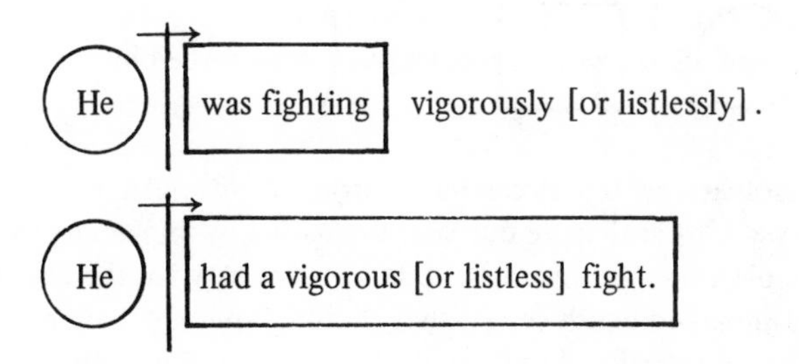

However, because "vigorously" modifies the complete phrase "was fighting" (Was fighting *how*?), it is diagramed outside the core box. "Vigorous", on the other hand, does not modify the complete "had" phrase but only "a fight" (What *kind* of fight?). Therefore, it is an inseparable part of the core. But more of this later.

To continue with our examples of similar constructions having different kinds of meaning, let us look at something else that is *undisturbed* and something else that *remained*. Our assertion about the treasure has a more precise meaning than

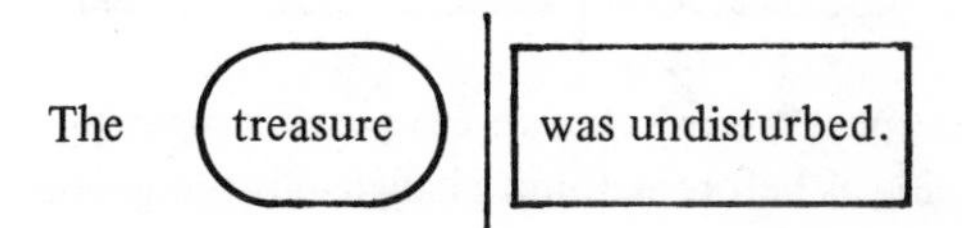

but the two meanings are of the same semantic kind. In both assertions the treasure is characterized as being undisturbed. But in

what is attributed to the man is not the characteristic of being undisturbed but the activity of working. "Undisturbed" here is a modifier – not of "man" alone or of "worked" alone but of the assertion as a whole. It provides information about the circumstances under which the man worked. The following expanded sentence, though we shall not stop to analyze it, should clearly show the difference between the modification of a thing ("old"), the modification of a function ("quickly"), and the modification of subject and attribute together ("undisturbed by the rain"):

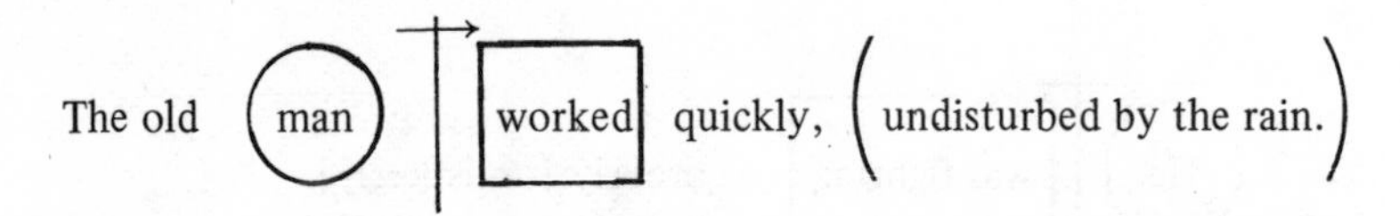

Because few idiomatic sentences can be constructed without the use of some modification, we must anticipate our later discussion by explaining those modificational diagraming conventions that are necessary for the discussion of assertions. Unmarked words (e. g. "the", "old", "quickly") are restrictive modifiers of the subassertional unit (subject or attribute) on their side of the assertion divider. Words and phrases in parentheses (e. g. "undisturbed by the rain") are restrictive modifiers of the assertion – they modify subject and attribute taken as a unit. The complete list of diagraming symbols can be found in Appendix B.

Finally, back to *remained*, here is something that remained in motion and is thus part of a function assertion:

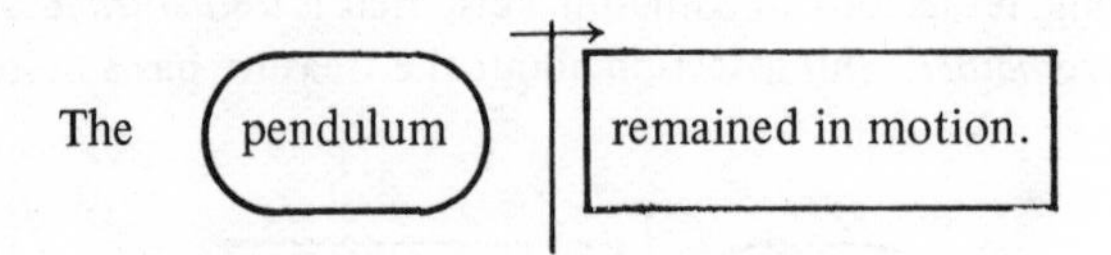

Unlike the six all-purpose 'verbs', *remain* has a stable meaning, but this meaning – continuing as before without change – is too general in itself to determine the semantic kind. Therefore, it is not properly thought of as an attribute core to which restrictive modification is appended. Rather, it is an indivisible part of a larger structure – indivisible, that is, in its attributeness. However, to anticipate our discussion of identity, here is someone who remained in a unique relationship and is thus part of an identity assertion:

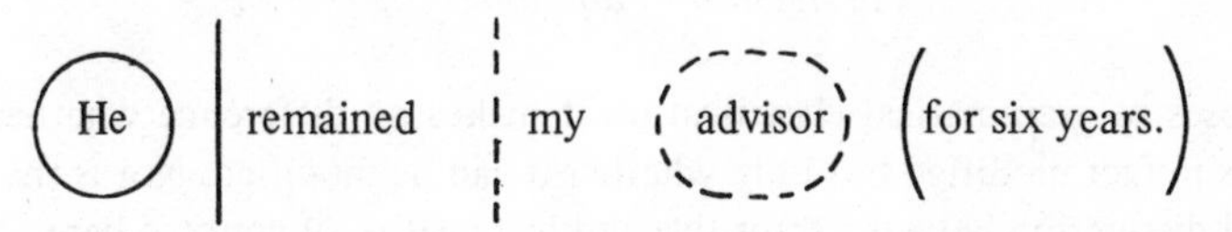

Remain is almost as ubiquitous as words like *be* and *have* – but not quite. *Remain* can stand alone as a common, idiomatic attribute and have a constant meaning as a characteristic assertion:

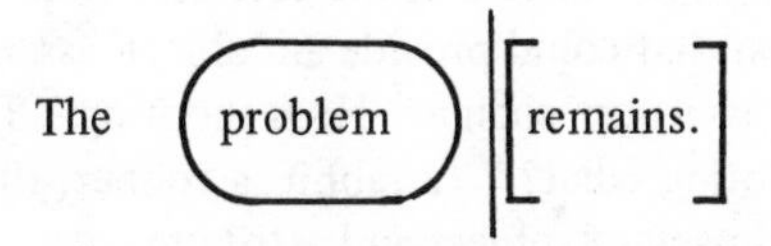

One of the very useful features of semantic grammar is the simplified system of analyzing modification. In the simplest sense, there are just two kinds of modifiers: restrictive and non-restrictive – those that qualify or make more precise what is modified and those that make additional assertions. A non-restrictive modifier can always be rewritten as a separate assertion without changing the semantic total. To emphasize the detachability of non-restrictive modifiers, we diagram them by enclosing them in brackets. The next step beyond this fundamental distinction between restrictive and non-restrictive is between those modifiers that modify subject *or* attribute and those that modify subject *and* attribute together. This distinction is of less importance for non-restrictive modifiers, which in any case are detachable from the sentence. But for restrictive modifiers it is an important aid to interpreting the meaning to be able to determine precisely what is being modified and what is not. Thus our diagraming distinguishes restrictive modifiers of subject or attribute by excluding them from the inclosed head word or phrase and using no other mark. It distinguishes restrictive assertion modifiers by inclosing them in parentheses. Moreover, because an assertion may have more than one assertion modifier and they may occur in more than one location, we will inclose in a separate set of parentheses each word or phrase that could stand alone as an assertion modifier by virtue of answering a different question. Though it can by no means show every grammatical distinction within a sentence, this simplified system of sentence diagraming does have the virtue of requiring no rearranging of the order in which the sentence was written, no transforming of it into something else, no learning of an elaborate set of diagraming symbols. Yet it nevertheless succeeds in indicating all of the assertional or rhetorical aspects of a sentence.

(1) *Agent by Function*

For purposes of grammatical classification it makes no difference whether a function is in fact modified but only whether it can be modified. Nor is the traditional distinction between transitive and intransitive of concern here. "She lifted", with its 'transitive verb' (i. e. taking an 'object') cannot stand as an idiomatic sentence. But the specifying of whatever she lifted (the club, his billfold, her eyes) is not part of the subject/attribute core. The 'object' exists as the answer to a question directed at the core assertion: She lifted what? It is the same question that could provide an 'object' assertion modifier of an 'intransitive verb' assertion, such as "He is shooting". The answer to the question, "He is shooting what? " (a rabbit, a robber, the rifle) is one step removed from the primacy of subject and attribute.

What does make a difference for the classifying of function assertions, however, is whether or not the subject is the agent that performs the function. This difference manifests itself as agent/function and object/function. The first point to be clear on is that the distinction between agent/function and object/function assertions is not entirely the same as the traditional distinction between active and passive constructions. All passive constructions are object/function, because in no passive construction is the subject the 'doer' of the function. But some active constructions, although their attribute is a function, cannot reasonably be interpreted as having a subject that performs or is the source of the function.

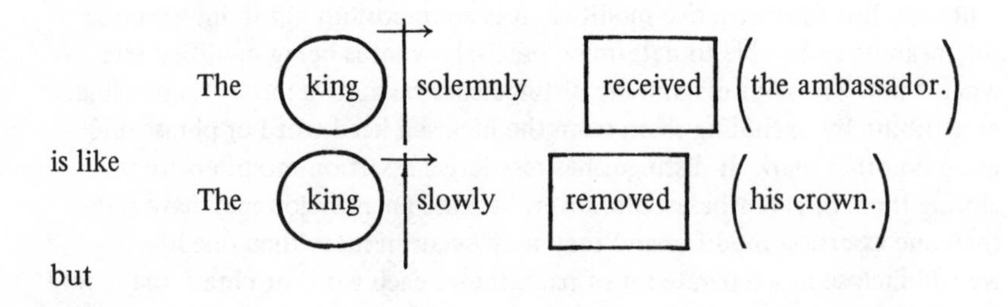

but

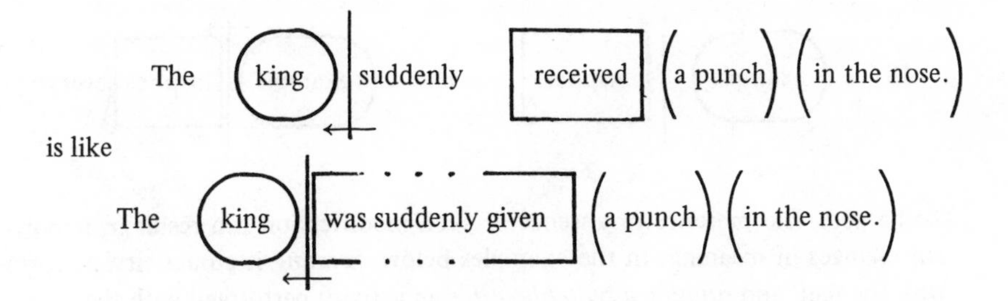

The first two assertions are traditionally labeled as 'active' and correspond to our agent/function. The fourth assertion is traditionally labeled 'passive' and corresponds to our object/function. But the third, though it is traditionally labeled 'active', is by our analysis an object/function. Whoever did the punching, and not the person who was punched, is the agent. The king in both the third and fourth assertions is the object of a giving function and not the agent of an accepting function.

This is not to say that the stated or implied agent of a function assertion must necessarily be a living creature capable of conscious and deliberate actions. It is simply to say that the *source* (animate or inanimate) of any temporal change, movement, or process must be the subject if the assertion is to qualify as agent/function. The three assertions below have non-living agents that are nonetheless doing something:

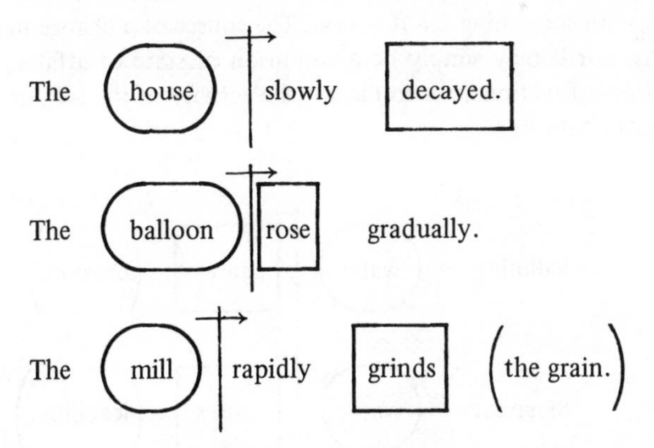

The first and second have no 'object' in the traditional sense; the third has one. But for agent/function assertions the presence or absence of this kind of assertion modifier does not affect the semantic classification. If an agent assertion "can take an object", then whether or not it does in fact do so is simply a matter of modification.

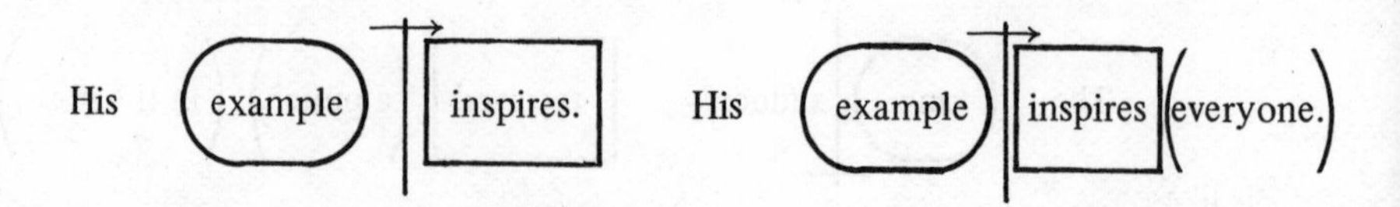

To be sure, the presence or absence of such modification can result in important changes in meaning. In the examples below, *running* is an activity performed with the feet, and *running a switchboard* is an activity performed with the hands. Both, nonetheless, are functions.

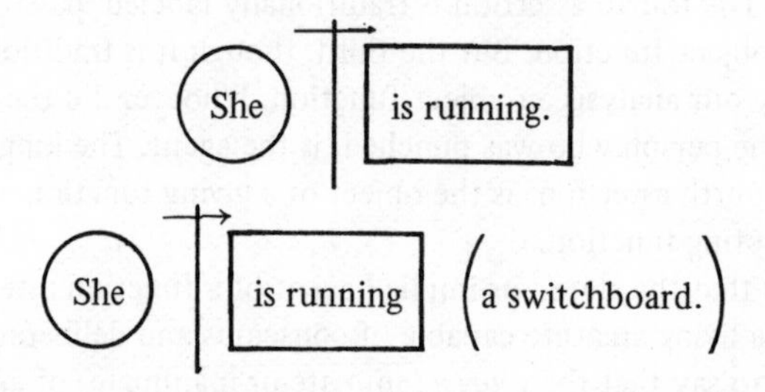

Our examples of agent/function assertions have heretofore emphasized the subject as an active participant in the function, but function is a more inclusive concept than activity. Any change that is claimed to result from or to correlate with something is a function. The source of a change may be itself an activity, or it may simply be a condition or state of affairs; what makes the assertion a function assertion is not the activity of the subject but the changes brought about by it.

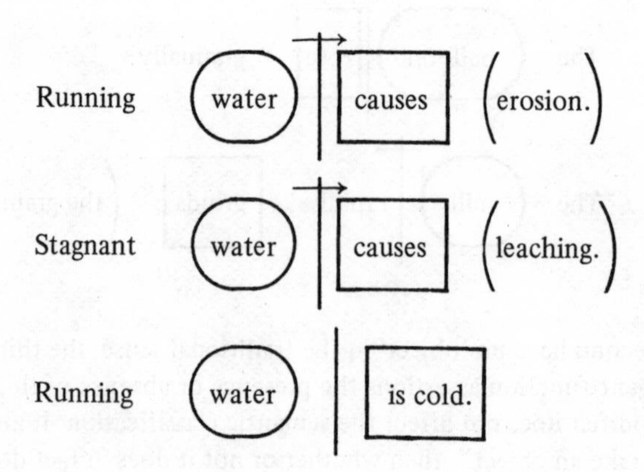

The first assertion is a function assertion not because the water is running but because the subject is claimed to give rise to a condition that did not exist until the subject created or helped to create it. The attribute of this assertion is not *running* but *causes*; *running* is a restrictive modifier of *water*. The assertion is not about any and all water but only water that is running. An assertion about water that is motionless (e. g. stagnant) can just as readily be about a function, and an assertion about water that is in motion can just as readily be about a non-function (e. g. being cold).

There is, to be sure, much imprecision in the use of causality as an attribute, but this difficulty is a problem of interpreting meaning rather than a problem of grammatical classification. And the lesson to be learned from it is that a grammar can be no more precise than the degree of conceptual precision maintained by the users of the language. A grammarian (semantic or otherwise) must be extremely cautious, however, about condemning certain usage as not good enough to bother analyzing, because it is just as likely that his grammatical system is not good enough to handle what is in fact an aspect of the language. If it is objected that some of the causality sentences to be analyzed here are not as precise as they should be, we would agree. The justification for treating them is that such usage is too widespread to ignore.

There are at least three distinct interpretations of causality as a function attribute: impetus, catalyst, and correlate. Probably the most common is *impetus*:

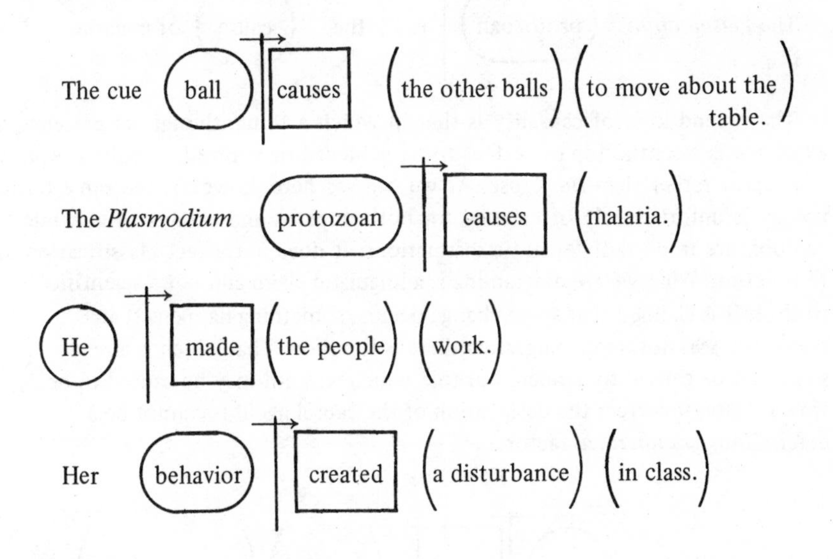

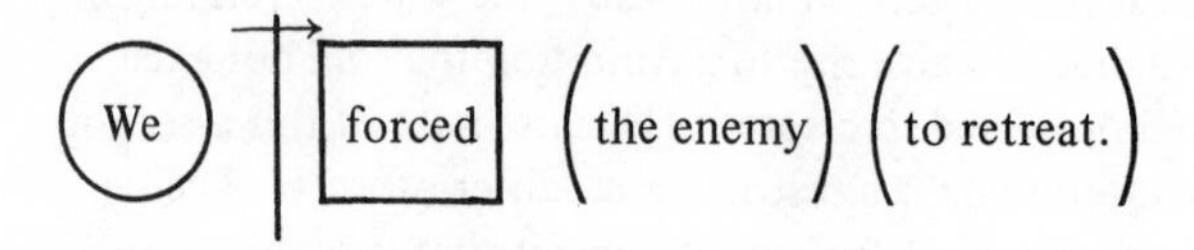

In all of these assertions some activity by the subject is claimed (rightly or wrongly, demonstrably or undemonstrably) to be a direct, determinable 'force' that is the impetus to some further change beyond itself. We need not stop to resolve the very legitimate physical and metaphysical dilemma of what exactly this means, or how such a relationship can ever be demonstrated, because our concern is primarily with the nature of claims rather than with the nature of ultimate reality. For our purpose, any assertion that refers to a change from one state or condition to another is a function assertion. This is not, however, to say that every reference to causality is necessarily a function assertion. For example, attributing *a cause* is classifying, and attributing *the cause* is identifying.

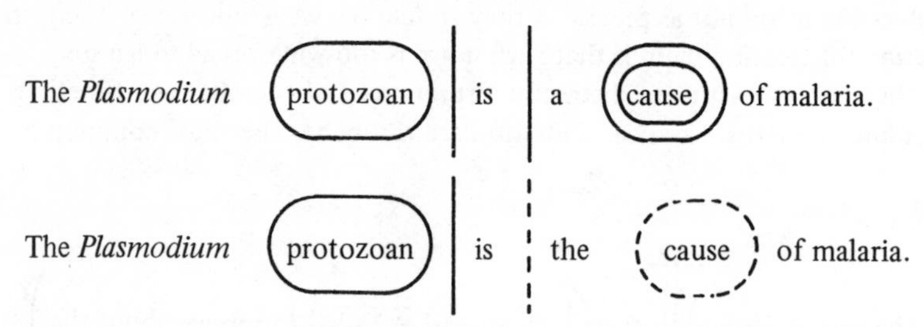

The second kind of causality is that in which a thing, though its presence or existence is essential for the effect to be achieved or realized, is only a *catalyst* – *a* factor rather than *the* cause. As we can see here, however, the same terminology is unfortunately often used for both impetus and catalyst. But while this can obscure important semantic distinctions, it does not affect classification as to function. What we are diagraming is a linguistic claim and not a scientific truth. If it is claimed that some change occurs, something happens that previously was not happening, then there is function. That which is already so cannot be caused to happen, but that which was not may be caused to be. How precise or correct the designation of the causal agent is cannot be a determining *grammatical* factor.

The slate table top causes the balls to move freely.

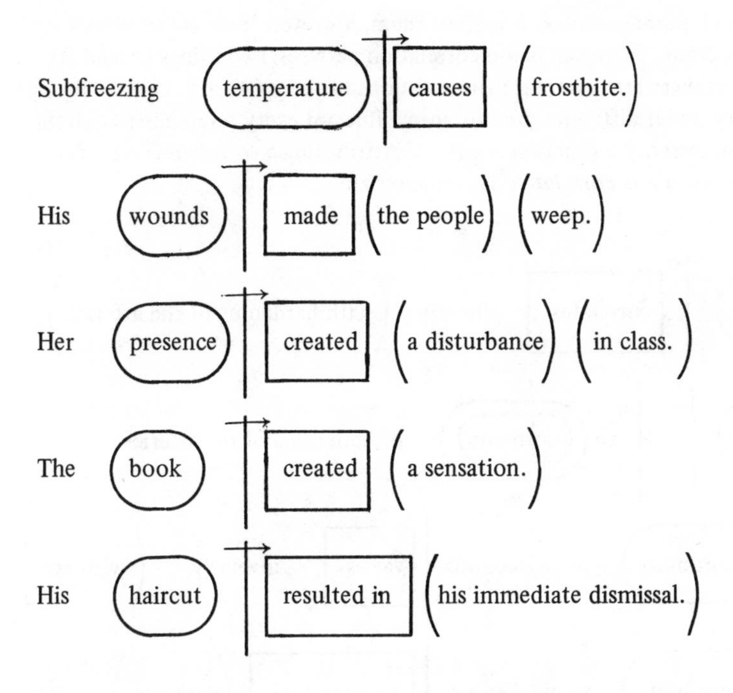

And just as all impetus causality need not be expressed as a function assertion, so it is with catalyst causality: *a factor* is a class, and *the factor* is an identity.

His haircut | was | an important factor in his dismissal.

His haircut | was ¦ the determining factor in his dismissal.

Third, and least likely to be ambiguous, is *correlate* causality. Though unlike causality in the more common senses already examined, correlation is treated here as causality because there are those who argue that no other conception of causality makes philosophical sense or serves any scientific purpose. A sequence of phenomena can be *described*, they say, but it cannot be *explained*. Correlation is a function in the mathematical sense of two things related in such a way that a change in one is reflected in a change in the other. The reflection may be a simple direct variation, an inverse variation, or something very much more complex. For all of them, however, there is variation – and thus function. There can be no correlation between two things (A and B) except as there are different manifestations of them (A_1 A_2 A_3) (B_1 B_2 B_3) that vary under different circumstances. But not every reference to correlation is necessarily a function assertion. Attributing *a correlate* is classifying, and attributing *is correlative* is characterizing.

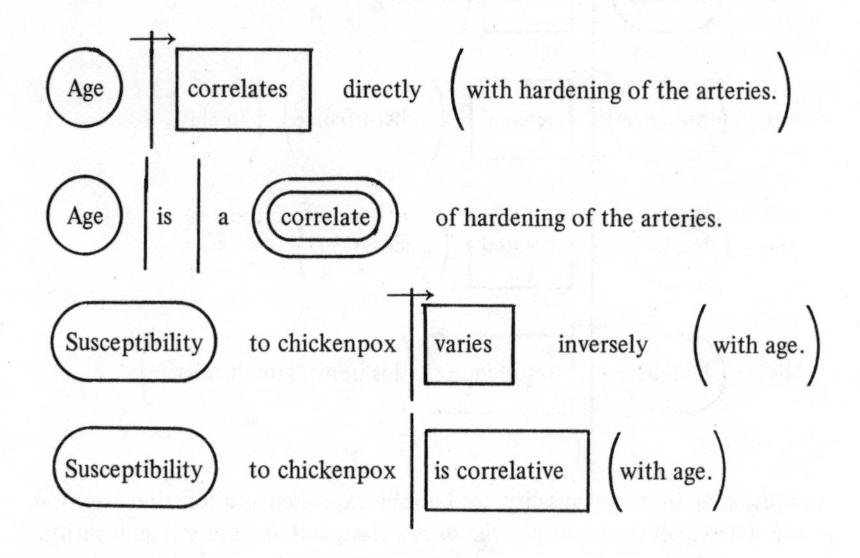

There is nothing here of causality in the sense of impetus or catalyst. Old age does not create hardening of the arteries nor does hardening of the arteries make one old. Susceptibility to chickenpox does not make one young nor does youth create a susceptibility to chickenpox. And herein lies the weakness of this least ambiguous of causality assertions – to frame a causality assertion as a simple correlation is to beg the kind of question we most want answered. What *is* the relation between the two things that are so clearly co-related? To say that

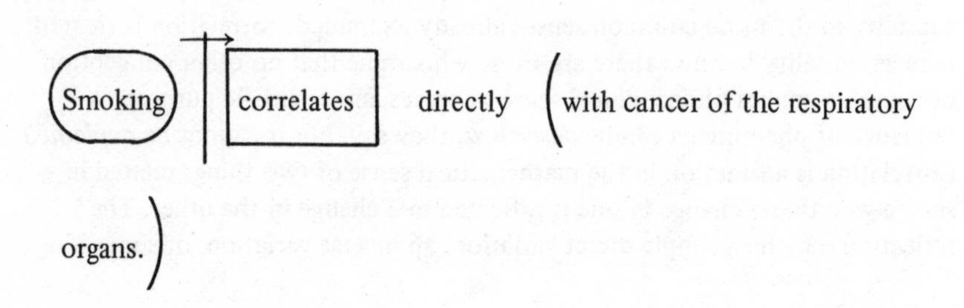

and yet to deny the legitimacy of saying that

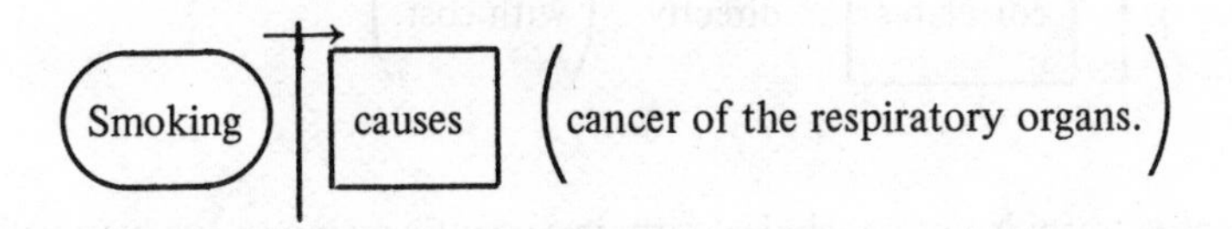

seems in effect to deny the legitimacy of ever establishing causal relations except as noncommittal correlations. Some relations are indeed no better understood than as correlations, and to frame these as impetus or catalyst assertions is to claim more than can be justified, with resulting ambiguity. But when knowledge is sufficiently detailed to warrant a more specific claim than correlation, a correlation assertion is not less ambiguous, only less precise.

Another problem associated with correlate assertions is more grammatical than semantical – insofar as the two can be distinguished. These are "the more the merrier" assertions, assertions that have long troubled grammarians because of their lack of a 'verb':

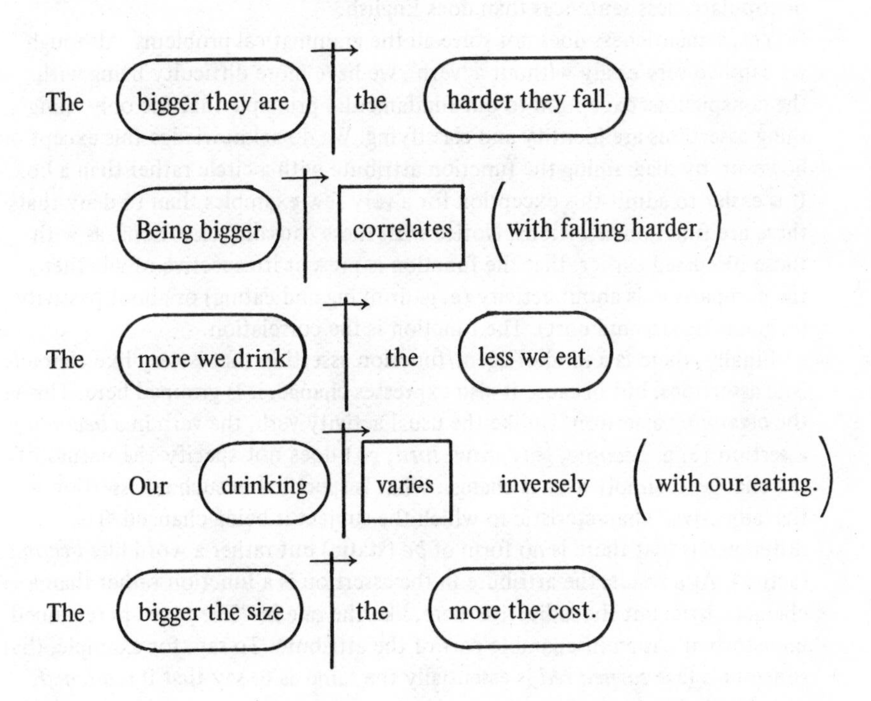

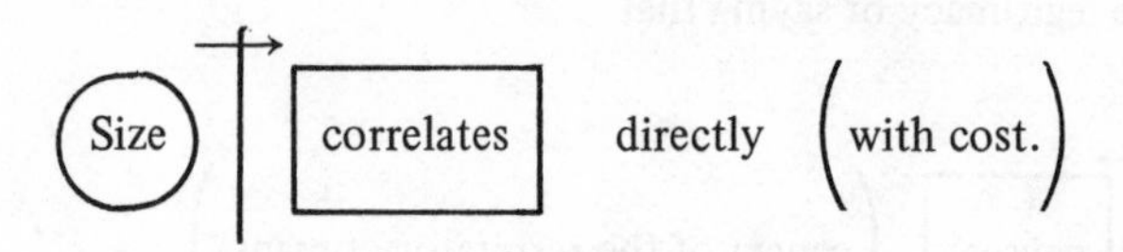

But because 'verb' is not a technical term in semantic grammar, we have little difficulty on this count in justifying these as assertions. What each does unquestionably have is a pair of things or states of affairs that correlate with each other. From this it is just a short step to labeling the first as a subject and the second as an attribute. The two are not synonyms in the sense of an identity assertion, and to say that the bigger they are the harder they fall is not necessarily to say that the harder they fall the bigger they are. All we need is a subject and an attribute, because the assertionness is expressed by the parallel features of the two phrases. The absence of a 'verb' here results in no ambiguity. Such a structure, unusual though it is in English grammar, can be interpreted only as a correlation. And, as an interesting comment by the by, some languages (e. g. Greek and Russian) have many more verbless or copulativeless sentences than does English.

Yet, semanticness does not solve all the grammatical problems. Although we can live very easily without a 'verb', we have more difficulty living with the conspicuous exception to our fundamental principle that the only thing/thing assertions are identity and classifying. We do acknowledge this exception, however, by diagraming the function attribute with a circle rather than a box. It is easier to admit this exception for a very few examples than to deny that these are function assertions. Notice with these causality assertions, as with those discussed earlier, that the function is present irrespective of whether the comparison is about activity (e. g. drinking and eating) or about passivity (e. g. having size and cost). The function is the correlation.

Finally, there is a kind of agent/function assertion that is very like characteristic assertions, but because it also expresses change, it is grouped here. This is the *becoming* assertion. Unlike the usual activity verb, the verb in a *becoming* assertion (e. g. *become*, *get*, *grow*, *turn*, *go*) does not specify the nature of the change; it simply asserts change. What is specified in such an assertion is the 'adjectival' characteristic to which the subject is being changed. The difference is that there is no form of *be* (static) but rather a word like *become* (active). As a result, the attribute in the assertion is a function rather than a characteristic; but the 'adjective' here, like the one in "The treasure remained undisturbed", is an inseparable part of the attribute. To say, for example, that someone's face *turned red* is essentially the same as to say that it *reddened*, and the diagraming reflects this:

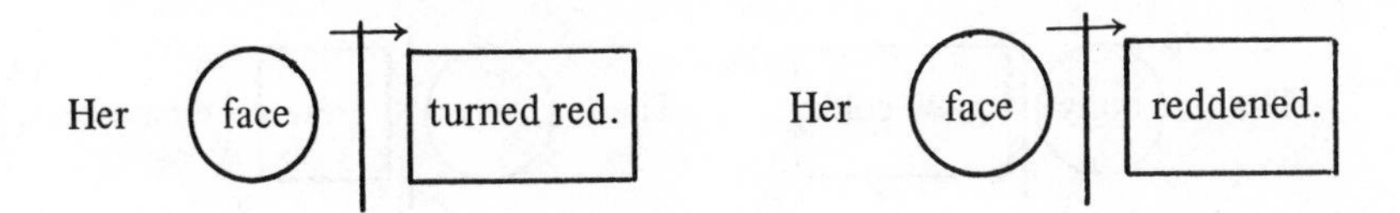

Notice, however, that the examples in the second column below have a *becoming* verb that does not result in a *becoming* assertion – sometimes, indeed, not even in a function assertion. The test for a *becoming* assertion is to substitute a form of *be* for the verb. If the result is a characteristic assertion that describes the subject after the change has taken place, then the original is a *becoming* assertion. For example, the result of

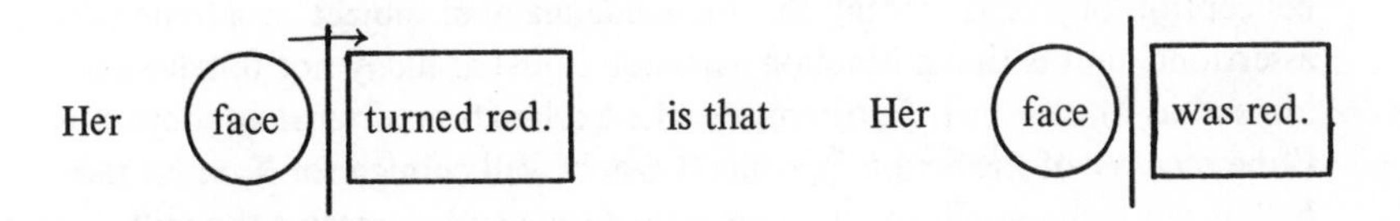

but the result of

Her (car) | turned (the corner.) is not that *Her car was the corner.

What the test does not, of course, prove is that the *becoming* assertion and the resulting characteristic assertion are synonymous.

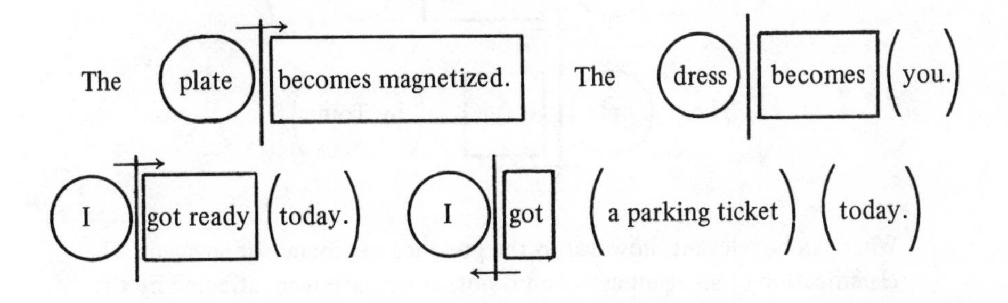

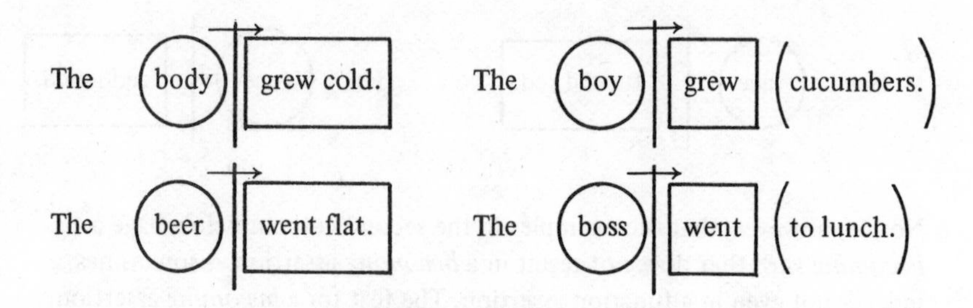

(2) *Object by Function*

In traditional grammar, and even in some modern linguistic analysis, the concept of 'object' is central. But the inadequacy of 'object' as a basic sub-assertional unit is that a function assertion is just as likely not to have an 'object' as to have one. Furthermore, the explanation of what an 'object' is ("the *receiver* of the *action*"), while it works well enough for *Tom hit the ball*, is not really applicable to *Tom sang a song* and *Tom runs the mile*. Thus our practice has been to treat these 'objects' simply as assertion modifiers and to reserve the term *object* for the subject of those function assertions in which the subject is not the agent. Whether or not the subject of an object/function assertion can reasonably be characterized as "receiver of the action" is thus irrelevant.

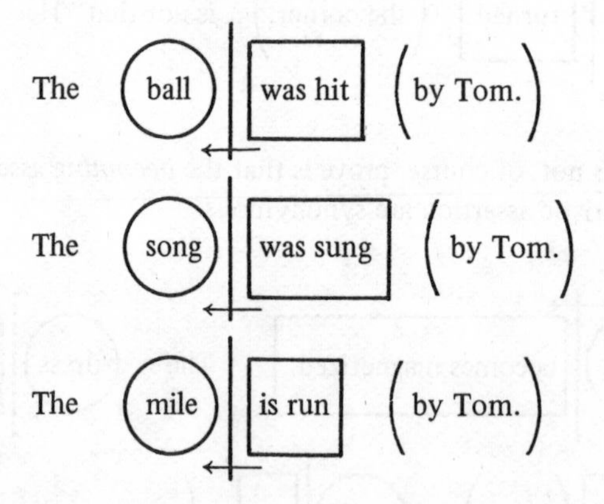

What can be relevant, however, is the presence or absence of an agent. The classification of an agent assertion is not, as we have seen, affected by the presence or absence of an object, but the classification of an object assertion may be affected by the presence or absence of an agent. This is understandable when we consider that a function necessarily has an agent, but it does not necessarily have an object distinct from that agent. All object assertions do in fact have an object, but in addition they necessarily state or imply an agent. Some object assertions that do state an agent cease to be function assertions when the agent is dropped because they do not necessarily imply an agent. When this is the case, the assertion is a characterizing one.

For the examples above, this is not the case. *Was hit*, *was sung*, and *is run* are functions that imply agents even if the agents are not stated. However, in the examples below, the nature of the assertion clearly changes depending on changes in modification. *Resulted* is always a function; but if something *resulted in*, it is an agent, and if something *resulted from*, it is an object:

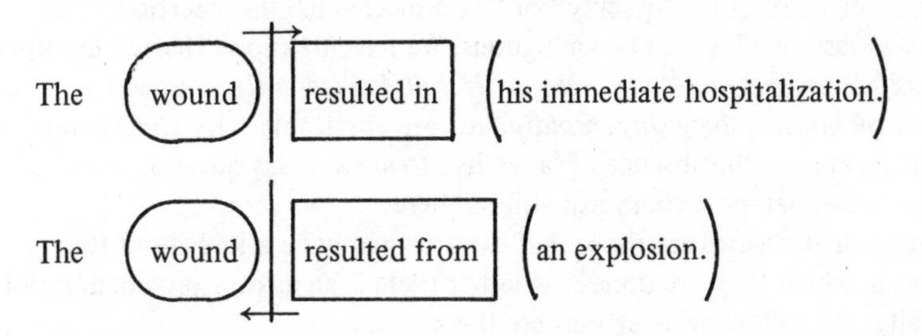

Resulted-in and *resulted-from* are two different words; in the absence of either *in* or *from*, we consistently interpret *result* as object/function:

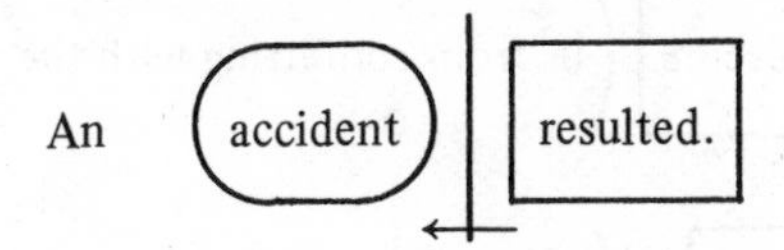

Fastened, on the other hand, may be either a function or a characteristic, depending on the modification. And what makes the example especially revealing is that each sentence has two different sorts of modifiers. These modifiers, though they result in important semantic differences between the two sentences, are formally exactly the same. The 'adverb' in the first assertion refers to how something *is* – it answers the question, "Is to what extent or degree? " The 'adverb' in the second assertion refers to how something *is done* – it answers the question, "Done in what manner? " But even without these attribute modifiers, the assertion modifiers obviously differ in kind from each other. A bolt is a *means*; a mechanic is an *agent*:

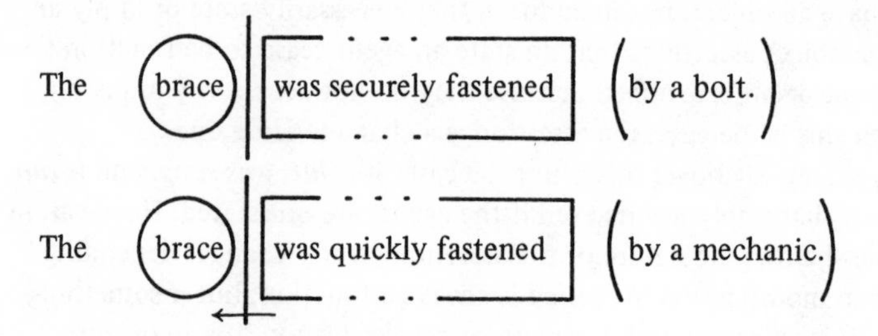

In the absence of either "quickly" or "by a mechanic" the assertion "The brace was fastened" would be ambiguous. We have to know whether modifiers like *willfully*, *regretfully*, *with care*, *with skill*, *belligerently*, *cautiously*, *efficiently*, *noisily*, *sluggishly*, *rapidly*, etc. are applicable. "By a mechanic" is sufficient, even in the absence of 'adverbs', to answer this question for us, but the 'adverbial' potential must still be there.

Function attributes are those that can reasonably be asked about the manner in which they are done – whether there is an answer provided or not. Formally, the following assertions are the same:

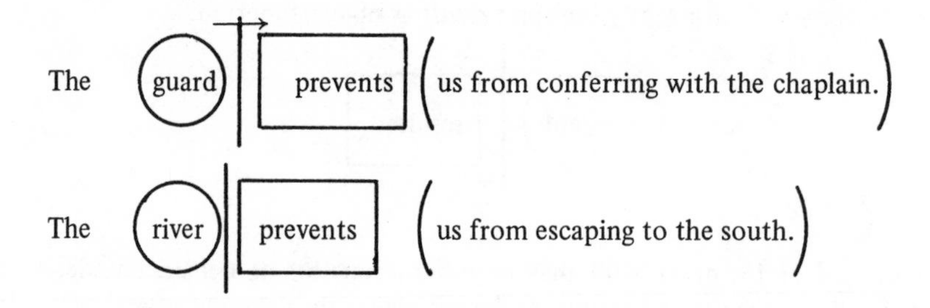

But semantically, the first one is reasonably asked about the manner in which the function is performed (e. g. *belligerently*), while the second one cannot be modified so as to provide such an answer. The river may flow rapidly and noisily, but it does not cut off our escape rapidly and noisily. And lest we seem to be implying that function modifiers are limited to single-word *–ly* forms of the *rapidly* and *slowly* sort, here are equally common answers to the basic question, "Done in what manner? "

with the energetic conviction of a born salesman.

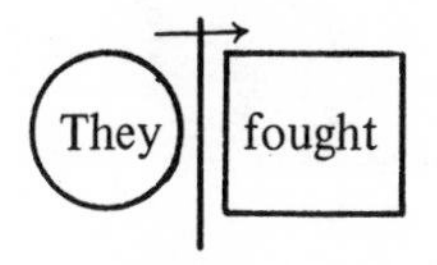

with callous disregard for the lives of their men.

There is one question that is applicable to both function and characteristic assertions, although more to the latter than to the former: "To what extent or degree? "

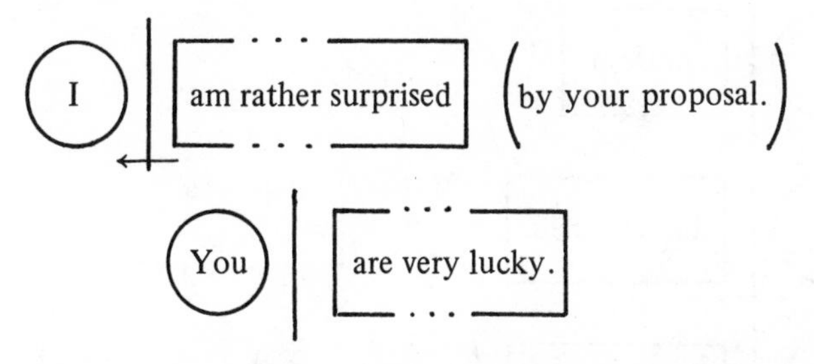

And herein lies a minor source of confusion. Attributes that can be modified by *rather* and *very* are, unless there is evidence to the contrary, characteristic. But some attributes that are essentially characteristic can be converted to object/function by the addition of an agent assertion modifier:

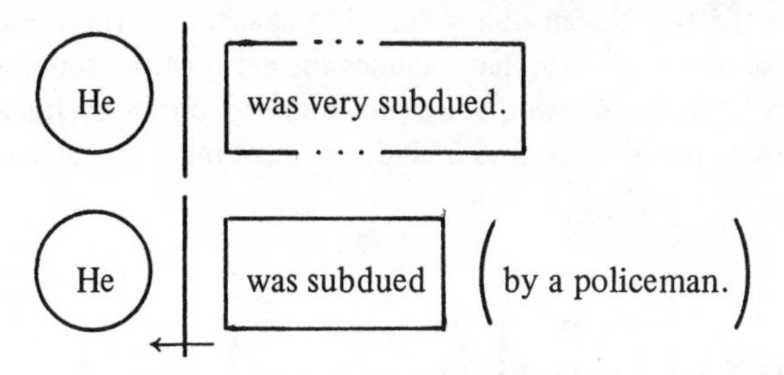

This is not a common source of confusion, however, because *very* is usually inapplicable as a modifier of function attributes (* He was very subdued by a policeman.) and because many words have variant forms that can distinguish between function and characteristic. "Complete" is distinguishable from "completed"; "fresh" is distinguishable from "refreshed". And thus function can be recognized in the following examples even when no agent is stated:

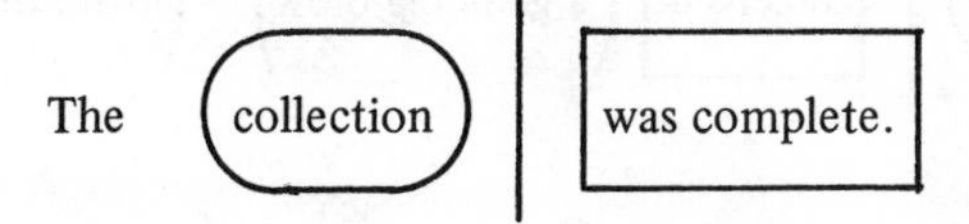

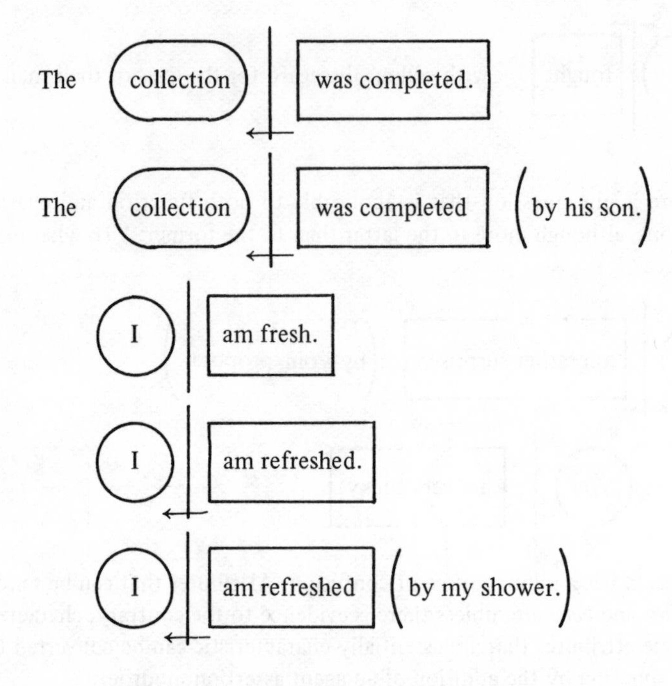

In most cases the test for an object/function assertion is the presence or potential presence of a *by* phrase that includes the agent of the function (e. g. "by his son", "by my shower"). But not every *by* phrase includes an agent, and not every phrase that does include an agent in an object assertion is a *by* phrase:

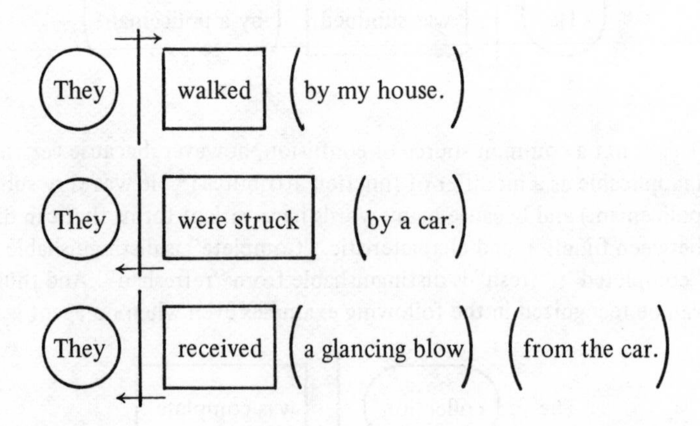

The lesson to be learned from this – which we have already emphasized and will be repeating over and over – is that grammar is as much a matter of meanings as it is of formal patterns. And to be a matter of meanings is by no means to be simply a question of words in and of themselves but to be a question of how words are used in specific contexts. In the last analysis, semantic subtlety may seem too delicate for either/or, workaday grammatical tools to do justice to. Does, for example, the very subtle difference between an image being created *in* a mirror and light rays being reflected *by* a mirror justify a fundamental difference of semantic kind?

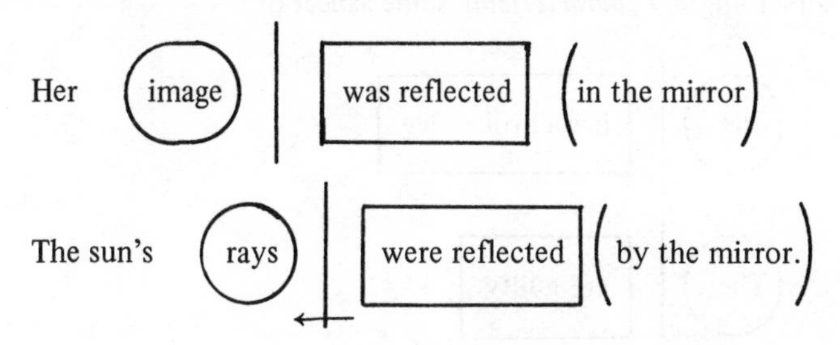

One man's difference of degree is another man's difference of kind; but in any case, there is a difference here in the nature of the reflecting, a difference that makes it possible for one assertion to take a 'passive' object and the other not to. A reflected image is part of the mirror and exists only as part of the mirror. A reflected ray, however, is acted upon by the mirror and distinguishable from it: "The sun's rays were reflected onto the opposite wall by the mirror".

In concluding our examination of function, we need to remember that on the level of maximum generality, all function assertions are semantically of the same kind. Within this unit, however, we found not only the two main divisions of agent and object assertions but also a series of subdivisions based upon semantic distinctions no less important than those that give rise to the six classes that form the basis of our grammar. These six classes, only two of which have yet been examined in any detail, are not ends in themselves; they are simply the necessary first step in developing a system of distinctions for the complete semantic interpretation of individual sentences. As we progress through the remaining four, we shall find equally important subdivisions appearing as a direct result of our efforts to determine the different ways that individual assertions qualify for inclusion in the larger classes. And when we reach the chapter on modification, we shall see how an understanding of modification is dependent on an ability to make precise distinctions among the different sorts of things modified. To understand what modifies what, and how, one must know what constitutes appropriate modification; and to determine what constitutes appropriate modification, one must understand what different sorts of things there are to be modified.

B. DESCRIBE SUBJECT BY NATURE

Nature assertions tell what a thing is rather than what it does (function) or what kind of thing it is (classification). There are two ways to describe the nature of something: by *characterizing* some aspect of it

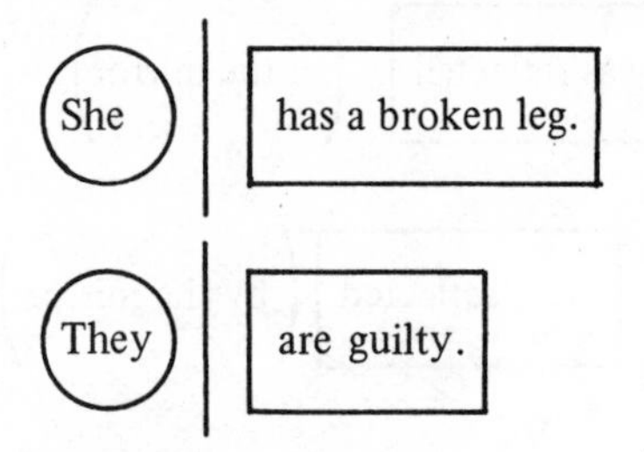

and by *identifying* it as a whole.

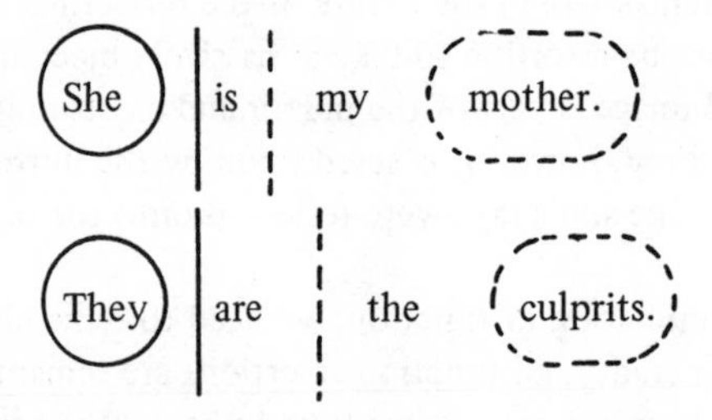

The two ways have in common attributes that are static rather than dynamic (distinguishing them from function) and that are descriptions rather than taxonomic relationships (distinguishing them from classification). However, characteristic and identity assertions differ in that the attribute in the former is just an aspect of the subject, while the attribute in the latter is the thing itself. As the diagrams on page 27 reveal, an identity assertion, and most obviously a negative version of it, is a thing/thing assertion. The subject is of course a thing, and the attribute, since it is or could be claimed to be identical with the subject, must also be a thing.

Thus, we return to our original problem in this chapter of deciding whether there are two basic kinds of assertions or three. If there are only two kinds, then agent/function, object/function, subject/characteristic, are grouped together formally by virtue of being about one thing rather than two. And subject/identity, individual/class, subclass/class, are grouped together by virtue of being about two things. In deciding on three basic kinds of assertions we are claiming that even though an identity assertion is formally like a relational assertion it makes more semantic sense to say that an identity assertion is actually about only one thing. By grouping together characteristic and identity assertions as subject/nature, we draw attention to important similarities as well as to important differences.

(1) *Subject by Characteristic*

The most amorphous of the six classes of assertion is characteristic. There are so many different manifestations of characteristic that it is much simpler to say what it is not than to say what it is. All assertions that are not about change or activity, that do not relate individual or subclass to class, that do not equate something with something else, are characteristic assertions. A thing may be characterized as to:

SIZE	is large, is tall, is short, is middle-sized, is six inches tall, is six feet tall, is six feet, rises eighty stories, drops fifty fathoms, number in the millions, runs to several thousand, has eighty stories
SHAPE	is oval, is square, is bent, curves, narrows, has a triangular shape
WEIGHT	is heavy, is light, is ten pounds, is over-weight, weighs a ton
COLOR	is blue, is blue-green, is colorful, is pale, has a reddish tinge
TEXTURE	is flat, is soft, is lumpy, continues to be slippery, has a rough texture
AGE	is young, is middle-aged, is old, is seventeen, is two days old, is two centuries old
LOCATION	is next to her, is next, is in a cave, is over the hill, is on the table, is below the horizon, is at home, is home, is under water, is near the tree, is near, is close, is here, is away, hangs from the ceiling, rests on a platform, spans the river
CONDITION	is undernourished, is full, is strong, is married, is true, is independent, is awkward, is over, is in shape, is at issue, is under discussion, kept quiet, remains hidden, exists, has a problem, has a toothache, has one tooth missing, takes two hours
RELATIONSHIP	has a baby, has an uncle, has an insurance agent, has an open-door policy

POSSESSION	owns a bicycle, has a car, has a slave, possesses great wealth
CONTENT	is about Greece, contains two errors, holds a pint, includes an index
FEELINGS	is composed, is happy, is interested, is resigned, is thoughtful, is depressed, is blue, has the blues
COMPOSITION	is four-wheeled, has four wheels, is wooden, is made of wood, is wood, is composed of hydrocarbons, consists of flour and water, is flour and water, has green eyes, has one tooth
VALUE	is good, is beautiful, is worthless, is evil, is invaluable, is disgusting, is below standard, possesses great value
IMPERATIVE	must remain, has to be waterproof, should be here, ought to be red

A certain semantic unity can be discerned here if we look ahead to classification assertions. Classification is also a static characterization but of a different sort. The class to which a thing belongs is not a part or aspect *of* it but a label imposed *upon* it. Characteristic, on the other hand, is more like a part-whole relationship. When we say that a car has a radio, or that the radio is part of the car, or that the radio comes with the car – we are talking about constituent elements. No matter whether the subject is the 'whole' or the 'part', the assertion is about components of a relationship. When we say that she has blue eyes or is blue-eyed, we are doing the same sort of thing. And these 'parts' need not be dissectible in a physical sense. When we say that she is seventeen years old, we are referring to something not separable from the subject itself but that is nonetheless an aspect of it and not a label. When we say that she has a music teacher, the music teacher is separable, but the relationship specified by "has a music teacher" is still an aspect of the woman in question. It is significantly different to say that she *is* a music teacher. Here we are labeling the subject by placing her in the large class of people who are teachers and in the more restricted class of people who are teachers of music.

Still, our list does emphasize the semantic variety of characteristic. And the formal variety is almost as great. There are more different ways of making a characteristic assertion than of making any of the other five semantic classes. As the chart below indicates, the traditional 'adjective' is by no means the only kind of characteristic. Not all characteristics are 'adjectives' and not all 'adjectives' are characteristics. Subjects can be designated by words traditionally distinguished as adjectives and thought to characterize things. The traditional form of the adjective may actually without alteration be a thing, whereas it cannot function without alteration (for example, by the addition of some form of *be*) as a characteristic in an assertion.

Black is a color, and thus *black* can serve as a thing – as the subject in a a function or nature assertion or as either the subject or the attribute in a classifying assertion. Blackness is also a thing, a condition or mode of existence, and thus *being black* can serve as a subject. However, blackness can also be a description, and thus only a slight change in the form of *be* results in *is black*, a characteristic.

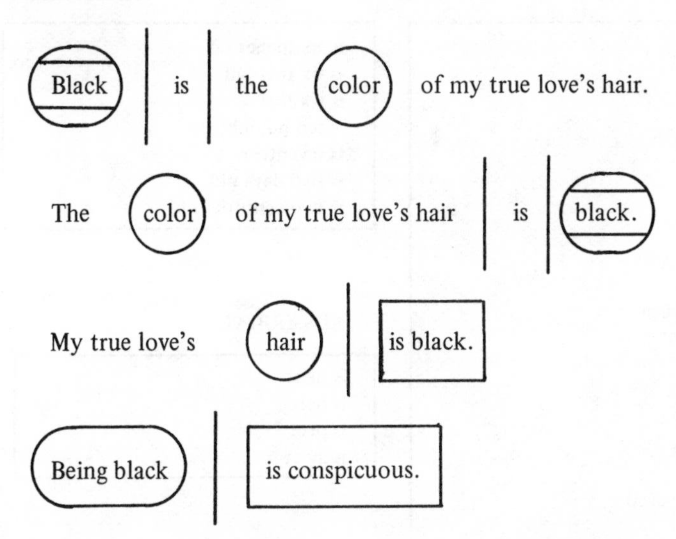

Black in the first sentence is a thing and the subject of the assertion, but since *color* is also a thing, this is a classifying assertion. The demonstration of this is that the two parts of the assertion can be reversed, with the old attribute becoming the new subject. In the third sentence, *hair* is a thing and the subject, but since *is black* is a characteristic, this is a nature assertion. To have said "Black is my true love's hair" would have been an unidiomatic reversal of the usual subject/attribute order but with subject and attribute still distinguishable. To have said "My true love's hair is black color" would have been erroneous, because my true love's hair is not a color but colored. In the fourth sentence *being black* is a thing not because of the 'participle' form but because of the meaning. The same form of *be* can occur as part of an attribute – where it signals the change from characteristic to function.

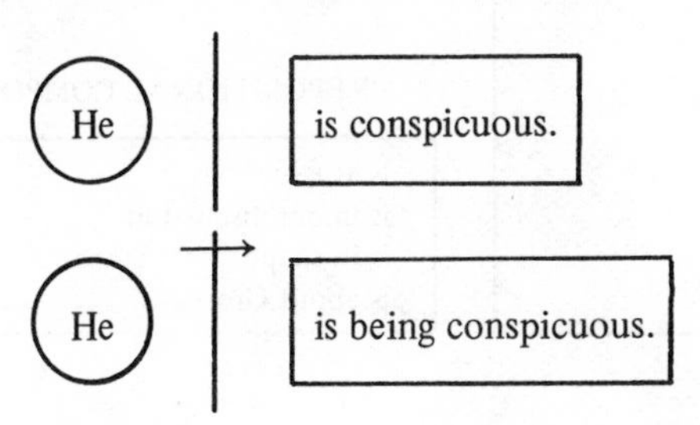

Is being is like *becoming*: both are used for unspecified function. However, not every state of being can serve as a function attribute – only those for which *acting* or *behaving* is substitutable for *being*.

ADJECTIVAL

is large
is tall
is short
is oval
is square
is bent
is heavy
is light
is overweight
is blue
is blue-green
is colorful
is pale
is flat
is soft
is lumpy
is young
is middle-aged
is old
is near
is close
is undernourished
is full
is strong
is true
is independent
is awkward
is four-wheeled
is wooden
is thoughtful
is happy
is good
is beautiful
is worthless
is invaluable
is evil

NUMERICAL

is six inches tall
is six feet tall
is six feet
is ten pounds
is seventeen
is two days old
is two centuries old

ADVERBIAL

is next
is here
is over
is away

PREPOSITIONAL

is next	to her
is in	a cave
is over	the hill
is on	the table
is below	the horizon
is at	home
is under	water
is near	the tree
is below	standard

PREPOSITIONAL COMPOUND

is at issue
is under discussion
is in shape
is about Greece

PARTICIPIAL

is made of wood
is composed of hydrocarbons
is composed
is interested
is resigned
is depressed
is underrated

NOMINAL

is wood
is home
is flour and water

VERBAL

rises eighty stories
drops fifty fathoms
number in the millions
runs to several thousand
weighs a ton
hangs
rests
spans
possesses great wealth
owns a bicycle
consists of flour and water
contains two errors
takes two hours
holds a pint
includes an index
possesses great value
curves
narrows
exists

HAVE

has eighty stories
has a triangular shape
has a reddish tinge
has a rough texture
has a problem
has a toothache
has a tooth missing
has one tooth
has green eyes
has an insurance agent
has a baby
has an open-door policy
has an uncle
has a car
has a slave
has the blues
has little value
has to be waterproof

VERBAL/ADJECTIVAL

continues to be slippery
remains hidden
kept quiet

MODAL

must remain
should be here
ought to be red

Traditional terms like 'adjective' and 'participle' are not semantical grammar terms, and the distinctions made by means of them are only for the purpose of correlating certain familiar (though imprecise) aspects of traditional grammar with semantic grammar. We want to see how many different manifestations of characteristic assertions we can find. For our purposes – as revealed in the chart above – there are eleven different manifestations of characteristic assertions.

Four of these eleven kinds need further attention because of their close resemblance to function attributes.

participle

verbal/adjectival

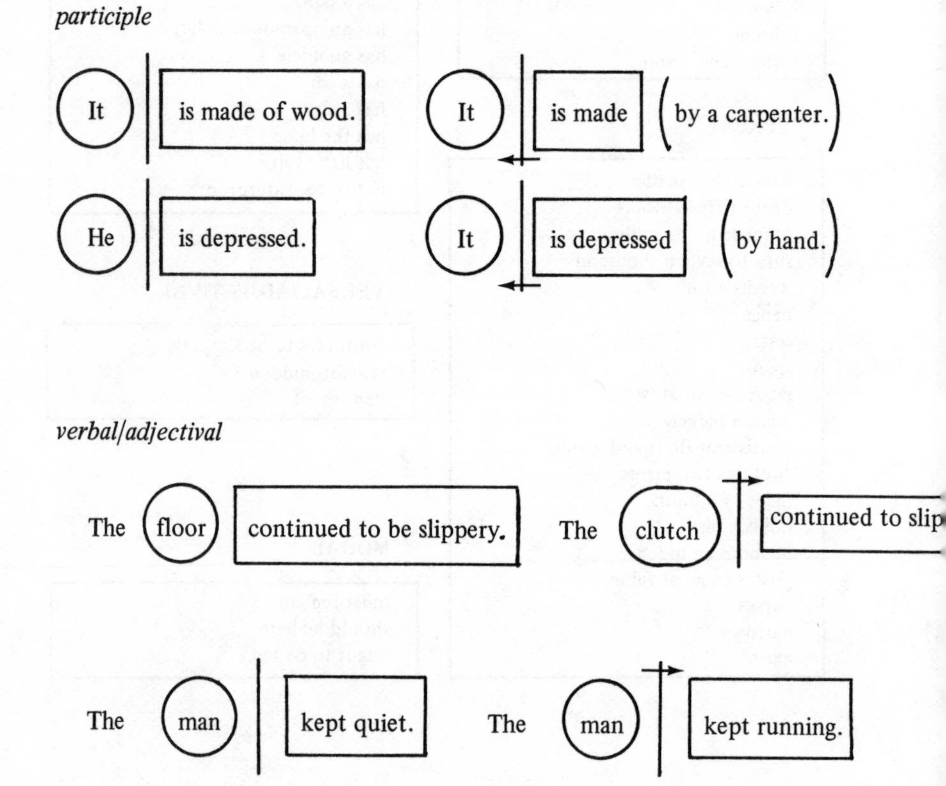

verbal

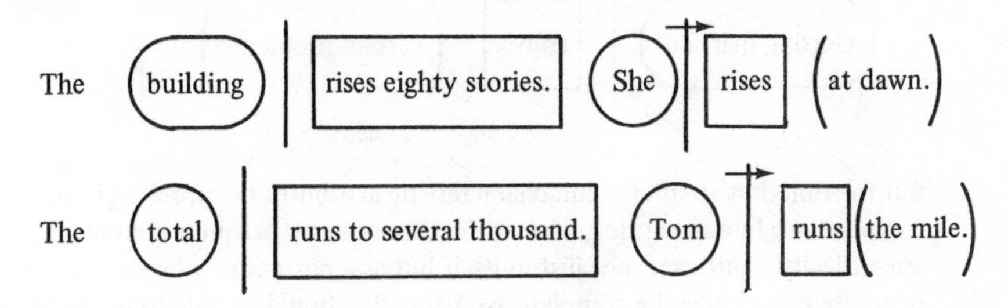

have

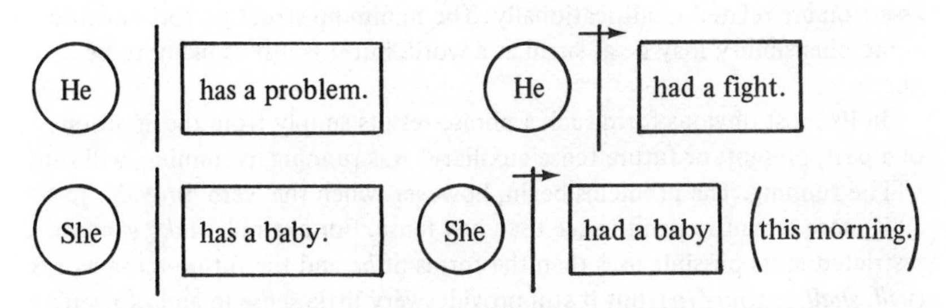

These examples raise again the question of compound attributes and subjects: What constitutes the core or headword and what are modifiers of it? In a semantic grammar it is as important to be able to articulate the principles for discerning compound semantic units as to articulate the principles for analyzing into ultimate constituents. For example, we cannot make a complete analysis of characteristic assertions without answering this question of semantic indivisibility; yet to attempt such an answer here would be to venture prematurely into a discussion of modification. For the present, a summary will have to suffice – though the basic rule of thumb is clear enough: words not semantically comprehensible in themselves and comprehensible in the same sense as revealed in the total assertion cannot serve as the core of a subject or attribute or as a modifier thereof.[3]

For *things* (subjects or attributes) the problem is relatively simple. The obvious exceptions to single-word cores are 'infinitives' and the 'present participles' of *be* and the becoming verbs:

To plant trees | is | to plan for the future.

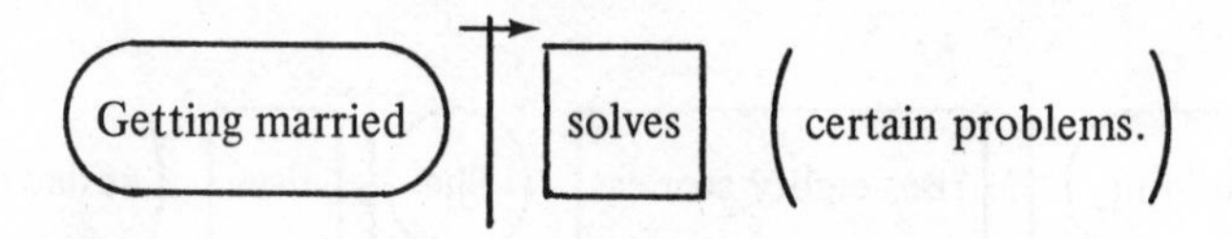

But for function attributes and characteristic attributes the problem is more complicated. In a semantic grammar the core of every attribute should be semantically significant, not just in itself but as a portent of whatever larger structure constitutes the complete assertion. We should be able to understand what kind of assertion we have by seeing only the simple subject and the simple attribute. Consequently, not all words that "go together" in an assertion are related modificationally. The minimum structure for semantic comprehensibility may be as small as a word, but it is just as likely to be a phrase.

In its most obvious form such a phrase results simply from the addition of a past, present, or future tense auxiliary: was running, is running, will run/ will be running. The problems begin, however, when the 'verb' provides just a bit more semantic significance than just tense. For example: *take* is more restricted in its possible uses than the forms of *be* and the future-tense words (*will*, *shall*, *is going to*), but it still provides very little sense in and of itself. Thus it is found in both function and characteristic assertions:

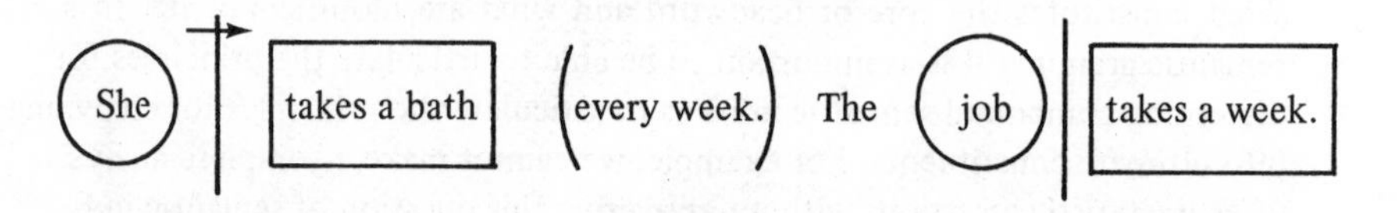

Taking a bath is something the subject does, but taking a week (like taking the cake) characterizes an aspect of the subject rather than stating what it does. She *reluctantly* takes a bath every week, but the job *requires* a week.

The confusion between function and characteristic attributes is probably most conspicuous when a 'direct object' is present. This is not a concept that is of much use in a semantic grammar, although as far as function assertions are concerned, we have no difficulty accounting for it as an assertion modifier answering the question "Do what or whom? " However, in a minority of cases the traditional 'direct object' is not the result of any *doing*.

He weighs *Weighs what 'direct object'?* the meat. / rock samples. / the contestants. / babies.

He weighs a ton.

To indicate this basic difference in semantic kind, we have diagramed the characteristic as an indivisible unit – to indicate that the meaning of the characteristic is more a matter of the 'direct object' than it is of the 'verb'.

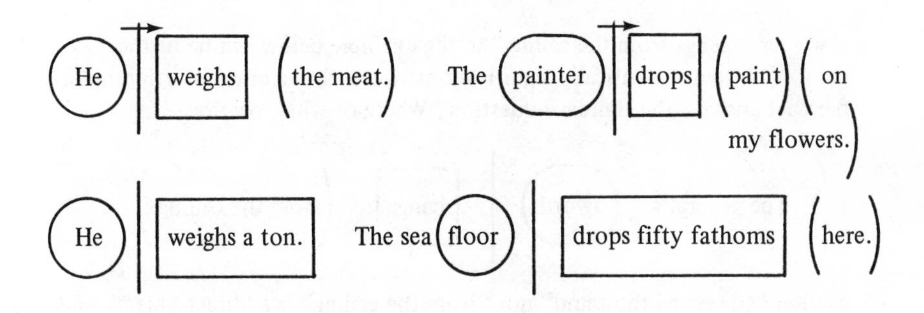

Distinguishing between separable (the ordinary) and inseparable (the extra-ordinary) attributes can be a means of making a significant kind of semantic distinction. However, it is occasionally possible for the ordinary meaning of a 'verb' to be a static characteristic and the extra-ordinary meaning to be the function:

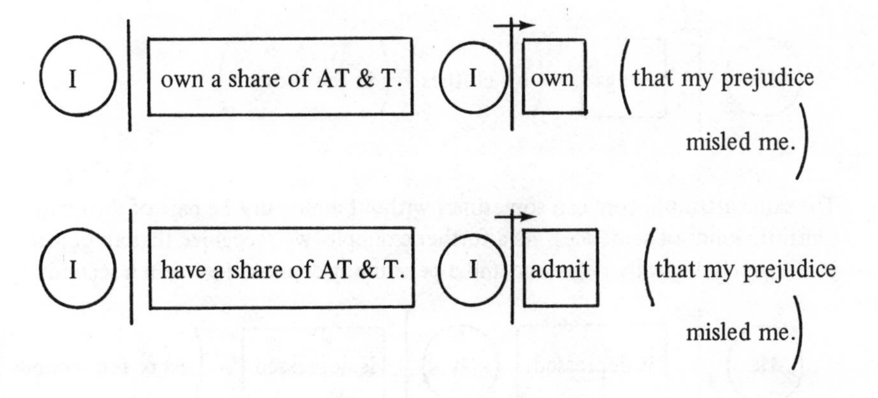

Yet the distinction of semantic kind remains the same.

When 'verbal' characteristics are not interpretable as containing a traditional 'direct object', the problem is a bit more complicated. We are still committed to making a consistent distinction between the two semantic kinds and to making the core attribute semantically significant in its own right. Thus "runs to several thousand" in the example below cannot be further reduced: "runs" in and of itself clearly implies a function, and the refugee population is not in any functional sense running.

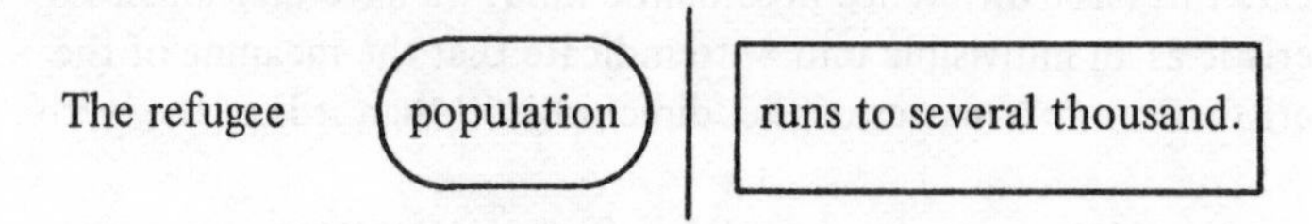

However, "hangs from the ceiling" in the example below *can* be further reduced: into a semantically significant attribute core and an assertion modifier that answers the standard question "Where or what location? "

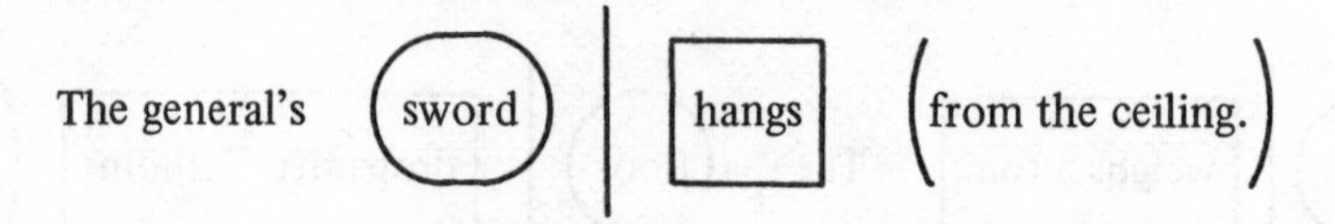

Neither "to several thousand" nor "from the ceiling" is a 'direct object', and neither one can provide an answer to the question "Do what or whom? " The difference here between a compound attribute core and a non-compound attribute core is simply that the "runs" is not what characterizes the population but that "hangs" *is* what characterizes the sword. But as a consequence of diagraming "hangs" as a characteristic, we are left with the possibility of the same word being a function attribute:

The same attribute core can sometimes without ambiguity be part of different semantic kinds of sentences. As a further example, we recognize that an object is not psychologically depressed and a person not depressed every ten seconds:

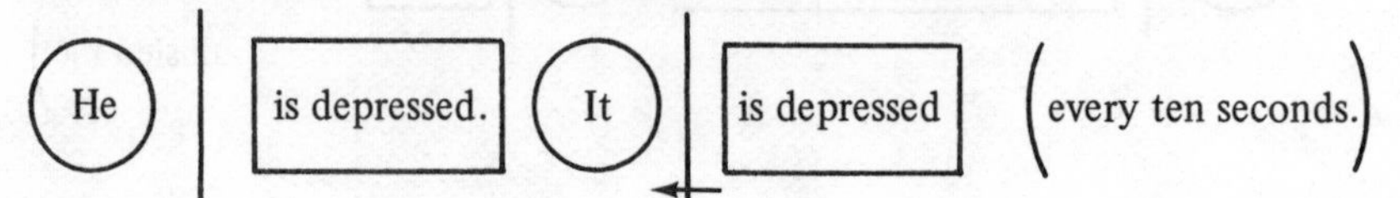

Finally, it is possible for an attribute core that is a phrase to include a word that by itself is without semantic significance. The prime example of this is ubiquitous *have*. *Have* is much more common in English grammar than the usual discussion of it as a tense auxiliary of the perfect tenses would lead one to think.[4]

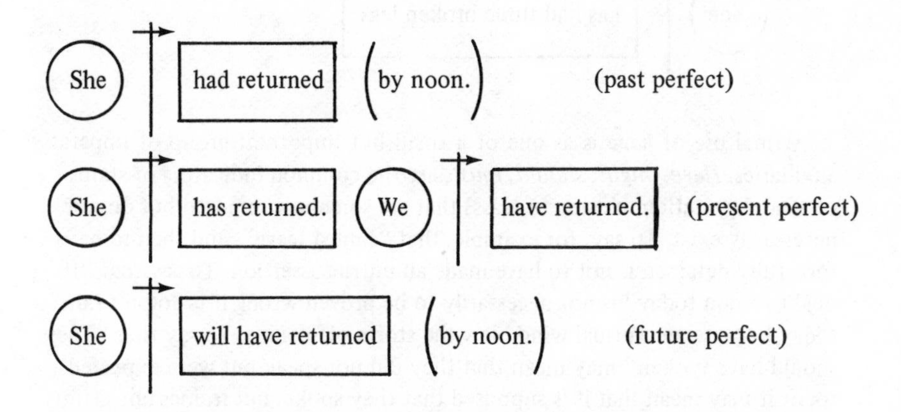

If we were to offer as the core of an assertion simply "she had", there would be no indication of which of three entirely different kinds of meaning was intended:

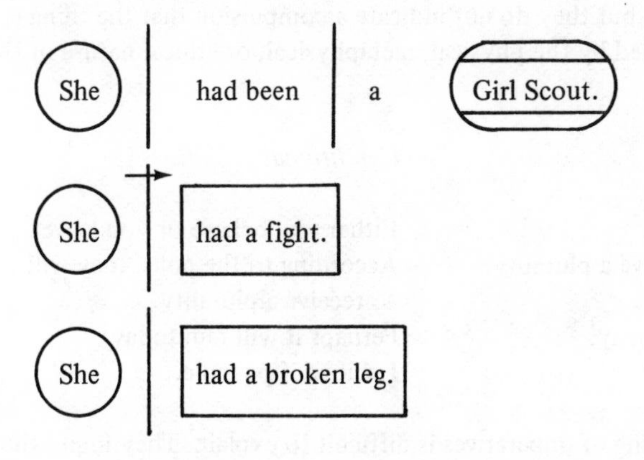

And, indeed, it is quite possible for *have* to be a tense auxiliary of a *have* attribute as a means of indicating a not yet terminated state of affairs:

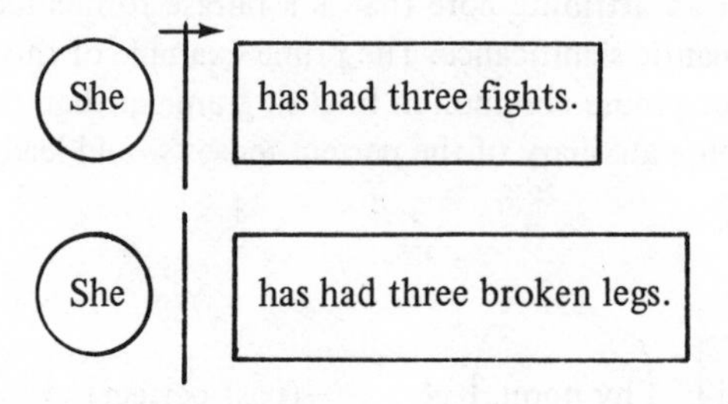

A final use of *have* is as one of a small but important group of imperative auxiliaries. *Have*, *ought*, *should*, *must*, are the common indicators of states of affairs (function, nature, or class) that are somehow required but do not necessarily exist. To say, for example, that "I must leave", and then to be forcefully detained is not to have made an untrue assertion. To say that "It ought to rain today" is not necessarily to be proven wrong if it doesn't rain today because an unusual wind blew the storm off course. To say that "They should have spoken" may mean that they did not speak but were expected to, or it may mean that it is supposed that they spoke, but it does **not** claim that they did in fact speak. These imperatives are a kind of conditional modification: they restrict the assertion by leaving open the possibility of things being other than required.[5] "I must leave" is like "Perhaps I will leave" in conditioning the assertion against the possibility of the something not happening. "Perhaps" or "if I don't get waited on soon" or "judging from the clouds" are qualifications, but they do not indicate a compulsion that the thing is somehow demanded by the physical, metaphysical, or ethical nature of things.

Imperative	*Conditional*
You must behave.	Either you behave or you leave.
They should receive a plurality.	According to the polls, they will receive a plurality.
It ought to rain today.	Perhaps it will rain today.
I have got to go.	I will go if possible.

The precise meaning of imperatives is difficult to explain. They imply the existence of powerful forces or standards that, however, are not always in accord with the facts. And thus imperatives are elements of assertions that are ultimately not subject to interpretation as to truth or falsity. Or, more precisely, we cannot determine the precise nature of the claim. As a result, there is a question as to whether an assertion that contains a function attribute is still a function assertion when an imperative auxiliary is added or whether it thereby becomes a characteristic assertion. There is no problem with characteristic attributes. "This ought to be red" (whatever its precise meaning) and "This is red" are both characterizing the subject – though of course the assertions do not mean the same thing. But with function attributes, the addition of an imperative seems to change the functional claim.

This problem is akin to the questions raised by negatives: e. g. , is "He is not walking" still a function assertion? Although we have not explained the reason for considering function to be function irrespective of negation, we have indicated our answer in the logical diagrams on page 26. The discussion of negatives must be postponed.[6] For the present let it suffice to say that imperatives are part of the core assertion because they can be explained as neither restrictive nor non-restrictive modifiers and because it makes for a significant difference in meaning if the claim is about what *is* or about what *is supposed to be*. But this difference of imperative or oughtness does not affect the semantic kind because semantic kinds are not distinguished by the 'mode' or attitude or realm of discourse of the asserting but by the nature of what in the simplest sense is attributed. To speak of working, for example, is to attribute function – irrespective of whether it is spoken of positively or negatively, equivocally or unequivocally, imperatively or matter-of-factly.

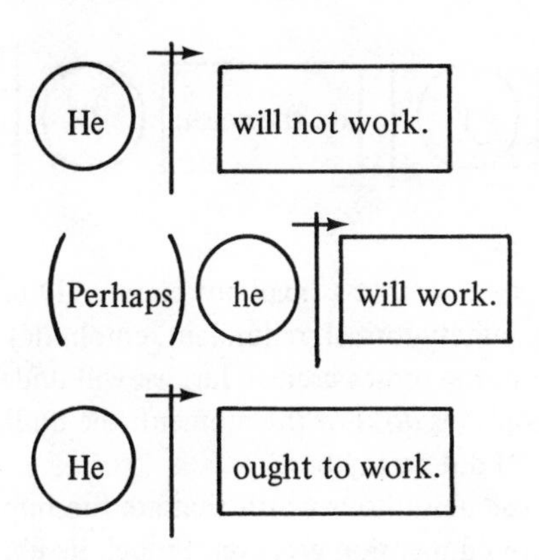

Matters of degree, specification of conditions, limitations in scope, are manifestations of restrictive modification (either assertional or subassertional), because the core assertion is still being claimed in one way or another even without the modifiers. But imperative and negative auxiliaries are necessarily (i. e. semantically) part of the core assertion because to remove them would result in a fundamentally different (though not different *kind* of) meaning.

A final consideration of the ubiquity of *have* in particular and of characteristic assertions in general is external relationships. Characteristic assertions are variable enough when we consider just the different ways that something can be described in and of itself, in whole or part. But while this takes care of my having blue eyes and having a toothache, it hardly seems to accord with my having an uncle, an insurance agent, an automobile, an open-door policy. Like *there* and *it* as all-purpose, and thus essentially semantically empty, subjects,[7] *have* relationships commit one to very little. *Have* provides nothing that is not contained in the meaning of the thing being had. I am related to an uncle (in a family way), to an insurance agent (in a business way), to an automobile (in a transportation way), to an open-door policy (in a diplomatic way). I can be characterized not just in and of myself but also in relation to things that impinge upon me from outside. There are no alternative ways of explaining these *have* relational assertions, but we are less than precise in labeling them as characteristic.

Similar to *have* in being able to serve as both tense auxiliary and verb is *do*. And like *have*, *take*, *become*, etc. , it is semantically too vague to ever serve as the core or headword of an attribute. It must derive its meaning and even its basic semantic kind from other words in the attribute. The meaning of *do* is never more precise than abstracted, unspecified function:

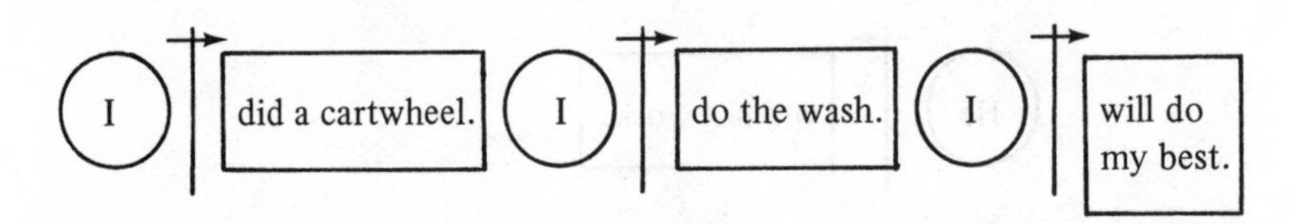

And when we discover, in Chapter 4, that a small but commonly used group of modifiers (called variously punctuational, redundant, emphatic) are neither restrictive nor non-restrictive in the senses used so far, we will understand better another use of the ubiquitous *do*. For the moment, the undiagramed example can speak for itself: "I did do my best".

While on the subject of those ubiquitous words that are too imprecise to serve as attribute cores, we should mention *get*, even though its ubiquity does not extend to characteristic assertions. *Get* can be subject/function, object/function, and imperative:

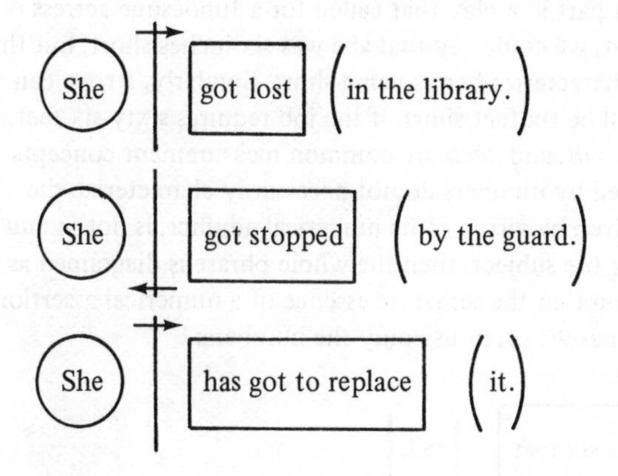

Two additional kinds of characteristic assertions that still need mentioning because of compound attributes are *numerical* and *prepositional compound*. Numerical attributes are very closely related to adjectival in that both use 'adjectives'. The difference hinges on whether or not the 'adjective' is a description of the subject (the first column) or a description of the kind of counting (the second column):

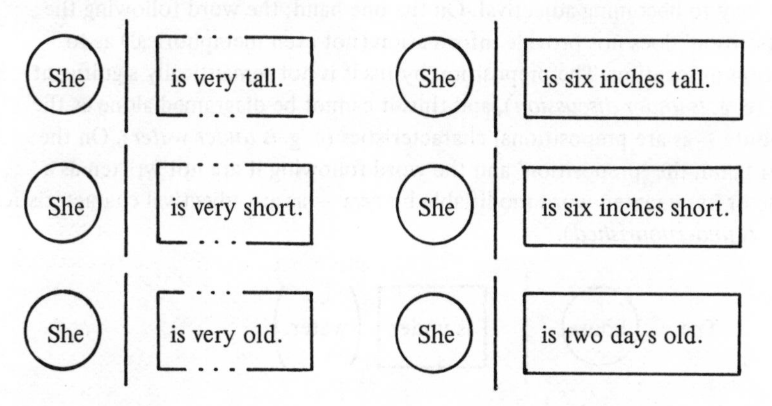

Adjectival characteristics can (with a few exceptions) be modified by *very*, and numerical characteristics cannot be. But more important than this formal test is the semantic one. To use a word like *tall*, *short*, or *old* without any numbers is obviously to characterize the subject as tall, short, or old. But to use these words with numbers is not necessarily to so characterize the subject. To describe someone as six inches tall is certainly not to characterize him as tall, and to describe him as six feet tall is not necessarily to do so. If a woman were auditioning for a part in a play that called for a Junoesque actress of at least six and a half feet, we could say that she was six inches short, but this would certainly not characterize her as being short. Similarly, a rope can be sixty feet long and still be six feet short, if the job requires sixty-six feet.[8] *Tall*, *long*, *short*, *old*, *high*, and *deep* are common measurement concepts that when accompanied by numbers do not necessarily characterize the subject. If the 'adjective', by virtue of its numerical adjunct, is not in and of itself characterizing the subject, then the whole phrase is diagramed as a unit. Further indication that the semantic essence of a numerical assertion is not the 'adjective' is that we often use only the numbers:

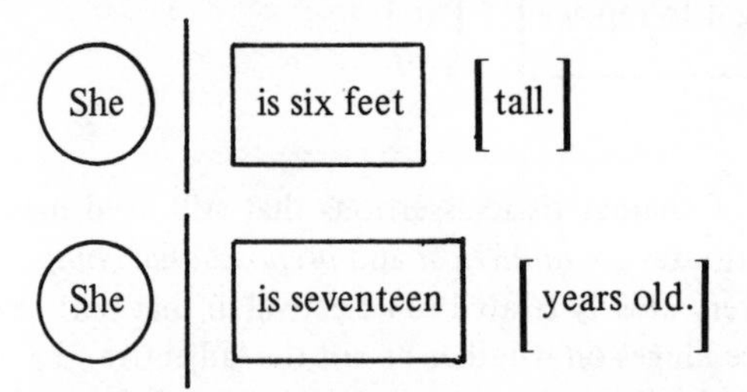

Prepositional compounds are prepositional phrases that could be said to be on their way to becoming adjectival. On the one hand, the word following the 'preposition' does not provide information (not even metaphorical) as to position or location. The preposition by itself is not semantically significant here (e. g. *is under discussion*), and thus it cannot be diagramed alone as the attribute – as are prepositional characteristics (e. g. *is under water*). On the other hand, the 'preposition' and the word following it are not written as a single or hyphenated word modifiable by *very* – as are adjectival characteristics (e. g. *is undernourished*).

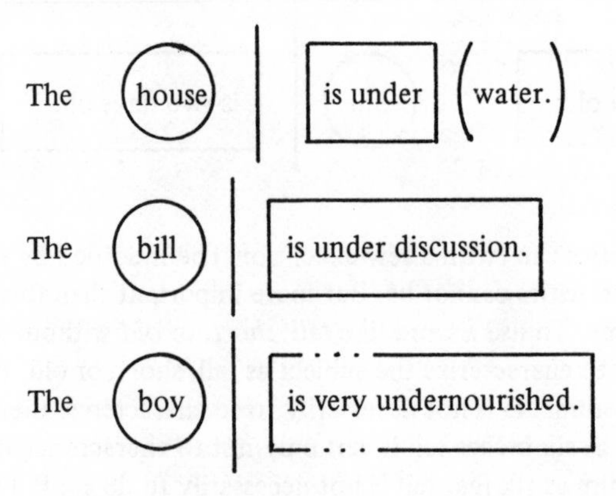

As a conclusion to this rather cursory treatment of what many grammarians have thought to constitute a host of basic grammatical features, we might offer this principle: *Word* is a very secondary grammatical concept because words are so variable in both form and meaning. If words are thought to be delimited simply by spacing on the page, then semantically some words are composites of other words, and some words are not truly words until joined into phrases.

long-lived	is-singing
four-wheeled	is-large
left-handed	is-six-inches-tall
high-pressure	is-next
out-of-date	is-at-issue
housefly	is-made-of-wood
hindsight	is-wood
overweight	remains-hidden
stepmother	rises-eighty-stories
bigwig	has-eighty-stories

Characteristic and function attributes would seem much less complicated if phrases that constituted inseparable semantical grammatical units were written as single or hyphenated words. Word delimitation in English, as compared for instance to German, is governed more by historical accident than by logic. And the resulting inconsistencies make grammatical analysis appear to be more complicated than is warranted by the amount of semantic distinctions made. Why should *bigwig* be written as one word and *big shot* be written as two? *Webster's Third* so lists them, even as it defines both as "a person of consequence". Why should *high* plus the comparative sign *er* be written as one word and *prepared* plus the comparative sign *more* be written as two? Why should the signs of past and present tense be incorporated into single words in *sang* and *sing* but be written as two words in *was large* and *is large*?

The fact that no semantic answers can be provided is not a criticism of English; all languages are the products of various processes of evolution that result in systems that are in part semantically explicable and partly not. No one is suggesting that we ought to begin hyphenating our compound attributes; the suggestion is rather that for understanding the semantic nature of assertions we can justifiably simplify our task by thinking of the compound attribute cores analyzed in this section as being indivisible single words.

Perhaps semantic grammar is in some respects more superficial in its analysis of similarities and differences than other kinds of grammars because of its frequent recourse to the concept of indivisible attribute cores. Certainly this will be seen by some as an attempt to gloss over crucial grammatical problems. Yet, one man's essential similarity is another man's essential difference and vice versa. There is no acknowledged court of final appeal, and in the last analysis it seems fair to say that, as compared for example to transformational-generative grammar, semantic grammar is no less precise, only different in emphasis. Some sentences that the transformationalists see as fundamentally the same appear fundamentally different to us, and some that they see as fundamentally different appear fundamentally the same to us. The only criteria are consistency and comprehensibility.

Here are three pairs of sentences commonly associated with and serving to justify transformational-generative grammar. No one denies that there are six different meanings here, but there is disagreement as to which pairs manifest essential similarity and which essential dissimilarity. The value of semantic grammar is that the nature of the semantic similarities and differences is consistently reflected in the diagraming of each sentence and that the sentence is comprehensible as it is written, without need to transform it into something else.

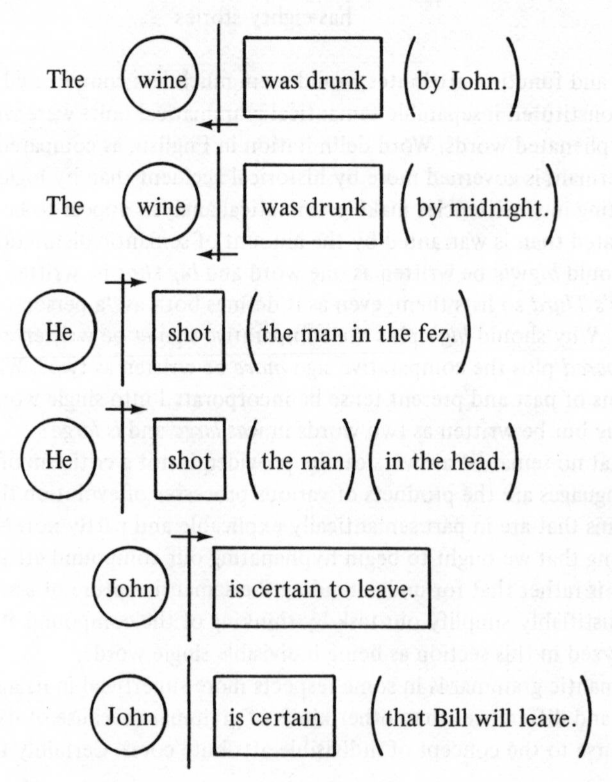

For the purposes of semantic grammar two assertions are essentially similar if they have the same subject and attribute cores and are of the same semantic kind. By this criterion the first two sentences are essentially similar. Assertions are equally object/function whether or not the doer of the function is stated. John did the drinking and midnight did not do the drinking; thus these assertion modifiers answer different questions ("Was drunk by whom? " and "Was drunk by what time? "). But either sentence could equally well specify the doer of the function, and both questions could be answered in the same sentence: "The wine was drunk by John by midnight". The fact that "by" functions essentially differently in the two sentences is beside the point here, because it occurs not in the subject or attribute cores but in the assertion modifiers.

The second two sentences are also essentially similar. Their difference lies only in the one having a single assertion modifier and the other having two. As to modificational function, "in the fez" is essentially different from "in the head": the first is a restrictive modifier of "man" (answering the question "What man? "); the second is a restrictive modifier of the whole assertion (answering the question "Shot him where? "). But again, this is a difference in assertion modifiers and does not affect the core of the assertion.

The third pair exemplifies essential dissimilarity: not only is the attribute core different, the difference is further reflected in a difference of semantic kinds. The meaning of "certain" in the two sentences is the same; the difference lies in the fact that two different people are certain. When I say "John is certain to leave" it is I who am claiming to be certain, not John. But when I say "John is certain that Bill will leave" it is John who is being claimed to be certain. In and of itself, "John is certain" can have only the second sort of meaning. It takes a special assertion modifier to convert the primary characteristic meaning of "certain" as *knows* to the secondary function meaning of *going to* or *will*. Though not strictly synonymous, "John is certain to leave" means essentially the same as "John is going to leave" and "John will leave". And by essentially the same we mean that all three would be diagramed the same to reflect the irreducible function attribute. "John is certain that Bill will leave" is essentially the same as "John knows that Bill will leave". John is not engaged in a function here – something that could be done slowly or rapidly, for instance – but is being characterized as to an aspect of his present psychology or state of mind.

(2) *Subject by Identity*

Characteristic assertions are the most complicated to explain, but identity assertions are the simplest. They are equations, with two different words or phrases designating exactly the same thing on either side of a linguistic equal sign.[9] Every kind of thing can serve as the subject/attribute of an identity assertion, and, as in an equation, the two parts are reversible.

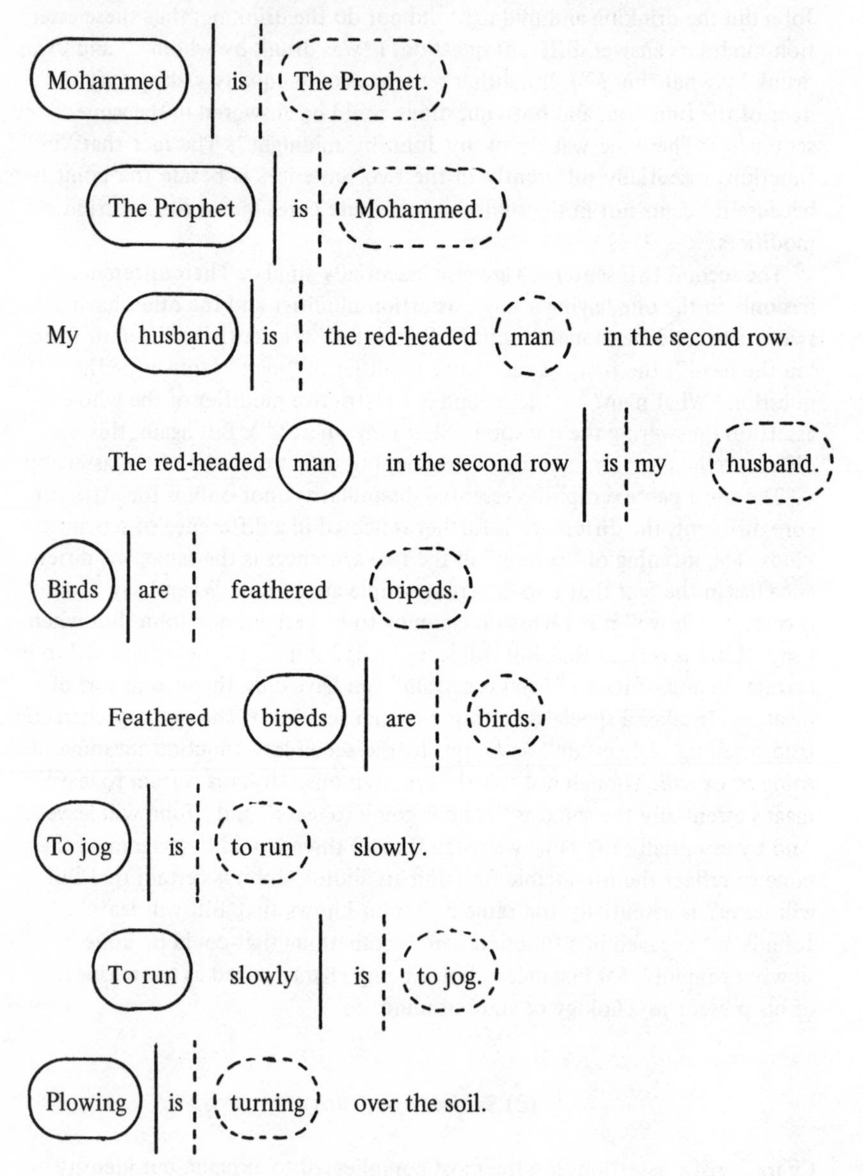

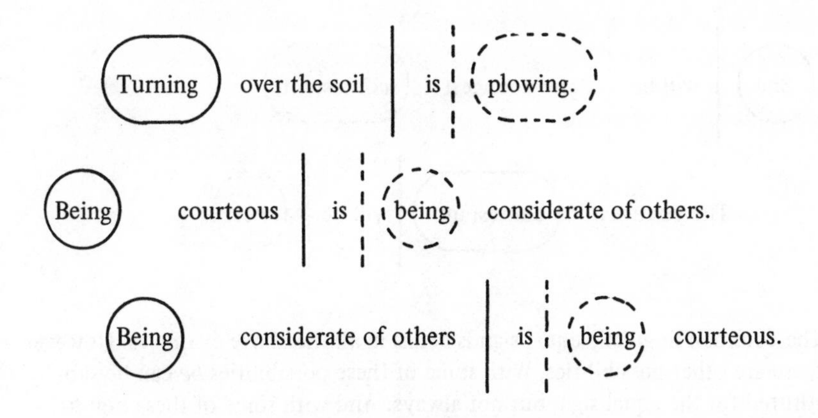

One small complicating factor with identity assertions is inflections, a problem that will arise again when we discuss parallel structure. Here the problem is primarily that of pronouns with different 'nominative' (*I*, *he*, *she*, *we*, *they*) and 'objective' (*me*, *him*, *her*, *us*, *them*) forms. From a semantic grammar point of view, the form of inflections is a secondary consideration to their meaning; and because *I* and *me* refer to exactly the same thing, they have the same meaning. For our purposes then, these differences are simply arbitrary variant spellings of the same word and as such are to be ignored in determining reversibility.

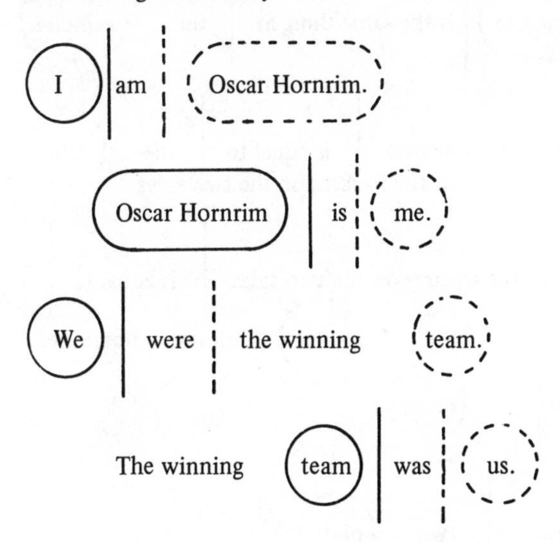

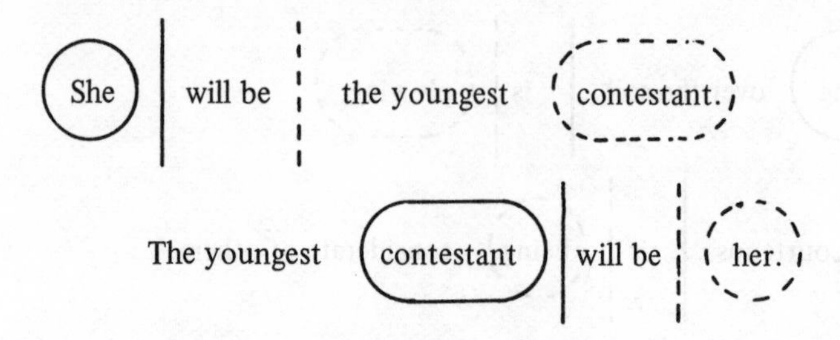

The common linguistic equal sign is *be*, as in all the above examples. However, there are other possibilities. With some of these possibilities *be* can be substituted for the equal sign, but not always. And with some of these non-*be* equal signs the equal sign remains the same after subject and attribute are reversed, but not always. The crucial question for identity is whether subject and attribute refer to the same thing and can be reversed without changing the meaning; the nature of the equal sign is not a factor.

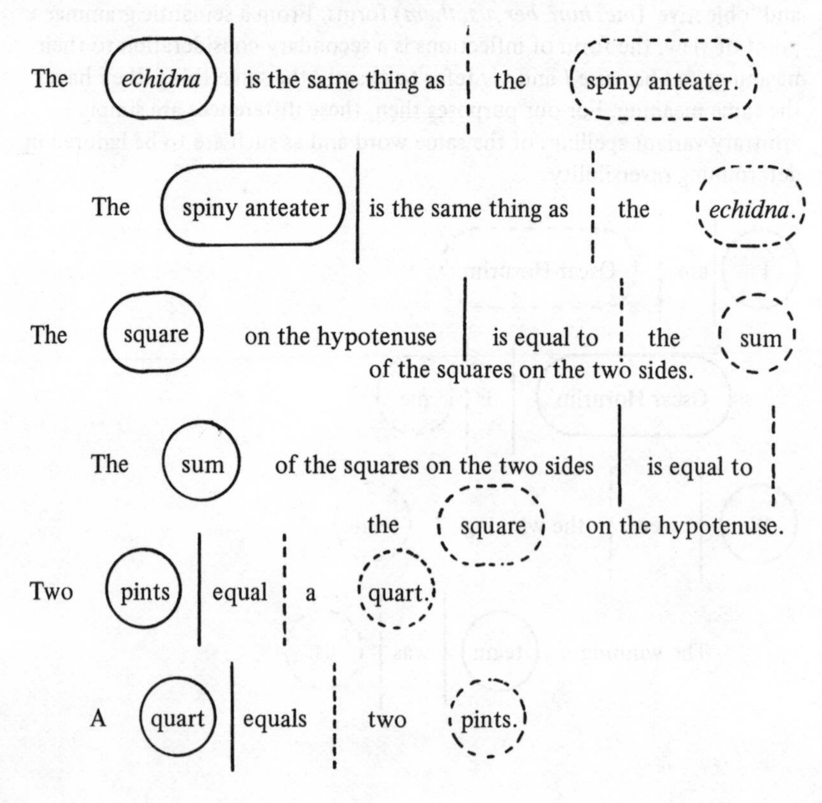

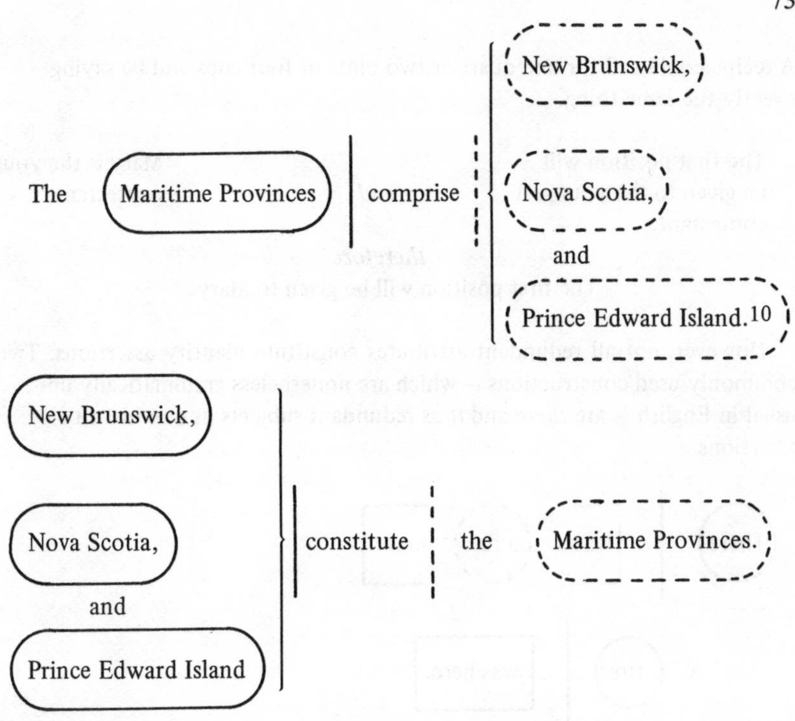

Diagraming the attribute in an identity assertion just as the subject is diagramed, except for the broken line, emphasizes the fact that subject and attribute designate the same thing. Or, we could say that the attribute, as far as reference goes, is redundant. In this sense all identity attributes are redundant. And the test for this redundancy is the logical axiom "things equal to the same thing are equal to each other".

A = C *and* B = C

therefore

A = B

If two pints equal a quart, then whatever else equals a quart must also equal two pints and be substitutable for either in all contexts.

Two pints equal a quart. *and* Four cups equal a quart.

therefore

Two pints equal four cups.

A recipe could call for one quart or two pints or four cups and be saying exactly the same thing.

The first position will be given to the youngest contestant.	*and*	Mary is the youngest contestant.

therefore

The first position will be given to Mary.

However, not all redundant attributes constitute identity assertions. Two very commonly used constructions – which are nonetheless grammatically unusual in English – are *there* and *it* as redundant subjects in non-identity assertions.

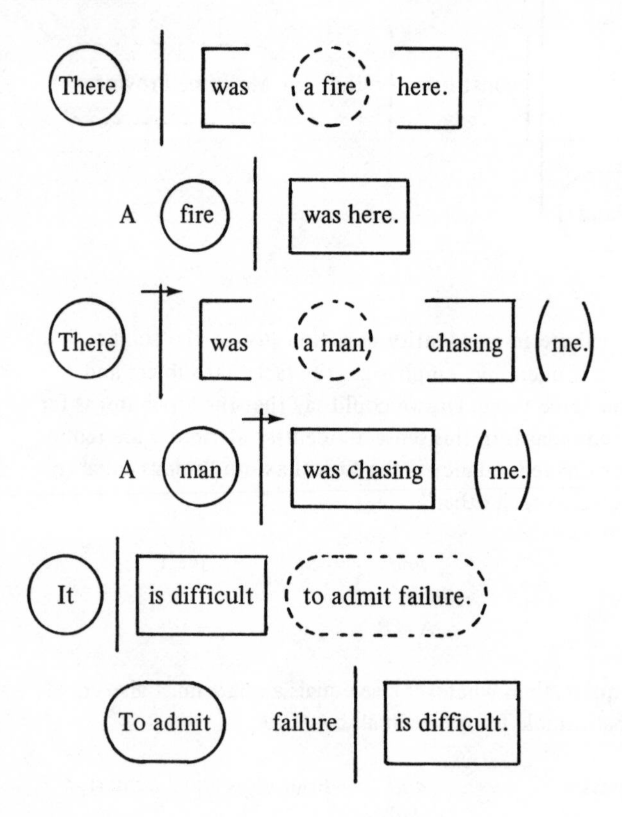

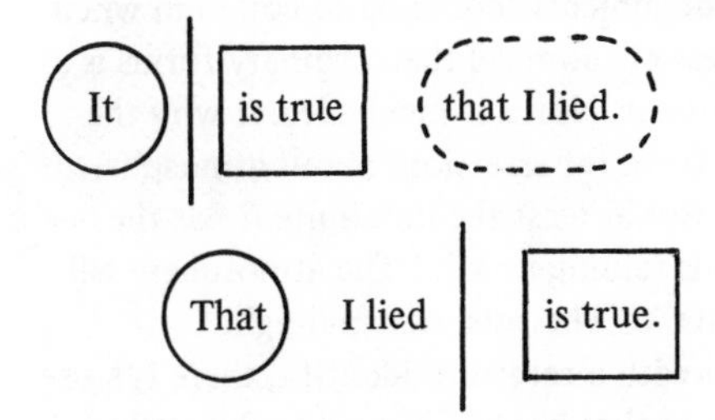

There as a redundant subject should not be confused with *there* as a demonstrative pronoun referring to place in an inverted sentence.

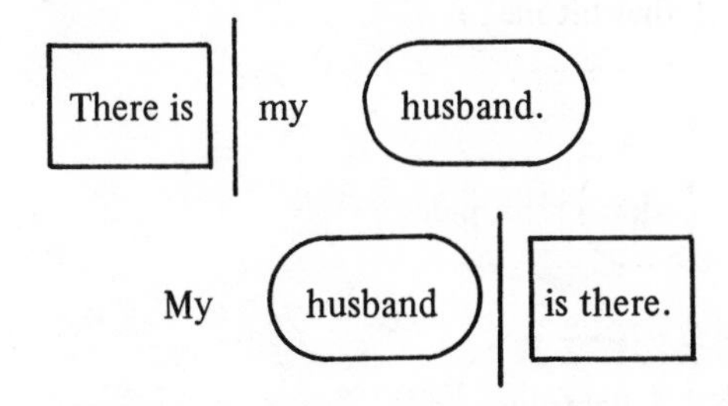

And *it* as a redundant subject should not be confused with *it* as a personal pronoun having an antecedent referent.

Nor is the redundant *it* to be confused with *it* as an indefinite pronoun having no stated referent, either before or after.

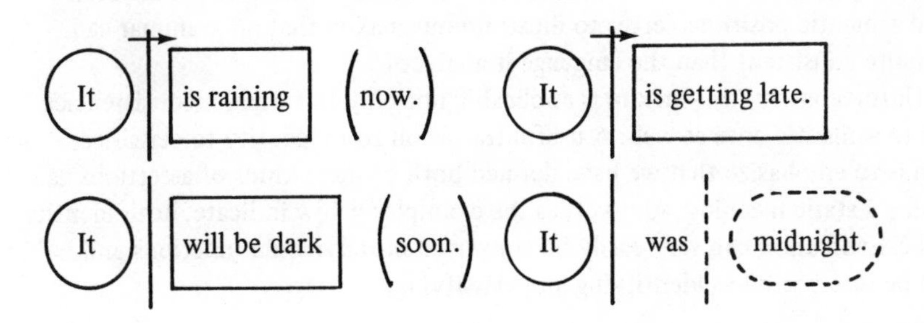

Why it is that *it* and *there* as redundant subjects should be so common when they are grammatically unusual and less economical than ordinary forms is a question no grammar seems able to answer. Nor is it much clearer why the indefinite *it* has become the standard form for assertions about atmosphere and time (both function and nature). But at least the indefinite *it* has the virtue of economy: "The atmosphere is raining now". "The atmosphere will be dark soon". "The time is getting late". "The time was midnight".

Finally, to conclude our discussion with a return to identity, there is a use of a redundant *it* in an identity assertion that has not just two subjects but three.

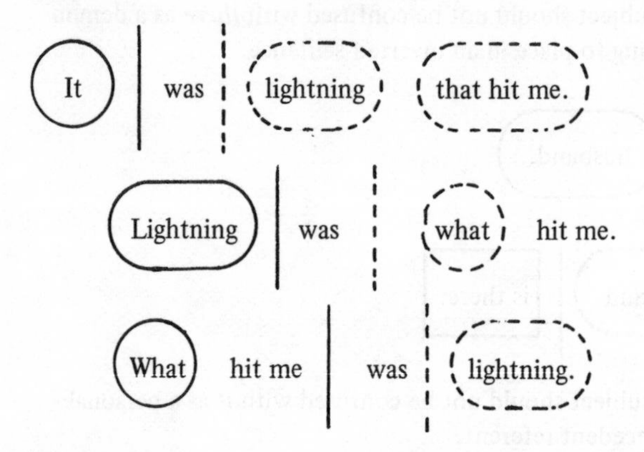

Once again there is a small complication resulting from inflectional variation. In modern standard English usage "that hit me" cannot function as either an independent subject or attribute, while "what hit me" is not permitted to be juxtaposed with an immediately preceding antecedent. Older or dialect usage would have allowed "It was lightning what hit me", and thus the complete reversibility of the three subjects would have been more obvious. The rise of this inexplicable formal distinction between *that* and *what* in what are identical semantic positions serves to illustrate our maxim that no grammar can be more consistent than the language it analyzes.

Unfortunately, this maxim is applicable not only to formal inconsistencies but to semantic ones as well. A useful transition from identity to classification is to emphasize that we have defined both of these kinds of assertions as having a static meaning. And yet, as the examples below indicate, both identity and classification can very easily be converted into dynamic functions and still be interpreted as identifying and classifying:

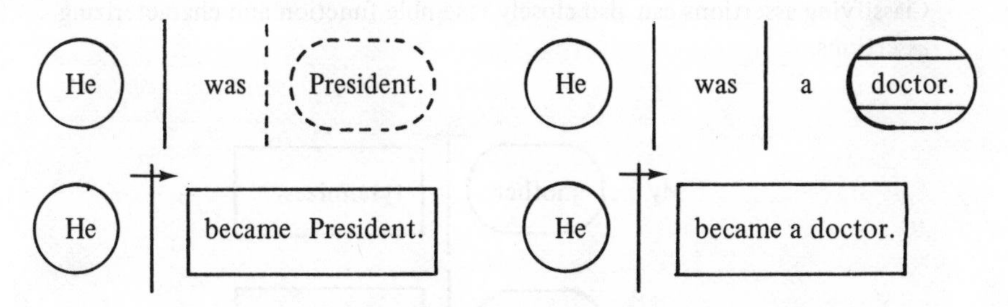

To *become* (function) is necessarily then to *be* (identity or classification), and thus it is as one-sided to diagram these becoming assertions as bipartite functions as to diagram them as tripartite identities and classifications. Yet once we have committed ourselves to the dynamic/static distinction, we seem obliged to give priority to function. Assertions that are about a function, whatever else they may be about, are not primarily static.

C. DESCRIBE SUBJECT BY CLASS

The line between identity and classifying assertions is a fine one.

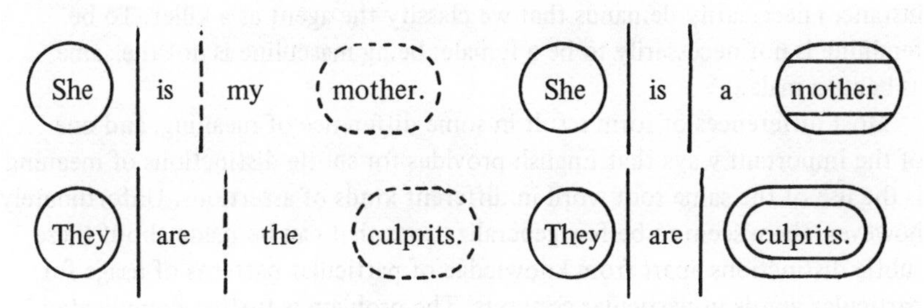

The difference is that with identity two things are equal, but with classification one thing is subordinated to the other. One of the two things in a classifying assertion is always a class, and the other is always either an individual or subclass that is part of the class.[11]

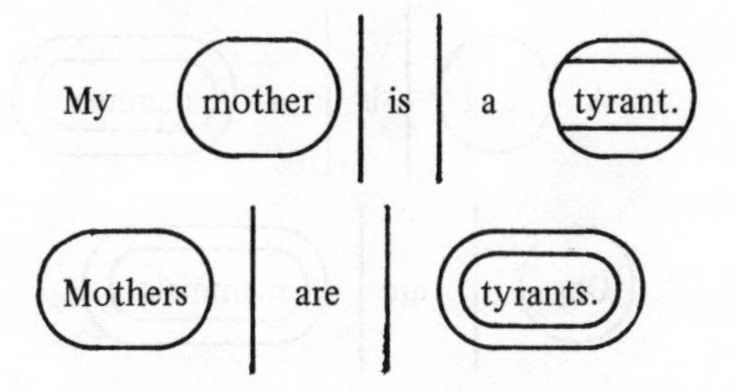

Classifying assertions can also closely resemble function and characterizing assertions.

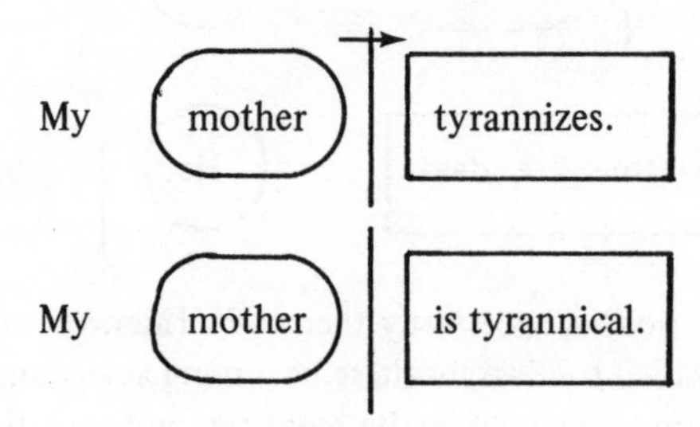

But the question of whether or not they have precisely the same meaning can usually be determined only in context. In some cases, however, sentences out of context are recognizable as being obviously different even though similar.[12] We may mean by a *tyrant* a person who *tyrannizes* and is thus *tyrannical*, but we sometimes find occasion for characterizing an act as tyrannical without being justified in claiming that the actor is a tyrant; not every act of tyranny renders the agent a tyrant. Similarly, not every act of killing (a mosquito, for instance) necessarily demands that we classify the agent as a killer. To be feminine is not necessarily to be a female; being masculine is not the same as being a male.

Most differences of form result in some difference of meaning, and one of the important ways that English provides for subtle distinctions of meaning is the use of the same root word in different kinds of assertions. Unfortunately, however, there seem to be few generalizations that can be made about these subtle distinctions apart from knowledge of particular patterns of usage for particular words in particular contexts. The problem is further complicated by the fact that not all differences of form do in fact reflect differences of meaning. One of the best examples of this comes from classifying assertions, where singular and plural forms do not necessarily correlate with individual/class and subclass/class. These two sentences, which we shall discuss later, have the same meaning:

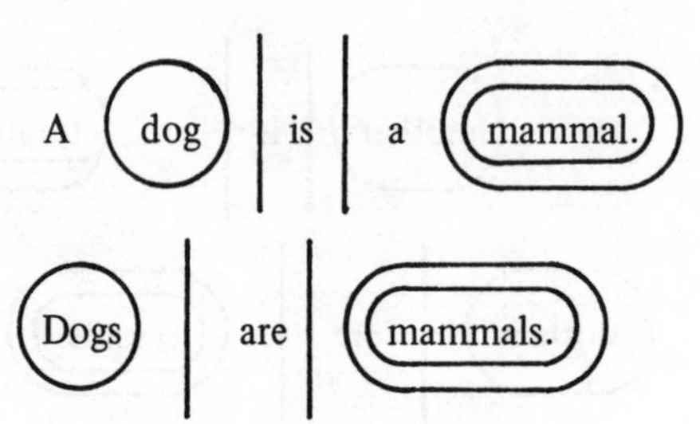

Both say that the subclass "dog" belongs to the class "mammal". The crucial consideration is not the form used to designate the class but whether the thing designated is the same.

All classes are made up of similar individuals; where there are no members it makes little sense to speak of a class. In addition, these individuals may also be grouped into subordinate classes. My dog (an individual) is a mammal (a class). My dog (an individual) is also an Airedale (a class). Airedale (a subclass) is a kind of mammal (a class). A group is a subclass or a class depending on whether it is the most inclusive group referred to in the assertion. Only "thing", the undifferentiated all-inclusive class, can never be a subclass.

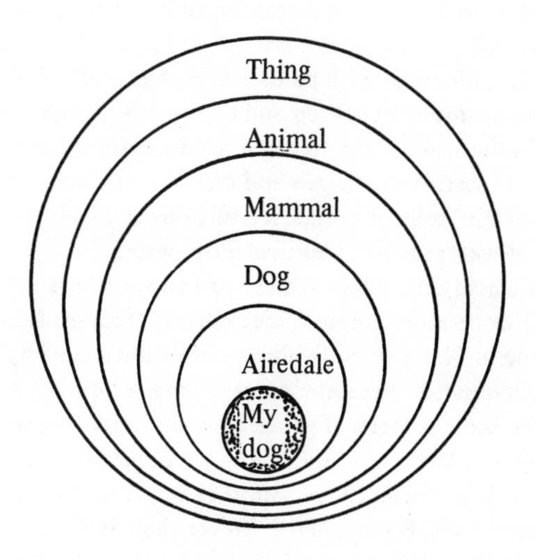

Biological taxonomy is not, however, the only appropriate model for classification. The same principles that make the concepts of atom and molecule essential to the physical scientist are those that distinguish individual and subclass in a wide variety of intellectual activity. Any homogeneous substance, from a piece of chalk to a drop of water, can be divided and subdivided into smaller and smaller units without destroying the essence (chalkness, waterness, etc.) of the substance. But this process cannot go on forever. Eventually the point is reached when division of the substance ceases to be a process of subdividing and becomes a process of destruction. In the physical sciences we say that at this point we have reached the line between molecules and atoms. The smallest possible unit of chalk or water is a molecule. Individual molecules taken together constitute the same substance as the molecule. But individual molecules further divided are no longer the same substance but constituent elements. In the physical sciences these constituent elements are atoms. A separate atom of oxygen and two separate atoms of hydrogen are quite different things than a molecule of water.

One drop of water is a class of thousands of water molecules. This drop, or class, can be divided and subdivided into smaller and smaller groups of molecules; two molecules together would still constitute a subclass of the drop. But one molecule of water is significantly different from two. One molecule is an individual; two molecules are a class (or subclass). Our committee is, by definition, identical with its members, but molecules of water are not identical with atoms of hydrogen and oxygen. It is impossible to have the ten members of a ten-man committee and not have the committee, but it is possible to have two parts of hydrogen and one of oxygen and not have water. Or, less technically, paste is composed of flour and water, but a pan of flour and a glass of water are not identical with paste.

The principles of classifying, while at the heart of science, are by no means confined to it, so let us be more commonplace in our analysis. Next door live the Lums – six of them. These six individuals constitute a class by virtue of many common characteristics: the same name, the same residence, the same source of income, the same pattern of genetic relationship. One way to subdivide this class is by sex. Mrs. Lum and Nancy are female Lums; Mr. Lum, Mark, Steven, and David are male Lums. Another way to subdivide is by age. Mr. and Mrs. Lum are adults; Nancy, Mark, Steven, and David are children. And we can subdivide the subdivisions. Having isolated a subclass of female Lums, we can distinguish between adult females and juvenile females. But at this point in our subdividing we no longer have subclasses; we are down to the level of individuals. Mrs. Lum is not a subclass of Lums; she is an individual Lum. We subdivided but no subclasses resulted. And at *this* point we can no longer even subdivide. To cut an individual Lum in half is not to get two Lums but to destroy the one we have. Parts and constituent elements are neither individuals nor classes; they are characteristics.

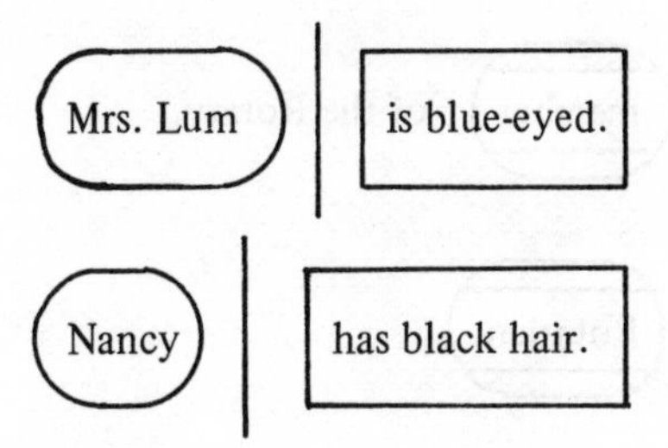

(1) *Individual by Class*

As with identity assertions, classifying assertions have a connecting link that may or may not be a form of *be*. And also like identity assertions, the subjects and attributes in classifying assertions can be reversed. An assertion moving from individual to class is most commonly linked by *be*, *belongs to*, and *be among*.

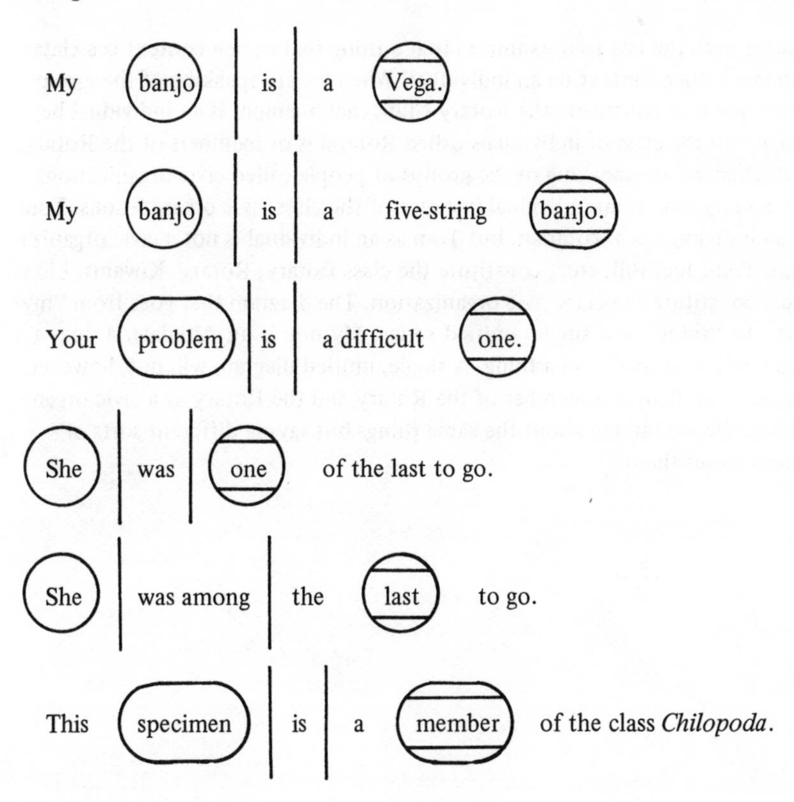

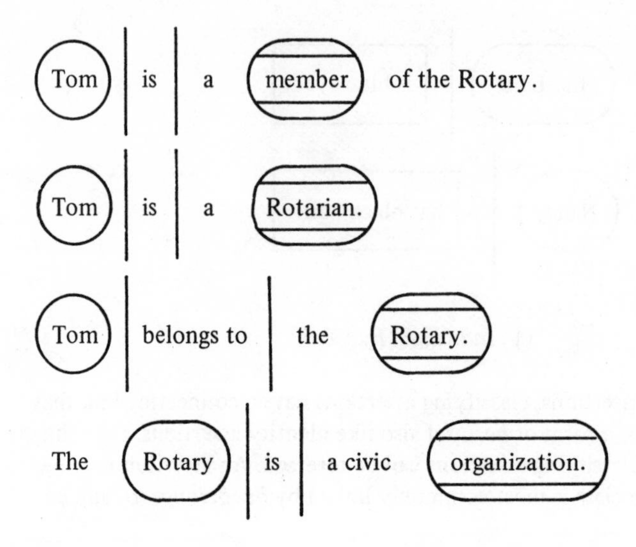

Notice with the last four examples that a thing that in one context is a class can in another context be an individual. When we are speaking of the group of people that constitute the Rotary Club, each member is an individual belonging to the class of individuals called Rotarians or members of the Rotary. But when we are speaking of the groups of people called civic organizations, the Rotary club is an individual instance of the class civic organizations. Tom as an individual is a Rotarian, but Tom as an individual is not a civic organization. Tom, Joe, Bill, etc. , constitute the class Rotary; Rotary, Kiwanis, Lions, etc. , constitute the class civic organization. The diagram that goes from "my dog" to "thing" is a single, unified series. My dog is an Airedale, a dog, a mammal, an animal, and a thing. A single, unified diagram will not, however, account for Tom as a member of the Rotary and the Rotary as a civic organization. We are talking about the same things but saying different sorts of things about them.

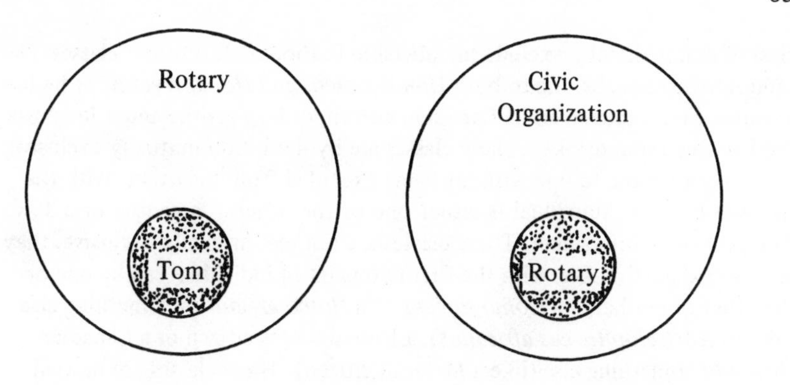

Classifying assertions, especially individual/class, are less likely to be reversed than are identity assertions. Those that are reversed are linked most commonly by *be*, *include*, and *be among*.

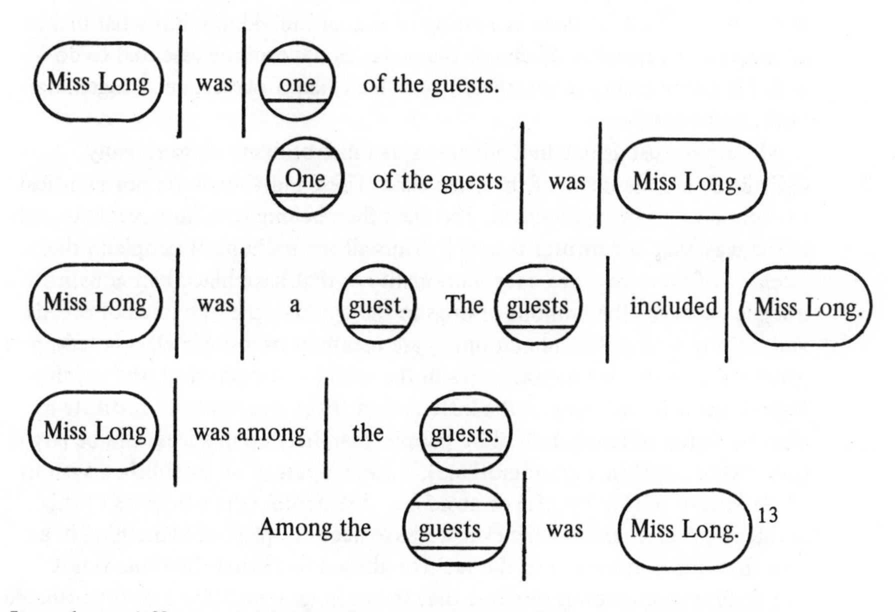

It made no difference with identity assertions which thing was subject and which attribute; the only way of distinguishing between the two identical things was by position in the sentence. Thus, whichever came first was the subject. In an identity assertion subject and attribute can be reversed, but there is no reverse order. In a classifying assertion, however, there is a subordinate relationship that is discernible regardless of whether the class comes first or second. The usual order is individual or subclass first and class second, but a reverse order is possible and is shown by the diagraming.

Important to keep in mind about classifying is that membership in one class does not thereby exclude membership in thousands of other classes. One cannot, of course, belong to both *Homo sapiens* and *Homo erectus*, or be both a United States citizen and a Canadian citizen, or be a gentile and a Jew, or a drinker and a non-drinker. These classes are by definition mutually exclusive; one cannot belong to one without being excluded from the other. With the last two pairs an individual is either one or the other – a gentile or a Jew, a drinker or a non-drinker. These classes are not just mutually exclusive, they are also exhaustive. But with the first two pairs an individual can be one or the other or neither – a *Homo sapiens* or a *Homo erectus* or something else (like an *Australopithecus africanus*), a United States citizen or a Canadian citizen or something else (like a Mexican citizen). These classes are mutually exclusive but not exhaustive. The great majority of classes, however, are neither mutually exclusive nor exhaustive. An individual can be at the same time a Rotarian, a banjo player, a father, a pillar of the community, an employer, an employee, an octogenarian, a nuisance, a writer, a home-owner, a world-traveler, a source of worry to his children, a delight to his grandchildren, etc. Each of these is a group of similar individuals, but what makes an individual a member of one of these classes has nothing essential to do with his membership in another. I may be a banjo player, an octogenarian, both, or neither.

Moreover, just as one individual is a member of many classes, many individuals are members of the same class. These individuals are not identical or even close to being identical. The class they belong to is homogeneous only in the way that constitutes the class. Thus all the millions of people in the world – of every sex, age, race, nationality – that have black hair constitute a single class. All the millions of dogs in the world – the hundreds of breeds and infinite mongrel combinations – are members of a single class based upon genetic similarity. All the pleasures in the world – the physical, the psychological, the spiritual, and all the instances of these pleasures – constitute a class by virtue of being desired by people. Membership in a class can be large (insects) or small (my grandmothers); it can be part of an established system of classification (*Chilopoda*) or an *ad hoc* distinction (the witnesses to this accident). A class exists whenever we have need to speak of something in a way that draws attention to the fact (or alleged fact) that the thing is not just similar to something else but that these things constitute a distinguishable group.

And just as membership in one class does not preclude membership in another class, being a subclass of one class does not preclude being a subclass of another class. The class "mode of transportation" and the class "source of food" have nothing essential in common. Transportation is not a kind of food, and food is not a kind of transportation. But camels (a subclass) are

both a mode of transportation (a class) and a source of food (a class).

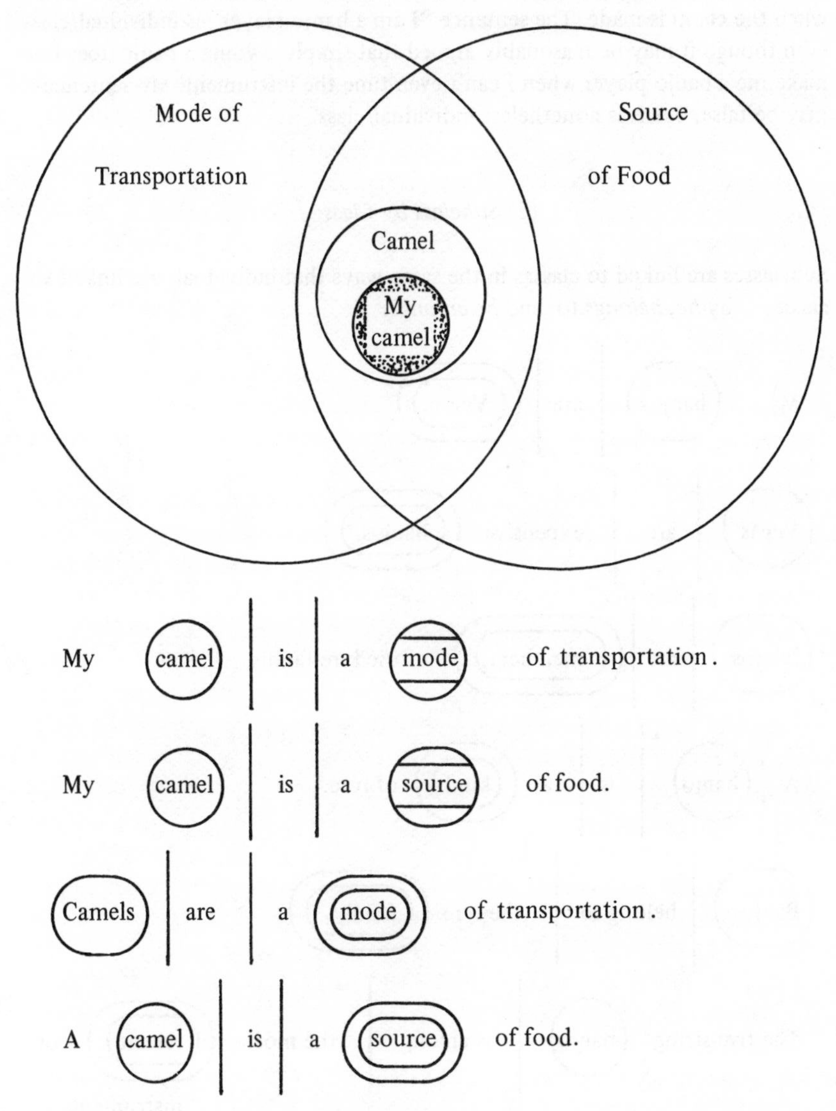

A group can be so precisely defined as to preclude most disagreement (e. g. *Homo sapiens*, hydrogen, Rotarian, octogenarian) or it may be so imprecisely defineu as to give rise to much disagreement (e. g. insanity, ether, pillar of the community, nuisance). But in either case an assertion is a classifying assertion when the claim is made. The sentence "I am a banjo player" is individual/class even though it may be reasonably argued that simply owning a banjo does not make me a banjo player when I can't even tune the instrument. My sentence may be false, but it is nonetheless individual/class.

(2) *Subclass by Class*

Subclasses are linked to classes in the same ways that individuals are linked to classes – by *be*, *belongs to*, and *be among*.

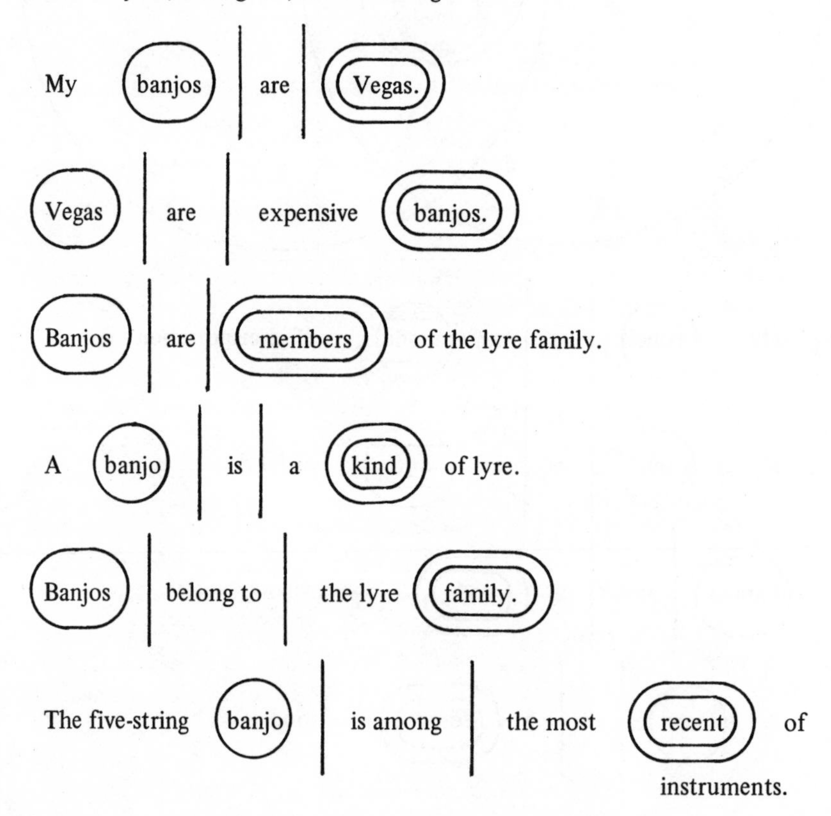

And like individual/class, subclass/class assertions can be reversed.

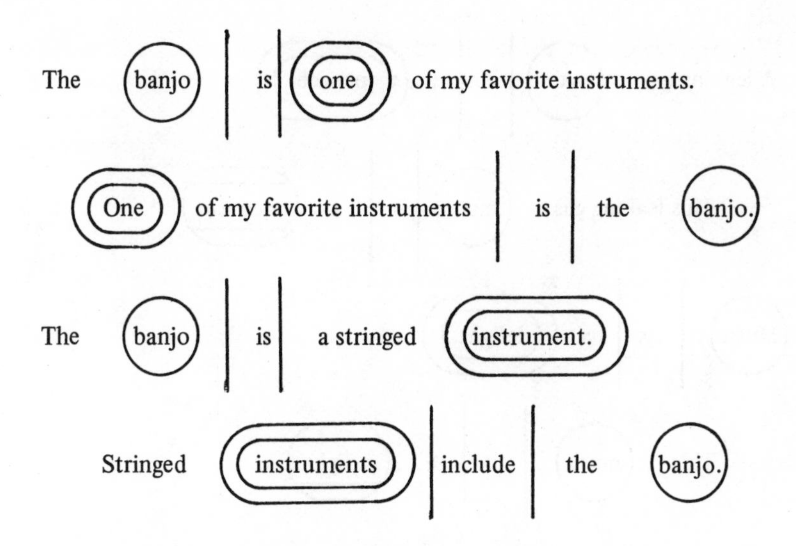

A complicating factor with subclass assertions is that a variety of grammatical forms is used. An individual is always singular, but a subclass can be not only plural but also singular with a definite article, singular with an indefinite article, and uncountable. The crucial test is whether or not there can be individual instances of the thing that do not exhaust it.

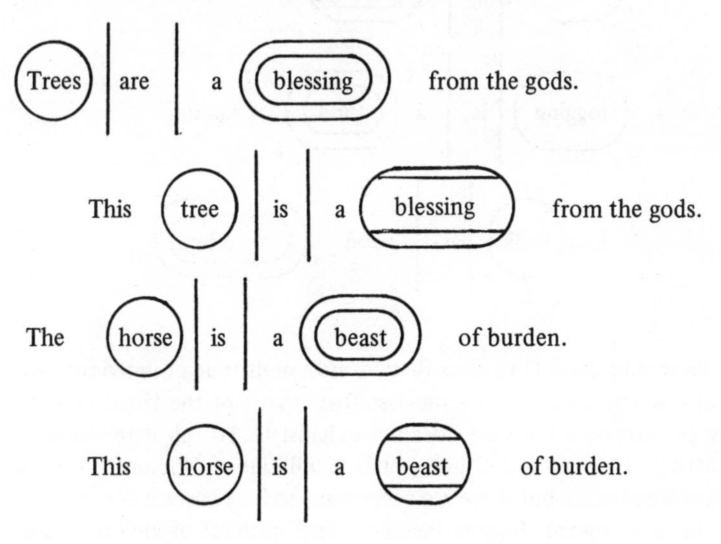

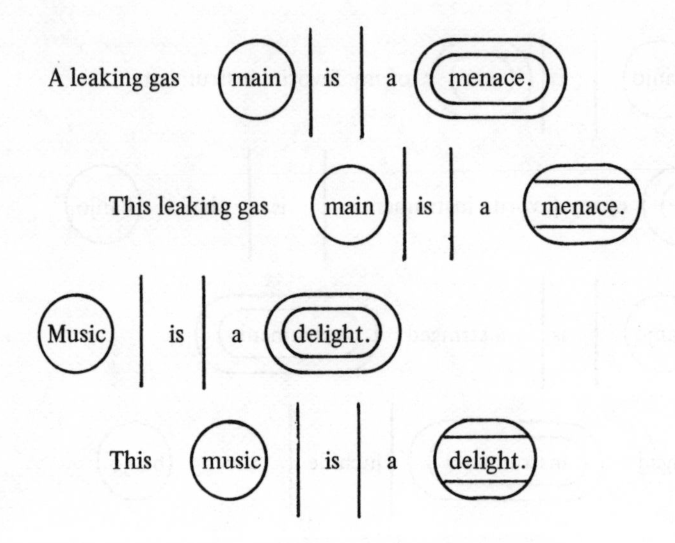

Into this last category fall also the various verbal forms that can function as things.

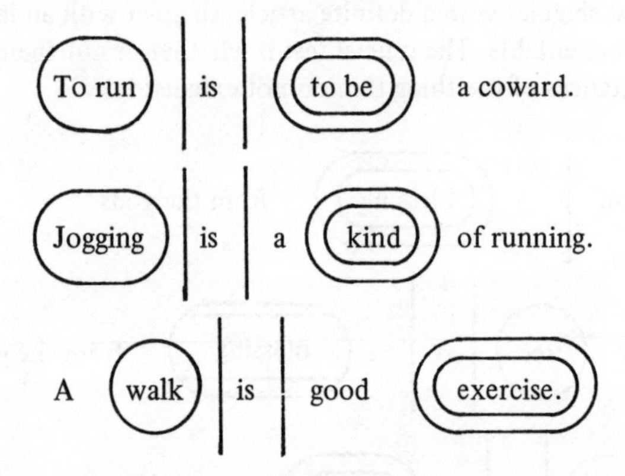

Each of these subjects is (1) a class that covers a multitude of individual instances of the activity and (2) a subclass that is part of the larger class designated by the attribute but that does not exhaust it. To run is to engage in a kind of activity that millions of individuals at millions of different times and places have engaged in, but there are other ways to be a coward – e. g. to grovel is to be a coward. Jogging includes every instance of anyone doing this at any time – what I did this morning, what you did last night, etc. But there are other kinds of running than jogging – sprinting, loping, etc. All jogging is running, but not all running is jogging. *A walk* is like *a banjo* in being a singular form used for any and all individual instances of the thing – my banjo, my walk last night. And *good exercise* is like *stringed instrument*, a class label that covers many particulars and more kinds than are designated by the subject – e. g. a swim is also good exercise.

By way of concluding our discussion of classes and sub-classes, let us have recourse to that most successful of classification systems – biological taxonomy.

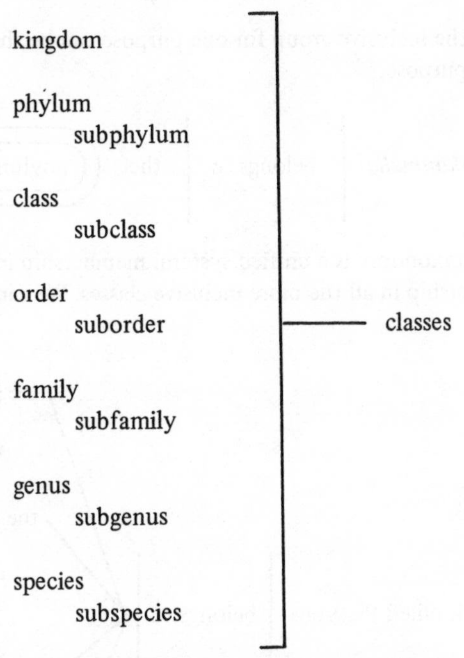

Each of these is a group of genetically similar individuals. No group, whether species or kingdom, is constituted by subordinate groups; it is constituted by individuals. These individuals can be grouped into a whole series of intermediate groups, but what constitutes these intermediate groups is the same thing that constitutes the inclusive group – individuals. It makes no difference that the biologist has chosen to label one of his many groups "class" and another "subclass"; generically, all are classes.

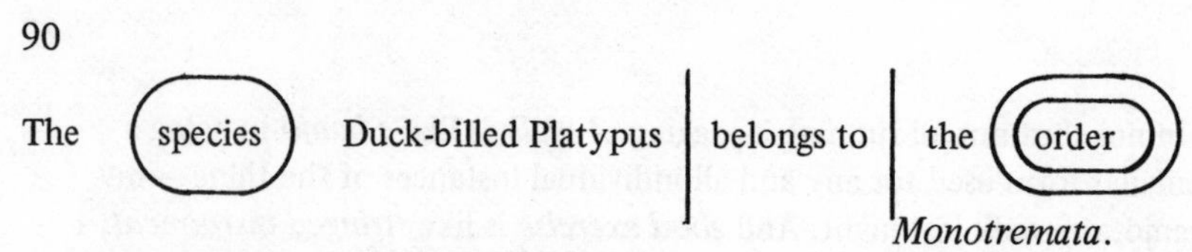

is no less a subclass/class assertion than is

The (subclass) *Prototheria* | belongs to | the ((class)) *Mammalia*.

And that which is the inclusive group for one purpose can be the subordinate group for another purpose.

The (class) *Mammalia* | belongs to | the ((phylum)) *Chordata*.

Because biological taxonomy is a unified system, membership in a subordinate class entails membership in all the more inclusive classes. We can thus say:

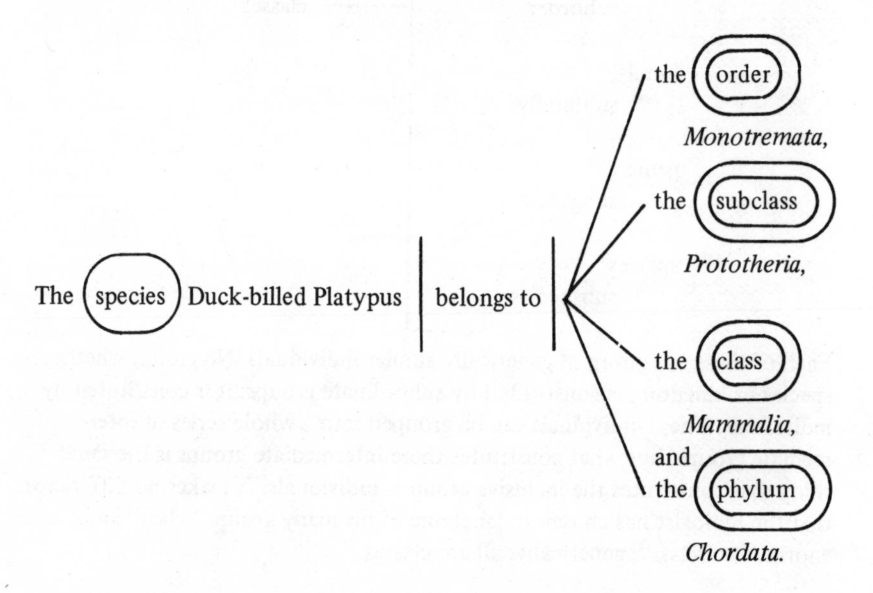

But at this point we have obviously moved beyond the level of individual assertions and into the realm of structure – our next topic.

NOTES

1 See Appendix A.
2 See also pp. 79, 83, 85.
3 See also pp. 255, 256, 268, 274.
4 See Appendix A.
5 For discussion of conditional modification see p. 155 ff.
6 See pp. 152-154.
7 Discussed on pp. 74-76.
8 For an extension of this discussion as applied to the analysis and diagraming of comparisons see pp. 178-179.
9 For a slight exception see p. 107.
10 For the discussion of unitary parallelism see p. 104 ff.
11 See the diagrams on p. 27.
12 See also p. 22-23.
13 For the discussion of positional anomalies like this see pp. 116-120.

3. THE STRUCTURE OF ASSERTIONS

To read well is to perceive the subordinate units in a composition and to understand the precise way that they are structured to make a unified whole. To write well is to structure various subordinate units in such a precise way that they do make a unified whole. A composition is not a collection; it is not a series; it is a pattern. The whole can be as small as a single sentence or as large as a multi-volumed work. The units can be assertions, sentences, paragraphs, chapters, volumes. But in any case subordination is the essence of composition – as, indeed, it is of all intellectual endeavor. To be sure, the larger the whole, the more the major subordinate units are determined by the subject of the composition. However, all compositions, large or small, are composed of assertions. Thus it is that semantic grammar focuses on assertions and inter-assertional relations rather than on larger units and their relations.

The structure of an assertion is the non-semantic relationship that it has with other assertions in the immediate context. It would be an over-statement to claim that such considerations are the essence of composition, but as soon as the writer aspires (which he inevitably does) to go beyond a list of simple sentences, then he is dependent for his success on a knowledge of the principles of structure. There are three basic kinds of assertion structure. An *independent* structure is one that exists as a separate sentence

My father suffered from gout.

or as an independent clause in a compound sentence

My father suffered from gout,

and

his father suffered from gout.

A *parallel* structure is one that results from two or more assertions sharing a common element (or elements) in a sentence or in an independent clause

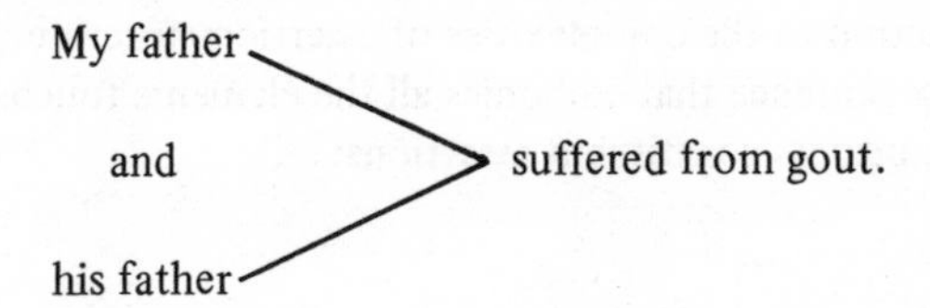

A *modificational* structure is one that results from the use of non-restrictive modification (enclosed here in brackets) within another independent or parallel structure. Non-restrictive modification is either post-positional

My father, [who was an alcoholic,] suffered from gout.

or pre-positional

My [alcoholic] father suffered from gout.

An independent assertion can exist by itself as a sentence, but there can be no parallel or modificational assertion existing alone as a sentence. A parallel assertion must have at least one mate or it cannot be part of a parallel construction. A modificational assertion, because it is dependent for its meaning on a completely expressed assertion, must also have a relationship to another assertion. But unlike parallel assertions – which are equal partners, or mates – modificational assertions are necessarily subordinated to or dependent on other assertions.

Sentences compounded of fully stated assertions (with or without the use of conjunctions) raise important questions of inter-assertional relations but not of assertional structure. The "independent" clauses in a compound sentence are just that – independent. There are three, and only three, ways in which multiple assertions can occur in a single sentence: by parallel structure, by non-restrictive modification, and by compounding. But only the first two are matters of *assertion* structure; the last is a matter of *sentence* structure.

Kinds of Assertion Structure	*Ways of Structuring Multiple Assertions in a Single Sentence*
Independent	
Parallel	Parallel
Modificational	Modificational
	Compound

As an introduction to the complexities of assertion structure, let us take a single complex sentence that embodies all the elements touched on so far and break it down into its constituent assertions:

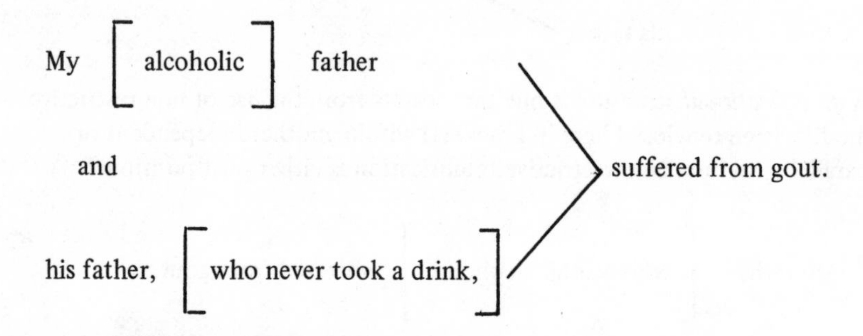

My father suffered from gout.
My father [was] alcoholic.
His father suffered from gout.
His father never took a drink.

What this does not, of course, embody is independent structure, either in the form of simple or compound sentences.

A. INDEPENDENT

Each of the four single-assertion sentences above has an independent structure. But an assertion can have extensive restrictive modification

> The man who lives next door sings loudly in the shower every morning at dawn to exercise his lungs.

and contain one or more instances of non-restrictive modification

> My father, [who lives next door,] leaves his [unpainted] cottage every morning at dawn to work in the fields.

and still have an independent structure.

By independent is meant only that the sentence (or independent clause in a compound sentence) has as a base one and only one assertion – an assertion that is not subordinated to or dependent on any other assertion. In the second example "My father lives next door" is a subordinate structure, because the relative pronoun "who" cannot function as an independent subject; "His cottage [is] unpainted" is a dependent structure, because it is dependent for part of its attribute on an implied but unstated form *be*.[1] But "My father leaves his cottage every morning at dawn to work in the fields", which is the core of the sentence, is an independent structure. To distinguish between the first example (with one assertion) and the second example (with one major assertion and two minor ones) we shall say that the assertion in the first sentence has a *simple independent structure* and that the major assertion in the second sentence has a *complex independent structure*. The structure is complex because it is the frame for elaboration that is not an essential part of the base assertion but rather adds to it.

That which is merely added (enclosed in brackets) can be subtracted without affecting the meaning of the base assertion. But that which provides a qualification or restriction cannot be omitted without affecting the meaning of the assertion of which it is a part. We shall continue to postpone the precise definition of this crucial distinction and a systematic analysis of sample sentences until we reach the section on modificational structure. Here we need only to understand that quite complicated assertions can exhibit independent structure.

Compound sentences – the juxtaposing of two or more fully stated separable assertions, with or without conjunctions – is the means of integrating multiple assertions into single sentences that is only one step removed from single-assertion sentences. It is a means of indicating a closer relationship than with separate sentences, but there is no increased economy. Unlike parallel structure and non-restrictive modification, compounding employs the same number of words as would be required to write out the assertions as separate sentences. Whatever is true of single-assertion sentences can be true of the component assertions in a compound sentence. The individual assertions may be simple or complex; they may or may not be linked by conjunctions; they may be limited to two or constitute a series (as, for example, this sentence). But whatever the variety, our diagraming convention is simply to juxtapose the individual assertions one under the other:

I am quiet,

    but

my neighbor is noisy.

I am quiet;

my neighbor is noisy.

I am quiet,

but

the man who lives next door sings loudly in the shower every morning at dawn to exercise his lungs.

The usual punctuation convention for distinguishing between compound sentences whose assertions are linked by conjunctions and those without conjunctions is to strengthen the stopping force of the punctuation mark when there is no conjunction and to mitigate the stopping force when there is a conjunction. Thus a comma is the usual mark with a conjunction, and a semi-colon is the usual mark without a conjunction. Much less commonly a dash can serve in either situation, and a colon can serve for the semi-colon. But though the presence or absence of a conjunction affects the punctuation, the component assertions are no less separable for being linked by a conjunction. As, for example, with the previous sentence, a sentence can begin with a conjunction that links it to the previous one. To define the sentence as an independent unit is not to claim for it, or any other instance of language, complete autonomy. Words, assertions, sentences, paragraphs, whole compositions, are meaningful in the final analysis because of the way we interpret them in the largest context we need to envision in order to make complete sense of them.

There are always more or less arbitrary conventions of linguistic usage that dictate matters of linguistic propriety, and one cannot wilfully ignore these without drawing attention to his prose that will interfere with the purpose of his composition. An example of this kind of more or less arbitrary convention relevant to the analysis of conjunctions in compound sentences is, what is termed in traditional grammar, 'subordinate' conjunctions. On the one hand, conjunctions like *although* and *because* can function between assertions like the more typical conjunctions *but* and *therefore*:

I am quiet,	I am quiet,
although	because
my neighbor is noisy.	noise pollution is a problem.

On the other hand, while the typical conjunctions can also begin a sentence, they must come between the two things being linked or conjoined. The sentence "But my neighbor is noisy" must follow another sentence to which it is being contrasted. This is not true of *although* and *because*, which are just as likely to introduce two assertions as to come between them:

Although	Because
I am quiet,	noise pollution is a problem,
my neighbor is noisy.	I am quiet.

The further complication is that, while *although* and *because* have the additional freedom of occurring at the beginning of a sentence, they have a restriction not imposed upon the other conjunctions of not being able to introduce a single-assertion sentence. On the one hand, "But my neighbor is noisy" and "Therefore I am quiet" can stand as independent sentences if the conjunctions are a link with previous sentences. On the other hand, "Although I am quiet" and "Because noise pollution is a problem" cannot stand as independent sentences even when *although* and *because* clearly serve as links with previous sentences.

The rationale for this is partly explained by the notion that a sentence can rely on previously stated elements as long as it itself is not left hanging. This explanation applies also to the common practice of using pronouns that would be quite inexplicable were it not for previously stated elements that specify what *it* or *those* or *he* refer to. And ordinarily we would say that the use of pronouns carries with it the obligation to specify *first* what is being referred to and not to use pronouns before the referent has been provided. Still, there is really no such thing as an absolutely semantically complete sentence. Therefore the conventions that allow us to begin pairs of assertions with some conjunctions but not with others, and to begin the second sentence in a pair of sentences with some conjunctions but not with others are a bit arbitrary.

This uncertainty of rationale is also reflected in the uncertainty of punctuation. For the most part, the convention of separating the independent clauses of a compound sentence with punctuation is one of the most useful and well-established in English composition. It is equally so whether or not the assertions are linked by conjunctions. Similarly with sentences *introduced* by subordinate conjunctions: the first assertion is almost always separated from the second by a comma, reflecting what is taken to be a reversal of the standard linking pattern. But when the subordinate conjunction comes *between* the two assertions, then there is much less consensus on the question of punctuation, and this reflects a lack of consensus on the question of whether or not sentences with subordinate conjunctions are to be thought of as compound. In a compound sentence the two or more component assertions are of equal value, equally separable. But if *although* and *because*, for example, are indeed *subordinate* conjunctions, then this is because they subordinate one assertion to another. In the sentence "I am quiet, because noise pollution is a problem" the comma is consistent with a conception of the sentence as compound. Without the comma, the implication is that "because noise pollution is a problem" is an assertion modifier of "I am quiet" and not a separable assertion.

The problem does not lend itself to an unequivocal solution, and different conceptions of grammar will include more or less within the class of compound sentences depending on the different goals being pursued. Since our goal is to emphasize the possibility of separating out individual assertions so as to discern the explicit and implicit inter-assertional relations, we will be treating subordinate conjunctions as simply a special case of conjunctions in general. We want particularly to be able to treat those very important kinds of inter-assertional relationships of support and conclude.[2] And thus we need to see *because* relationships as no more than the counterpart of *therefore* relationships. The simple system of assertion diagraming used here distinguishes between assertions in and of themselves and inter-assertional conjunctions, no matter where in the sentence they may occur. Thus, if the assertion can stand alone when the conjunction is detached, then we will consider it independent even if the conventions of usage dictate that it cannot be independent when accompanied by the conjunction.

For the present, we need pursue this one manifestation of the much larger subject of inter-assertional relations no further, but in Chapter 6 the subject will be examined in detail. Here we need only make the point that in semantic grammar the question of independent assertions can be divorced from the question of the presence, absence, or kind of inter-assertional conjunction.

Our final point about compound sentences is made only for the sake of completeness; it does not reflect common usage. Sometimes a complete assertion will be inserted into another assertion rather than the one follow the other

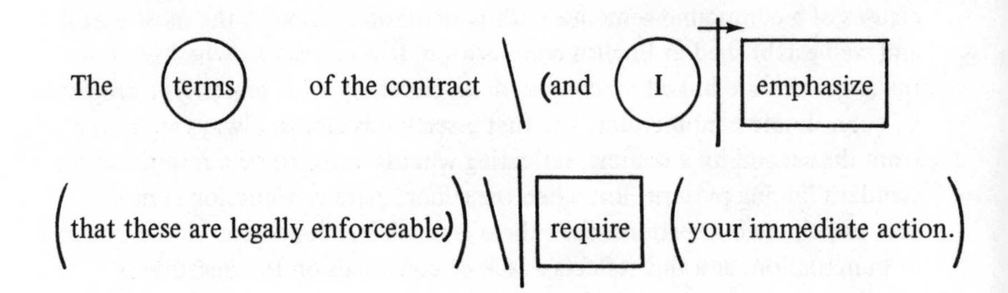

A more common structure would have been a non-restrictive modifier, which would have had the advantage of increased economy but perhaps have lacked the advantage of emphasis:

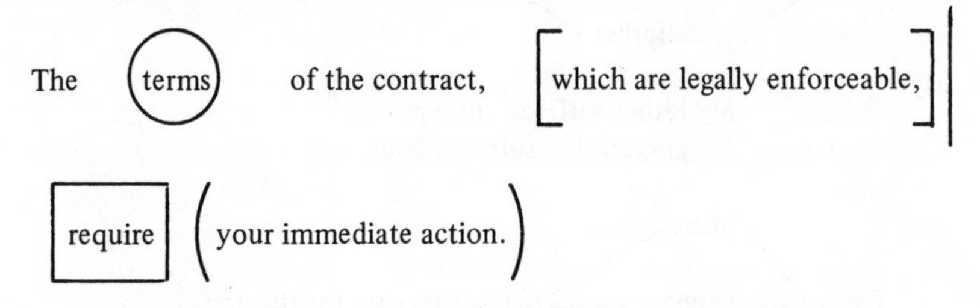

But discussion of non-restrictive modification must be deferred until we have treated parallel structure.[3]

B. PARALLEL

In the strict sense, parallel structure is the presentation of multiple assertions in a single sentence by means of two or more words or phrases that rely on a single word or phrase as a common element in the two or more assertions. The test for such structure is to read the assertions independently of each other; if this can be done without distorting the meaning of them as they appear together, then the assertions are parallel. Any part of an assertion can be parallel: subject, subject modifier, attribute, attribute modifier, assertion modifier. The parallel items can be the major part of a sentence or a minor part. The different parallel assertions may be of the same semantic kind or of different kinds. A parallel item can itself lead into further parallel items, and there may be separate sets of parallels. The sole criterion is that each parallel item must when joined to the common element result in a complete and separable assertion.

The following are examples of parallel subjects:

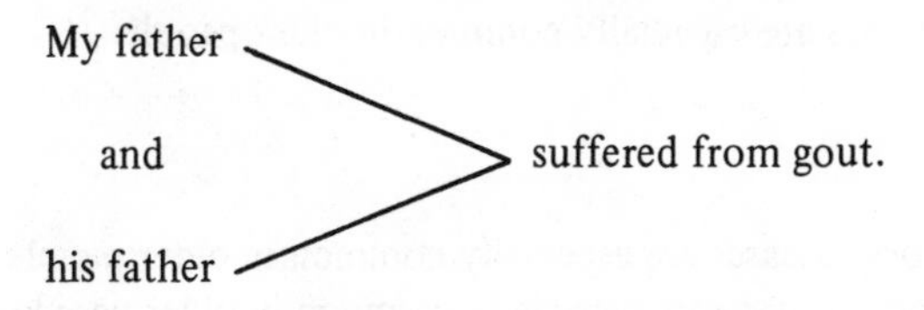

My father suffered from gout.
His father suffered from gout.

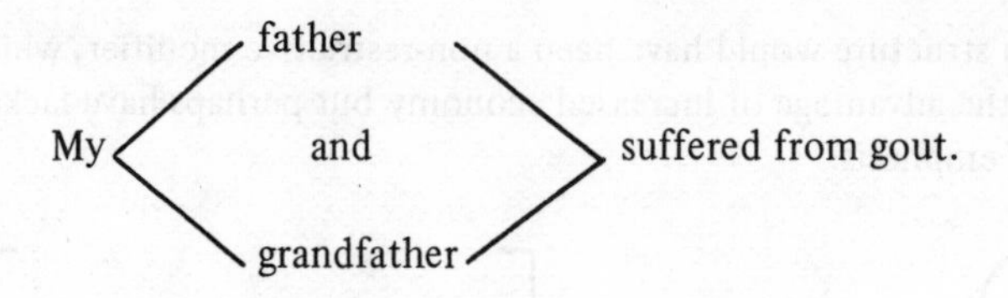

My father suffered from gout.
My grandfather suffered from gout.

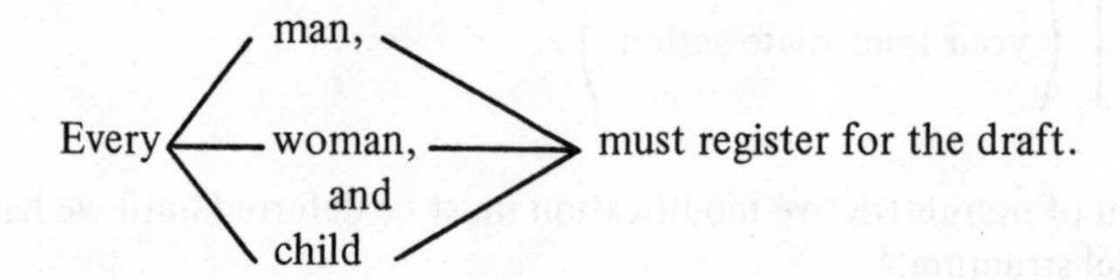

Every man must register for the draft.
Every woman must register for the draft.
Every child must register for the draft.

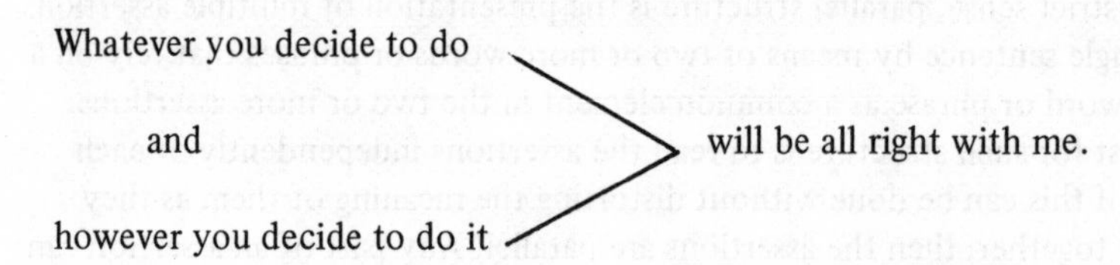

Whatever you decide to do will be all right with me.
However you decide to do it will be all right with me.

And here is an example of parallel subject modifier without the headword of the subject also being parallel:

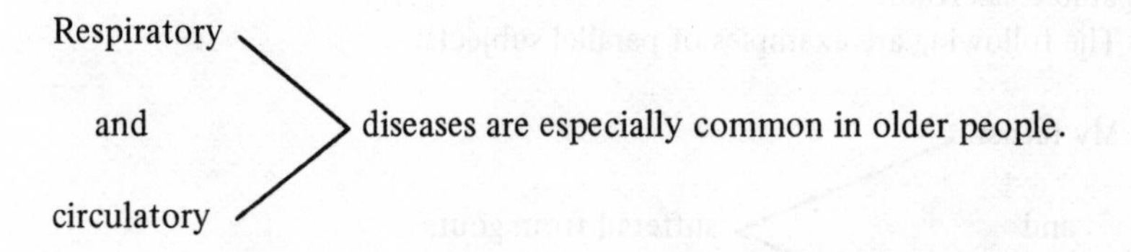

Respiratory diseases are especially common in older people.
Circulatory diseases are especially common in older people.

The following represent some of the many possibilities for parallel attributes and attribute modifiers:

We can succeed.
We will succeed.

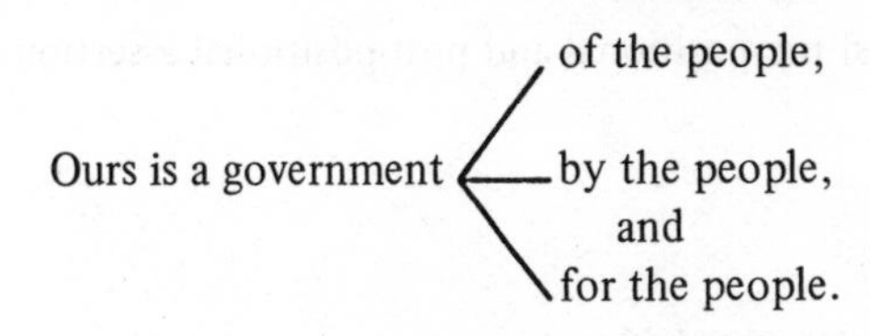

Ours is a government of the people.
Ours is a government by the people.
Ours is a government for the people.

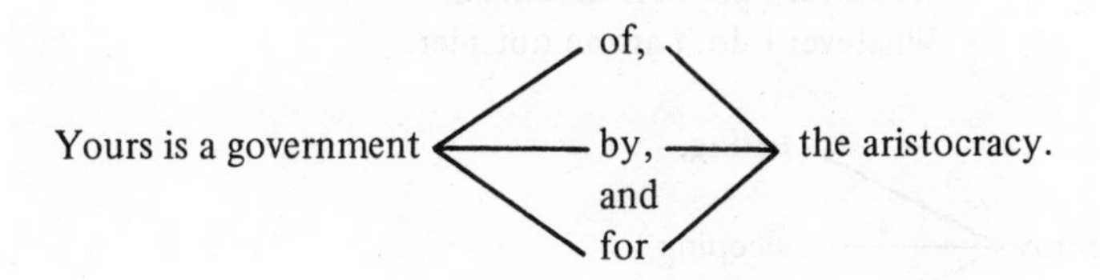

Yours is a government of the aristocracy.
Yours is a government by the aristocracy.
Yours is a government for the aristocracy.

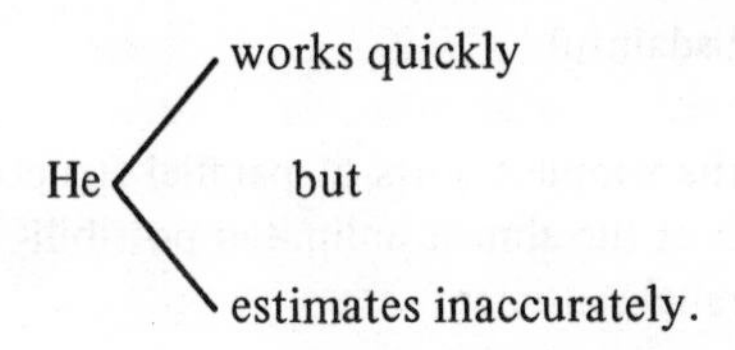

He works quickly.
He estimates inaccurately.

And here is an example of parallel attribute modifier without the headword of the attribute also being modified:

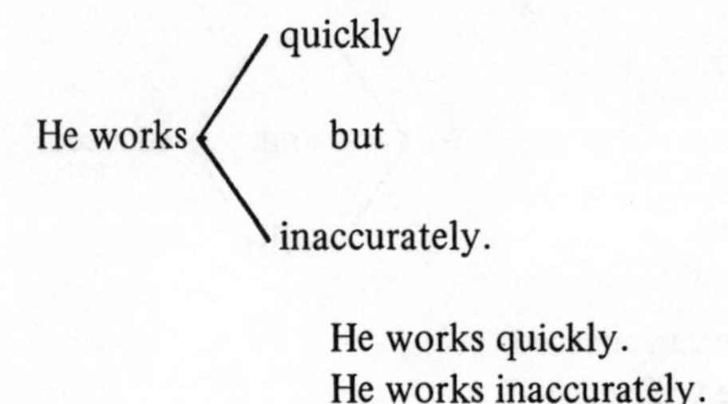

He works quickly.
He works inaccurately.

The following sentences contrast pre-positional and post-positional assertion modifiers:

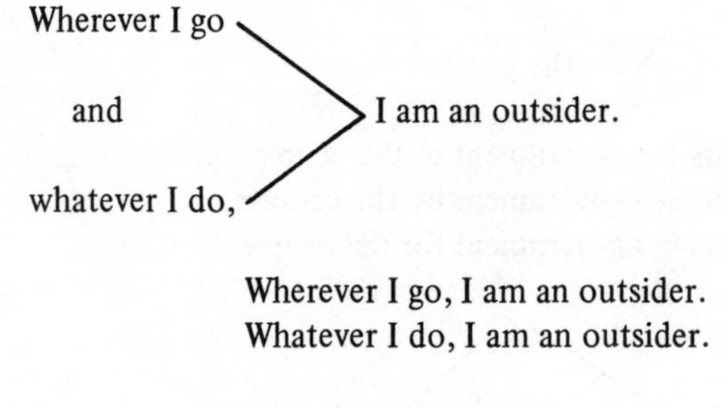

Wherever I go, I am an outsider.
Whatever I do, I am an outsider.

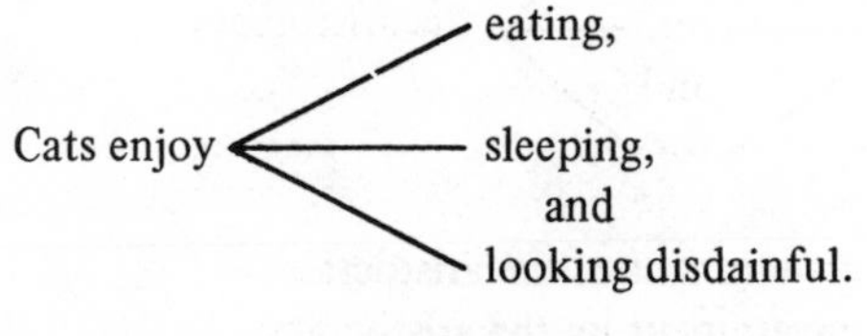

Cats enjoy eating.
Cats enjoy sleeping.
Cats enjoy looking disdainful.

Our examples so far have been only the simplest sorts of parallel structure. The following sentences give an indication of the almost unlimited possibilities for elaborating the simple two-leg parallel sentence:

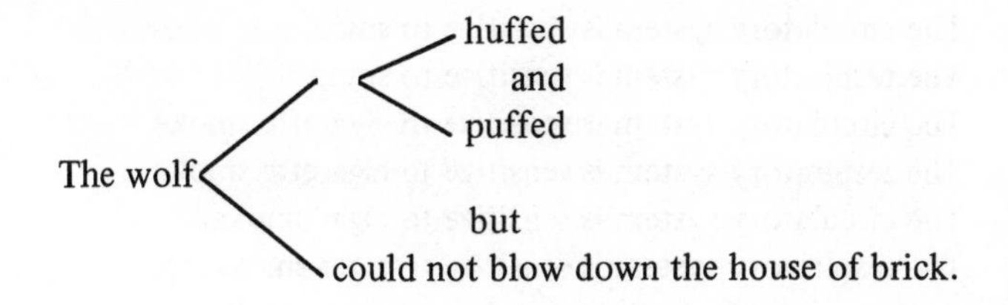

The wolf huffed.
The wolf puffed.
The wolf could not blow down the house of brick.

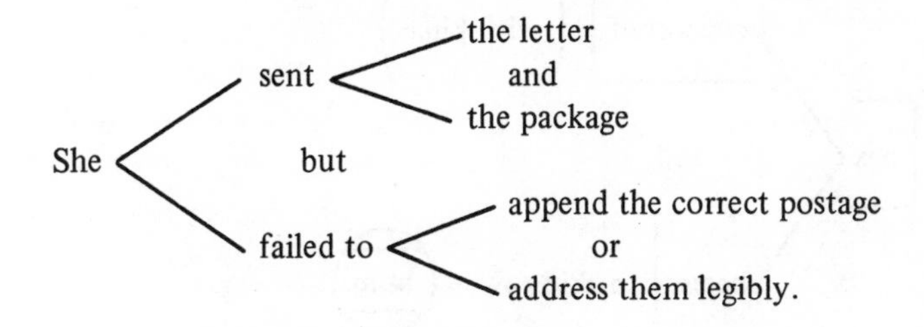

She sent the letter.
She sent the package.
She failed to append the correct postage.
She failed to address them legibly.

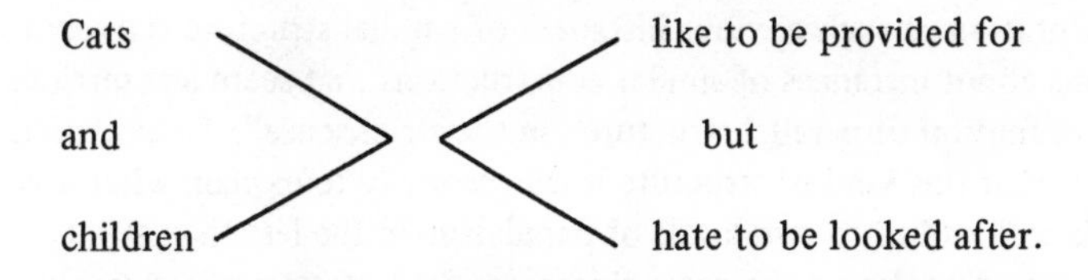

Cats like to be provided for.
Children like to be provided for.
Cats hate to be looked after.
Children hate to be looked after.

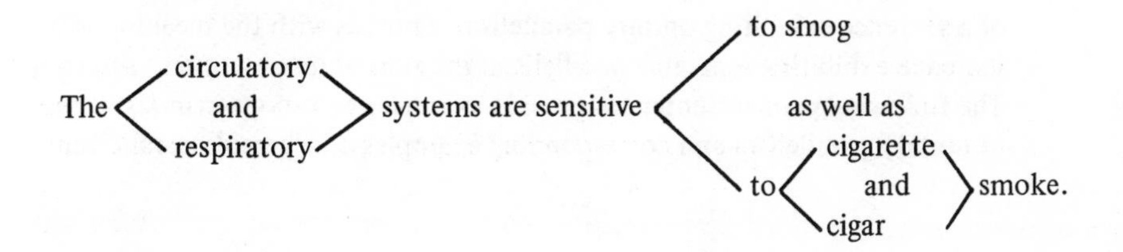

The circulatory system is sensitive to smog.
The respiratory system is sensitive to smog.
The circulatory system is sensitive to cigarette smoke.
The respiratory system is sensitive to cigarette smoke.
The circulatory system is sensitive to cigar smoke.
The respiratory system is sensitive to cigar smoke.

Last, and probably least (as far as frequency is concerned), we have a parallel sentence in which the legs are of different semantic kinds:

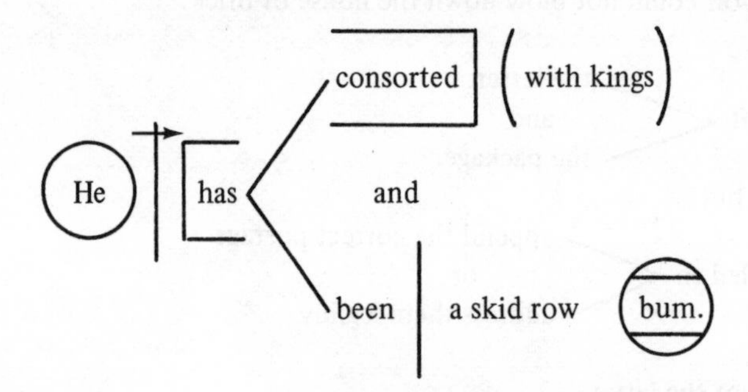

He has consorted with kings.
He has been a skid row bum.

As they stand, these eighteen examples are for the most part self-explanatory. But the presentation of such obvious instances of parallel structure is likely to raise questions about instances of similar constructions that seem less obviously to fit our definition of parallel structure "in the strict sense". To explain in greater detail what this kind of structure is is necessarily to explain what it is not. And this will lead us to two kinds of parallelism in the less than strict sense. All of the examples on the preceding pages are instances of *separable* parallelism. Besides this, there is a kind of parallelism that does not create additional separate assertions (*unitary*) and a kind of parallelism that does create additional assertions but accomplishes this by means of non-restrictive modification as well as parallel structure (*appositive*).

Unitary parallelism is parallel in structure but not in meaning. The meaning of a sentence exhibiting unitary parallelism is not, as with the meaning of a sentence exhibiting separable parallelism, the sum of its constituent assertions. The following pairs of sentences provide examples of various manifestations of unitary parallelism and corresponding examples of separable parallelism:

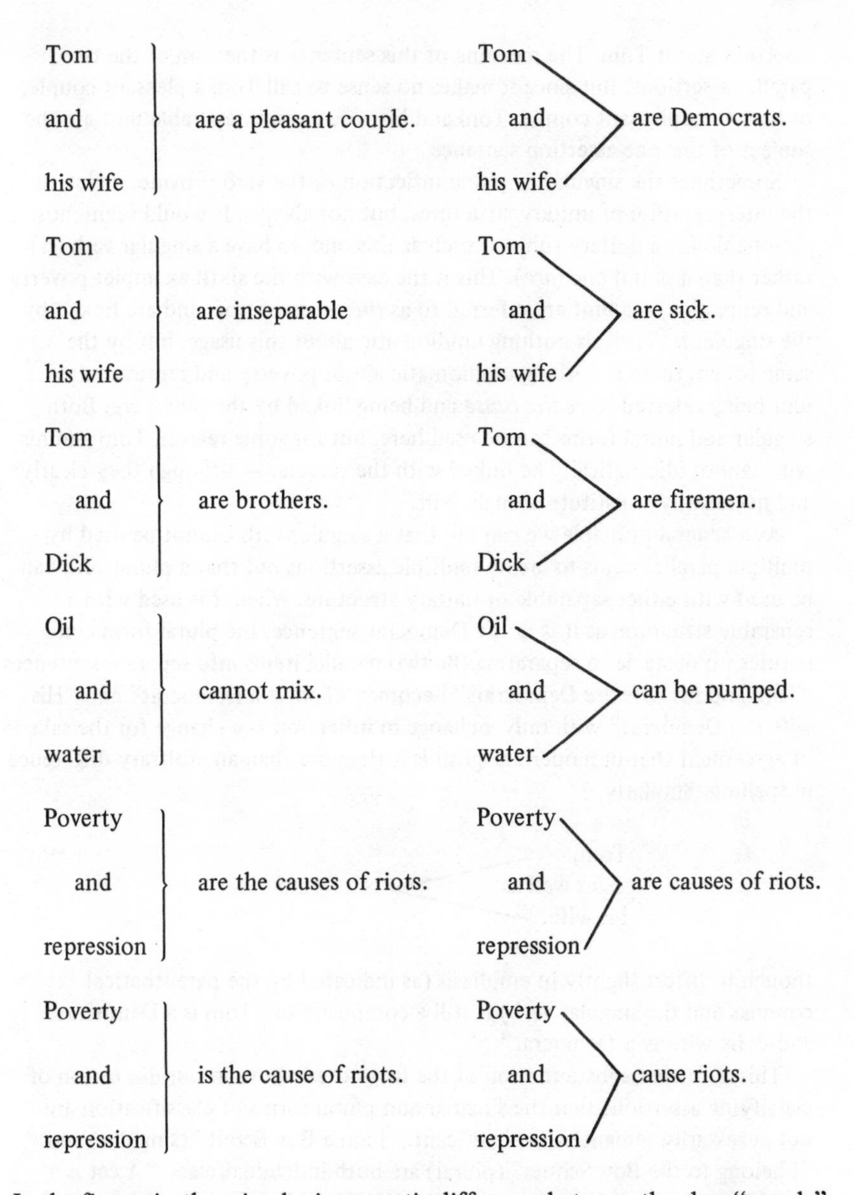

In the first pair, there is a basic semantic difference between the class "couple" and the class "Democrat". One person can be a Democrat, but one person can never be a couple. An instance of couple is by definition two-part. Tom is a Democrat, and this is complete and separable from his wife being a Democrat. Likewise, the assertion about his wife is complete and separable from the assertion about Tom. The meaning of this sentence is the sum of the two parallel assertions. But since it makes no sense to call Tom a pleasant couple, or his wife a pleasant couple, Tom and his wife as an inseparable unit are the subject of this one-assertion sentence.

Sometimes the singular or plural inflection of the verb provides a clue to the interpretation of unitary structures, but not always. It would seem most reasonable for a unitary subject, such as this one, to have a singular verb (*is*) rather than a plural one (*are*). This is the case with the sixth example: poverty and repression as a unit are referred to as *the cause* of riots and are linked by the singular *is*. There is nothing unidiomatic about this usage, but by the same token, there is nothing unidiomatic about poverty and repression as a unit being referred to as *the cause* and being linked by the plural *are*. Both singular and plural forms can be used here, but for some reason, Tom and his wife cannot idiomatically be linked with the singular – although they clearly and necessarily constitute a single unit.

As a general principle we can say that a singular verb cannot be used by multiple parallel items to create multiple assertions but that a plural verb can be used with either separable or unitary structure. When it is used with a separable structure, as it is in the Democrat sentence, the plural form constitutes no obstacle to separating the two parallel items into separate sentences. "Tom and his wife *are* Democrats" becomes "Tom *is* a Democrat" and "His wife *is* a Democrat" with only a change in inflection – a change for the sake of agreement that in modern English is little more than an arbitrary difference in spelling. Similarly,

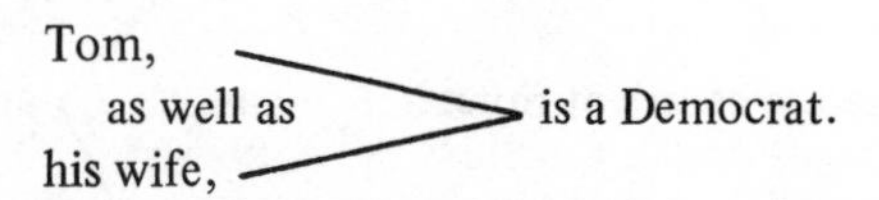

though it differs slightly in emphasis (as indicated by the parenthetical commas and the singular verb) is still a composite of "Tom is a Democrat" and "His wife is a Democrat".

This is further substantiation of the fact noted above in our discussion of classifying assertions that the singular and plural forms of classification are not necessarily semantically significant. "I am a Boy Scout" (singular) and "I belong to the Boy Scouts" (plural) are both individual/class. "A cat is a worthless creature" (singular) and "Cats are worthless creatures" (plural) are both subclass/class.

In the third pair, being firemen is like being Democrats, but being brothers is not like being a couple. Two brothers do not constitute a unit in the way that husband and wife constitute a unit but belong to a class by virtue of the mutual (i. e. identical) relationship they bear each other. Thus, it is possible for "Tom is a brother" and "Dick is a brother" to make sense as separate assertions, although Tom being a brother and Dick being a brother does not add up to Tom and Dick being each other's brother – which is the meaning of "Tom and Dick are brothers". On the other hand, "Tom is a fireman" and "Dick is a fireman" do add up to "Tom and Dick are firemen".

The basic kind of unitary parallelism is the relationship of inseparability (Tom and his wife) and its counterpart, immiscibility (oil and water). To say that two things are either inseparable or cannot mix is not to say that each has this characteristic but that the single relationship between them is so characterized. Thus, we continue to find instances of formal similarity that are no help in recognizing basic semantic differences and formal dissimilarities that are no help in recognizing basic semantic similarities. Parallel structure as the formal linking of two things will not in and of itself tell the reader whether the two things are parts of two separate assertions or whether they are parts of one assertion. And both a singular form and a plural form can be used to create a plurality of assertions.

A bit more complicated than our other examples is a unitary parallelism that is very like identity assertions.

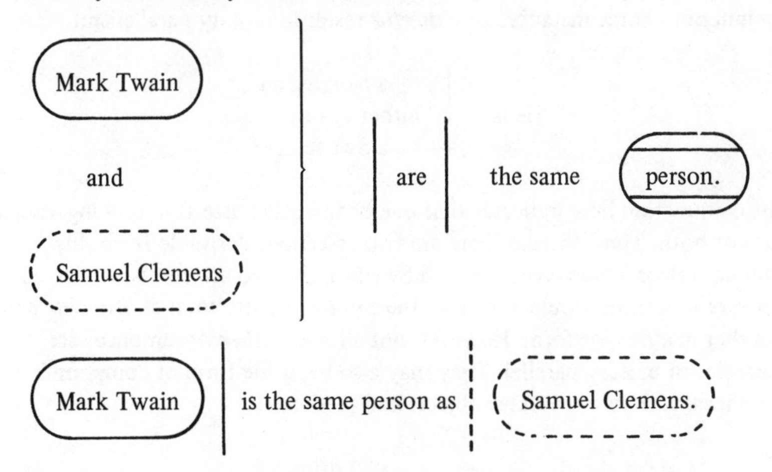

Like all unitary parallels, this one cannot be broken down into separate assertions; but unlike other unitary parallels, the two parallel items here do not refer to different things but to one and the same thing. Mark Twain and Samuel Clemens do not constitute a unit in the way that Tom and his wife constitute a couple, nor do they bear a mutual relationship to each other in the way that Tom and Bill are each other's brother. The man named both Mark Twain and Samuel Clemens belongs to the same class as the man that bears the titles Vice President and Presiding Officer of the Senate – the class of individuals who have more than one label. The crucial point for diagraming, however, is that structurally there is a conjunction linking two parallel items and yet only one assertion.

Finally, we need to note that subjects are not the only elements that can occur as unitary parallels. In addition to the reversal of subject and attribute in identity assertions (Poverty and repression is the cause of riots / The cause of riots is poverty and repression) a common kind of unitary attribute results from the use of *or* to mean *somewhere in between*:

They were gone { two / or / three } hours.

This assertion does not mean that they were gone *either* two *or* three hours. *Two* and *three* are unitary because they specify the limits of an approximation. The assertion is not false if they were in fact gone two and a half hours, but it is false if they were gone one and a half.

A final example of unitary parallelism results from the use of the *either/or* conjunction. Some instances of *either/or* result in unitary parallelism:

He is { a Norwegian / either . . . or / a Swede.

The conjunction here indicates that one or the other assertion is being asserted but not both. Thus, though there are two assertions derivable from this sentence (He is a Norwegian. He is a Swede.), the two assertions written as separate sentences would not have the same semantic total as the two written together in *either/or* form. However, not all such *either/or* sentences are examples of unitary parallel. They may also be in the form of compound sentences, with two separate subjects and predicates:

Either . . . or: you drink / you don't drink.

But in any case the two assertions are still mutually exclusive. And like most formal distinctions, this one can be used for quite different semantic functions. Usage, if not logic, finds quite acceptable a sentence in which *either/or* results in multiple assertions:

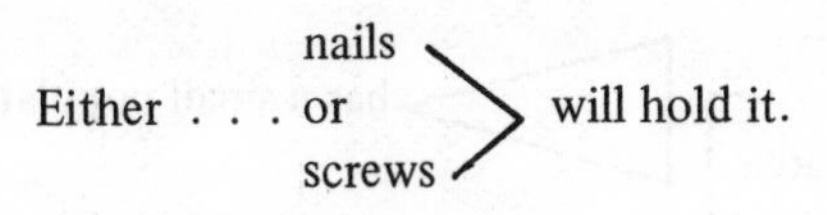

Nails will hold it.
Screws will hold it.

Similar to this last example of *either/or* is *neither/nor*:

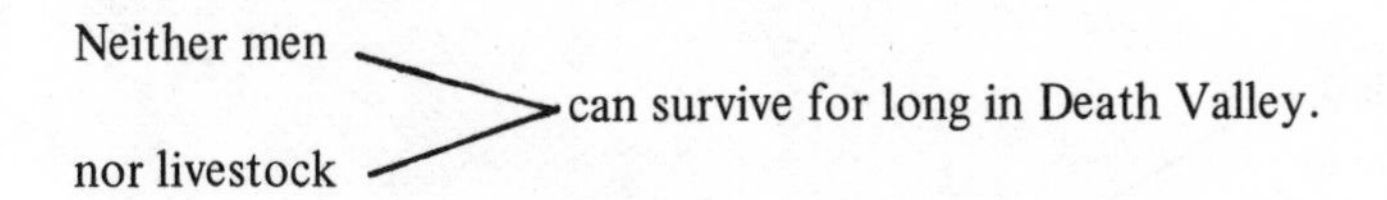

No men can survive for long in Death Valley.
No livestock can survive for long in Death Valley.

The grafting of the negative elements onto *either* and *or* makes these two conjunctions semantically significant in their own right quite apart from their function as conjunctions. This is made especially obvious by the inflectional modification that is required in writing the two assertions as separate sentences. This can be done by ignoring the *-either* and *-or* but not by ignoring the *n-* and *n-*.

C. MODIFICATIONAL

Appositive parallelism, the third and last kind of parallel structure, is also our introduction to non-restrictive modification. The multiple items can be read separately as complete and independent assertions, but unlike the items in separable parallelism, these items refer to the same thing. As a result, all succeeding items function as non-restrictive modification of the first item. A succeeding item may be a synonym for the first:

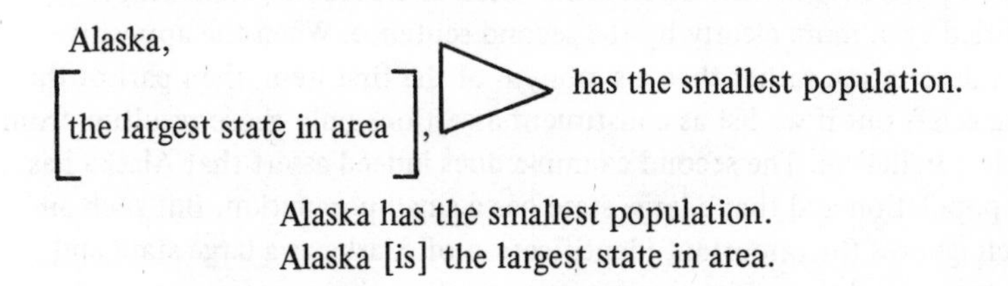

Alaska has the smallest population.
Alaska [is] the largest state in area.

or it may be a description of it:

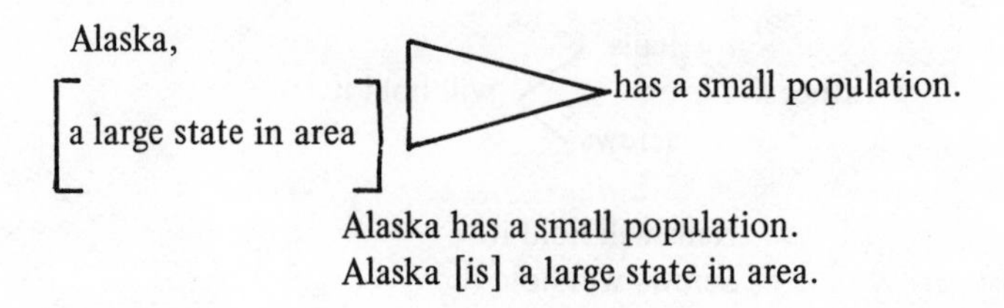

Alaska has a small population.
Alaska [is] a large state in area.

But in neither case does the second parallel item mean anything basically different from the first – as it always does in separable parallelism:

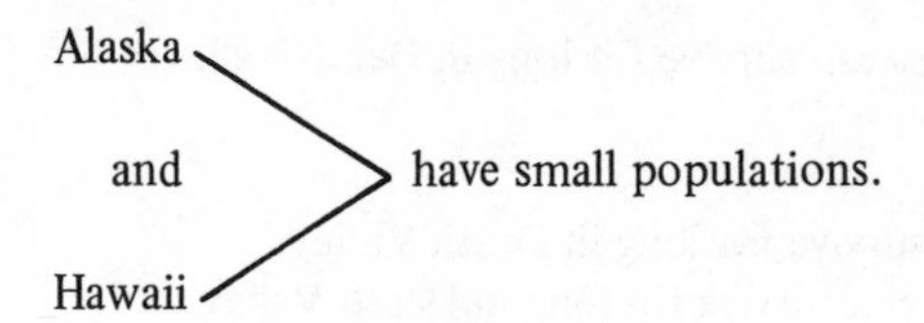

Alaska has a small population.
Hawaii has a small population.

For this reason, the multiple assertions do not really result from linking the multiple parallel items with the common element in the sentence, as they do in separable parallelism. Instead, they result from taking the succeeding parallel items to be attributes of the first parallel item. The first example does indeed assert that Alaska has the smallest population and that the largest state in area has the smallest population, but the point of an appositive construction is not to say the same thing differently but to say two different things about the subject: Alaska has the smallest population, and Alaska is the largest state in area. And, of course, if these are both true, then it necessarily follows that the largest state in area has the smallest population. But to say that this sentence is composed of three, rather than two, separate assertions seems misleading and unnecessarily repetitive.

The justification for taking the constituent assertions of appositive parallelism as non-restrictive modification rather than as separable parallelism is exemplified even more clearly by the second sentence. When the appositive item is a description rather than a synonym of the first item, then part of the meaning is left out if we list as constituent assertions only those resulting from separable parallelism. The second example does indeed assert that Alaska has a small population and that a large state has a small population. But such an approach ignores the important identification of Alaska as a large state and substitutes instead the misleadingly vague assertion that some unspecified large state has a small population.

The following sentences are a representative sampling of the various manifestations of appositive parallelism. By and large their diagrams make them self-explanatory. To the extent that they do not, it is because we have yet to define precisely what is meant by non-restrictive modification. Thus, rather than stop to analyze these sentences, we will proceed at once to the discussion of modificational structure.

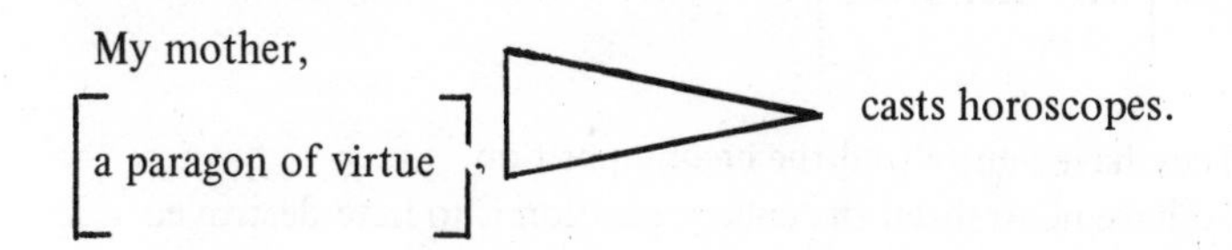

My mother casts horoscopes.
My mother [is] a paragon of virtue.

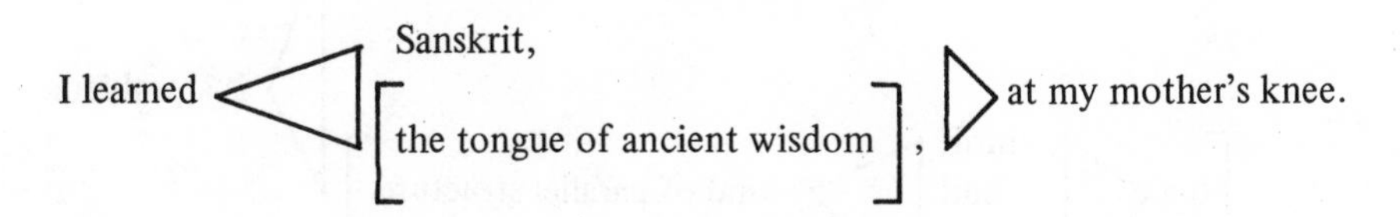

I learned Sanskrit at my mother's knee.
Sanskrit [is] the tongue of ancient wisdom.

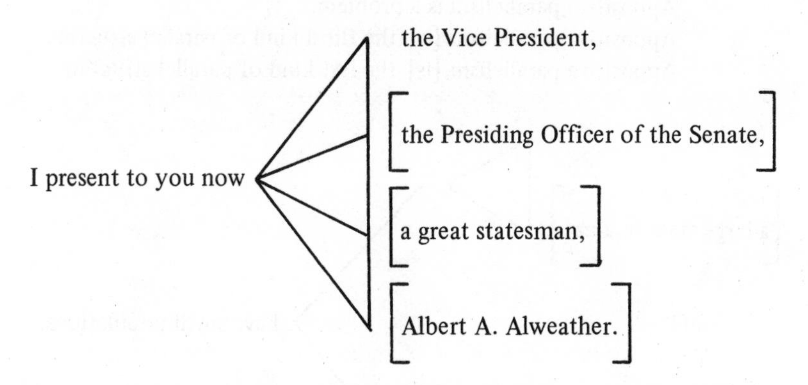

I present to you now the Vice President.
The Vice President [is] the Presiding Officer of the Senate.
The Vice President [is] a great statesman.
The Vice President [is] Albert A. Alweather.

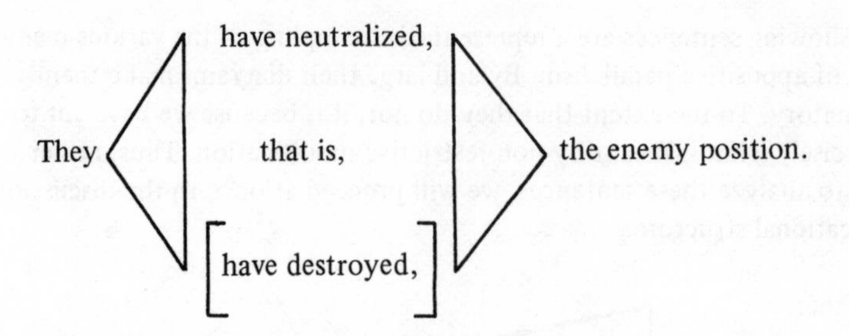

They have neutralized the enemy position.
To have neutralized the enemy position is to have destroyed the enemy position.

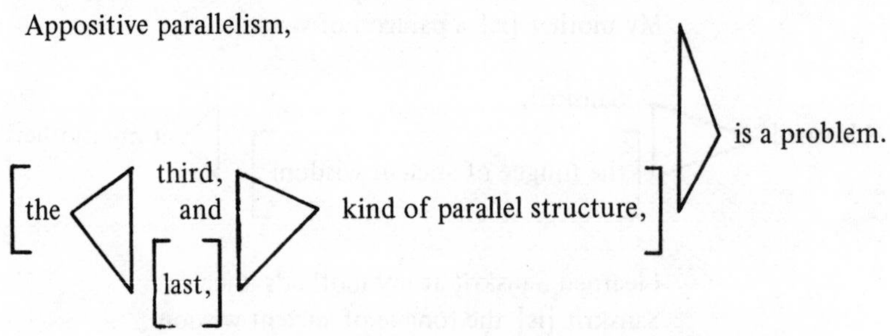

Appositive parallelism is a problem.
Appositive parallelism [is] the third kind of parallel structure.
Appositive parallelism [is] the last kind of parallel structure.

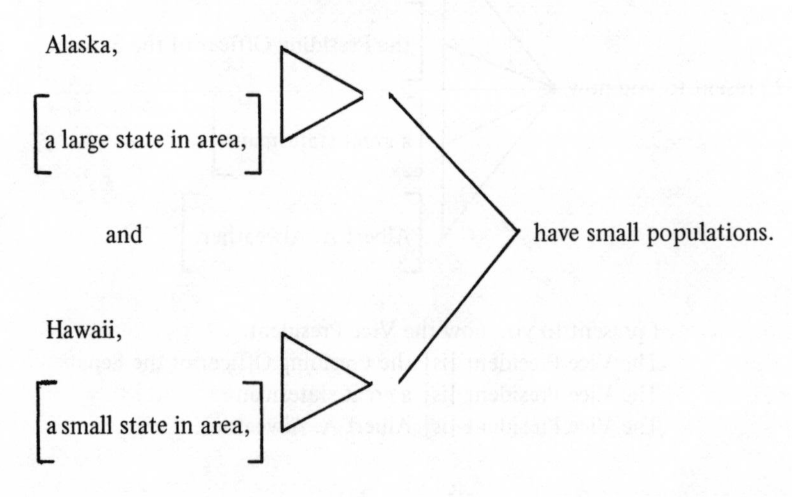

Alaska has a small population.
Alaska [is] a large state in area.
Hawaii has a small population.
Hawaii [is] a small state in area.

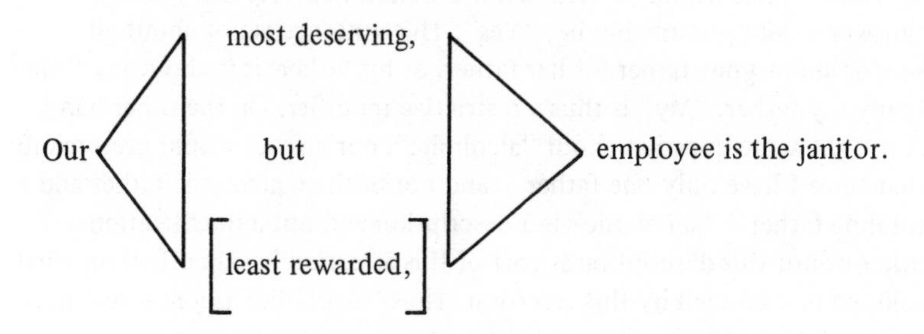

Our most deserving employee is the janitor.
Our most deserving employee [is] our least rewarded employee.

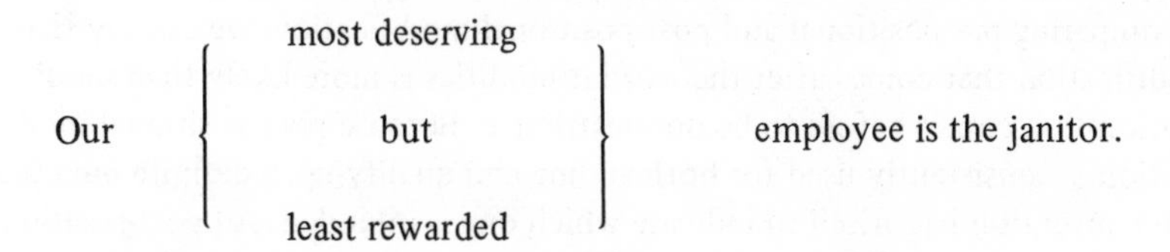

Our most deserving but least rewarded employee is the janitor.

The next chapter will take us down the many byways of modification, but in explaining non-restrictive structure we shall be content here to remain on the highway and to distinguish only the two broad classes of restrictive and non-restrictive. Within an assertion, modification can qualify that assertion or it can create an additional assertion. The test for restrictive modification is the question: Does the modifier serve to exclude certain possibilities from being asserted that could be included if the modifier were not present? In the sentence "Lazy people are unreliable", "lazy" modifies "people". If we ask the question, "Does 'lazy' serve to exclude certain things from being asserted that would be included if the modifier were not present? " our answer would presumably be, "Yes". This sentence is not about all people, or white people, or young people, or old people. It claims that people who are lazy – no more and no less – are unreliable. The sentence says neither that people in general are unreliable nor that people in general are lazy. It serves only to exclude people who are energetic. Thus, "lazy" is a restrictive modifier, not a non-restrictive one, and the sentence makes only one assertion.

Most commonly, modification that comes before the word it modifies is restrictive rather than non-restrictive, but not always. In the sentence "My alcoholic father suffered from gout", "my" and "alcoholic" both modify "father". If we ask the question, "does 'my' exclude certain things from being asserted that would be included if the modifier were not present", our answer would presumably be, "Yes". This sentence is not about all fathers or about your father, or her father, or his father; it is about my father and only my father. "My" is thus a restrictive modifier. On the other hand, if we ask the same question about "alcoholic", our answer would presumably be that since I have only one father – and not both an alcoholic father and a teetotaling father – "alcoholic" is a description and not a qualification. Whether or not this description is part of this assertion has no effect on what is included or excluded by this assertion. Thus "alcoholic" is a non-restrictive modifier, not a restrictive one, and the sentence makes two assertions.

Modification in sophisticated writing is more often than not qualifying rather than additive. Long sentences are not primarily the means for making many assertions but the means for making increasingly precise assertions. But in comparing pre-positional and post-positional modification, we can say that modification that comes after the word it modifies is more likely than modification that comes before to be non-restrictive. Because post-positional modification is consistently used for both adding and qualifying, a definite punctuation convention has arisen to indicate which one is intended. All post-positional non-restrictive modification is set off by punctuation (commas, dashes, parentheses); post-positional restrictive modification is not set off by punctuation. Unfortunately, this convention does not also apply to pre-positional modification, although it would be a great help if it did.

With this much in mind, we should be able to clarify any problems that may have arisen with our examples of appositive parallelism. In the first sentence there is a parallel subject: "my mother" and "a paragon of virtue" can both serve as the subject of "casts horoscopes". However, the second of these subjects is set off by commas and functions as an attribute of the first subject. In this case, the appositive modifier is not a synonym for the thing modified but is a description of it. Not all paragons of virtue are equated with my mother, and not all paragons of virtue are claimed to cast horoscopes.

In the second sentence an assertion modifier rather than the subject is parallel. And unlike the parallel in the first sentence, the second of the parallel items here is synonymous with the first item. Sanskrit is claimed to be *the* tongue of ancient wisdom, and *the* tongue of ancient wisdom is claimed to be Sanskrit. But again, the second of the two parallel items is set off as non-restrictive modification by commas.

The third sentence is like the second except that it contains more parallel items, and these are examples of both descriptive and synonymous relationships. The Vice President, the Presiding Officer of the Senate, and Albert A. Alweather are one and the same person; but "a great statesman" is not confined to this one person but is rather a class to which this person, among others, belongs. If we did not mind a good deal of non-significant repetition, we could combine the elements of this sentence into ten assertions:

I present to you now the Vice President.
I present to you now the Presiding Officer of the Senate.
I present to you now a great statesman.
I present to you now Albert A. Alweather.
The Vice President [is] the Presiding Officer of the Senate.
The Vice President [is] a great statesman.
The Vice President [is] Albert A. Alweather.
The Presiding Officer of the Senate [is] a great statesman.
The Presiding Officer of the Senate [is] Albert A. Alweather.
A great statesman [is] Albert A. Alweather.

The fourth sentence is a rarity among appositive parallels because it actually contains a form of *be* linking the two items. To have neutralized the enemy position is to have destroyed it. We do not usually think of the phrase *that is* as functioning as a conjunction, but in the sense that it clearly and unequivocally joins two parallel items, it is as much a conjunction as is *and*. But however we choose to characterize this particular parallel, it differs from all our other examples of appositive parallelism by virtue of providing, and not just implying, a form of *be* to link the first item as a subject to the second item as an attribute.

The sentence about appositive parallelism, which occurred earlier in the text as a quite unintended use of what was being explained, is interesting because it contains an appositive parallel within an appositive parallel. And correspondingly, the third parallel item is set off by commas within the second as well as the second being set off by commas from the first. But as far as the constituent assertions are concerned, the parallel items function the same as they did in the Vice President sentence, where the items were all structurally parallel to each other. Here both the second parallel item and the parallel item within the second are attributes of the first one.

The Alaska example shows the difference, within a single sentence, between separable parallelism and appositive parallelism. And this gives us the opportunity to note that, although *and* as a conjunction occurs in the great majority of separable constructions, it does not occur in appositive constructions, where it would be ambiguous. Indeed, only rarely, as in the fourth example, does any conjunction occur with appositives; the basic means for indicating apposition is to juxtapose with punctuation but without conjunctions.

The kind of ambiguity that can occur with conjunctions is illustrated by the last two examples. If the writer were not careful with his use of punctuation and the reader not clear on what the writer meant by his punctuation, such an instance of post-positional modification within pre-positional modification could result in two different meanings. The question here is whether the sentence is asserting that the most deserving employee is also the least rewarded employee or whether it is simply referring to the most deserving employee *who is the least rewarded employee*. If "least rewarded" is a qualifying modifier, then it distinguishes the most deserving employee who is the most rewarded (perhaps the president) from the most deserving employee who is the least rewarded. When "least rewarded" is set off by commas, it is a non-restrictive modifier, and the sentence has two assertions; when it is not set off by commas, it is a restrictive modifier, and the sentence has just one assertion.

With these two examples, we complete our survey of appositive parallelism and return to the distinction with which we began – restrictive and non-restrictive modification. For introducing basic structural distinctions this is as detailed as we need to be in analyzing modification. In the next chapter we will examine at greater length the different subcategories within both restrictive and non-restrictive modification. But before concluding our discussion of structure we need to confront two complicating factors that render our diagraming system less universally applicable than we have made it appear to be. The first of these is displaced assertion structure. The second is elliptical structure. In the first, all of the words that would appear in regular structure are present, but the word order is modified. In the second, some of the words are actually missing.

For the purpose of facilitating the transition from one sentence or independent clause to the next, the structure of the second sentence is sometimes displaced or inverted:

The house is surrounded by a wall.

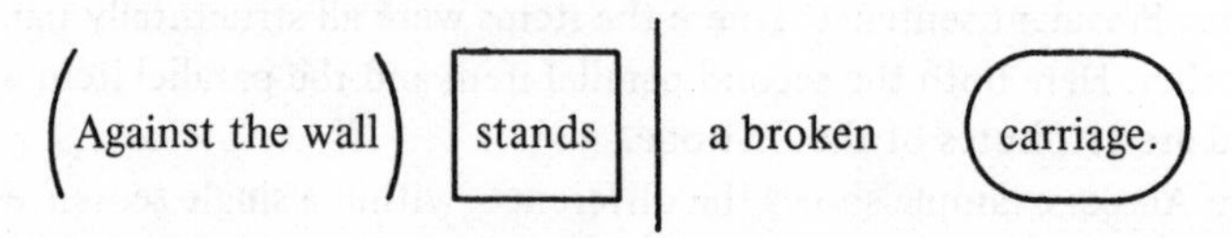

The last element of the first sentence is used as the first element of the second, but neither semantically nor grammatically is the second sentence significantly different from the standard subject/predicate form:

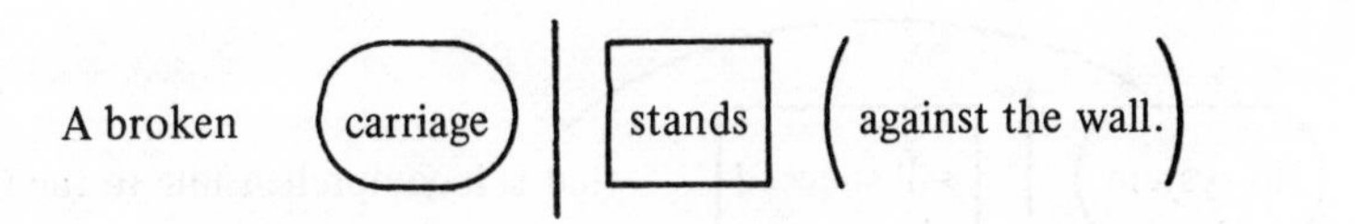

One of the common kinds of inverted structure is these place or 'prepositional' predicates:

Below the hill is a cave. On the stone is an inscription.

Lying at my feet was the weapon. Across the street is a doctor.

These cannot always be accounted for by transitional reasons; sometimes we simply have to say, vaguely but probably legitimately, that the displaced element seems to be the most important part of the sentence and receives more attention by coming ahead of schedule. English syntax provides, for some kinds of sentences at least, quite a variety of positional possibilities – to facilitate transition, for emphasis, sometimes simply for variety. The possibilities are especially multiplied when there is a complex but indivisible attribute:

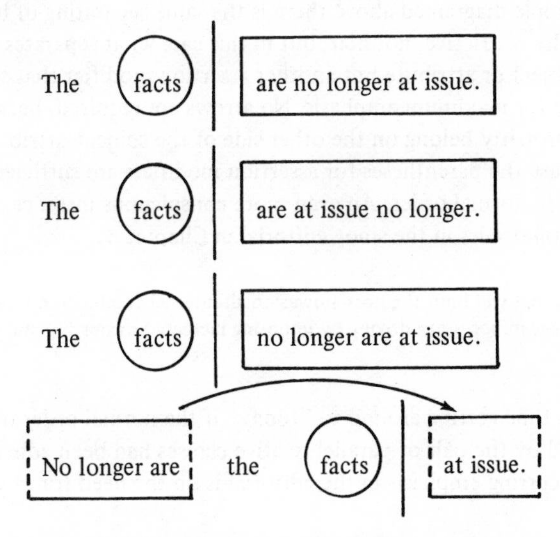

The truism that proximity to the thing modified is the basic formal evidence of modification is open to exceptions when primary emphasis seems to be defeated by the usual order.

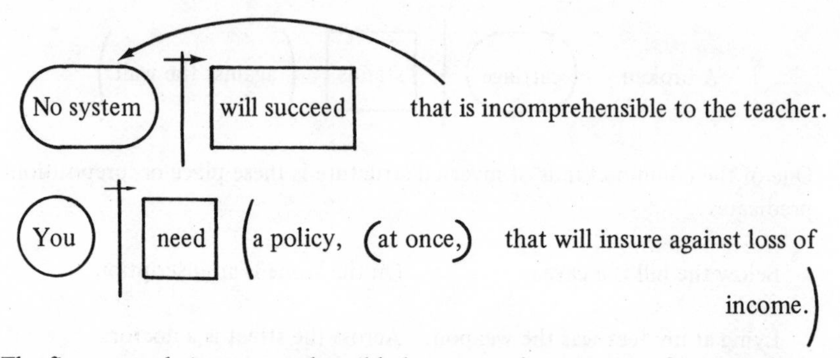

The first example is a comprehensible but unusual separation of a core subject from its lengthy restrictive modifier. Presumably, the rationale is that "will succeed" is too basic a part of the sentence to be left (in German fashion) to the very end. An even more conspicuous example, but one too long to diagram here, is this sentence from the Introduction:

No system of linguistic analysis will become established that is not comprehensible to those whose task it is to teach it, at the elementary as well as the advanced levels.

In the second example diagramed above there is the same separating of headword from a lengthy restrictive modifier, but in this case what separates it is not a displaced subject or attribute but another assertion modifier that seems to be inserted here for maximum emphasis. No arrows are required, because it does not more properly belong on the other side of the subject/attribute division, and because the parentheses for assertion modifiers are sufficient to indicate the break in normal order. An even more conspicuous instance of this kind of construction occurs in the smog editorial in Chapter 8:

We need laws, today, that will limit the horsepower on all internal combustion vehicles and that will discourage unnecessary driving by imposing increased ownership and use taxes.

It would be a long time getting around to "today" if the normal order of headword followed by the pair of parallel relative clauses had been adhered to. And yet the recurring emphasis in the editorial is on the need for *immediate* action.

The use of arrows is indicative of the limits beyond which the diagraming system cannot proceed without losing its simplicity and thus much of its usefulness. It is one thing to have a complete inversion, with complete attribute first and complete subject second, or to have one assertion modifier inserted within another. It is quite another to have part of the subject or attribute on one side of the central division and part on the other side. This calls for some kind of jury-rig.

As we have seen in discussing classifying assertions, this problem of displaced structure is not restricted to bipartite structure:

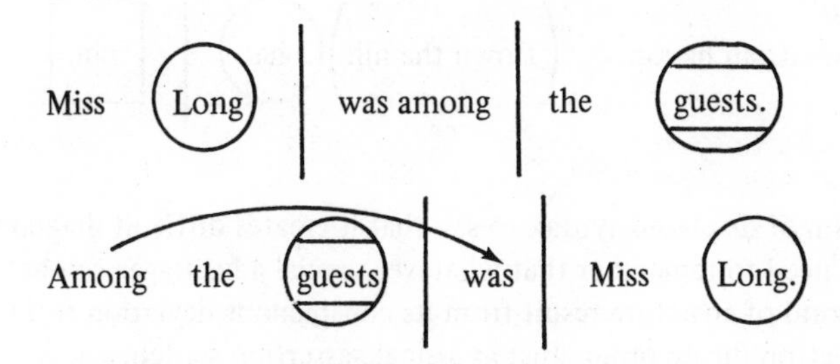

Yet it is not classifying assertions but function assertions that most commonly manifest displaced structure. Especially likely to be out of place are 'adverbs' – both in our sense of a function modifier and in the traditional sense of a verb-adverb combination.

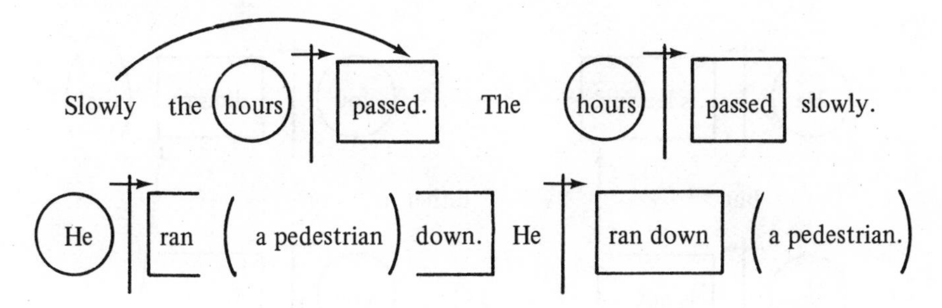

The difference in diagraming the attributes reflects the difference between a function modifier of a core attribute and an indivisible (although displaced) attribute core. To run down a pedestrian is not the same sort of activity as to run down a hill.

He ran down the hill.

And, lest we seem to be implying that English syntax allows for every possibility of positional variation, here is a bit of evidence for the greater indivisibility of verb-adverb attribute cores than of attributes and assertion modifiers:

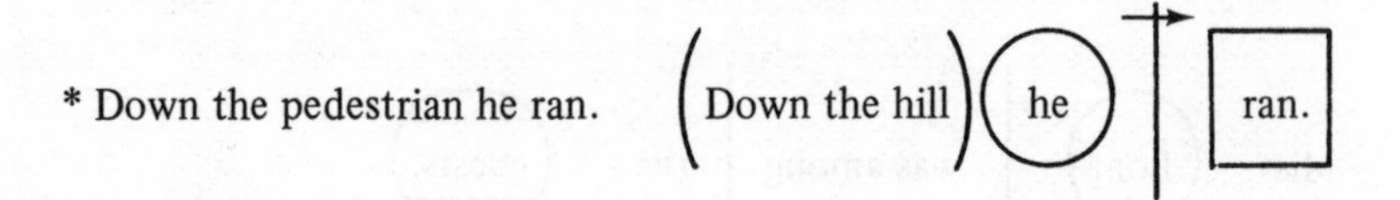

It is no criticism of displaced syntax to say that it creates difficult diagraming problems; but we need to remember that whatever special advantages can be gained from this kind of structure result from its conspicuous deviation from the norm of subject/predicate order. Just as a single-assertion sentence and a single-sentence paragraph can be useful for emphasis when used sparingly, so an inverted sentence structure can be useful when used sparingly.

The explanation for elliptical constructions is more obvious: economy. Ellipsis is like parallel structure and additive modification in making double use of single words or phrases, but its non-elliptical form is usually compound:

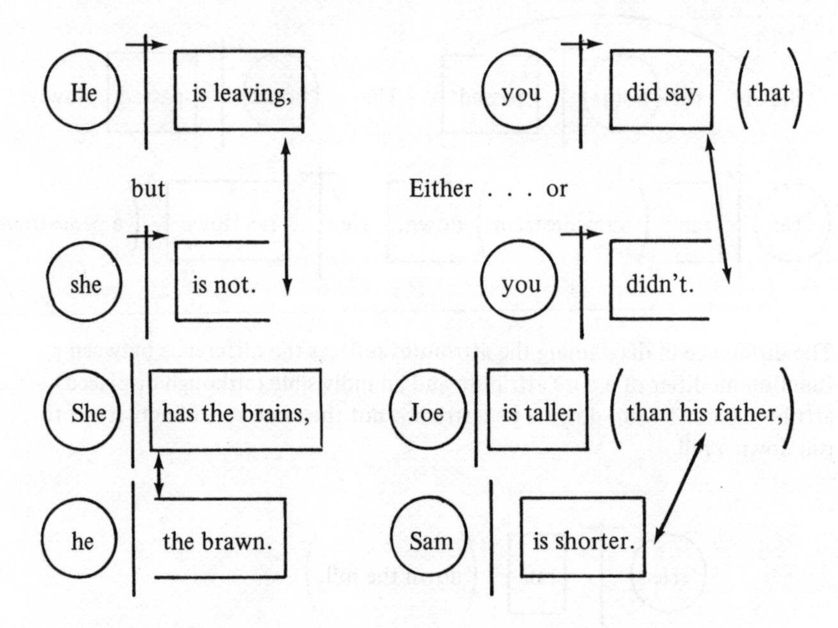

The single pointed arrows, for displaced structure, indicated that part of the sentence was to be moved from one place to another; the double pointed arrows, for elliptical structure, indicate that part of the sentence is to be used in another place even as it must remain where it is. Admittedly, these are quite simple examples, and with the addition of other complicating factors, the use of arrows would become rather cumbersome.

Simple or complex, however, the principle remains the same: whatever the varieties of assertion structure, if we are dealing with assertions we are dealing with explicitly presented elements. Elliptical constructions differ from ordinary parallel constructions only in the arrangement of the words, not in their presence or absence. In parallel structure the shared element can come before or after the two or more parallel elements but not in the midst of them, which would result in ellipsis instead. There are different ways that these elements can be arranged and do multiple duty, but for both parallel and ellipsis the elements must be there. For the purposes of analysis – separating out the individual assertions – we can change positions and inflectional forms, but we cannot assume to be present elements that in fact are not present.

Some comparisons are like pronouns: crucial semantic reference need not always occur in the sentence that relies on such reference. Our "taller/shorter" example above was a single sentence, but just as idiomatic are separate sentences like "Sam is shorter" and "Sue is more beautiful". Thus, such constructions are not in the strictest sense elliptical. They are semantically dependent on prior reference, but they are formally independent. "He the brawn" cannot stand as an independent sentence because a crucial part of the attribute core is missing, but when only an assertion modifier (e. g. "than his father") is missing, independence is possible. The only other anomaly to note here is the difference between inflected forms for comparative and superlative degrees (*-er*, *-est*) and additional words (*more*, *most*, *less*, *least*). The former are diagramed as part of the core; the latter are diagramed as modifiers of the core. The standard of comparison is an assertion modifier answering the question, "Compared to what? " The degree to which the standard is met is part of the attribute (modifier or otherwise) answering the question, "To what extent or degree? "

NOTES

1 For further explanation of these two kinds of non-restrictive modifiers see Chapter 4, p. 123 ff.
2 The subject of section B in Chapter 6.
3 Further discussion of this internal compounding and of the pair of slash marks with which they are diagramed occurs on page 198.

4. THE USES OF MODIFICATION

The expansion, contraction, and general clarification of meaning is called modification. The thing modified can be a word, a phrase, or a whole assertion; and the modifier can be a word, a phrase, or a whole assertion. When the thing modified and the modifier become larger than individual assertions, we tend to think of the relationship as one of organization rather than modification. But the difference between the two is simply a matter of perspective. When a composition is viewed from the bottom up – adding word to word, assertion to assertion – the relationship is one of modification. When a composition is viewed from the top down – separating part from whole – the relationship is one of organization. But the composition is the same.

A. NON-RESTRICTIVE

We have already introduced the two primary kinds of modification (restrictive and non-restrictive), but we need to recognize that while these are exhaustive distinctions, we have heretofore been exemplifying them with only certain kinds of modifiers. For example, our discussion of non-restrictive modifiers has treated only what, for lack of a traditional term, we will call *additive*– modifiers that make additional assertions. Another kind of modification that does not restrict (and thus by default must be considered non-restrictive) but does not make additional assertions is simply emphatic, redundant, punctuational. The terms will vary depending on the examples, but for the sake of a general label, one that presents an obvious contrast to additive, we will refer to this kind of modifier as *redundant*. To be redundant is not to restrict, but neither is it to add an assertion.

But before examining this new kind, let us conclude our discussion of non-restrictive additive modification as the third of the three ways of making assertions. We need to analyze at greater length its two different manifestations – subordinate structure and dependent structure. With some important exceptions, like appositive parallels, this is a difference between modifiers that come after the thing modified and modifiers that come before. For the purposes of grammatical analysis the subordinate/dependent distinction is the basic one, and it is with this that we shall begin. But for the purposes of composition the post-positional/pre-positional distinction is the most relevant, and it is with this that we shall conclude.

(1) *Additive*

Additive modification that is subordinate makes a complete assertion when the words of the modification are joined to the term modified. Additive modification that is dependent makes a complete assertion when the words of the modification are joined to the term modified *by means of the form of "be" that is necessarily implied by but not included in the sentence itself*. To write out a subordinate additive modifier as a separate assertion is to make use of only the words, or their inflected forms, provided in the sentence. To write out a dependent additive modifier as a separate assertion is necessarily to provide in brackets a form of *be* to make formally complete what is already semantically complete.

Perhaps the best way to list our examples of subordinate additive structure is to group them according to the things they modify. All subordinate modification is post-positional and is introduced by the relative pronouns *which* and *who* (including the possessive inflected form *whose* and, rather archaically, the 'objective' form *whom*). There are, however, four different things that it can come after and modify. It can modify the subject of the independent assertion (the most common), the attribute of the assertion, an assertion modifier, or the whole assertion (the least common). A point to notice about the positioning of all additive modifiers is that they are juxtaposed with what they modify. Even when they modify the whole assertion and even though this can sometimes create ambiguity, juxtaposition is the rule. Unequivocally restrictive meaning allows for the possibility of displaced restrictive modifiers – as we saw in the previous chapter – but additive modifiers do not have this potential.

modification of subject

My mother, [who is a paragon of virtue,] casts horoscopes.

My mother casts horoscopes.
My mother is a paragon of virtue.

Her birthday, [which comes once every four years,] is February 29.

Her birthday is February 29.
Her birthday comes once every four years.

Her birthday, [which she celebrates with a fast,] is February 29.

Her birthday is February 29.
She celebrates her birthday with a fast.

modification of attribute

This is your draft card, [which must be carried with you at all times.]

This is your draft card.
Your draft card must be carried with you at all times.

It is a Meadowlark, [which is a species of Blackbird.]

It is a Meadowlark.
A Meadowlark is a species of Blackbird.

modification of assertion modifier

She was born on February 29, [which comes once every four years.]

She was born on February 29.
February 29 comes once every four years.

Tom arrived with Dick, [whose wife I had met earlier.]

Tom arrived with Dick.
I had met Dick's wife earlier.

Dick arrived with his wife, [whom I had met earlier.]

Dick arrived with his wife.
I had met his wife earlier.

modification of assertion

Tom arrived late, [which was unusual for him.]

Tom arrived late.
Tom's arriving late was unusual for him.

They are Republicans, [which precludes any agreement.]

They are Republicans.
Their being Republicans precludes any agreement.

Dependent additive modification makes a complete assertion when the words of the modification are coupled with the term modified by means of the form of *be* that is implied by but not included in the sentence itself. Thus, to write out a dependent additive modifier as a separate assertion is necessarily to provide in brackets a form of *be* to make the assertion formally complete. Also, the term modified, no matter what its function in its own assertion, becomes the subject of the dependent assertion. In this respect dependent modification differs from subordinate, which, as we saw in three of our previous examples, can contain its own subject:

Her birthday, [which she celebrates with a fast,] is February 29.

Her birthday is February 29.
She celebrates her birthday with a fast.

A further difference is that dependent modification, unlike subordinate, is the basic way of creating appositive parallelism. Except for the one example of subordinate parallelism (using "that is") noted in the previous chapter, all the examples of appositive parallelism were also examples of dependent structure. However, most subordinate additive modification takes the form of post-positional relative clauses (i. e. , introduced by the relative pronouns *who* and *which*); and there are no dependent additive modifiers that are relative clauses.

There is, however, dependent structure that begins with *when* and *where* – words that are integral parts of the added assertions rather than simply introductions to them.

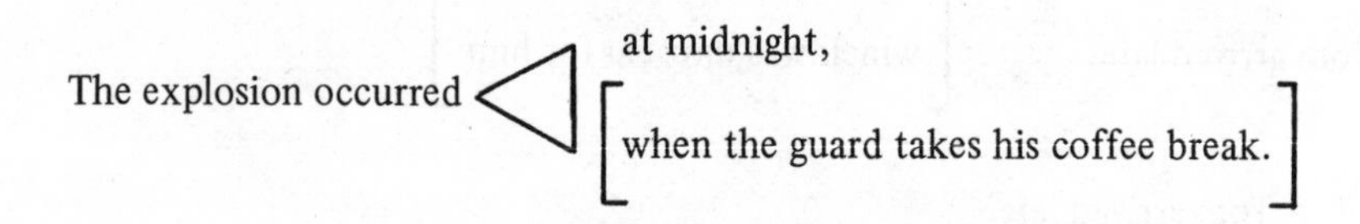

The explosion occurred at midnight.
At midnight [is] when the guard takes his coffee break.

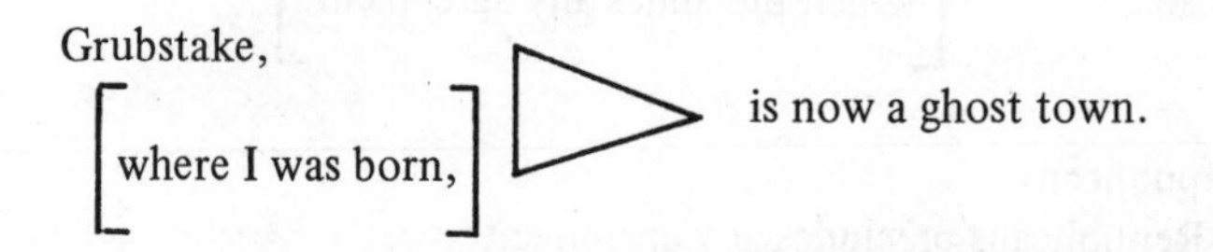

Grubstake is now a ghost town.
Grubstake [is] where I was born.

Each of the dependent clauses is part of a parallel because each can also be joined independently to the single elements without distortion of meaning.

The explosion occurred when the guard takes his coffee break.

Where I was born is now a ghost town.

But now consider the use of *which* and *who*. Both of these relative pronouns are subordinators and as such can introduce but cannot be part of additional assertions.

The explosion occurred on Main, [which is a heavily traveled street.]

The explosion occurred on Main.
Main is a heavily traveled street.

Grubstake O'Rourke, [who was my grandfather,] is now a ghost.

Grubstake O'Rourke is now a ghost.
Grubstake O'Rourke was my grandfather.

We cannot say idiomatically

* The explosion occurred on which is a heavily traveled street.
* Who was my grandfather is now a ghost.

If we had wanted to say

The explosion occurred on a heavily traveled street.
My grandfather is now a ghost.

then we would have had to use a dependent appositive construction.

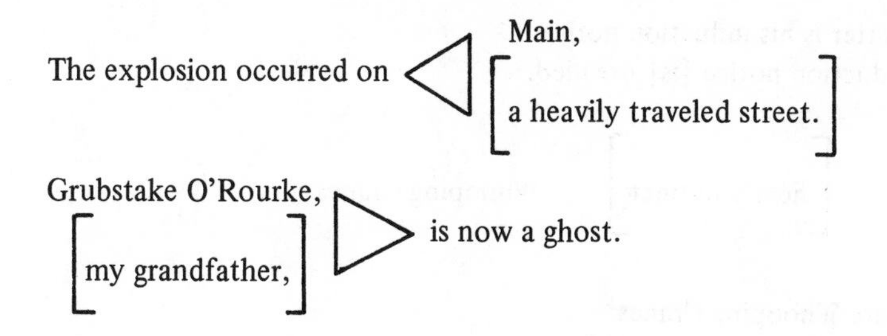

We shall list our examples of non-parallel dependent modification in the same way that we listed the subordinate ones – according to the things they modify. Dependent structure can modify the subject of the independent assertion, the attribute, or an assertion modifier. But unlike subordinate structure, dependent structure cannot modify an assertion as a whole.

modification of subject

My [alcoholic] father suffered from gout.

My father suffered from gout.
My father [was] alcoholic.

[Lazy] Tom is still in bed.

Tom is still in bed.
Tom [is] lazy.

modification of attribute

This letter is his [dreaded] induction notice.

This letter is his induction notice.
His induction notice [is] dreaded.

They are [nearly extinct] Whooping Cranes.

They are Whooping Cranes.
Whooping Cranes [are] nearly extinct.

modification of assertion modifier

Dick arrived with his [long-suffering] wife.

Dick arrived with his wife.
His wife [is] long-suffering.

She lost her [meager] savings.

She lost her savings.
Her savings [were] meager.

The chart on this and on the next page lists all the additive modifiers that have appeared in this chapter and makes obvious an important principle of composition: additive modification is handled better post-positionally than pre-positionally. Every kind of independent assertion can be structured as post-positional additive modification,

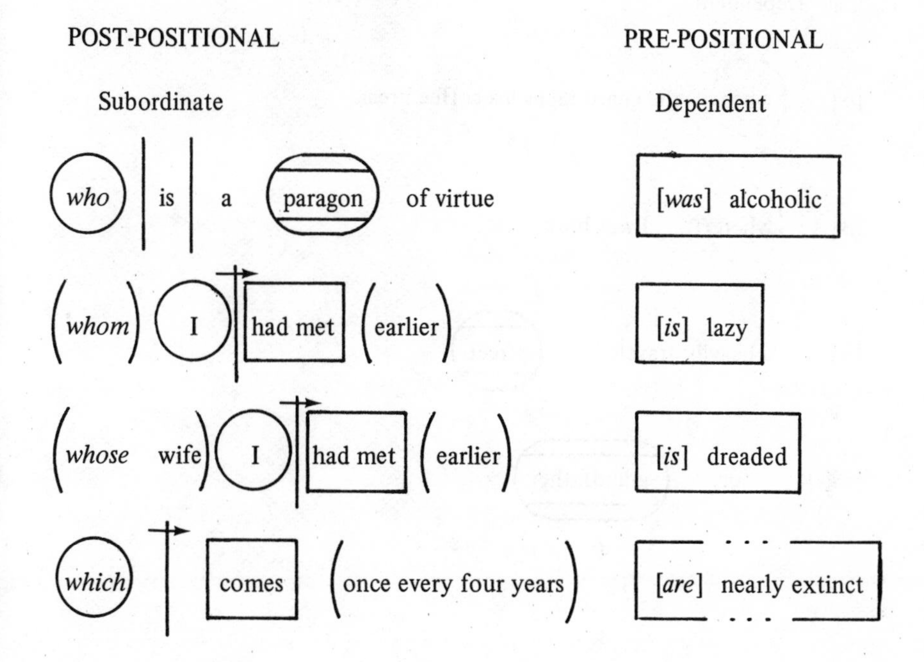

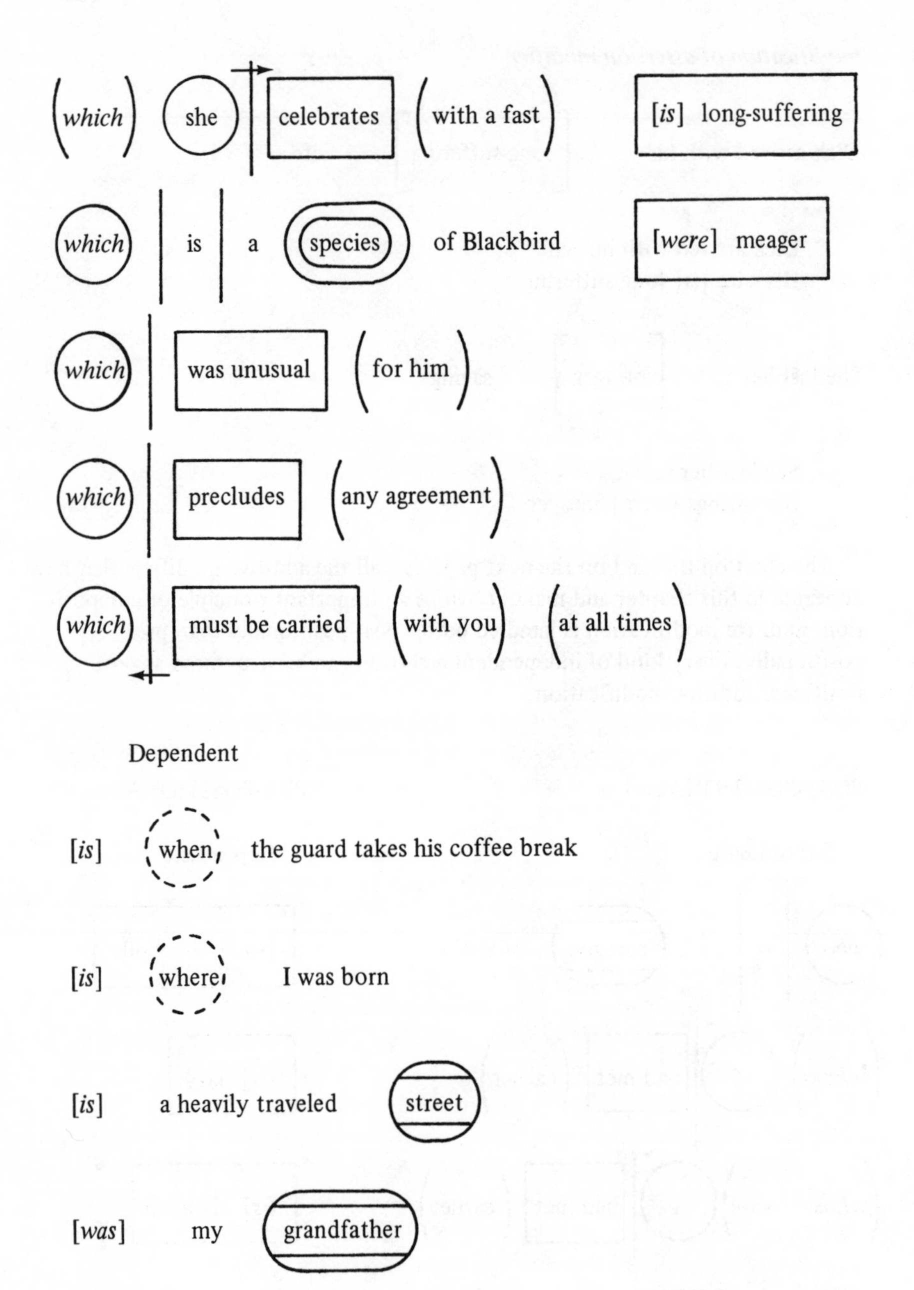
which
she
celebrates
with a fast
[is] long-suffering
which
is
a
species
of Blackbird
[were] meager
which
was unusual
for him
which
precludes
any agreement
which
must be carried
with you
at all times
Dependent
[is]
when
the guard takes his coffee break
[is]
where
I was born
[is]
a heavily traveled
street
[was]
my
grandfather

but only characteristic assertions can be structured pre-positionally. Pre-positional additive modifiers have the virtue of economy, but they have the shortcomings of limited use and possible ambiguity. The post-position can handle additive and restrictive modification equally well, but, as we shall see in the next section, pre-positional modification is better suited to restrictive than to additive modification.

All of these dependent pre-positional modifiers can be formulated post-positionally:

my father, who was alcoholic
Tom, who is lazy
his induction notice, which is dreaded
Whooping Cranes, which are nearly extinct
his wife, who is long-suffering
her savings, which were meager

But none of these subordinate post-positional modifiers can be formulated pre-positionally:

* This is your must-be-carried-with-you-at-all-times draft card.

Only a few post-positional additive modifiers are not relative clauses, and thus in only a few instances are post-positional modifiers convertible to pre-positional:

Her husband, [now deceased,] was a fireman.

Her [now deceased] husband was a fireman.

These two sentences employ exactly the same words and have exactly the same meaning; the only difference is the punctuation. And this is perhaps an appropriate place to repeat our earlier contention that English punctuation would be made more consistent and pre-positional additive modification easier to interpret if the convention of setting off additive modifiers with punctuation applied to pre-positional as well as to post-positional.

What, in the absence of punctuation, makes pre-positional additive modification possible to interpret is a thing to be modified that is not ordinarily restricted because it is just one of a kind. The repeated use of *mother* and *father* in our examples is not a reflection of parental preoccupation; these are simply the most obvious and unambiguous words for attaching additive modifiers to. If I were to refer to my alcoholic brother, I might be characterizing my one brother as alcoholic (additive) or distinguishing one brother who is alcoholic from one or more brothers who are not (restrictive). Except for proper names, the number of suitable words for attaching pre-positional additive modifiers to is not large, and thus the opportunities for such modification are limited.

mother and *father*	but not *grandmother, grandfather, sister, brother, aunt, uncle*
nose and *mouth*	but not *eye, ear, arm, leg, tooth*
husband and *wife*	but less so with the increase in divorces and remarriages
home	but not necessarily *house*

It is usually assumed that a person has no more than one mother, father, nose, mouth, husband, wife, home. But it is not unlikely that a person has or has had more than one brother, arm or house.

However, even with proper names and words like those in the first column, the final test is still semantic interpretation, because every thing that can be modified one way can be modified another. And furthermore, both additive and restrictive modifiers can be attached to the same word at the same time. Once *mother* has been restricted by the modifier *his*, we would ordinarily expect that any other modifiers would be additive (e. g. , *his aged mother*), but in the phrase *his foster mother* both *his* and *foster* are restrictive. *His* distinguishes one mother from the class of all women called mothers, and *foster* distinguishes among those women called mothers between those who are so labeled because of the function they perform and those who are so labeled because of biological reasons. Similarly with proper names: we assume that the modifier of an individual person, place, or thing is additive (e. g. , "lazy Tom", "busy Main Street ", "invincible Excalibur"). But in the following sentence the restrictive modifier "good" has been called for because the proper name alone was ambiguous:

I mean good Senator McCarthy.

To understand the meaning of this sentence we must go beyond grammatical analysis and draw upon our knowledge of recent political events. The existence of two prominent Senators McCarthy of such opposing views and personalities as to have given rise (among certain people) to a moral evaluation as a means of identification must be known about in order for "good" here to be recognized as a restrictive modifier. On the other hand, the uniqueness (among senators) of the name "Inouye" makes "good" below an additive modifier:

I mean good Senator Inouye.

I mean Senator Inouye.
Senator Inouye [is] good.

We have nothing to say about the admittedly quite important grammatical problem of the order of multiple modifiers. What modifies what within a complex structure of restrictive modification is not our concern as long as it is recognized as being restrictive. The traditional rule of thumb that modifiers increasingly removed from the headword or phrase modify increasingly larger units and that farthest removed is most specific is quite acceptable to semantic grammar as long as it does not obscure the semantic realities. In the sentence "Some very old Chinese women got off the boat", the restrictive modification of "women" is first "Chinese". Then "Chinese women" are modified by "old", but "old" is separately modified by "very" (a slight but common and readily acknowledged exception to the general rule). Therefore "old" as modified by "very" is the next step. Finally, "some" modifies the entire phrase "very old Chinese women". The largest category is women. All women? No, just Chinese women. All Chinese women? No, just old Chinese women. All old Chinese women? No, just very old Chinese women. All very old Chinese women? No, just some very old Chinese women.[1]

However, this principle of working away from the headword is not so readily applicable to non-restrictive modification. We can work backward from the headword with increasing specificity, but this pattern bears no necessary relation to the presence or location of a non-restrictive modifier. This is the case not just with mother and father type headwords but with restrictive modifiers that specify uniqueness.

My [alcoholic] father suffers from gout.

This [three-credit] course is open to freshmen.

"Three-credit" could be said to modify "course" by way of distinguishing among all courses irrespective of credit or amount of credit those that grant three credits. "This" could then be said to modify "three-credit course" by way of distinguishing among all three-credit courses a particular one. But a crucial difference has been overlooked in this admittedly restrictive progression away from the headword. "This", like "my" in the previous example, is sufficient in and of itself to provide all the possible restrictive modification. To render unique is to undercut the restrictive function of all less-than-unique modification of the same headword. What without the presence of the unique modifier would function restrictively becomes in its presence an additive modifier.

Heretofore we have confined our analysis to sentences with only one additive modifier, but before leaving additive modification we should note that there is no such limitation. A sentence may have a pre-positional and a post-positional modifier; it may have multiple pre-positional modifiers; and it may have multiple post-positional modifiers.

[Once green] Honolulu, [which is now a concrete jungle,] is a portent.

Honolulu is a portent.
Honolulu [was] once green.
Honolulu is now a concrete jungle.

[great]

I voted for and Albert A. Alweather.

[good]

I voted for Albert A. Alweather.
Albert A. Alweather [is] great.
Albert A. Alweather [is] good.

[who won the race,]

Joe, but refused to give up the trophy.

[who was later disqualified,]

Joe refused to give up the trophy.
Joe won the race.
Joe was later disqualified.

The multiple modifiers in the second and third sentences are parallel in the sense that two different words or phrases have a common relationship with a single element in the sentence, and for this reason they have been written one on top of another. But because these parallels are not integral to the sentences – as were all our examples of separable, unitary, and appositive parallel – there is no special parallel symbol used. Additive modification, of whatever kind and of whatever position, is an adjunct and has no effect on the assertion of which it is a part.

(2) *Redundant*

To be concise or economical is a cardinal virtue in composition, but it does not follow from this that to be redundant is necessarily a vice. Even a favorite whipping boy like "consensus of opinion", while not recommended, does have a certain justification. "Of opinion" is not the redundance of emphasis but the redundance of appending a more commonly understood word to a less commonly understood one so as to insure understanding. This is quite similar to a much less frowned upon construction like "linked together". How things could be linked in any way other than together is very difficult to see.

For the most part, however, redundant modification functions either to provide emphasis or to provide punctuational guidelines. The two are not necessarily distinct, but insofar as they are, we can say that the first four examples below are emphatic:

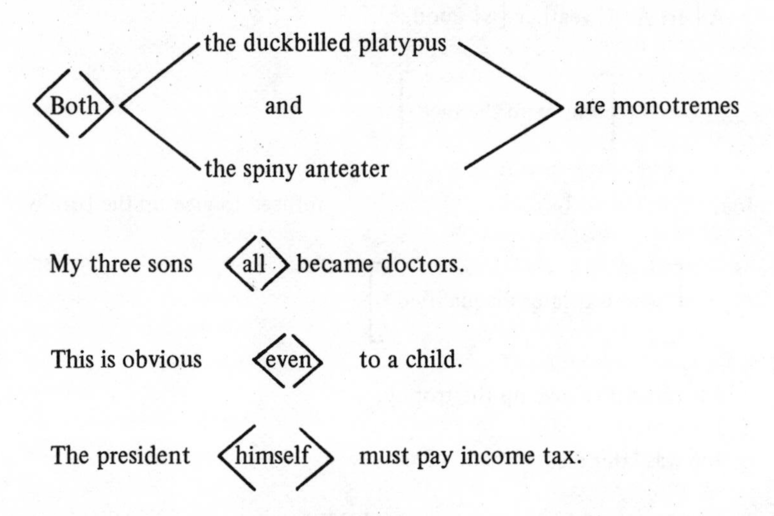

Judging the sentences in and of themselves, and not as part of larger compositions, no semantic essentials are lost by eliminating "both", "all", "even", and "himself". These words serve important *compositional* functions but *assertionally* they are redundant. This is not, however, to so characterize these words in every context. For example, the presence and absence of "all" can result in various kinds of semantic interpretations depending on the different contexts:

All Scotchmen are thrifty. Scotchmen are thrifty.

To refer specifically to my sons is to refer to all of them unless otherwise restrictively modified, but to refer to Scotchmen in general is not necessarily to refer to every single one of them. Our first example above can be false at the same time that the second example is true. A generalization can absorb exceptions; an unequivocal, all-inclusive assertion cannot. "All" is thus a restrictive modifier here – excluding, for example, such possibilities as "some" and "many".

Let us attempt brief explanations of the possible rationales behind the use of the emphasis modifiers in the examples above. The platypus, with its duckbill, and the anteater, with its spines, seem superficially to be quite different creatures. The assertion that they are in fact the same sort of creature thus takes more emphasis; it must counter what the speaker knows to be a different conception. The second sentence is also a matter of countering common expectations. Considering how desirable many parents think it is to have a son who is a doctor, and how difficult it is to become one, and how few parents have even one, the "all" clearly serves to draw attention to the extraordinary achievement of making a clean sweep. The use of "even" with "child" in the third example is presumably a means of implying that what is obvious to an untutored, inexperienced child would necessarily be obvious to the bulk of us knowledgeable, experienced adults. Like the final example, this emphatic is primarily a means of reinforcing a comparison or contrast. Our last sentence involves the traditional 'reflexive pronoun'. With the child, something must be so because the lowest sort of person is capable of it. With the president, something must be so because the highest sort of person is obliged to do it. These are not asserted, only implied, but what we choose to emphasize partly determines what implications will be drawn from our assertions. Redundance may be simply superfluous (as with "linked together"), but it may also be a key to implied meaning.

Our second set of redundant modifiers are emphatics only in the sense that they help to emphasize the structure of our assertions. We thus refer to these as punctuational.

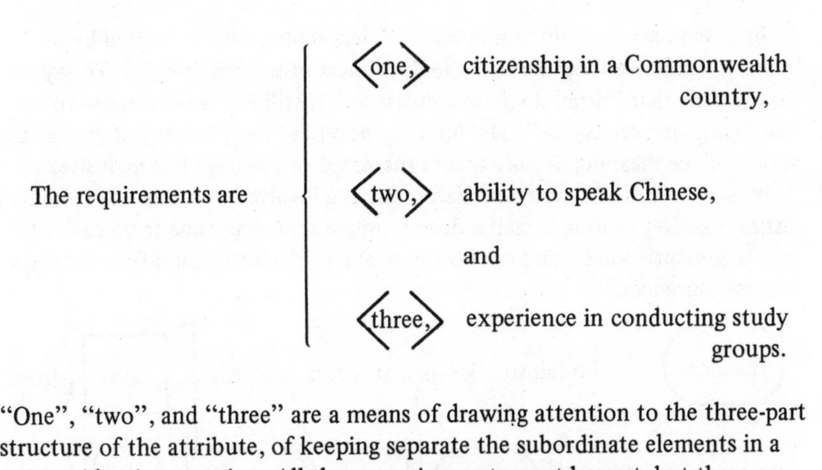

"One", "two", and "three" are a means of drawing attention to the three-part structure of the attribute, of keeping separate the subordinate elements in a unitary identity assertion. All three requirements must be met, but there are three distinct counts on which a condidate can fail. Satisfying one or two of them is not sufficient.

Other words and phrases that might have been discussed here as redundant modifiers (e. g. "however", and "on the one hand . . . on the other hand") will be taken up as conjunctions and discussed in Chapter 6.

B. RESTRICTIVE

The test for restrictive modification is the question: "Does the modifier serve to exclude certain possibilities from being asserted that could be included if the modifier were nor present? " Simple as the question is, however, there is a variety of different kinds of answers and thus more complexity to cover in this section than in our discussion of non-restrictive modification. A point made earlier is worth repeating here: complex modification is primarily a means of creating one precise assertion rather than of multiplying the number of assertions. The major kind of restrictive modification is limiting, but there are also two other kinds – conditional and inclusive/exclusive. Our examples of restrictive modification have heretofore been limiting, and the examples in the next section will be the same. Just as non-restrictive modification is, unless otherwise indicated, additive, restrictive modification is, unless otherwise indicated, limiting.

(1) *Limiting*

To limit is to say the same thing but with less scope; what is limited by a limiting restrictive modifier is the inclusiveness of what is asserted. To say for example that "Stray dogs are a nuisance", is still in a general sense to say that "Dogs are a nuisance". The limiting modifier "stray" does not change the nature of the meaning; it only makes the scope of coverage less inclusive.

By way of introduction, and before getting involved in a series of systematic distinctions, let us look at half a dozen sample sentences (one from each of the six semantic kinds) and see how crucial a role limiting modification plays in most sentences.[2]

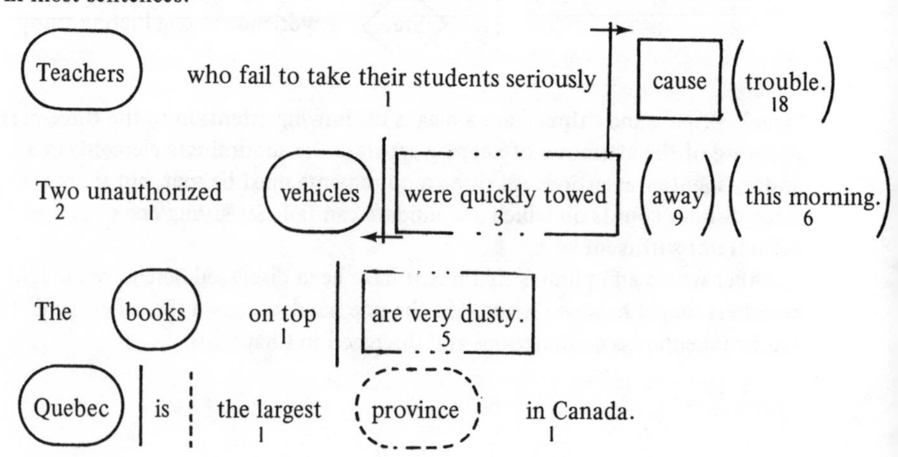

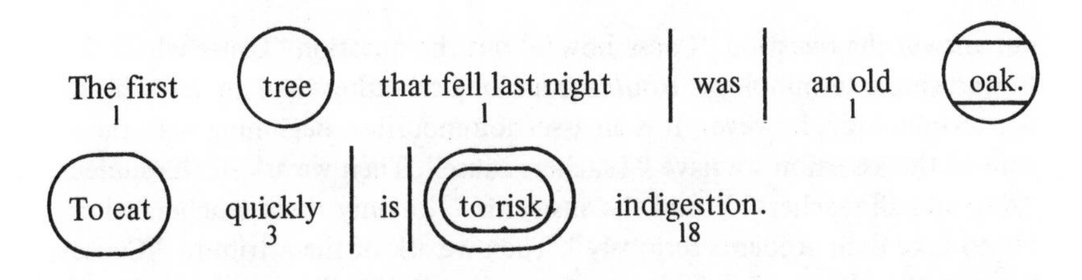

The numbers under the limiting modifiers are the keys to the different questions being answered. The chart on page 143 provides the list of questions and page 144 shows further numbered examples. There is nothing absolute about these questions, however. For example, as long as we recognize "for short-range commuting" as a limiting modifier in the sentence below, it is a minor difference whether we think of it as answering "Under what circumstances? " or "Why? ".

For short-range commuting, a bicycle is more useful than a car.

Similar disagreement can arise over our decision to treat words like "almost" as attribute modifiers in function and characteristic sentences (e. g. , "He almost won".) and as assertion modifiers in identity and classification sentences (e. g. , "He is almost a doctor".) The crucial point of agreement is that both are limiting modifiers answering the general question, "To what extent or degree? " Perhaps our questions are not as precisely phrased as they could be. Perhaps they are too many or too few. But in any case, they are a useful means of emphasizing the diversity of meaning that occurs within the unity of single assertions. Each of these sentences, though it provides much information, makes just one assertion. The information in each assertion serves to limit the meaning of the one assertion in such a way that the information cannot be broken down into different separate assertions and preserve exactly the same meaning. If this could be done, the modification would be non-restrictive rather than restrictive.

In the first sentence the subject is *teachers*, but not all teachers – only those *who fail to take their students seriously*. Excluded from this subject are all other teachers. Whatever virtues and vices a teacher may have, if he takes his students seriously he is excluded by this limiting modifier of the subject. Not all teachers fail to take their students seriously, and not all teachers who cause trouble do so because they do not take their students seriously (for example, teachers who are poorly prepared also cause trouble). *Cause* is the attribute in this sentence; it is a function, and could be modified in a way characteristic of change or process – for example, *quickly cause*. In this particular sentence, however, there is no such modifier. *Trouble* does not answer the question "Cause how? " but the question "Cause what? " In traditional terminology, *trouble* is an 'object' rather than an 'adverb'. In our terminology, however, it is an assertion modifier. Beginning with the core of the assertion we have "Teachers cause". Then we ask of the subject "Any and all teachers? " And the answer is "No, only those teachers who fail to take their students seriously". Then we ask of the attribute "Cause in any particular way? " And there is no answer. Finally, we ask of the subject and attribute together "Teachers who fail to take their students seriously cause what in particular? " And the answer is "They cause trouble". Teachers who fail to take their students seriously could and probably do cause other things. For instance, they could cause teachers who *do* take their students seriously to be better appreciated. But such possibilities as this are excluded by the assertion modifier *trouble*.

The subject of the second sentence is *vehicles*, and the attribute of this object function assertion is *were towed*. When we ask the question "How did the function function? " we are provided with an answer – *quickly*. Necessarily excluded by this modifier is a possibility like *slowly*. The subject is also restricted. When we ask the question "Any and all vehicles? " the answer is "No, only unauthorized vehicles". And when we ask the question again "Any and all unauthorized vehicles? " the answer is "No, only two unauthorized vehicles". We could go on and ask of this doubly restricted subject "Which two unauthorized vehicles? " And although there could be an answer (e. g. , the two unauthorized vehicles parked in my driveway), this sentence does not provide one. The last two modifiers in the sentence are *away* and *this morning*; both are assertion modifiers. *Away* does not modify the attribute, because it does not answer the question "How were they towed? " Rather, it answers the question "Where were they towed? " To have said that the vehicles were towed *here* would have been quite different than to have said that they were towed *away*. Similarly with *this morning* – it does not answer the question "How towed? " but "When towed? " And the answer makes the sentence more precise by excluding such possibilities as last night and this afternoon.

There are as many different assertion modifiers as there are different questions answered. Any word or phrase that restricts the meaning of the assertion but does not modify either the subject or the attribute necessarily modifies the assertion as a whole. All traditional "objects" are assertion modifiers, but so are many other sentence elements.

Unlike the first two sentences, the third has no assertion modifier. The subject is *books* – not all the books but only those *on top*. This form of the modifier, rather than the full relative clause, is a common abridgement. But it has the same meaning as *the books that are on top*. And like all unabridged limiting relative clauses, the abridged form is not set off by punctuation – thus maintaining the crucial punctuation distinction between non-restrictive and restrictive relative modifiers. The attribute of this assertion is the characteristic *are dusty*, and the question we ask of such a characteristic is "To what extent or degree? " The answer provided here is *very*, and it serves to exclude possibilities like *slightly dusty*.

The identity sentence has neither subject modifier not assertion modifier, but it does have a complex attribute modifier. The headword in the attribute is *province*. "Every province? " "No, just a province in Canada". "Any province in Canada? " "No, just the largest one". Excluded by these modifiers are, first, all provinces in France, Argentina, etc. , and, second, all of the nine smaller provinces in Canada.

The fifth sentence has a simple attribute modifier and a complex subject modifier but no assertion modifier. Beginning with *tree* as the subject, we first exclude from this class of things all those that are still standing or were cut down. Then we further exclude all members of this class that fell but did so at a time other than last night. Finally, we exclude from those that did fall last night all but the one that fell first. How many trees did in fact fall last night is not stated, but clearly implied is that more than one did. The attribute here is *oaks*. "Every oak? " "No, just the old ones". Excluded by the limiting modifier *old* is everything from saplings to middle-aged specimens.

The last sentence is subclass/class: all instances of eating quickly are said to risk indigestion, but there are other ways to risk indigestion. For example, to over-eat (however slowly) is also to risk indigestion. Thus, we would not say conversely that "To risk indigestion is to eat quickly". *Quickly* here, like *quickly* in the second sentence is a limiting modifier. Eating slowly, for instance, is not said to risk indigestion – just as the second sentence excludes the possibility of the vehicles being slowly towed away. But unlike the first *quickly*, which is a modifier of a function attribute, the second *quickly* is a thing modifier of a subject. *To eat* (like *eating*) can be restricted just as non-verbal things can be restricted, but the questions we ask and the kinds of answers that are appropriate are different. Of *tree* in the fifth sentence we asked "Which individual"? And the answering modification was "the first that fell last night". Of *teachers* in the first sentence was asked "Which subclass? " And the answering modification was "who fail to take their students seriously". But neither one of these questions is appropriate to an activity, whereas the question "Do in what manner? " is appropriate. Similarly, we would never ask of non-verbal things "Do what? " This is a question whose answer is ordinarily an assertion modifier. In the first sentence, for example, we ask of subject and attribute together, "Teachers cause what? " And the answer is the assertion modifier *trouble*. But any question that is appropriate for a function assertion is also appropriate for an activity verb used as a thing. Thus we can ask of the attribute *to risk*, "Risk what? " And the answer is the attribute modifier *indigestion*. Excluded by this limiting modifier are such possibilities as lung cancer and falling arches. The determining factor in recognizing limiting modification of verbal things is not the form of the modifier but whether it does serve to exclude certain things from being asserted.

The key to limiting modification, whether subassertional or assertional, is a list of basic questions that a reader either consciously or unconsciously addresses to the sentence he reads and that a writer provides answers to with the modification he uses. The chart on the next page gives an ambitious but probably incomplete list, and several of the questions will be recognized as having already been used in our analysis of modification. There are, however, some kinds of quasi-limiting modification that do not unequivocally fit in with these: cumulative 'adverbial' clusters, articles, and negatives. With the first two the problem is to decide the extent to which there is an actual limiting function being performed by the modification; with the third one the problem is to decide the extent to which there is an actual modificational function being performed or whether the negative is essentially a part of the assertional core.

Function sentences like "He advanced slowly" and characteristic sentences like "He was very large" present no problems in their use of limiting attribute modifiers. But when a single general 'adverb' like "slowly" or "very" gives way to a series or cluster of specific modifying phrases, then the modification has something of an additive look about it:

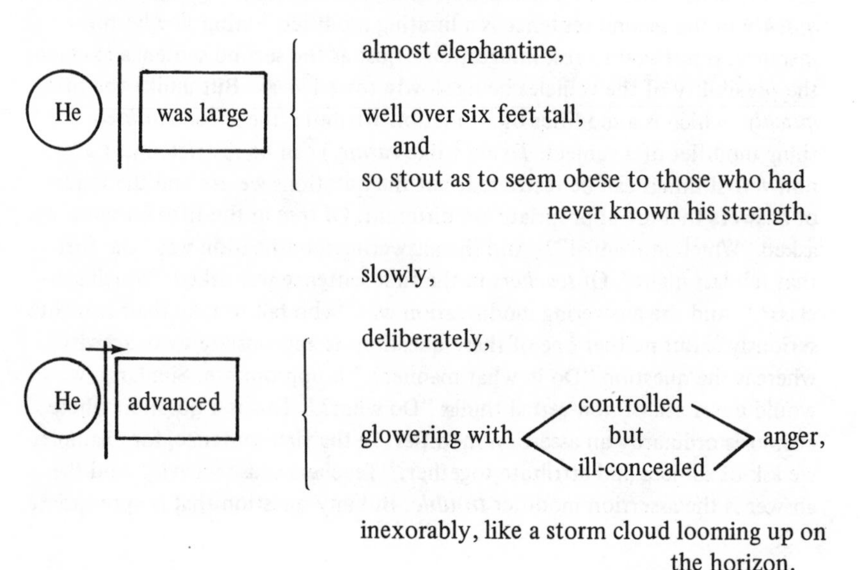

QUESTIONS THAT ELICIT LIMITING MODIFIERS

Of Things (subjects and class attributes)

1. which one or kind?
2. what quantity?

Except for these, all of the questions are also applicable to verbal things (e. g. *exercising*, *to exercise*).

Of Functions

3. do in what manner?
4. to what extent or degree?

Of Characteristics

5. to what extent or degree?

Of Assertions

6. what time?
7. what location?
8. directed toward what or whom?
9. from where, what, or whom?
10. under what circumstances?
11. why or because of what or whom?
12. what means or basis?
13. how often?
14. how long a time?
15. how far a distance?
16. to what extent or degree?
17. compared to what or whom?
18. do what or whom?
19. by what agent?
20. what end?
21. what idea or about what topic?
22. together with what or whom?
23. how labeled?
24. in what respect?

LIMITING ASSERTION MODIFIERS

We were almost defeated (by them) (because of our cockiness.)
19 11

He was (almost) a millionaire, but he died (a beggar.)
16 20

We elected (Dick) (president) by a wide margin (in 1971.)
18 20 6

(Once a year) we give (them) (a treatment) (with this serum.)
13 8 18 12

(Swimming beyond the reef,) he was attacked (by a shark.)
10 19

The barn is painted (yellow) (to match the house.)
20 11

The shutters blew (off) (yesterday) (in the wind.)
20 6 10

I built (my parents) (a house) (fifty miles from here.)
11 18 15

He made (the boys) (happy) (by giving out candy) (while examining them.)
18 20 12 10

(For short-range commuting,) a bicycle is more useful (than a car.)
10 17

(For exercise) I swim (an hour or two) (every day) (at the Y.)
11 14 13 7

I met (a man (at Oxford) who had been a French Legionnaire in Algeria.)
7 18

The keys were taken (from me) and given (to Mary.)
9 8

We hiked (as far as you did) (in half the time.)
15 14

Ebor is as far (as Tamworth) and farther (than Walcha.)
17 17

He ran (out of the house) (with only a towel on) (when the alarm rang.)
9 22 6

He talked (shop) (with Fred) (until midnight) (under a street light.)
21 22 14 7

We will speak (to the manager) (about our grievance.)
8 21

We are eager (to speak to the manager about our grievance.)
21

We thought (him an inefficient president.)
21

We thought (that he was an inefficient president.)
21

The company was (twice) robbed of its entire weekly payroll.
13

He is called (a prophet) (by some) and accused (of treason) (by others.)
23 19 23 19

She was successful (in business) but a failure (as a teacher.)
24 24

(Financially,) it was a failure.
24

The guard prevents (us from conferring with the chaplain.)
18

The guard prevents (our conferring with the chaplain.)
18

The guard makes (us) (stand at attention.)
18 20

The guard forces (us) (to stand at attention.)
18 20

The river prevents (us from escaping to the south.)
20

The river prevents (our escaping to the south.)
20

The terms of the contract require (your immediate action.)
20

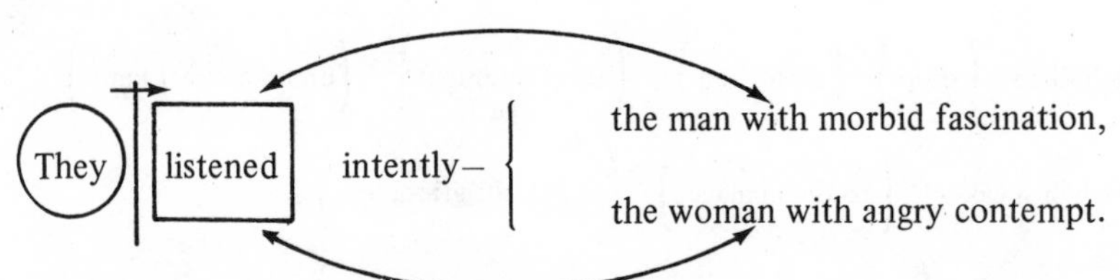

As the diagrams indicate, we have resisted the temptation to treat these modifiers as additive, but the problem remains. A good case can be made for parallel structure in the first sentence. He was: (1) large, (2) almost elephantine, (3) well over six feet tall, and (4) so stout as to seem obese to those who had never known his strength. And, indeed, our unitary diagram fails to reflect the fact that "large" can fill, at least formally, the same syntactical slot as the other three. But on the other hand, the use of the dash is evidence for the correctness of our diagram. The problem is to decide whether "almost elephantine", for example, functions primarily as an attribute of "he" (and thus makes an additional assertion) or whether it functions primarily as a modifier of "large" by answering the question "to what extent or degree? " (and is thus limiting). Perhaps we will have to admit that it is both, with no great difference in meaning one way or the other. But if we do, this will be no great praise of the sentence.

"Was large" is made more precise by the addition of "almost elephantine, well over six feet tall, and so stout as to seem obese to those who had never known his strength". To be these is certainly to be large, but many things are properly characterized as large without being properly characterized in these terms. Although one could reasonably refer to more than this particular person in these terms, one could hardly apply them to a large spider or a large briefcase, for example. Our decision to diagram the sentence as we did was based in the last analysis on the generic nature of "large": it does not have a different meaning than "almost elephantine" but neither is it synonymous with it. Rather, "large" is an inclusive concept that covers many restricted manifestations, such as "almost elephantine, well over six feet tall, and so stout as to seem obese to those who had never known his strength". If we demand to know what manifestations are excluded by these as limiting modifiers, we might answer: "mountainous", "fifty stories high", "capable of containing an entire infantry division". But admittedly, these are as much a matter of particular characterizing as of general limiting.

And herein lies the basic objection to these cumulative constructions: like introductory 'participial' phrases (which we have postponed until Chapter 6), cumulative 'adverbial' clusters are often a means of surreptitiously adding information under the misleading guise of restrictive modification. They allow the writer to avoid making up his mind as to whether restriction is needed. A good case could be made for thinking that our first example above would have been both more concise and more precise written this way:

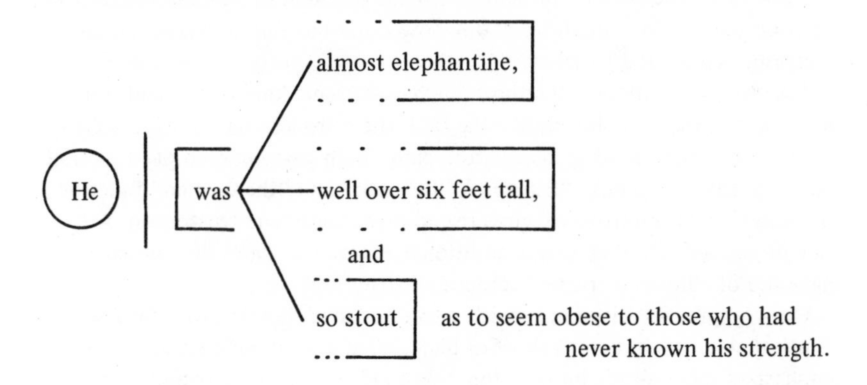

By eliminating attributes modifying attributes we eliminate possible ambiguity with no loss of meaning. Whatever else these three attributes mean, they certainly mean large.

The second example above differs from the first both as to semantic kind and as to conciseness. Everything after the dash answers the question "advanced in what manner? " Nothing before the dash answers that question. And as far as "slowly" and "deliberately" are concerned, there is no problem with interpreting limiting modification of the attribute. Slowly and deliberately are general ways of advancing quite apart from the subject that is doing the advancing. But the last two modifiers are like "so stout as to seem obese to those who had never known his strength" in being more obviously about the subject in particular than about the attribute in general. Why, then, do we treat these as assertion modifiers rather than attribute modifiers? Or better yet, why not treat them as the basis of four different assertions in a separable parallel structure? All that can be said in reply is that each of the four modifiers in this sentence answers the same question, and while there is indeed a difference in specificity, there is only a difference of degree between "slowly" and "inexorably, like a storm cloud looming up on the horizon". The subject is not doing four different things nor the same thing at four different times or places. He is doing one thing, and the multiple modification serves only to make the statement of this one thing more precise than the attribute in and of itself specifies.

A further difference between the second sentence and the first is that we are dealing here not just with a series of parallel function modifiers but with a function modifier of a function modifier: Advanced in what manner? Advanced glowering. Advanced glowering in what manner? Advanced glowering with controlled but ill-concealed anger. The modifier of "inexorably" in the last leg of the parallel presents a similar problem of attenuation, but the question elicits not a modifier about how done but one in answer to the question, "compared to what? "

Like the first sentence, the third one has the same kind of elements on both sides of the dash; but unlike the first, the third also has multiple subjects. Not only do "with morbid fascination" and "with angry contempt" function like "intently" to modify "listened", "the man" and "the woman" function like "they". This multiplicity gives rise to quite legitimate frustration. Are they modifiers? Do they create additional assertions? Does the sentence make use of ellipsis to create a compound structure?

Our compromise diagram is neither fish nor fowl. It acknowledges the elliptical elements but stops short of diagraming a compound structure; it emphasizes the multiple limiting function modifiers of the attribute but stops short of treating these three modifiers in the same way. Again, our justification for this unitary parallel interpretation is the same as in the first example: "with morbid fascination" and "with angry contempt" are subordinate manifestations of the general concept "listened intently". If we emphasized the additional information provided by "the man" and "the woman" as new subjects, we would have no way of showing the essential limiting function that results from answering the question "listened intently in what manner? " Unlike the first example, this third one shows us a modifier of an already modified attribute. As the dash here clearly indicates, "the man with morbid fascination" and "the woman with angry contempt" are not on a semantic par with "intently", even though the three could be diagramed as formally parallel. Thus, the argument against treating the sentence as essentially compound is ultimately that what follows the dash is semantically subordinate to what precedes the dash. This does not explain away the problem of a subject in a limiting 'adverbial' modifier; it simply recognizes an unavoidable conflict and opts for a semantic rather than a formal compromise.

Proponents of the cumulative sentence will be less than satisfied with our treatment of it, not only because we emphasize its limitations but also partly because our examples have not reflected the full rhythmic potential of narrative written in this fashion. The more the potential is revealed, however, the more conspicuous become the pitfalls. Here is full narrative complexity in a single sentence:

He advanced – slowly at first, with ears pricked forward, looking expectantly from side to side, then rapidly as the trail broadened and his quarry came into view, finally in a headlong rush, with ears laid back, covering the last eighth of a mile in seconds.

The sentence is not just part of a narrative context; it is in and of itself narrative because it reflects moment-by-moment an action in time. In the sense that different things are happening at different times and places, then there are multiple assertions here. But in the sense that "he" is the subject, and "advanced" is the attribute, and everything else answers the question "advanced in what manner? " then there is just one assertion here.

In our previous examples we adhered to the principle that multiple restrictive function modification does not make for multiple assertions, but in none of these sentences was there differentiation through time. And, in addition to the seeming multiplicity of assertions resulting from different stages of the advance ("slowly at first","then rapidly", "finally in a headlong rush"), there is the further implication of assertions in restrictive modification such as "the trail broadened". What is gained, we might reasonably ask, by turning so many potential assertions into restrictive modifiers? Here is a possible alternative version of the above sentence that minimizes the reliance on 'adverbial' clusters by increasing the number of separate assertions:

He advanced slowly. His head, with ears pricked forward, turned expectantly from side to side. The trail broadened, and his quarry came into view. His pace quickened. His ears lay back. Then in a final headlong rush he covered the last eighth of a mile in seconds.

There is, admittedly, something of an arbitrary element in the decision to present information as separate assertions or as restrictive modification, but there is also a penchant in some writers to restrict whenever possible despite the lack of discernible restrictive rationale. The logic of this when pushed to absurdity would sanction the writing not only of Faulkner's page-long sentences but even the writing of an "advance" or "quest" story like *Huckleberry Finn* as a single assertion repeatedly modified moment-by-moment by new but still restrictive bits of information. Our creature above (perhaps a tiger) may advance a few feet or a few miles or across half a continent and be described in the greatest detail simply by answering the question "How did he advance? " In terms of what principle do we decide that there are multiple answers in a single sentence and thus multiple assertions? Or better yet, in terms of what principle do we decide that a cumulative sentence has accumulated too much for restrictive structure to conveniently and intelligibly handle?

The first question is easier to answer than the second. We can say that discernible stages in a function result in multiple assertions even though the function modified is unitary. This principle results in three assertions for the original sentence rather than the seven of the rewritten version above:

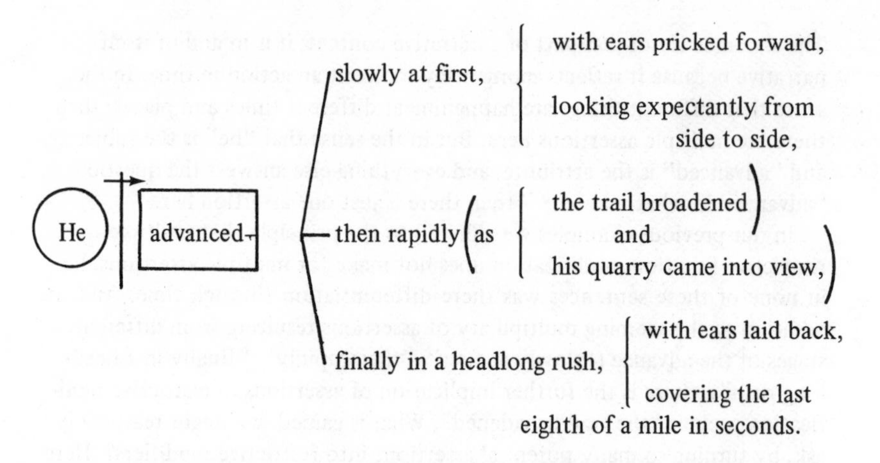

This seems more in accord with the amount of information in the sentence but does not really pierce to the heart of the matter, which is the rationale for wholesale use of restrictive modification when the subject seems to require not a limitation of scope but an addition of information. Not only does each of the three assertions consist of a restrictive modifying phrase of the attribute ("slowly at first", "then rapidly", "finally in a headlong rush") but also each of these differently modified attributes is further restrictively modified by a pair of modifying phrases. In the first and third legs of the parallel these second-level unitary parallels are further answers of the "How done? " sort. In the second leg they are assertion modifiers answering the questions "Where? " and "under what circumstances? "

We can only conclude that, although the distinction between restrictive and non-restrictive modification is one of fundamental importance, the language allows certain leeway in the presentation of information. Yet, the limits on restrictive presentation of information are much greater than on non-restrictive, because syntax is not just a matter of beads on a string. It is not the length of the above sentence that pushes it to the upper limits of its type but the difficulty of interpreting it. For the reader who understands the pervasive and important distinction of restrictive and non-restrictive modification, this kind of sentence is frustrating: for all its complexity it does seem to be little more than beads on a string.

In answer to our second question, about a principle for deciding when too much has been accumulated, we can say at least this much: Syntactical complexity is not a virtue in itself. We go beyond a list of atomistic assertions because we need to show various kinds of relationships, and the price we must pay is an understanding of complex sentence structure. But if we pay the price and get nothing in return, then the whole endeavor has been a net loss. And not only is it a waste as far as the individual attempt is concerned, it is a deterrent to future use of a principle that may come to seem more arbitrary than consistent.

A writer can go all his life without producing such clusters and no one will laugh and point. Indeed, a grammar would not be conspicuously derelict if it ignored them altogether. But the same is not true of the second problem case among limiting modifiers. One of the most vexing aspects of English grammar – an aspect that vexes the semantic grammarian as much as it does the formal grammarian – is the problem of articles (*a*, *an*, *the*). Articles are the last aspect of English to be mastered by a non-native speaker because neither semantic explanations nor formal explanations can give a consistent account of idiomatic usage. The most conspicuous inconsistency is in those classifying assertions that can have the same meaning using an indefinite article, a definite article, or no article at all:

A horse is a beast of burden.
The horse is a beast of burden.
Horses are beasts of burden.

Whatever else they may be, *a* and *the* can hardly be termed limiting modifiers here.

Articles cannot simply be ignored, however, because they often are the means of making significant distinctions:

A horse is in my yard.	Two horses are in my yard.
The horse is in my yard.	Your horse is in my yard.

The indefinite article in the first example is essentially a synonym for *one* (as distinguished from two, three, twenty, etc.) and is thus a limiting modifier. The definite article in the second example is best thought of as a pronoun; it has no specific meaning in itself but rather refers to an antecedent specification of what particular horse is being discussed. Thus, this article is also limiting; it distinguishes one particular horse from all other horses. With both examples the presence and kind of the article is not simply a matter of idiomatic usage; it is a matter of making the meaning more precise than it would have been without the article.

But now consider these examples:

The Eiffel Tower is a tourist attraction.
London Bridge is a tourist attraction.

It would be quite unidiomatic to say "Eiffel Tower is a tourist attraction", yet it would be perfectly comprehensible and semantically identical with the idiomatic version. There is only one Eiffel Tower and thus no possibility of modifying it restrictively. However, for no discernible reason, it is quite idiomatic to refer to London Bridge without an article.

Cursory as this glance at articles has been, we can still make some useful generalizations about this complicated aspect of English usage. (1) Articles may be quite superfluous, with the same meaning being idiomatically possible with and without them. (2) Articles may be required for idiomatic expressions but be semantically quite superfluous. (3) Articles may perform important limiting modification. We can only conclude from this state of affairs that the problem of articles cannot be solved with a few simple principles. As every teacher of foreign students can readily attest, the problem can be laid to rest only by consigning it to the small but conspicuous area of usage that is easier to memorize than to understand.

The question here is to decide how best to diagram articles. Articles seem more likely than not to be limiting. Also, diagrams can easily become more cumbersome than their value warrants – for example, an article that is not limiting may be separated from the rest of the headword by much intervening additive and limiting modification:

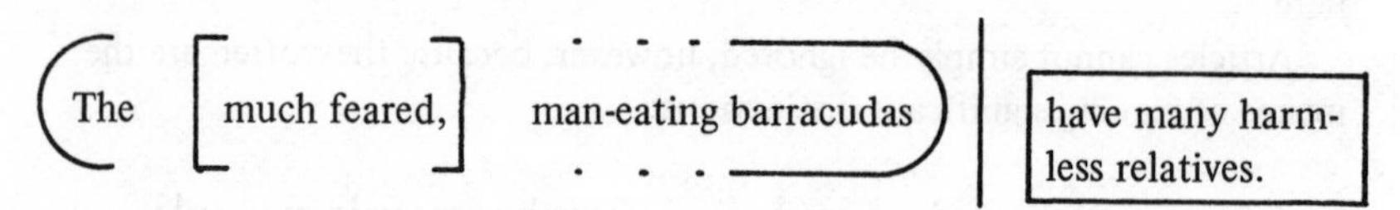

Thus, in the absence of a completely satisfactory way to diagram articles, the simplest method suggests itself as the best for our purposes. In separating out the headword in subject or attribute, irrespective of whether the article is in fact limiting, irrespective of whether there is other modification, we will leave all articles unmarked in the same way as we do limiting modifiers:

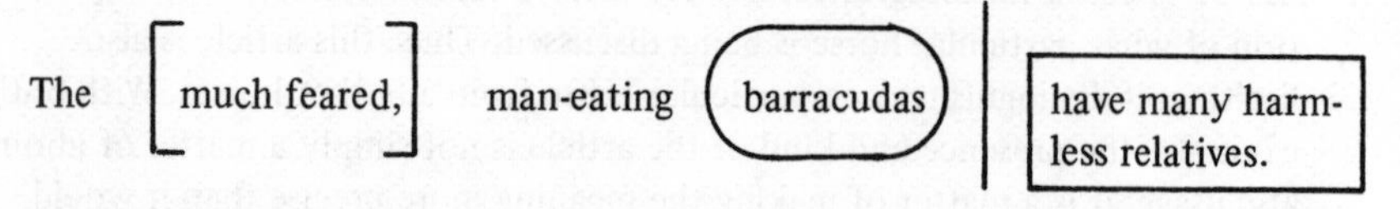

But while it is easy enough to simplify diagraming conventions, one is never absolved from the necessity of interpreting the meaning of assertions as accurately as possible. Articles not only can but often do play a crucial role in presenting the meaning of assertions.

Almost as difficult a question as articles is that of negatives. The trouble with taking limiting modification as representing the essence of restrictive modification is that it seems to deny the legitimacy of classifying negatives as restrictive. Yet there can hardly be a more undetachable, crucial sort of semantic unit in an assertion than a negative 'modifier'. The answer to the question thus turns on whether negatives are properly considered as modifiers or as part of the core assertion. The following two sets of assertions exemplify the case for and against considering negatives to be modifiers:

He is a non-participant.	He is not a participant.
He is unreliable.	He is not reliable.

In the first pair, being a non-participant can have a different meaning than not being a participant. In the second pair, being unreliable seems semantically indistinguishable from being not reliable; and thus it would be reasonable to treat "not" the same as "un – ", as part of an indivisible attribute core. Those in attendance at a conference, for instance, are often divided into two classes: participants and non-participants. To be designated as either carries with it the implication of having been present, and probably having been officially acknowledged as such. But to say that someone is not a participant is vaguer than this. He may not even have been present; he may have been present but only physically (e. g. the janitor, a waitress, someone who stepped in out of the rain). "Non-participant" can thus designate an actual class, but "not a participant" merely denies class membership.

Yet, lest we think of bound forms as simply negating the attribute (as in "unreliable"), here are negatives that are bound to what seem to be assertion modifiers:

I went nowhere	I never went.

Instead of saying "I did not go", these assertions say that I did go. But on being queried as to where and when, the assertion modifiers answer "nowhere" and "never". If we are required to give assertion modifiers priority, then we can take the negative neither to be a restrictive modifier in itself nor to be an indivisible part of the core assertion. However, if the core assertion takes priority, then we could say that such a semantically crucial part of an assertion as a negative must go into the core no matter what it may drag in with it.

We must not think, furthermore, that negative elements are candidates for just attributes and assertion modifiers. Here are what seem to be subjects modified by negatives:

No man is an island.	None returned.

Does the first of these, for example, say that man is an island and then modify it? And if this is the case, is "no" a restrictive modifier? "No" cannot be an additive modifier because it cannot be removed without making a significant change in the meaning of what remains. But then it cannot be a limiting modifier either because its effect on "man" is not to limit the scope of "man" (a white man, the man who robbed me, every man in this outfit) but to eliminate the scope entirely. Must we then set up a special category of restrictive modifiers to accommodate negatives? But if we do, a sentence like "No one returned" would have a restrictive modifier, and a sentence like "None returned" would not.

It is difficult to escape the negative conclusion that whatever we decide to do with negatives we cannot reasonably call them limiting or restrictive modifiers. In no sense could they be said to limit or restrict. And whatever our positive conclusion, it ought reasonably to treat "none" and "no man" the same. At this point we have not just reduced our options, we have excluded every possibility except treating all negatives – free forms or bound forms – as part of the core assertion.

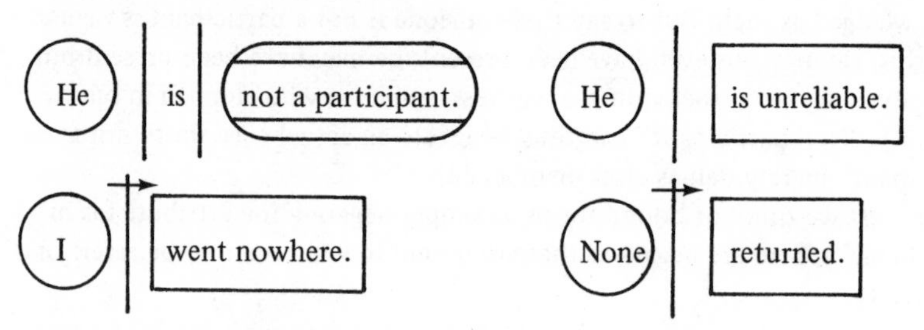

Negation does not affect the semantic kind because semantic kinds are determined by the topic or subject matter. But negation does affect the nature of the core assertion because a core assertion is a core assertion by virtue of establishing the irrevocable meaning of the assertion as a whole. However, since the core of identity and classification assertions is tripartite, then there is no ultimate significance to diagraming the negative as part of the attribute or as part of the link between subject and attribute. We have adhered to the former only as a matter of consistency.

To deny is not to modify, but anything short of denial, short of unequivocal negation, can be accommodated within restrictive modification – if not within limiting modification, then within conditional or inclusive/exclusive.

(2) *Conditional*

The simplest sort of conditional restrictive modification indicates degrees of certainty of the assertion as a whole:

(Perhaps) he qualifies for a junior position.

He (probably) qualifies for a junior position.

He qualifies for a junior position (almost certainly.)

But radiating out from these unequivocal examples are two different sorts of problem modifiers.

The first of these is modeled on the *-ly* form but seems to demand a different sort of meaning:

Hopefully he will come. He unfortunately lost.

This usage is often characterized by grammarians as recent and erroneous. And the reason is clear enough: these modifiers do not just indicate degrees of assertional certainty but verge on the creation of new assertions. But they do not quite succeed in creating new assertions because so much is left to implication. In the sentence "Probably he will come" the core assertion is "he will come", and the assertion modifier indicates the degree of certainty with which it is offered. However, in the sentence "Hopefully he will come", the core assertion seems to be less "he will come" than "I hope". The problem is to decide whether "Hopefully he will come means the same thing as "I hope he will come". It is easy enough to claim that the two are synonymous, but much more difficult to explain how the meaning of the "hopefully" sentence correlates with or derives out of its grammar. Where does the subject come from? And with the "unfortunately" sentence we must derive even more from implication. Not only must we supply a subject ("It" or "that"), we must also supply part of the attribute ("is"): It is unfortunate he lost. That he lost is unfortunate.

On this problem semantic grammar has no more adequate explanation than traditional. The temptation is to go along with those who condemn the usage as inexplicable. A language cannot absorb an unlimited amount of idiomatic but grammatically inexplicable usage without losing both its flexibility and its precision. The spector of written Chinese haunts the grammarian: the possibility that a language can become so idiomatic that it constitutes an almost unbearable burden of memory cannot be ignored. That grammarians have very much to say about the ultimate course of linguistic trends, however, may well be doubted. At this stage in the evolution of words like "hopefully" and "unfortunately" on the model of "certainly" and "probably" we can still reasonably say that usage is not unequivocally established. But insofar as a practical grammar is obliged to take some sort of stand on all conspicuous problems of usage, let us make these tentative distinctions among *-ly* modifiers:

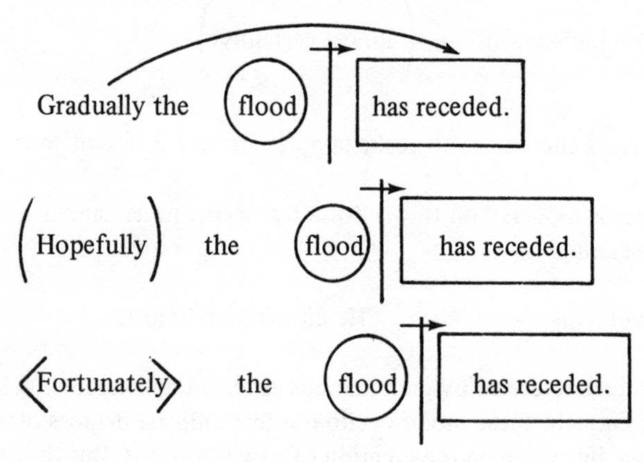

"Gradually" is an attribute modifier: it answers the function question, "Do in what manner? " This interpretation is unequivocally demanded. "Hopefully" is unequivocally demanded as a conditional modifier because it is a hedge against the truth of the assertion that it modifies. However, it is a bit equivocal insofar as it seems also to imply an additional assertion: I hope that the flood has receded. "Fortunately" is the least adequately handled. In labeling it as punctuational we are denying it the status of an assertion and saying instead that it is little more than a smile or a rising intonation pattern – an appended device for aiding in the interpretation of an assertion whose assertional meaning is unaffected by its presence or absence. Not only is the *-ly* form of no help in determining the kind of function in the sentence, the position is of no help. All three kinds can occur at the beginning of the sentence, at the end of the sentence, after the subject, and in the middle of the attribute.

The second kind of problem example radiating out from the degree-of-certainty conditional modifiers is one usually associated with 'modal auxiliaries', such as *should* and *must*.

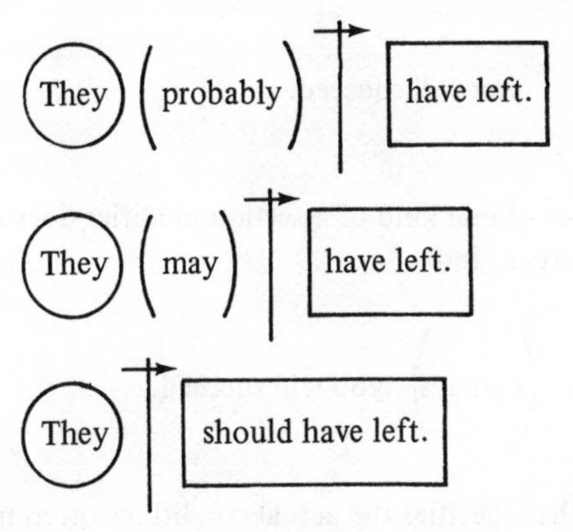

May is like *should* in being linked closely to the verb; there is no place in the sentence that these two can occur except after the subject and before the verb. *Probably*, on the other hand exhibits the general characteristic of assertion modifiers of being able to occur in various positions: Probably they have left. They probably have left. They have probably left. They have left probably. But this is only a formal difference. Semantically *may* more closely resembles *probably* then it does *should*. "They probably have left" and "They may have left" both assert that "They have left". And they both append a qualification as to the degree of certainty with which the assertion is being offered. "They should have left", on the other hand, is not so much a claim about what happened as about what properly ought to have happened. Both assertions are protected against the charge of falsity in the face of evidence that in fact the people have not left. But while the *may* assertion invites invalidation only on the grounds of factual knowledge, the *should* assertion invites invalidation primarily on the grounds of judgments based on some kind of norms, standards, or rules. Thus the *may* assertion is essentially a claim about leaving, while the *should* assertion is essentially an imperative claim. To remove the conditional assertion modifiers *probably* and *may* does not change the meaning of the core assertion, but to remove *should* is to remove part of the attribute core and thus to change the meaning.

The next kind of conditional modification is not merely a matter of degree of certainty but a matter of specifying the actual condition under which the core assertion will or will not be true.

(Unless you study,) you will fail.

(If you study,) you will succeed.

And, of course, the presence of one kind of assertion modifier does not preclude the possibility of another kind.

(If you study,) (perhaps) you will succeed.

Conditional modification that specifies the actual conditions often manifests itself as unitary parallel structure.

(If you {are a citizen and have no criminal record}) you can join.

The structure is unitary because there is no indication that meeting one condition without meeting the other is sufficient. Such indication is provided, however, in this sentence by the "or":

(If you < are a citizen,) or have declared your intention of becoming one,) > you can join.

And this conjunction introduces us to the last kind of conditional modification – *either/or*. The sentence above is composed of two assertions: If you are a citizen, you can join. If you have declared your intention of becoming one, you can join. But in an *either/or* conditional sentence there is just one assertion. Examples of this – both in compound and parallel form – were given on page 108. What is worth emphasizing again, however, is the unreliability of assuming the meaning simply on the basis of one function of the conjunction.

One meaning of *or* links two different assertions about two alternative possibilities. In the example above, for instance, a person cannot both be a citizen and have declared his intention of becoming one, but there is no unitary conditional modification here because two assertions can be made about the two possibilities. Another meaning of *or* is the conditional *one or the other but not both*: He is a Norwegian or a Swede. A third meaning of *or* is the non-conditional *both* or *that is to say*: These are echidna, or spiny anteaters. The result of this appositive parallel is two assertions: These are echidna. Echidna are spiny anteaters.

Similar to the different uses of *or* are the different uses of the *either/or* conjunction. "The doctor is either a Norwegian or a Swede" employs conditional modification that results in just one assertion. "The doctor cannot see you either today or tomorrow" employs the same *either/or* conjunction but in a way that results in two assertions: The doctor cannot see you today. The doctor cannot see you tomorrow. The usual meaning of *either/or* is that of a unitary conditional modifier, but just as idiomatic is the non-conditional use of it as a continuing modifier like *and.*

(3) *Inclusive/Exclusive*

Just a handful of modifiers constitute this sub-class of restrictive modifiers, but they are very important and very commonly employed. The major inclusive modifiers are *all*, *every*, *each*, *any*, *entire*, *complete*, *whole*. Less important are phrases like *without exception*. The obvious exclusive modifiers are *only*, *simply*, *just* and, less obviously, phrases like *nothing but* and *except for*.

As the following examples reveal, inclusive modifiers can occur not only in various places in an assertion but also can be piled up together for emphasis. Inclusives can be similar in this respect to redundant non-restrictive modifiers; to multiply the inclusive modification is to convert some of it into redundant.

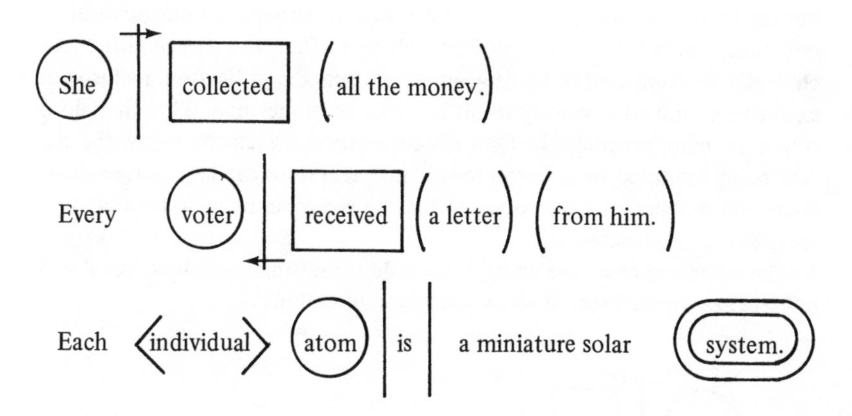

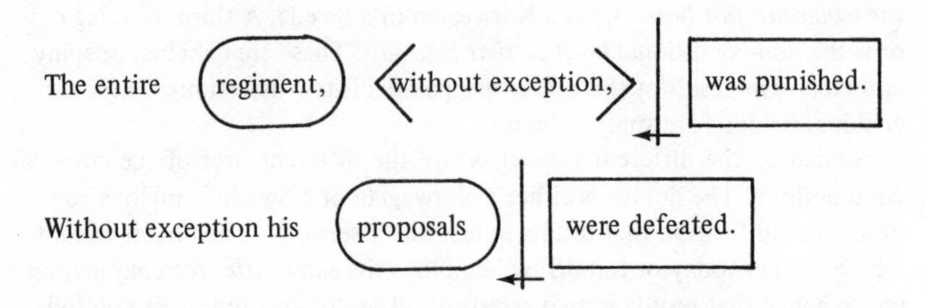

Inclusives are not so difficult to explain as being restrictive modification as are negatives, but the problem is similar: neither seems in the strict sense to restrict. Negatives restrict to the point of denial, and inclusives restrict only in the sense that they restrict the possibility (to the point of denial) of limiting modifiers. Both negatives and inclusives are thus absolutes, and insofar as restrictive modification is literally restrictive and modificational, it is not absolute but partial. The crucial difference between negatives and inclusives – crucial for denying modificational status to negatives and for granting restrictive modificational status to inclusives – is that the addition of an inclusive modifier does not make a basic difference of meaning in the core assertion. "She collected the money" and "His proposals were defeated" are not so unequivocal as are the above examples with their inclusive modifiers, but this is a matter of degree rather than kind. And where we can speak of matters of degree resulting from the presence or absence of words we can properly speak of modification. Like all restrictive modifiers, inclusives make the meaning more precise than it would have been without them.

In the traditional courtroom phrase "the truth, the whole truth, and nothing but the truth" the first part makes the basic but perhaps not unequivocal reference. The second part modifies inclusively. The third part modifies exclusively. As compared to limiting and conditional modification, inclusive and exclusive do not so obviously result in a change of meaning. What they do do is to draw more precisely the lines of demarcation – inclusive below the concept being modified so as to insure that no exceptions can leak out, exclusive above the concept, as a lid, to insure that no more can be included than is specified by the headword.

The following exclusive examples should speak for themselves, but this is not true, as we shall see, of all exclusive modification:

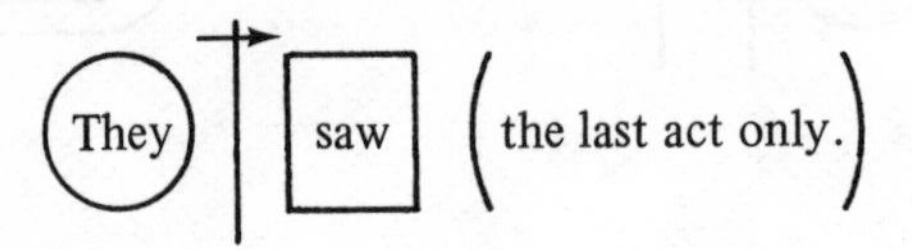

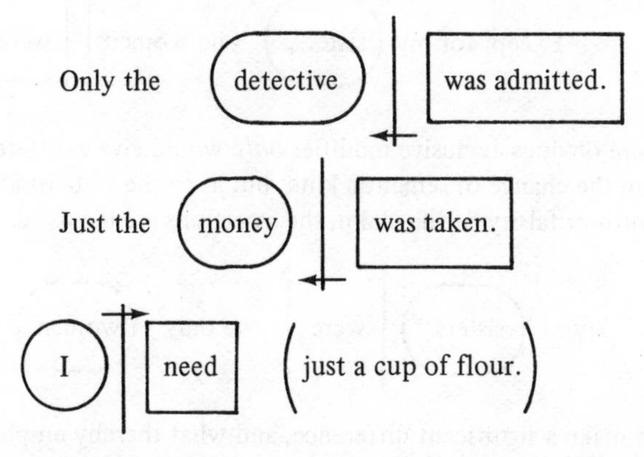

But now let us compare the sentence "Only the detective was admitted" with the sentence "No one but the detective was admitted". Not many grammarians – traditional, contemporary, or whatever – would be willing to admit that the subject of the second sentence could be other than "one" or "no one". And theirs would seem to be the reasonable interpretation when considered in light of how readily the sentence can be rewritten as "No one was admitted but the detective".

This interpertation may be in accord with formal principles, but is it in accord with semantic principles? The answer is no. Whether the structure is regular or inverted, the core of the assertion cannot claim, consistently with the assertion as a whole, that no one was admitted. As in our discussion of negatives, we see here a manifestation of purported modification denying the meaning of what is modified. The principles of semantic grammar can allow for no subject but "detective".

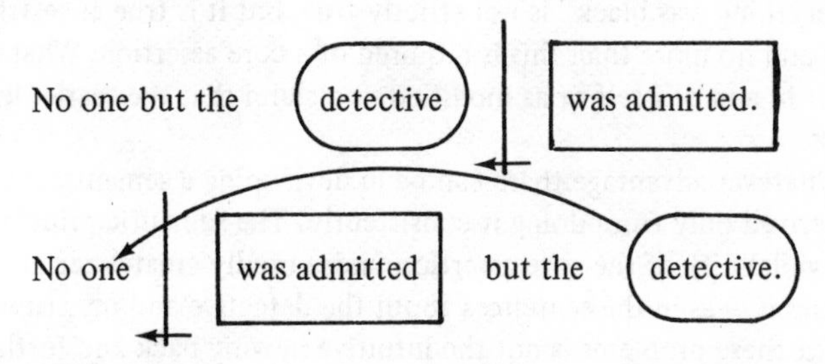

Similarly with the phrase *except for*: the emphasis may be on the rule rather than the exception, but if the assertion about the exception is strictly true and the assertion about the rule is not strictly true, then the core of the assertion must be the exception.

Using the more obvious exclusive modifier *only* would give a different emphasis resulting from the change of semantic kind, but as to the state of affairs referred to and the truth or falsity of the claim, the assertions are identical.

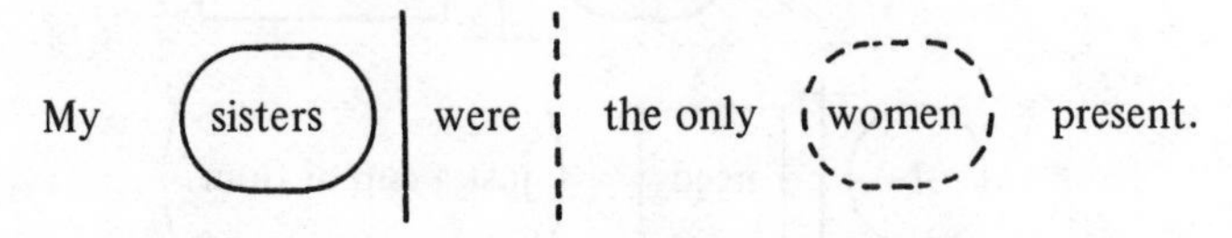

What does make a significant difference, and what thereby emphasizes the strictly semantic nature of our interpretation, is the stating of single-exception assertions positively rather than negatively. What makes the significant difference is that in a *nothing but* (negative) assertion the exception is true as stated, while in an *everything but* (positive) assertion the exception is not true as stated.

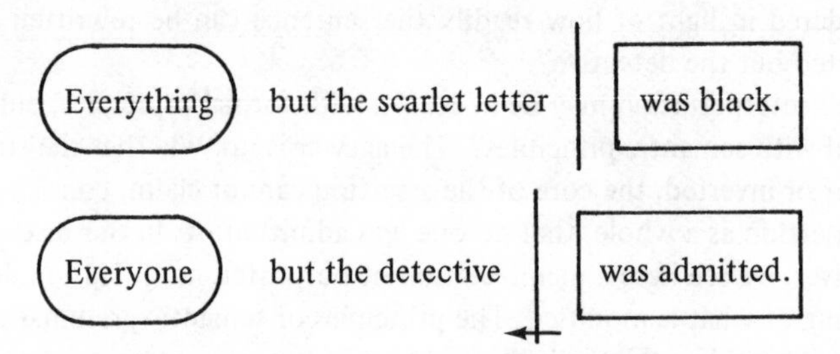

"Everything was black" is not strictly true, but it is true as restrictively modified; and no more than this is required of a core assertion. What is not true, either in and of itself or as modified, is a claim that the scarlet letter was black.

Whatever advantage there can be in developing a semantic grammar can be derived only from doing it consistently. The semantic principle of the non-violability of the core assertion undoubtedly creates certain kinds of problems – as in the sentences about the detective and my sisters – but one of these problems is not the intuitive moving back and forth between formal and semantic principles in analyzing assertions. Where the semantic elements and the formal elements seem not to correlate, then we are obliged to give priority in our analysis to one or the other. We endeavor here to choose always the semantic over the formal. This maxim was first employed back in Chapter 2 with the decision to diagram "She is blue-eyed" and "She has blue eyes" exactly the same way, because, out of context at least, these have the same meaning. We cannot, of course, say that all sentences diagramed the same way have the same meaning, but we should be reluctant to diagram differently sentences of the same semantic kind that have the same meaning.

If, for example, "To please John is easy" and "John is easy to please" are semantically indistinguishable, then we would expect the diagrams to reflect this.

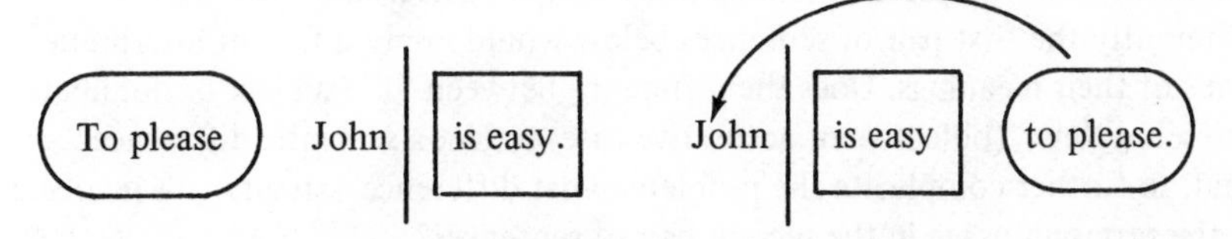

What is easy is not John but the act of pleasing. The controlling factor here is not found in the 'infinitive' form but in the meaning. A *to* phrase can function as a subject (and thus as the attribute core in identity and classification assertions). It can function (as we noted on page 68 above) as part of the core attribute in a future time assertion. It can function as an assertion modifier in sentences like "John asked to leave" and "John is eager to please".

John being eager is restricted by a specification of what he is eager about, but the core meaning is the same with and without this specification. However, to please is not a restriction of John being easy. It is, rather, the specification of what is easy. This is not in any useful way thought of as a matter of deep structure differences; it is simply another instance of the arbitrariness with which some formal differences are used to make semantic distinctions and some formal differences result in the same meaning. The two different positions of "to please" in the sentences above result in no semantic distinctions. But in these two sentences, position is all:

John insulted Hank. Hank insulted John.

There are, moreover, other options confronting the grammarian than just meaning being dependent on form and meaning being independent of form. As we have repeatedly noted, inflectional distinctions may be idiomatically required, but violation of these does not result in difference or distortion of meaning. If instead of such uninflected words as *John* we substitute inflected pronouns, then idiomatic reversibility is not possible. "Him insulted we" is both unidiomatic and semantically ambiguous, but only a matter of degree separates this from a more or less idiomatic and quite semantically unambiguous sentence like, "He insulted we of the Third Battalion". *We* may be 'grammatically wrong' as an object, but the deviation from *us* neither changes nor distorts the meaning. Who did what to who (or whom) remains quite comprehensible. Just as the 'nominative' and 'objective' distinction of *who* and *whom* is unquestionably a disappearing feature of English grammar, so is the *we/us* distinction showing signs of uncertainty among native speakers of English.

This matter of inflectional constraints is not just a problem of correctness. Among equally 'correct' variations of a sentence, there can arise questions of synonymy and thus of diagraming. For example, a decision to diagram differently the first pair of sentences below would imply different interpretations of their meanings. Does the difference between "I" (subject or nominative case) and "me" (objective or accusative case) reflect a semantic difference? And, to further complicate the problem, what difference – if any – is involved in the pronoun usage in the second pair of sentences?

She urged that I submit a proposal.
She urged me to submit a proposal.

She urged my wife and I to submit a proposal.
She urged my wife and me to submit a proposal.

The traditional grammarian would say that "I" must be used in the first sentence because a 'nominative' form is required for the subject of "submit a proposal" – this despite the fact that "I" is not in the subject of this single-assertion sentence but in the predicate. On the other hand, "me" must be used in the second sentence because an 'objective' form is required for the 'direct object' of "She urged". But as far as semantic grammar is concerned, these two sentences have just a single assertion modifier, which answers the question, "What idea or about what topic? " And, out of context at least, there is no discernible semantic difference between the alternate versions of the answer. Thus, the two are diagramed the same:

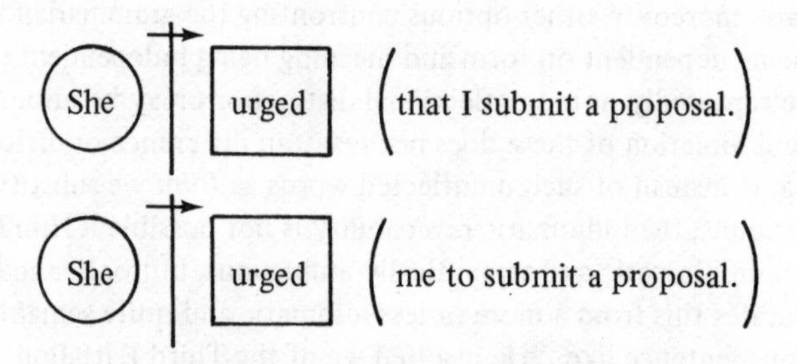

The complex topic or subject matter of what is thought, said, believed, urged, etc. , can be formulated idiomatically either as a relative clause (that is, in assertion form) or as a two-part juxtaposition that is not in assertion form. But if the meaning is the same and just the single question is being answered, then the diagram of the assertion modifier should reflect this. The inflected form of a pronoun here is semantically irrelevant. As is shown by the pair below, the synonymous counterpart of a double assertion modifier is different from the synonymous counterpart of a single assertion modifier:

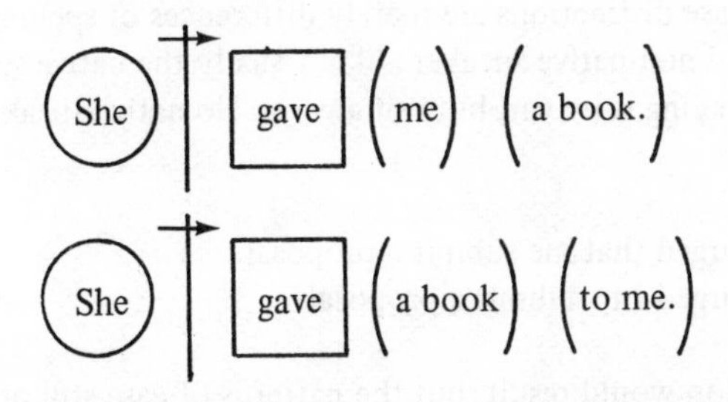

There is no formal possibility for a relative clause here and no semantic possibility of thinking that "me" is part of what was given.

Let us carry this kind of analysis a step further. As with changes in inflections, changes in position may or may not reflect differences in meaning. We can add to "She gave me a book" the answer to another question, "When? " And the result is three assertion modifiers: "today", "me", "a book". There is no possible way that "today" in the following sentence, no matter where it occurs, could be other than a third assertion modifier answering the question, "When did she give? "

> Today she gave me a book.
> She gave me a book today.
> She gave me today a book.

However, we can add "today" to our other examples in two possible ways: as an additional assertion modifier or as part of the original assertion modifier:

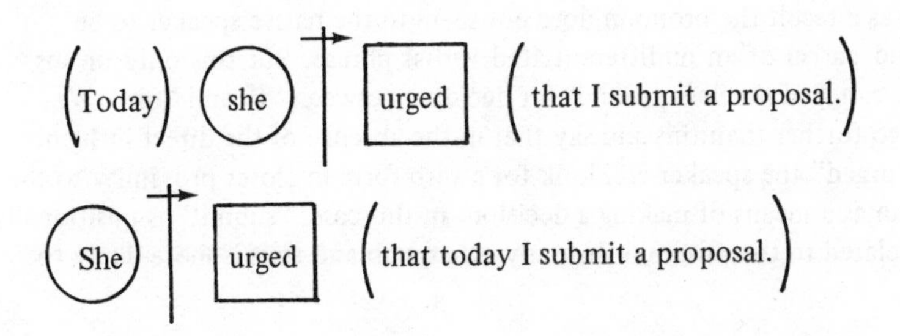

"Today" can be part of *what was urged* (like the pronoun), or it can provide information as to *when it was urged*. And just as there is no formal sign here to indicate the different functions of the word for time, there is no formal sign here that indicates different functions of the pronouns. The difference is that "today" looks the same in either function, but the pronoun, because of the lingering remnants of case in English, appears as either "I" or "me". Like the human appendix, the pronoun distinctions in these examples are quite real but quite functionless.

As often as not case distinctions are merely differences of spelling – pitfalls for native and non-native speaker alike. Usually the native speaker can get by simply playing it by ear, but not always. No native speaker would say

> * She urged that me submit a proposal.
> * She urged I to submit a proposal.

No semantic confusion would result, but the patterns of case still prevail in these sorts of situations. However, when the word or phrase that is said to 'govern' the case of the pronoun becomes separated from the pronoun by intervening words, then confusion results. And when no difference of meaning exists to maintain the consistency of usage, the arbitrary inflectional differences will predictably be used arbitrarily. Whether one says

> She urged my wife and I to submit a proposal.

or

> She urged my wife and me to submit a proposal.

is no longer a matter of consistent usage and therefore no longer properly spoken of as correct or incorrect.

Indeed, we might even go so far as to suggest that more than negative reasoning is involved in explaining "my wife and I". The uninflected "My wife" intervenes between the pronoun and the 'verb' that is said to 'govern' it, and as a result the pronoun does not seem to the native speaker to be part and parcel of an undifferentiated verbal phrase. But this only means that he can find no clear grounds for deciding between "I" and "me". We might go further than this and say that in the absence of the direct influence from "urged" the speaker will look for a verb form in closer proximity to the pronoun as a means of making a decision. In this case, "submit" is positionally more related to the pronoun than any other verb and thus is more likely to 'govern' it than any other. But the relation of the pronoun to this verb is as a subject, whereas the relation of the pronoun to "urged" is as an object. Thus, when the native speaker reasons (albeit unconsciously) that "I" is called for rather than "me" he is probably looking at the verb that follows. This is hardly to be labeled as correct, but neither is it incorrect. Case, in this instance, has degenerated to the point where only the pedant would condemn the use of "I". But this does not make "me" incorrect either. We simply are confronted with the most current manifestation of a process of case simplification and elimination that has been going on in English for many centuries.

Case inflections are just one manifestation of the general disintegration of inflection in English. Let us conclude this digression into the inconsistencies between formal and semantic principles with an example of the general problem as manifested in number, in the attempt to consistently distinguish singular and plural meanings by singular and plural forms:

She is one of the few people who like(s) buttermilk.

Is "like" to be governed by "one" (one likes buttermilk) or by "people" (people like buttermilk)? Both inflectional possibilities are equally idiomatic. The inescapable conclusion is that the presence or absence of the "s" form makes absolutely no difference either in the meaning of the sentence or its clarity.

NOTES

1 For a systematic examination of the problems involved in such analysis of modification see Chapter V of *The Limits of Grammar*, "The Limits of Hierarchical Analysis".
2 Unmarked words and phrases restrict the subassertional unit (subject or attribute) on one side of the assertion divider. Words and phrases in parentheses restrict the subject and attribute taken together.

5. THE PROBLEM OF IMPLICATION

The problem of implication is two-fold: how assertions are distinguished from implications and how much implied meaning is a necessary or a permitted part of semantical grammatical analysis. Difficult as these questions are to answer, they must be met head on or grammatical analysis remains shrouded in a mist of inconsistent intuition. It is certain that different reasonable answers are possible, but as a bare minimum we must strive to be consistent. And to be consistent is impossible without clearly formulated principles to serve as criteria of judgment. One of the basic inadequacies of transformational-generative grammar, for example, is the indiscriminate lumping together of assertions and implications in the realm of 'deep structure'.

By this point in our analysis we should be clear enough on what constitutes assertions. The problem now is to determine what is definable as *implied* assertions and still distinct from *actual* assertions. To be of maximum use our conception of implication should exclude from consideration the infinitely great penumbra of suggestions made up of what individual readers at specific times and places can discern to their own satisfaction but that are not confirmable by any reasonable sampling of intelligent, disinterested readers. To construct various sorts of symbolic or iconic analyses or to draw out stream-of-consciousness connections is not what is meant here by implication. Only agreed-upon interpretation can form the basis of grammatical and rhetorical analysis, and insofar as implications are agreed upon, they are as much a matter of convention as are the interpretations of assertions. Thus our notion of implication is perhaps closer to that of assertion than it is to the usual notion of suggestion.

Indeed, one of our two basic categories of implication is "necessarily implied". Here the meaning is not strictly speaking asserted but must of necessity be assumed by virtue of what is asserted. One may disagree with the truth of a necessary implication, but one cannot rationally deny its necessarily implied character. There is, of course, more to implication than this, but by emphasizing this we are emphasizing the assertional basis of our conception of implication and discouraging the common attempt to find unlimited semantic significance in a composition. In characterizing the various manifestations of implication we might quite properly begin with a more positive principle than "discouraging the common attempt to find unlimited semantic significance in a composition". But this is easier said than done. The easiest way to proceed, and probably the easiest to comprehend, is to begin with necessary implications. What is not necessarily implied is not necessarily agreed upon. Thus we will find very helpful an initial understanding about kinds of implication that no one could rationally deny.

A. NECESSARILY IMPLIED

An obvious sort of necessary implication is the syllogism of traditional Aristotelian logic. To assert that all men are mortal and that Socrates is a man necessarily implies that Socrates is mortal. And this is what we mean by necessarily implied: that asserting something precludes the legitimacy of denying something else. It does not mean that such an implication has actually been asserted; it only means that to assert the one and deny the other is inconsistent. Assertions are asserted; implications are not asserted. But an assertion can be just as inconsistent with an implication as it can be with another assertion.

The syllogism, however, is not a prime example of what we mean here by necessarily implied because it involves a minimum of two separate assertions as the means of implying a third assertion. Perhaps we could refer to this as rhetorical implication and distinguish it from grammatical implication. Rhetorical implications are those that arise out of the relationships between assertions; grammatical implications arise out of single assertions. Before saying more about rhetorical implication, let us focus on simpler manifestations – on single restrictive modifiers that, in addition to providing a necessary qualification, necessarily imply another assertion.

The first kind of necessarily implied assertion results from the special kind of truth word being modified.

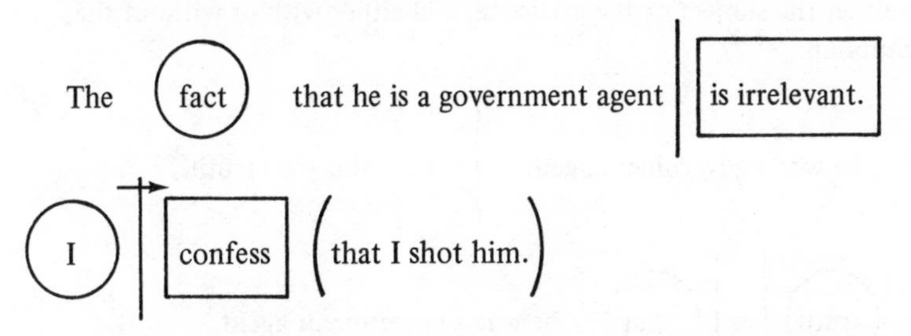

There can be no dispute with these sentences as to what is subject, attribute, assertion modifier. Unlike the exclusive modifiers discussed above – where there were alternative conceptions of the subject and one subject resulted in an assertion inconsistent with the assertion resulting from the other subject – the problem of interpretation here arises from a restrictive modifier that seems in and of itself to make an additional assertion. "That he is a government agent" clearly limits the scope of "fact" so as to exclude all but the one manifestation of the class. In this respect it is just like

But with "fear" there is no possibility that the restrictive modifier makes a necessarily implied assertion. To restrictively modify a word like "fact" is different from restrictively modifying the great bulk of the words and phrases, because to call something a fact or a kind of fact precludes a denial of having committed oneself to its truth. I can assert "The fear that he is a government agent is widespread" and still reasonably deny that he is in fact a government agent. What is feared is not necessarily so. But I cannot assert "The fact that he is a government agent is irrelevant" and still reasonably deny that he is a government agent.

Similarly, I cannot assert "I confess that I shot him" and still reasonably deny that I shot him. "That I shot him" is a limiting modifier, because "I confess" is not a claim to confessing everything; the scope of the function is severely limited, and everything but my shooting him is excluded by virtue of the modifier. However, "I shot him" is a necessarily implied assertion, because one cannot confess to something and reasonably deny the truth of what was confessed. To retract one's confession is thus necessarily to deny the original assertion.

A related form of truth assertion results from the use of identity sentences. Instead of a relative clause being the modifier of a truth word, the clause becomes either the subject or the attribute, and either with or without the relative pronoun:

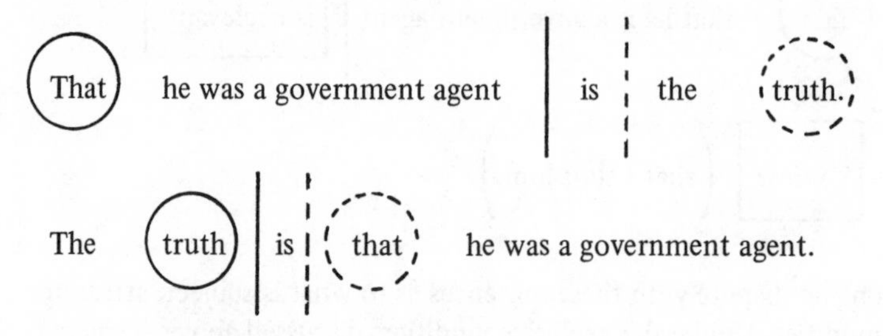

One cannot make these assertions and at the same time deny that he was a government agent. But in the following example, one can make the similar identity assertion and at the same time deny that he will not return:

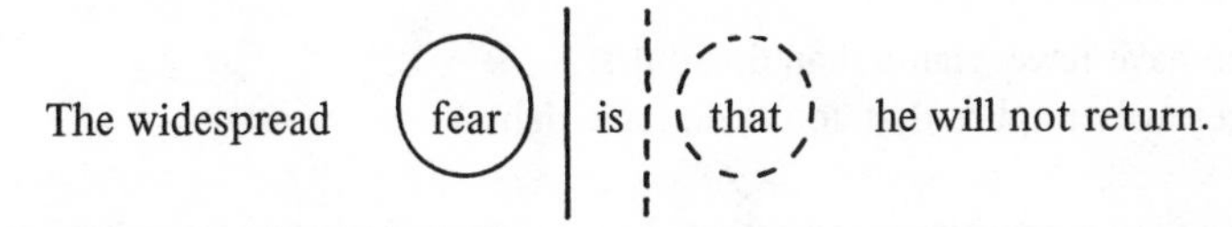

One's report about what exists as a widespread fear does not necessarily include oneself among those who fear, nor does it equate what is feared will happen with what is known will happen.

The second category of necessarily implied assertions results from comparisons or contrasts. By no means all such assertions necessarily imply an additional assertion. For example, "Sam has more friends than Don" can be taken to imply that Don has friends, but there is nothing necessary in this interpretation because the assertion is equally true if Don has no friends at all: "Sam has more friends than Don; indeed, Don really has no friends at all" is quite a reasonable sentence. But in the assertion "Sam has fewer friends than Don" we are obliged to infer that Don has friends because the comparison makes sense only insofar as Don provides the standard of comparison. If it makes sense to say that something is less or fewer than something else, it is because that something else is more or greater. And to have more or greater is necessarily to have. This difference between necessary and not necessary implication is not strictly speaking a matter of elliptical constructions. Neither of these two non-elliptical forms is quite idiomatic, but the second one still necessarily implies that Don has friends and the first one does not:

Sam has more friends than Don *has friends*.

Sam has fewer friends than Don *has friends*.

For the moment, this is all that needs to be said about comparison and contrast. The more common interpretation of such assertions is of the not-necessarily implied sort, and these will be discussed in the next section. The point to emphasize here is that reference to something in a comparison may necessarily imply its existence but may not. What makes the difference is not so much a semantic understanding of the sorts of things being compared as it is a formal understanding of the sort of comparison being made. To be *less* than something else *necessarily implies* an assertion about the existence of the more:

Poverty has less influence than does affluence.
(necessarily implies that affluence does have influence)

Children have fewer rights than do adults.
(necessarily implies that adults do have rights)

To be *more* than something else *implies*, but *not necessarily*, an assertion about the existence of the less:

Affluence has greater influence than does poverty.
(poverty may have no influence)

Adults have more rights than do children.
(children may have no rights)

The third logical possibility for a comparison is that the things compared are equal, but for our purposes of deciding between necessarily and not necessarily implied, these are like the last pair of examples: they do not necessarily imply an additional assertion:

I am as rich as he is.

They are as quiet as a herd of elephants.

Someone may previously have claimed that he is rich or someone may have asked if they are quiet, but the two assertions of ours are equivocal on the existence of richness and quiet. All they commit us to is equality in relation to the pertinent standards.

We would not be concerning ourselves at such length about the problem of implication if all that was involved was such obvious kinds of necessary implication. Implication is a problem because some aspects of assertions seem semantically essential yet neither are asserted nor necessarily implied – at least in the logical senses analyzed above. The most obvious manifestation of the problem is the reference to things without ever asserting their existence. In any ordinary, practical language use it seems to go without saying that we talk about what exists and thus feel no obligation to systematically assert the existence of everything we go on and talk about. To say that "The family upstairs is as quiet as a herd of elephants" or that "Ice floats on water" does not require in any usual discourse prefatory remarks such as: "There is a family upstairs" and "Water exists". Indeed, to get really precise we could say that the first assertion would require a background of: "I exist". "Families exist". "Upstairs exist". "Herds exist". "Elephants exist". "There is an upstairs where I am". "There is a family upstairs where I am". "Herds of elephants exist".

If it is not necessary to assert all this preparatory to making a responsible assertion that "The family upstairs is as quiet as a herd of elephants", is it because these eight assertions are necessarily implied by the inclusive assertion? One argument for thinking that these eight are *not* necessarily implied is that to think so would preclude the legitimacy of such assertions as the following except as prefaced by disclaimers of non-existence:

Ether was much discussed in nineteenth-century physics.

Mount Olympus was the residence of the Greek deities.

Othello strangles Desdemona in a fit of insane jealousy.

What the native speaker cannot understand cannot be part of the grammar.

Ether, Greek deities, Othello, Desdemona, the native speaker – these do not exist. Yet they can reasonably be referred to and talked about. We are no more obliged in practice to assert their non-existence than we are to assert the existence of Mount Olympus or nineteenth-century physics.

But even more important than the not infrequent need to refer to hypothetical and fictional things is the need to distinguish the elements of assertions from the meaning that is asserted by means of the elements. There may or may not be a compelling need in the logical 'grammars' of artificial computer 'languages' to reduce individual assertions to a collection of supporting assertions that convert every element of the main assertion into a separate assertion. But such a procedure is self-defeating in developing the grammar of a natural language. Here, the difference between what is actually asserted and what is not asserted is fundamental. It is possible to assert existence in and of itself, and to do this is an important matter of emphasis by virtue of the contrast it makes with the usual procedure: "Ether does exist". "Macbeth was a real person". Yet if we say that the grammar requires that this be done, in either explicit or implicit fashion, then we seem to require that language use be considered as primarily a matter of referring. This, of course, is the familiar positivistic theory of meaning. At this late stage in the debate we can simply indicate our approval of the recent decline of such proposals. But quite aside from a fundamental disagreement with the theoretical validity of positivism's atomistic conception of meaning and of linguistic analysis, the goal we are seeking – to make possible the systematic analysis of extended discourse – would be impossible to reach if every assertion had to be reduced to a dozen or so sub-assertions before the main assertion could be related to the assertions coming before and after. Requiring the reduction of every *sentence* into its component *assertions* is quite a different matter from requiring the reduction of every *assertion* into its existential implications.

Reference to something implies, in the absence of indications to the contrary, its existence, but this implication is never necessary. A grammar book, full – as it necessarily is – of various kinds of sample assertions, would be almost meaningless, or at least certainly false, if we were obliged to infer that every reference to "my wife", "my husband", "my alcoholic father", "Albert A. Alweather", necessarily implied the existence of such. Sustained composition would be an impossible business if we were required always to assert existence, and it would be almost as bad if we were required always to infer existence. We must thus conclude that, while we can usually assume that reference implies existence, this will by no means always be the proper inference in a given instance.

The principle behind our refusal to make reference equivalent to necessary implication applies equally to restrictive modifiers as to what they modify. Whether the restrictive modifiers are mere single-word references to or whether they contain the full subject-predicate elements of an assertion, their restrictive function is the governing factor. Take for example the following pair of sentences:

My tent collapsed. The tent I slept in collapsed.

Each sentence contains just a single assertion, but the second one has a more detailed implied assertion by virtue of the subject-predicate form of the modifier: I slept in a tent. Restrictive modifiers (e. g. "My" and "I slept in") cannot be detached from what they modify and be made separate sentences without changing the meaning of the original assertions. "Lincoln was the president who freed the slaves" is not reducible to "Lincoln was a president" and "A president freed the slaves". "The tent I slept in collapsed" is not reducible to "A tent collapsed" and "I slept in a tent". But the question of necessary implication goes beyond this.

It is probably safe to say that every restrictive modifier implies something beyond its role of limiting or qualifying what is modified. But where more than one thing seems implied and different people have different formulations of what precisely is being implied, then there is no one necessary implication that every rational person is logically obliged to recognize. In the sentence "My tent collapsed" there are several plausible candidates, and thus no certainty exists in accepting one as necessarily implied: I owned a tent. I rented a tent. I lived in a tent. I pitched a tent. I slept in a tent. Not unexpectedly, we find that the gain in economy made possible by pre-positional modification results in corresponding disadvantages. Not only is there a possible ambiguity in taking the modifier to be both restrictive and non-restrictive, there is a possible uncertainty in deciding what precisely is being implied. Admittedly, in many cases there is no problem. And in many others the differences between alternative interpretations will be of minor significance. But problems can and do arise, and the fact of the matter is that a full subject-predicate form of post-positional modification is a means of reducing confusion.

There is an important difference between the pre-positional "My tent collapsed" and the post-positional "The tent I slept in collapsed", but this is a difference in precision of implication, not in different kinds of implication. In the latter the implication is precisely that I slept in a tent. However, there is nothing logically compelling about this implication. Different contexts could lend different existential interpretations to this restrictive modifier. Grammatically it is no different from

Greek tragedy was conceived on the day *Zeus raped Leda*.

One is free to infer that Zeus did in fact rape Leda, but he can still deny it without having to deny the whole sentence as a meaningful, appropriate assertion in a particular context. And this is the case irrespective of whether the relative pronoun is used. "Greek tragedy was conceived on the day *that* Zeus raped Leda", with its relative pronoun, has the same overall assertional meaning and the same not-necessary implication.

And while on the subject of relative pronouns, we might note examples of *when* and *where* clauses. These result in restrictive assertion modifiers even when they include complete subject and predicate elements:

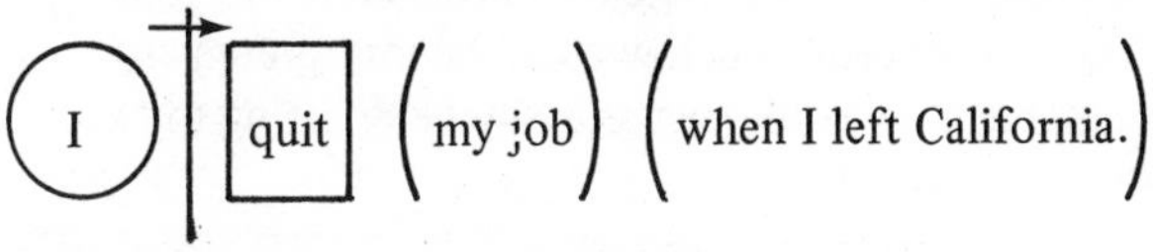

I quit (my job) (when I left California.)

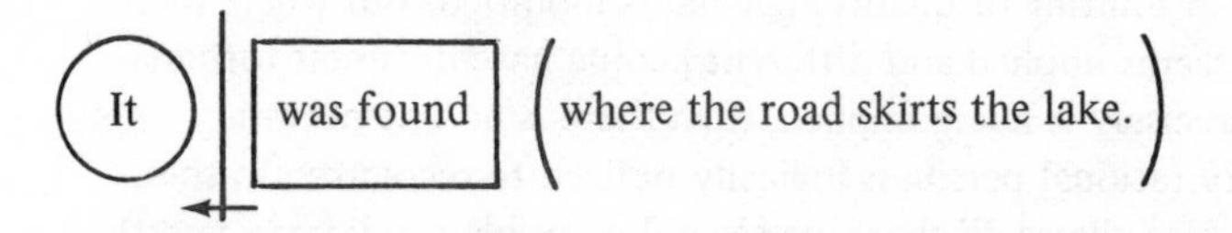

As to function in the sentence, these clauses are no different from

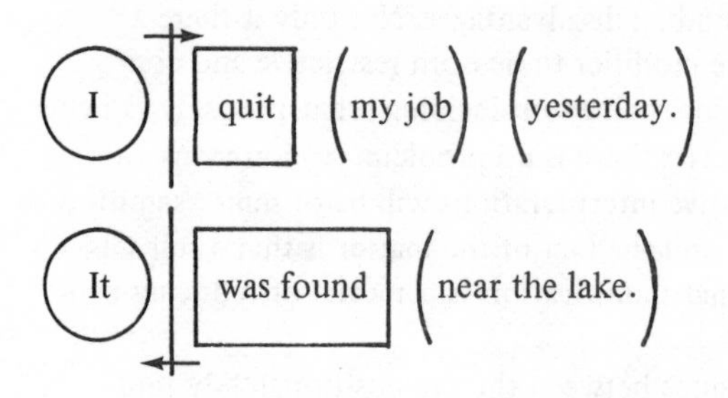

And thus there are no necessary implications.

A further complication results from strings of, what the transformational-generative grammarian refers to as, "left-branching modifiers". These are the pre-positional ones, the ones that are much more idiomatically multiplied than are the post-positional ones. But the idiomaticness of an example like the following does not thereby invalidate the basic distinction between single-assertion sentences and multiple-assertion sentences:

A new red Ford pickup truck is parked outside.

Can we infer from this sentence that other trucks are parked outside? that other pickup trucks are? that other Ford trucks are? that other red trucks are? that other new trucks are? The important question is not whether these are necessary implications but whether they are implications at all. We need to determine first whether the multiple modifiers result in multiple explicit assertions, because the source of implications is structures of restrictive modification.

Our example is clearly and unequivocally referring to just a single truck; thus we cannot treat the four modifiers as parallel and separate out four individual assertions. The four assertions below could be interpreted as referring to a single truck, but they could just as easily be referring to two, or three, or four trucks:

A new truck is parked outside.
A red truck is parked outside.
A Ford truck is parked outside.
A pickup truck is parked outside.

Consequently, the four modifiers are restrictive, and as such they can give rise to implied assertions. In a given context we may or may not be justified in inferring from this sentence that other trucks are parked outside. Even out of context it is reasonable to assume that there are trucks in existence that are not new, not red, not Fords, not pickups. But there is nothing logically necessary in the rule of thumb that a distinction made implies the existence of an actual contrast.

It is occasionally possible for multiple pre-positional modifiers to result in multiple explicit assertions; however, this requires some semantic means of making a precise distinction between multiple characteristics of one thing and multiple things being characterized:

He has a large red truck.

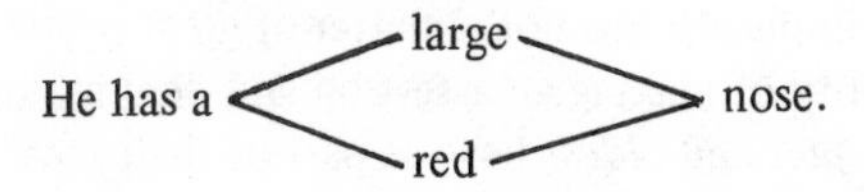

The first example is not necessarily the same as "He has a large truck" plus "He has a red truck", because these two sentences could be referring to two different trucks. However, the second example does clearly and unequivocally refer to one man's one nose, regardless of whether there is one sentence with multiple modifiers or two sentences with single modifiers. Theoretically, we would expect that separable parallel modifiers could always be conjoined by *and*. In practice, this is not always idiomatically the case, although it frequently is:

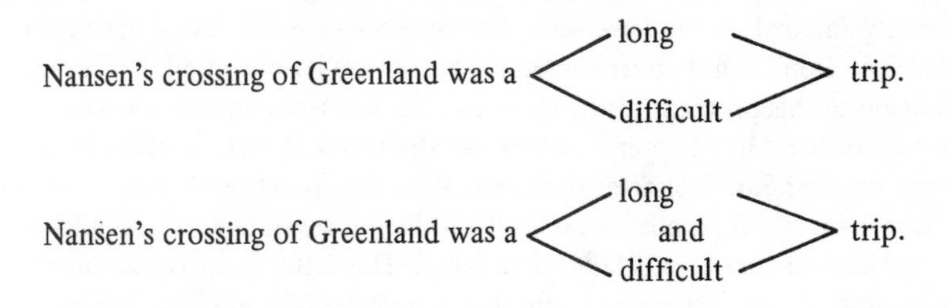

What is involved in the interpretation of "A new red Ford pickup truck is parked outside" is not primarily a matter of implication beyond what is explicitly stated but a matter of recognizing the different elements of an explicit assertion. No assertion is semantically atomistic. "A truck is parked outside" is a composite of several unified ideas, and the addition of four restrictive modifiers to the subject does not change this. The problem of implication is not a matter of extracting atoms of ideas from an assertion but of constructing additional assertions on the basis of what is explicitly asserted. Grammatical implications are structures of restrictive modification that are interpreted as assertions even as their restrictive grammatical function remains unchanged.

As a general rule we assume that a distinction made implies the need for it and thus that we can infer some kind of contrast. To refer to "my oldest brother" implies that I have more than one brother. Indeed, we can go so far as to claim that this is a necessary implication, because the superlative degree of comparison could not logically have been used if I had only one brother. If I refer to "my older brother", this too implies that I have more than one brother, but it may be that the comparative degree indicates only that I have one brother and that he is older than I. Thus we cannot term this a necessary implication. Necessary implication is not a matter of great probability but of the logical impossibility of making an assertion and denying the resulting implication. Words like *fact* and *oldest* have as part of their meaning this ready potential for indicating logical, either/or, necessity. However, most words are like *new*, *red*, *Ford*, *pickup*, and *truck* in having for the most part potential only for equivocal implications.

B. NOT NECESSARILY IMPLIED

We need to do little more than refer back to our discussion of comparison and contrast by way of noting that this type of construction never states more than one assertion, but it does imply more than one. Some of these are necessarily implied, as we have seen, but by no means all. "Sam has fewer friends than Don" is not contradicted if Sam has no friends at all. However, in addition to this problem of the more and the less is the problem touched upon briefly back in Chapter 2, where we discussed numerical characteristics.[1]

If we say that Sam is shorter than Don, does this assert or necessarily imply that Sam is short? If Sam is six feet tall and Don is seven feet tall, should we have said instead that Don is taller than Sam? This latter transformation would seem to preclude any objection to finding as a necessarily implied assertion that Don is tall.

The difficulty is two-fold. First, there is no place in a continuum of tall and short, or big and little, or heavy and light that carries any agreement as to where the one pole ceases to govern and the other pole takes over. Not only is there a difference from subject to subject but also for the same subject from one context to another. Second, there is no consistent pattern in actual usage. People seem just as likely to speak of big things in terms of smallness as of big things in terms of bigness. If the subject of the assertion is less than the thing serving as the standard, then no matter what its dimensions it will be spoken of as less.

We may in individual instances infer as much as we like from a comparison, but this will not be a necessary implication unless the conditions previously discussed have been met. Just as we decided in Chapter 2 that the core of a numerical attribute could not be the kind of measurement (tall, short, old, deep, high, etc.) but was the actual measurement as a whole (is six inches tall, is six inches short, is two days old), so we must conclude that, whatever may be inferred in individual instances, there is no necessary implication simply by virtue of there being a comparison.

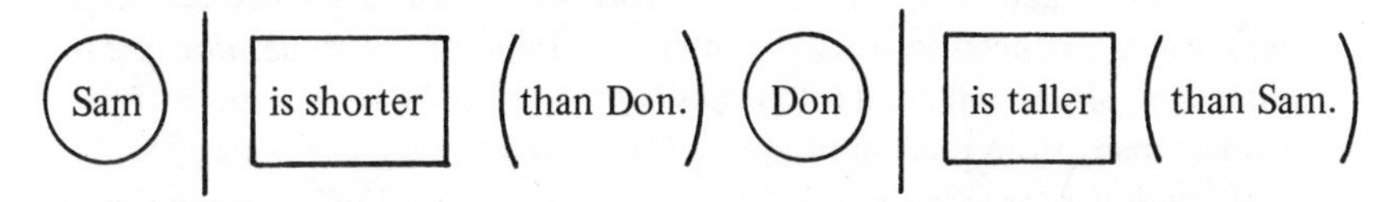

To say that Sam is shorter than Don *means* that Don is taller than Sam. It would be pointlessly redundant for the two assertions to be stated together. The question is only whether we can infer from "Sam is shorter than Don" that Sam is short, or that Don is short, or that Don is tall. Depending on the context, any of these is a possible inference, but in no context (because context is ultimately irrelevant for necessary implication) is one of these necessarily implied.

Similar to comparisons are sentences like the following:

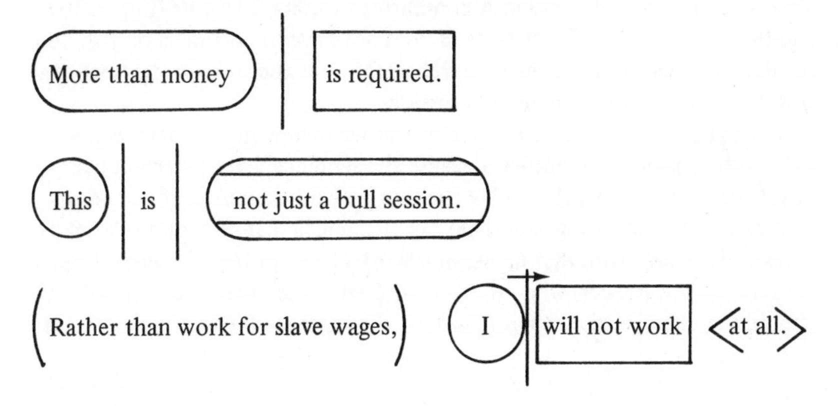

Are we obliged to infer that money (among other things) is required? and that whatever else this session may be it is also a bull session? Would it (as a matter of context) ever make sense to say that more than money is required and then to deny that money is required? Is it (as a matter of logical or semantic analysis) ever possible to say that being more than something does not include as part of itself that which it is more than?

Volunteers are called for on a stormy night to man a lifeboat; someone pulls out his wallet and offers to support the venture. He is curtly informed that more than money is required. Indeed, there is no substitute here for courage, strength, and endurance. Perhaps there is an element of irony in the answer; perhaps it is a deliberate understatement; perhaps the most precise answer would have been that money is not required. But ironic or not, such an answer would have been appropriate and comprehensible under the circumstances.

However, we are not really obliged to invent fictional situations to test the question. The concept of *more than* can, of course, be interpreted in terms of *more of the same*: More than a couple of dollars is required to buy this camera. More than your half-hearted effort is required to gain a place on this team. But the concept can also be interpreted in terms of *something else more important*: More than good intentions is required to become a successful business man. More than an inside tip is required to play the horses.

Many dollars are required to buy this camera. *All-out effort* is required to gain a place on this team. These are more-of-the-same comparisons. *Ruthlessness* is required to become a successful business man. *Money* is required to play the horses. Because one can be a successful business man without good intentions and play the horses without inside tips, these are something-else-more-important comparisons. We are thus not able to say that such assertions necessarily imply that the specified criterion is included, even though insufficient. In the sentence about the bull session we might make this point more obvious than it is in its "not just" form by rewriting the sentence thus: This is not a mere bull session. A committee meeting that is drifting further and further from the subject at hand does not have to become a bull session for the chairman to make the comprehensible and appropriate statement that this is not just, or not a mere, bull session.

In the third example, we must take "rather than work for slave wages" as a limiting assertion modifier, because the sentence does not unequivocally assert that I will not work. Unlike the two previous sentences, this one has an assertion modifier; but like them, its meaning is that of a comparison. The speaker does *not* claim that he will not work at all nor that he will not work for slave wages. Rather, when the two alternatives are presented, he will choose the one over the other. However, the sentence leaves open the possibility that he might be forced to work for slave wages and the possibility that he will be able to work for non-slave wages. It is probably fair to infer from the sentence that the speaker will not work for slave wages. We assume as a Constitutional right that "Neither slavery nor involuntary servitude, except as punishment for crime whereof the party shall have been duly convicted, shall exist within the United States, or any place subject to their jurisdiction". But there is nothing logically compelling about an inference based on such an assumption.

Rather than often functions as a negative, but only by implication. In essence it is a comparison, like *more* and *less*; but unlike them, it does not create a necessary implication. Where the phrase does occasionally occur with an explicit negation, it is redundant. In sentences like "He is twenty rather than twenty-one" and "He is a Swede rather than a Norwegian", nothing new is added by the "rather than" phrase. To say that someone is twenty *means*, among other things, that he is not twenty-one; to say that he is a Swede means, among other things, that he is not a Norwegian.

The next general category of not necessarily implied implications is rhetorical questions. An explicit question is not, of course, in itself an assertion. It may contain within itself as an additive modifier a separable assertion:

Why do you, [the least qualified,] claim the greatest reward?

"You [are] the least qualified" is unequivocally asserted; there is nothing inferential about it; it can be lifted out of the context without altering the nature of the question. There are, however, two possibilities for implications: You claim the greatest reward. You shouldn't claim the greatest reward.

The first of these cannot be treated as a separate assertion because to lift it out of context would destroy the question. "Why do you claim the greatest reward" is not a composite of "You claim the greatest reward" and "Why do you claim? " The precise nature of the claim is lost this way. We can, however, interpret the question as necessarily implying that you claim the greatest reward. The difficulty with this interpretation is that our standard test for necessary implication is not really applicable to questions. We cannot ask whether asserting one thing and denying another is logically inconsistent, because there is not a stated assertion and an implied assertion but rather a question and an implied assertion. This gives rise to the frustrating kind of situation exemplified by the question, "Have you stopped beating your wife yet? " The answer called for is either "Yes" or "No". But if you have not in fact been beating your wife, how do you answer? The question clearly implies that you have been beating your wife, but just as clearly there is nothing necessarily implied by it because there is no possibility of demonstrating a necessary inconsistency between what is questioned and what is implied. A reasonable retort is "I have never beaten my wife". But a disagreement does not necessarily prove a logical inconsistency.

"You claim the greatest reward" is much closer to being necessarily implied than is "You shouldn't claim the greatest reward", but it still falls short of strict necessity because strict necessity requires the possibility of two inconsistent assertions – one actually asserted and one implied by the one that is actually asserted.

The kind of implication characteristic of rhetorical questions is exemplified by the last example: an implied answer. Not all rhetorical questions clearly imply an answer; some are simply the means of introducing a new subject or a new stage in the discussion or of admitting ignorance of something. But many rhetorical questions function more as answers than as real questions. Certainly in the above question it is hard to deny that if the person addressed is indeed the least qualified it is hardly right that he claims the greatest reward. Unless there is argument to the contrary, we usually assume that least qualified should correlate with smallest reward and that most qualified should correlate with greatest reward. Thus the obvious incongruity between "least" and "greatest" in this question implies (though not necessarily) a negative answer.

The great bulk of not-necessarily implied assertions is not, however, a matter of comparison and contrast or of rhetorical questions; it is a matter of reference and restrictive modification. To speak of something is to imply its existence, and in the absence of evidence to the contrary, we are usually justified in assuming that reference to something is sufficient to indicate its existence. But this assumption is a matter of semantic interpretation rather than formal signs.

The man in the upstairs apartment is not seen during the day.
    The man in the moon is not seen during the day.
The rape of the Bangladesh women will not go unpunished.
    The rape of Mother Nature will not go unpunished.

And not only do the second and fourth examples indicate the need for caution in assuming that reference implies existence, they also indicate how limited is the positivistic equating of meaning and reference. The second and fourth are no less meaningful than the first and third. Not just the realm of hypothetical and fictional references but also the widespread use of metaphorical references is invalidated by such a narrow conception of meaning.

Yet, while a reference like "The rape of Mother Nature" cannot be taken to imply existence in the way that "the rape of the Bangladesh women" can be, there are additional kinds of implicational possibilities not available to true/false referential assertions. Metaphorical assertions imply, although of course not necessarily, important similarities between things from quite different realms of discourse. To speak of the natural, biological, non-cultural, non-technological processes of the Earth in terms of motherhood is to imply that this aspect of our world deserves the highest respect and consideration we are capable of, even as we are allowed great familiarity with the object of respect. This is the traditional metaphorical implication. To take this traditional metaphor as the basis of a new metaphor is to create a further realm of implication. If motherhood is deserving of the highest respect and consideration because it is the very source of our existence, growth, and development, then the ultimate violation of this source, its pollution, is deserving of the greatest condemnation. This kind of metaphorical statement implies a kind and intensity of value judgment that could hardly result from a reference, for example, to "the ecological imbalance". To speak of an imbalance seems to imply that it is possible to restore the balance, but to speak of a rape seems to imply that something irrevocable has happened, akin perhaps to gaining the knowledge of good and evil.

Of necessity, metaphors always imply, but the individual implications are never necessary ones. We are a long way here from "I confess that I shot him". But what is equally true of the two examples of the two kinds of implication is that the meaning of each sentence is not completely interpreted until we have articulated the inevitable implications. The fact that most implications are a matter of disputable interpretation does not gainsay their presence.

This chapter, coming as it does before the discussion of inter-assertional relations, is essentially concerned with grammatical rather than rhetorical implications. However, by way of introducing the discussion of the latter (the subject of the next chapter), we might profitably examine a special sort of inter-assertional implication that arises out of a standard grammatical pattern. This is the implied causality of 'participial' constructions. The use of 'participials', especially *having* and *being*, as a means of making an *explicit* additive assertion and an *implicit* causal relationship is common, but this convention slips easily into problem cases – where not only is the implication unclear but also where the distinction between restrictive and non-restrictive modification is unclear.

First, let us make clear the sort of *having* and *being* constructions that are not at issue here. When the 'participial' form is the subject or the attribute, there is no additive modifier and no question of a causal implication:

Being a woman is a disadvantage when applying to medical schools.
Having a headache is no excuse.
Having children is having a life-time commitment.

As additive modifiers, *have* and *be* phrases are set off by punctuation, although their usual position is before rather than after the thing modified:

[Having failed her exam,] she was ineligible.

She was ineligible.
She had failed her exam.

His daughter, [having married a bum,] is living on welfare.

His daughter is living on welfare.
His daughter has married a bum.

[Being a woman,] she was ineligible.

She was ineligible.
She was a woman.

Written as *explicit* rather than *implicit* causals, these sentences readily lend themselves to parallel structure:

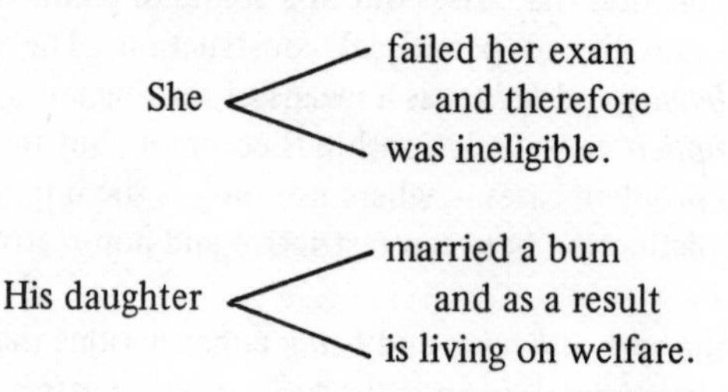

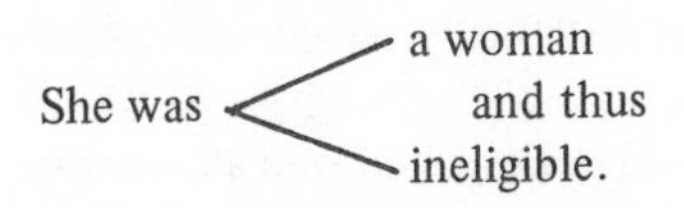

The following two sentences each contain a pair of assertions but with different subjects as well as different attributes; consequently, there is no structure of modification. However, in treating them as compound structure, we will be stretching a bit our conception of two completely independent clauses. "Having" and "being" are the subordinating forms of "has" and "was", but these are just inflectional variations and thus will not prevent us (in the absence of any more adequate alternatives) from diagraming such sentences as compound:

The course having no prerequisites,

even freshmen are enrolled.

The course has no prerequisites.

Even freshmen are enrolled.

The taxi being late,

we missed the first act.

The taxi was late.

We missed the first act.

Written as explicit causals, these continue to manifest compound structure:

Because

the course has no prerequisites,

even freshmen are enrolled.

The taxi was late;

therefore,

we missed the first act.

A problem that commonly arises because the additive form has no separate subject is that despite obvious causal implication, the subject of the core assertion will not serve as the common subject:

* Having eaten our lunch, the boat departed.
* Having argued in vain all evening, it was finally agreed to submit to arbitration.
* Being unable to write on the assigned topic, the teacher agreed to another.

* Being weak with hunger, food was finally served.

The boat did not eat our lunch; *it* did not argue in vain all evening; *the teacher* was not the one unable to write on the assigned topic; *food* was not weak with hunger.

The counterpart of this problem is obvious syntactical parallelism but ambiguity of implication. The use of *having* and *being* in additive modification clearly establishes a prior condition, and the semantic convention seems fairly well established here that *post hoc, ergo propter hoc*: to come after is to be the result of. There seems to be no other special rationale for the pre-positional 'participial' form. But sometimes such constructions seem simply to be *post hoc*, and the reader looks in vain for a *because/therefore* relationship where nothing but *and* can be justified:

Having left the theater, they walked toward the delicatessen.
They left the theater *and* walked toward the delicatessen.

Packed as full as practicable by automatic machines, it contains the full weight indicated.
It was packed as full as practicable by automatic machines *and* contains the full weight indicated.

At this point our topic of 'participial' modifiers begins to expand beyond *having* and *being*, but the problem is familiar: deciding whether we are confronted with one assertion or two. There is no problem with the two parallel sentences above: they are composed of pairs of assertions. But with the modificational counterparts a case can be made for "having left the theater" and "packed as full as practicable by automatic machines" as being either restrictive or non-restrictive. Partly this kind of problem results from our insistence on imposing an either/or conception of analysis on modification, but partly it results from the latent ambiguity in this kind of sentence structure. As long as the 'participial' phrase uses just *having* or *being* and as long as there is a reasonable causal interpretation, then we are dealing with non-restrictive modification. The proof of such an interpretation is the converting of the modificational structure into a parallel structure and the providing of an explicit causal conjunction (e. g. *because* or *therefore*).

An alternative possibility to parallel structure as a more adequate formulation of some of these 'participials' is as restrictive modification. The phrase may simply be the answer to questions of when, where, or under what circumstances:

Returning from lunch, I was accosted by four men.

Hanging from the gallows, his corpse is a warning to all traitors.

Swimming beyond the reef, he was attacked by a shark.

"When were you accosted? " "Where is his corpse? " "Under what circumstances was he attacked? " Answers to these questions provide restrictive assertion modifiers. But is there, in addition to this kind of interpretation, a causal implication in these sentences? On the one hand, it seems to make little sense to say that I returned from lunch and *therefore* was accosted by four men. On the other hand, it is not unreasonable to say that there is some kind of causal relationship between the corpse hanging from the gallows and the reaction of traitors who see it. Yet the second sentence is not about what the hanging corpse *causes* but what it *is*. We are not told that traitors are taking warning but only that the corpse is a warning. No more than the first sentence can the second one be restructured as a causal relationship without altering the meaning. The third sentence is more obviously causal than the first one (being attacked by a shark seems more likely to accompany swimming beyond the reef than being accosted by four men is likely to accompany returning from lunch). But unlike the second one, it is a matter of mere accompaniment rather than of essential connection.

This causal ambiguity arises because of a tendency in English to treat this sort of pre-positional modification as a deliberate deviation for causal purposes from the more usual post-positional structure:

I was accosted by four men when returning from lunch.

His corpse hanging from the gallows is a warning to all traitors.

He was attacked by a shark while swimming beyond the reef.

These restrictive assertion modifiers clearly and unambiguously answer questions of when, where, and under what circumstances and raise no causal implications. The journalese tendency topile on unintegrated information at the beginning of a sentence results in more than "a stylistic monstrosity" (as one commentator labels it); it often results in causal implications that are not clearly in accord with the explicit meaning.

It would be fortunate if all of our difficulties with these 'participial' constructions could be attributed to the innate ambiguity of the form, or at least to the illegitimacy of attempting causal implications except with *having* and *being*. Unfortunately, however, there are some sentences that seem to be quite acceptable manifestations of causal implication without *having* or *being* and at the same time meet the criteria of restrictive modification. In the last analysis we may be forced to admit that a sentence like the following is so close to the borderline between restrictive and non-restrictive as to render the distinction inappropriate:

Living among the natives, I came to understand their point of view.

In the first place, it seems quite in accord with the basic meaning of the sentence to rewrite the sentence as an explicit causal using parallel structure:

I lived among the natives and as a result came to understand their point of view.

In the second place, the phrase "living among the natives" seems clearly to answer the question "under what circumstances? "

Does the causal implication render the 'participial' modifier non-restrictive? Does the answer to a restrictive question necessarily qualify as a restrictive modifier? Can a modifier be both restrictive and non-restrictive? These questions cannot be ignored, but they are better treated in the next chapter, where the complexities of causality can be examined at greater length than would be appropriate in this chapter on implication.

Before going on to explain explicit causality, a final kind of implicit causality should be noted. This is a minor point, yet it constitutes a conspicuous exception to one of our well-established principles. There is a kind of dependent additive modifier that requires *have* instead of *be*. As an inflectional adjunct to an attribute core, *have*, as we have seen, is hardly less ubiquitous than *be*. However, it is rarely required for rewriting an additive modifier as a separate assertion. Where it is required is in certain modifiers that are introduced by *with* and imply a causal relationship:

Australia, [with extensive deserts,] is a sparsely populated country.

Australia is a sparsely populated country.
Australia [has] extensive deserts.

We reasonably infer that Australia is a sparsely populated country *because* it has extensive deserts, but this is not necessarily implied.

In summarizing this subject we can say that the analysis of implication involves the distinction not just between necessarily and not necessarily implied but also between ambiguous and unambiguous implication. It is no criticism to refer to something as being not necessarily implied, but it is a criticism to refer to it as an ambiguous implication.

NOTES

1 Pp. 65-66.

6. INTER-ASSERTIONAL RELATIONS

The concept of inter-assertional relations is very much a transitional notion: it is a matter of grammar insofar as multiple assertions are integrated into single sentences; it is a matter of rhetoric insofar as multiple sentences are involved. And insofar as the decision to make multiple assertions multiple sentences or to integrate them into single sentences can be more or less arbitrary, so the distinction between grammar and rhetoric can be more or less arbitrary. Much more significant than distinguishing between grammar and rhetoric is distinguishing between the *strengths and weaknesses of the different kinds of formal assertion structure*. And even more significant than this is distinguishing the *kinds of semantic relationships that can pertain between assertions*, irrespective of whether these inter-assertional relations are within a sentence or between sentences.

The literal meaning of an assertion is independent of its structure: the same assertion can appear as an independent sentence, as part of a compound sentence, as part of a parallel structure, or as an additive modifier. But the role it plays in a composition, its relationships with other assertions, can be affected by the different structural possibilities. For example, parallel structure is a means of showing commonality among two or more assertions. In contrast to this structure is independent structure. A fundamental advantage of independent structure is as a means of emphasizing an individual assertion. This is obviously not what parallel structure is best suited for because in parallel structure two or more assertions receive equal emphasis.

It must be understood, however, that the various kinds of strengths and weaknesses to be found in the different kinds of structure are very general and thus not always unequivocally obvious in every instance. Also, we are dealing here not with correct and incorrect but with legitimately competing considerations. Thus, for example, the desire for maximum explicitness and maximum conciseness will never be completely satisfied because, though equally important, the one goal is achieved by adding words and assertions, while the other goal is achieved by subtracting them. Nor are we always justified in thinking that a one-assertion sentence is being given special emphasis; it may simply be that the desire to show commonality was thwarted by the need to include in the single assertion such extensive restrictive modification as to make it unable to also develop parallel assertions. The criterion of emphasis is not the only one on which single-assertion sentences rank high; the desire to be explicit, to spell out in maximum detail, may be the best explanation of a particular single-assertion sentence. But relativity is always a factor: a statement that in one context might be thought to be belaboring the obvious might be thought too cryptic in another context.

The following three pairs of structural criteria are all matters of degree, and in given instances may be more or less arbitrary, but they have the value of being essentially formal – of being equally applicable to assertions on any subject.

EXPLICIT independent/compound parallel additive *CONCISE*

EMPHATIC independent compound parallel additive *SUBORDINATE*

COMMON parallel additive compound independent *DIFFERENT*

In a sense, things semantic are *sui generis* – that is, significant for the very fact that they are unique. Thus, there could be only formal principles of structure (what is common to different compositions regardless of subject matter); there could be no semantic principles (what is unique to each composition). But in another sense, we have already committed ourselves to a basic semantic principle in the implied dialog nature of discourse. Quite apart from its form or structure, the meaning of each assertion is an answer to a question elicited by a previous assertion. The basic premise of generative rhetoric is this principle of implied dialog as the fundamental semantic tool for generating and analyzing the meaning of discourse. But the question remains: are there more specific tools of semantic analysis that are still general principles and not simply the explication of individual compositions?

When simple assertions are integrated to form a unified composition, there are indeed general semantic relationships that the assertions – whatever their form or structure – can have with each other. The dialog relationship is not just a matter of implicit question and answer; it is also a relationship of explicit assertions. More important than relative *degrees* of relationship between two opposite poles (explicit-concise, emphatic-subordinate, common-different) are the *kinds* of relationships. Most commonly an assertion is related to the previous assertion as a *continuation*. Less common is the relationship of *contrast*. Relatively uncommon are the relationships of *concluding* and *supporting*. Least common is the relationship of explicit *questioning* and explicit *answering* of explicit questions. Although of no great significance, we can correlate the general frequency of occurrence with the availability of conjunctions:

Continuing is more common than Contrasting, which is more common than Concluding, which is more common than Supporting, which is more common than Questioning, which is more common than Answering (though both the latter lack conjunctions). These six kinds of semantic relationships, together with characteristic inter-assertional conjunctions, are listed below, grouped together in the point-counterpoint pairs that are necessary for explaining the nature of each:

DESCRIPTIVE

Continue	*and, in addition, furthermore, indeed, even, also, similarly, namely, among, while, then, or, nor, for example, that is, as well as, in other words, by the same token, neither . . . nor, not only . . . but also*
Contrast	*but, however, although, yet, or, nonetheless, nevertheless, despite, even so, even though, either . . . or, on the one hand . . . on the other hand, while*

EXPLANATORY

Conclude	*therefore, thus, consequently, hence, so, accordingly, as a result*
Support	*because, since, for, as a result of, as, so that*

RHETORICAL

Question

Answer

By no means, however, do all inter-assertional relations use an explicit conjunction. Not only are there no standard ones to link an explicit question with the assertion that elicits it and an explicit answer with an explicit question, but also relationships are often simply implied – especially for continuing. And even aside from this influence exerted by the kind of semantic relationship, the kind of structural relationship can militate against explicit conjunctions; additive modifiers are rarely linked to the core assertion by conjunctions, yet there is nonetheless some kind of inter-assertional relationship. Furthermore, not all conjunctions that do occur function as inter-assertional links, as we have already seen with unitary parallel. Nor do all assertional conjunctions necessarily occur between the assertions. For example, *because* can occur at the beginning of a pair of assertions and within the first of the pair. Others, like *not only . . . but also*, are separable conjunctions, with part introducing a pair and part linking them. Finally, there are those like *however*, *indeed*, and *therefore* that can occur in the standard intermediate position linking two assertions but that can also occur somewhere in the middle of the second assertion.

The analysis of inter-assertional relations is, then, partly a matter of different semantic kinds, partly a matter of different structural possibilities, and partly a matter of the explicit vs. the implicit conjunction.

A. DESCRIPTIVE – CONTINUE AND CONTRAST

Any of the five conjunction positions may be occupied in descriptive inter-assertional relationships: a conjunction between the two assertions, a conjunction introducing a pair of assertions, a separable conjunction introducing and linking the two assertions, a conjunction within the first assertion, a conjunction within the second assertion. Or no conjunction may be used at all. Furthermore, both continuing and contrasting conjunctions (e. g. *and* and *but*) can be employed for other functions than to link assertions. Finally, as already noted, the individual assertions can have independent structure, parallel structure, or modificational structure.

Of the first sort, the ordinary inter-assertional conjunction, we are already over-supplied with examples from our discussion of compound and parallel structure. But our previous examples have been very limited in the range of conjunctions used. We do not need any more simple *and* and *but* examples; we do, however, need to emphasize how many different words function syntactically the same as do these two standbys. And we also need to recognize that two assertions can be linked by multiple conjunctions of different types and of the same type.

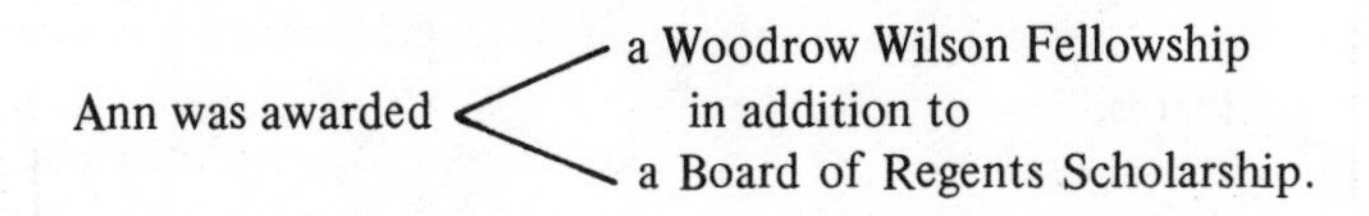

Her grade-point is high;
  but, in addition,
she is the daughter of migrant farm workers.

  Indeed,
Ann herself was a migrant farm worker for several years;
  that is,
she worked as part of a family engaged in contract fruit picking.

As compared to *and*, *in addition to* is probably a means of providing greater emphasis on the cumulativeness of the attributes, but this is a matter of fine shades of meaning rather than of different kinds of inter-assertional relations. The two conjunctions in the second sentence do not cancel each other out but rather point to the two different kinds of relationships between the two assertions. On the one hand, the two assertions have in common the fact that both reflect reasons why Ann was awarded these two valuable and prestigious grants; on the other hand, the two assertions reflect fundamentally different criteria of worthiness.

There was no conjunction between the first and second sentences (the usual case), and our concern at the moment is not with implied relationships. However, between the second and third sentences there is a conjunction. As we noted in our study of redundant or punctuational modification, *indeed* can occur within an assertion and function as a means of special emphasis in addition to being an indicator of the continuing sort of inter-assertional relationship. When it does occur between assertions, its punctuational function is less conspicuous, and we will be content to let it stand simply as a conjunction. Yet, whether we mark it or not, *indeed* has as part of its basic meaning an intensification that *and* lacks. In this particular sentence we can say that *indeed* is primarily a conjunction because *herself* is the primary means of intensification. But *indeed* in and of itself is sufficient to indicate a continuing inter-assertional relationship no matter where it occurs or what other words occur in addition to it.

The final conjunction (*that is*) recalls our example, in the discussion of appositive parallelism, about neutralizing the enemy position. In this case there is no appositive parallel – although there easily could have been:

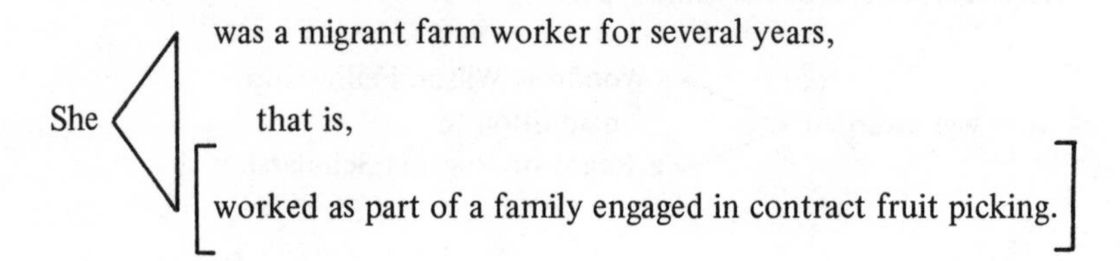

Appositive conjunctions can raise questions about what precisely is the modifier and what the head. Our policy, albeit unstated, has been always to treat the first leg of an appositive parallel as the head and the succeeding leg or legs as modifiers. But sometimes the first leg needs to be recognized as the modifier:

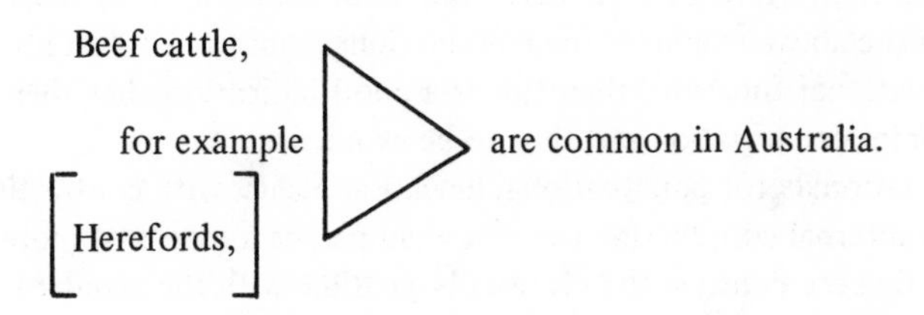

The only way that "Herefords" can qualify as an additive modifier is for us to provide extra words beyond the inflectional "be": "Beef cattle [include] Herefords". It perverts the sense of this classification relationship to say "Beef cattle [are] Herefords", because there are many beef cattle that are not Herefords. However, we can say that "Herefords [are] beef cattle". "For example Herefords" is parenthetical, a subordinate part of the primary assertion, and consequently we have been reluctant to diagram "beef cattle" as the additive modifier. Yet in listing the component assertions of this sentence, we have no options but these:

Beef cattle are common in Australia.
Herefords are common in Australia.
Herefords [are] beef cattle.

For no very clear reason some continuing and contrasting conjunctions (e. g. *that is*, *indeed*, *in addition*, *however*, *nevertheless*) can occur both between assertions and within the second assertion:

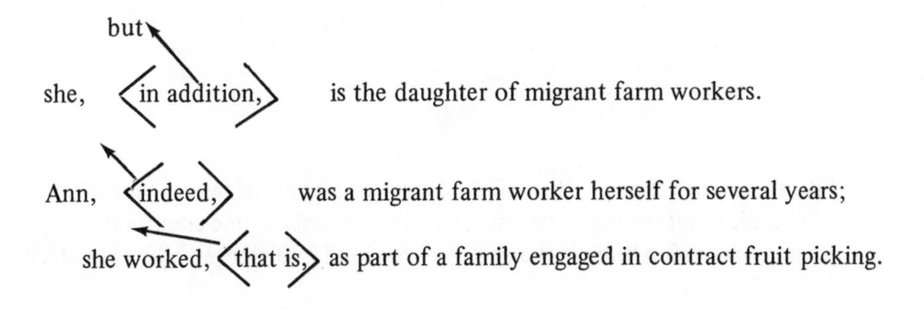

There should be reasons why in individual instances we might prefer one position over its alternative, but in general the two are equally acceptable. We assume that the deviation from standard form, of putting the conjunction within the second assertion, is for some purpose – presumably for emphasis, for a punctuational purpose. And consequently we diagram the conjunction as such in addition to indicating its standard conjunctional position by means of an arrow. If in the above examples the conjunctions seem to manifest no very clear punctuational function, then this is a good indication that their positioning is a pointless deviation and thus to be avoided.

A more likely rationale for punctuational deviation occurs with contrasting conjunctions. An internal conjunction can, for example, be a means of more precisely pinpointing the contrast than is usually possible with the standard inter-assertional conjunction:

Her faith in him is unbounded;

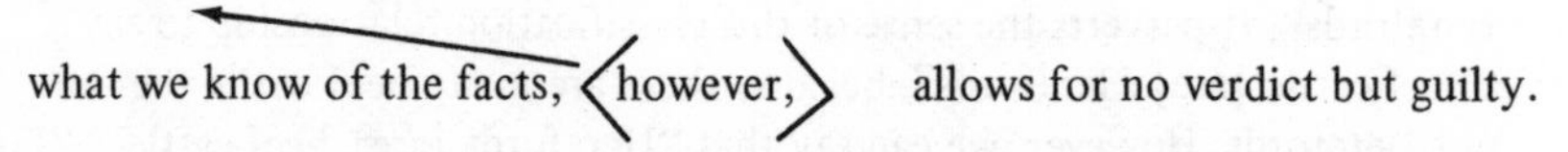

In the general sense the contrast here is between the first independent clause and the second independent clause, and this justifies us in labeling "however" an inter-assertional conjunction and employing the arrow to indicate its standard position between the two assertions. But more precisely, the contrast is between "faith" and "facts". A very close variation of this sentence could be achieved by means of underlining:

Her faith in him is unbounded;
however,
what we know of the *facts* allows for no verdict but guilty.

A similar kind of rationale for displacing a contrasting conjunction to a later position is manifested in this sentence:

The *Titanic* was called unsinkable.

She sank, nevertheless.

Like the above example, this one has a contrasting set of terms: "unsinkable" and "sank". But we might be able to carry our analysis one step further. By placing the conjunction at the end of the second assertion we allow the starkness of "she sank" to speak in large measure for itself; the "nevertheless" does little more than keep our pair of sentences from sounding paradoxical. We would say then that "nevertheless" here is characterized as redundant just as well as punctuational; its function is not merely to underline "sank" but also to show the writer's awareness of the obvious contrast between his two sentences.

The additional function of these punctuational or redundant conjunctions tends to be reflected in the punctuation. Whereas *and* and *but* are simply preceded by commas in compound sentences, conjunctions that can occur in different positions tend to be preceded by semi-colons and followed by commas when inter-assertional and similarly to be set off by punctuation fore and aft when intra-assertional. And in the same vein, some two-part or separable conjunctions are more heavily punctuated than are ordinary inter-assertional ones:

On the one hand,
you refuse to fight for the common defense;
on the other hand,
you incite others to aggressive violence.

But this cannot be called a general rule.

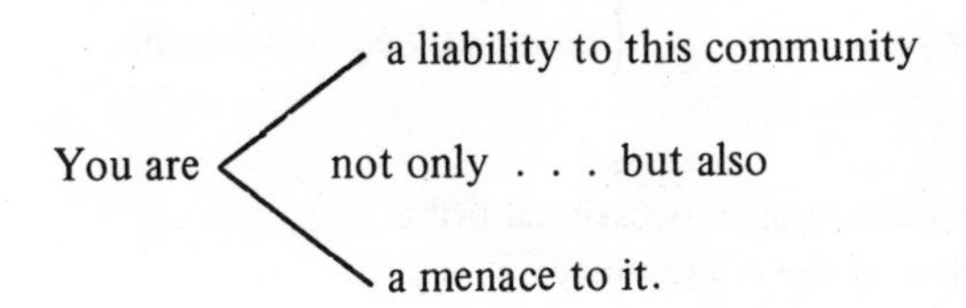

This difference in punctuation is not a result of the difference between compound structure and parallel structure, as we can see when the parallel structure is recast as compound:

Not only

are you a liability to the community;

you are (also) a menace to it.

This is an entirely idiomatic sentence, but what accounts for the displaced subject in the first assertion and the displaced conjunction in the second is not at all clear. Nor is it clear why the *but* drops out in the compound version.

Yet what remains constant, and thus makes the two sentences semantically identical, is the same two component assertions ("You are a liability to the community". "You are a menace to it".) linked in a continuing inter-assertional relationship.

A relatively uncommon possibility for joining assertions by means of conjunctions was briefly touched on in the discussion of compound sentences.[1] This is the inserting of both the conjunction and the second assertion into the middle of the first assertion. The conjunction within the first assertion may introduce either an independent clause or an additive modifier:

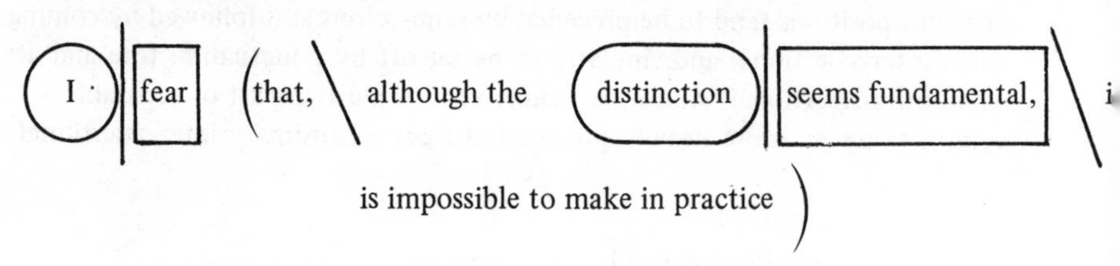

The distinction seems fundamental.
I fear that it is impossible to make in practice.

The mayor, [although a pillar of the community,] is not above taking an occasional bribe.

The mayor is not above taking an occasional bribe.
The mayor [is] a pillar of the community.

In order to be able to distinguish the two independent clauses in this rather unusual kind of relationship, we introduce the pair of slash marks. And, because both clauses have complete and independent subjects and predicates (as contrasted to the additive modifiers), we diagram each clause separately.

A variation of the additive modifier above is to begin the sentence with the conjunction; this is possible with both continuing and contrasting conjunctions:

[In addition to being a movie star,] he is a part-time preacher.

[Despite having had a heart attack,] he continues to work full time.

Our diagraming system makes it almost impossible to separate out the conjunctions that are part of additive modifiers, but there are conjunctions here nonetheless. And to make the point that continuing and contrasting inter-assertional relationships cannot be implied as easily as they can be designated, notice what happens to the above sentences when the conjunctions are removed:

Being a movie star, he is a part-time preacher.

Having had a heart attack, he continues to work full time.

Here are the same pairs of assertions but with a clearly implied causal relationship resulting from the participial forms of *be* and *have*. Implied inter-assertional relationships, common though they are, can be a definite source of trouble; and while we can probably agree on rejecting the above sentences as illogical simply on semantic grounds, this would not be true of all such sentences. The following two sentences could be reasonably interpreted in two different ways depending on whether the conjunctions were present or not:

In addition to being a priest, he is a man of discretion.

Despite having lost the election, she really understands precinct politics.

He may simply happen to be a priest *and* a man of discretion; he could still be a priest and indiscrete. However, he may be a priest and *therefore* a man of discretion, because discretion is a characteristic of priests. She may really understand precinct politics *even though* she lost the election; or she may really understand precinct politics *because* she lost the election. On the one hand, one could reasonably claim that losing the election demonstrated a lack of understanding of precinct politics; on the other hand, one could reasonably claim that only those scarred in battle can really understand precinct politics.

The category of implied inter-assertional relations of the continuing and contrasting sort is almost too amorphous to characterize. Every assertion is in one respect or another both like and unlike the previous assertion. In the absence of a context to aid the interpretation, the following sentence could just as well exemplify continuing or contrasting inter-assertional relationship:

My older brother is in the army;

my younger brother is in the navy.

If the primary point is that both brothers are in the military, then the two independent clauses could be joined by *and*. But the emphasis might just as well be the contrast between older en younger and army and navy – in which case the two independent clauses would be joined by *but*.

Not all such compound sentences would be so inter-assertionally ambiguous. In the following sentence the contrast between "professor" and "pickpocket" seems more crucial than any of the similarities, and the absence of a conjunction is no obstacle to interpreting the inter-assertional relationship as contrast:

My older brother is a professor;

my younger brother is a pickpocket.

However, such easily interpreted contrast in the absence of a conjunction is not common. The great bulk of unmarked inter-assertional relationships are continuing. For example, the assertions in this paragraph that are not introduced by conjunctions ("In the following . . . " and "The great bulk . . .") are both related to the preceding assertions as continuations.

In the absence of conjunctions, it is sometimes possible to establish a continuing relationship simply by means of punctuation. A common use of the colon is as a shorthand substitute for a continuing conjunction. The first two paragraphs of this chapter happen to have been introduced by sentences using colons as inter-assertional continuing links:

The concept of inter-assertional relations is very much a transitional notion: it is a matter of grammar insofar as multiple assertions are integrated into single sentences; it is a matter of rhetoric insofar as multiple sentences are involved.

The literal meaning of an assertion is independent of its structure: the same assertion can appear as an independent sentence, as part of a compound sentence, as part of a parallel structure, or as an additive modifier.

Usually the colon introduces multiple items (as in the above examples), but the link may simply be between two assertions. From the third paragraph in this chapter comes such an example:

But relativity is always a factor: a statement that in one context might be thought to be belaboring the obvious might be thought too cryptic in another context.

To conclude our discussion of continuing and contrasting conjunctions we need to refer back to our discussion of unitary parallel, where *and* functioned as a link between assertionally unseparable items. But not only are there examples like "Tom and his wife are a pleasant couple", there are examples that employ contrasting conjunctions:

If you are always asking questions but never listening to the answers, your teachers will cease to take you seriously.

And and *but* in unitary parallels present no great problem of analysis, because we can recognize that similar things are being linked (e. g. two people or conditions) even though these are not assertions. However, in the next section, where we examine explanatory or causal relationships, we will find ourselves obliged to explain the presence of what seem to be concluding and supporting conjunctions in contexts that are not so clearly made up of two similar things.

B. EXPLANATORY – CONCLUDE AND SUPPORT

To continue where the previous section left off is to take up explanatory relationships at the most difficult point. But to do so is to emphasize the inconsistencies in traditional conceptions of conjunctions. Just as our rather unorthodox list of conjunctions includes all words and phrases that can function in a similar fashion, so we exclude from consideration as conjunctions words on that list when in given instances they do not strictly speaking link two similar things.

The prime example of this on-and-off-again conception of conjunctions is the traditional 'coordinate' conjunction *for*. And this on-and-off nature is unrelated to the traditional distinction between 'coordinate' and 'subordinate' conjunctions – in this case between *for* and *because*. In the following sentence the two conjunctions seem to be strictly synonymous:

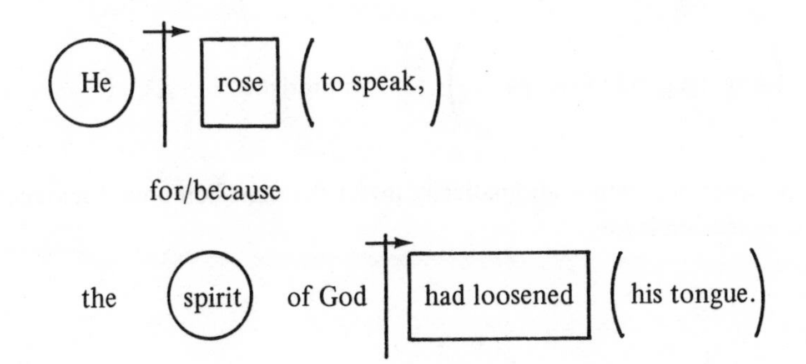

Similarly, *for* and *because of* are quite interchangeable in the next example, but with the crucial difference that they do not function as conjunctions:

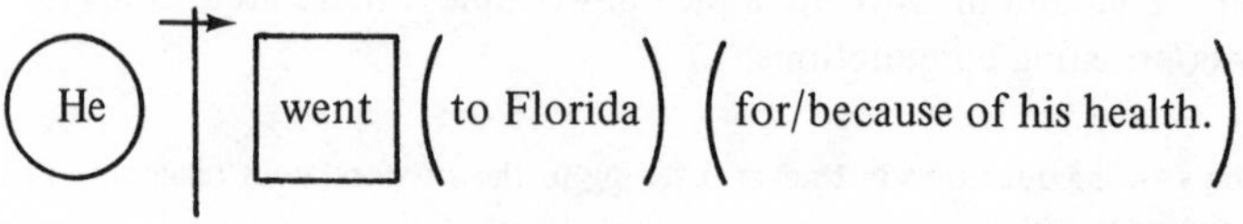

He | went (to Florida) (for/because of his health.)

The assertion modifier "for/because of his health" in the second sentence functions the same as the assertion modifier "to speak" in the first sentence: in answer to the question, "Why? " In neither case is there an additional separable assertion, as there are, for example, in these sentences:

He rose,
because
he wanted to speak

He went to Florida,
because
his health was deteriorating in the cold winters.

The position of such assertion modifiers – either at the beginning or the end of the sentence – is not a factor in determining the meaning. Just as we can idiomatically invert the above compound examples

Because
his health was deteriorating in the cold winters,
he went to Florida.

we can invert an independent structure:

I will resign (for the good of the party.)

(For the good of the party,) I will resign.

However, we cannot idiomatically invert the same compound sentence if the conjunction is *for*:

* For his health was deteriorating in the cold winters,
he went to Florida.

This is simply a matter of idiom, however, not of ascertaining the number and relationship of the assertions.

As we were forced to admit in the previous chapter, ascertaining the number and relationship of assertions in such sentences can be a problem. We need to return at this point to the problem we left hanging there – the difficulty of deciding whether a sentence such as the following does or does not contain multiple assertions and does or does not imply a causal relationship:

Living among the natives, I came to understand their point of view.

In the strictest sense, this construction must be judged ambiguous. A slight modification in one direction or the other will result either in two assertions linked causally or in a single assertion with an "Under what circumstances?" assertion modifier:

[As a result of living among the natives,] I came to understand their point of view.

(While living among the natives,) I came to understand their point of view.

Undeniably, these two sentences are very close in meaning; indeed, in some contexts they could function synonymously. But when questioned in the most precise manner about the exact relationship of the "living among" to the "came to understand", there are two distinct possibilities: (1) that the former is the cause of the latter, (2) that the former is simply the context of the latter. We are by no means obliged to commit ourselves on such a difficult topic as the nature of causality or to posit specific causal relationships. The grammar provides quite acceptable means of making associations that stop short of asserting causality. However, this is not to claim that the two are essentially the same. The use of the causal conjunction ("as a result of") makes, rightly or wrongly, an unequivocal claim about a certain kind of relationship. The assertion modifier ("while living among the natives") may or may not be taken to imply such a relationship, but it does not imply it necessarily and it does not assert it.

Just as *for* may or may not function as a supporting conjunction, *as a result of* may or may not function as a concluding conjunction. In the above example there are two assertions: I came to understand their point of view. I lived among the natives. But in the examples below there is just one assertion:

(As a result of the drought,) he lost his farm.

(Considering her qualifications,) Mary should have been promoted.

Causality is an explicit part of the meaning in these two sentences, but there are no conjunctions and no inter-assertional relationships. Whether we say in general that these assertion modifiers answer the question, "Under what circumstances? " or in particular, "Under what causal circumstances? " there is no way of deriving multiple assertions. The fundamental principle remains in effect: referring to something is not the same as asserting its existence.

The corollary of this principle is that the concept of conjunction is strictly a functional one, not a matter of word classes or parts of speech. It makes no difference whether "as a result" is replaced by "because". Conjunctions exist only as the means of joining two or more similar elements.

We have already noted the special flexibility of *because* and *therefore* as conjunctions – occurring not just before and between but also within:

Because
you are on probation,
you cannot take this course.

She left
because
we arrived.

He is the librarian;
therefore,
he gets a sabbatical.

Joe, because he lost, had to pay.

She won the case;
she therefore collected.

It is also possible to have a separable conjunction of sorts with causal inter-assertional relationships, but this is less common than with continuing and contrasting, and more obviously redundant. *Because* and *therefore* can be used together in the same sentence but with no different meaning than if either one or the other is used alone:

> Because
> you are a three-time loser,
> I must therefore sentence you to life imprisonment.

And indeed, in this particular case, the absence of both conjunctions would have little effect on the inter-assertional relationship, whose causal meaning is quite clear simply from an understanding of the individual assertions. But however satisfactory is the implied relationship in this sentence, causal or explanatory relationships are much less likely to be left without explicit conjunctions than are continuing relationships. What can be linked as conclusion or support by means of a conjunction is often interpreted simply as continuing in the absence of such conjunctions. In contrast to the significance of conjunctions in supporting and concluding relationships is the complete lack of conjunctions for our next category.

C. RHETORICAL – QUESTION AND ANSWER

The lack of conjunctions for rhetorical relationships is in large measure explained by the fact that the relationship of an assertion to the explicit question elicited by it and the relationship of an explicit question to an assertion answering it are not strictly speaking inter-assertional. It is one thing to posit implicit questions as rhetorical links between the assertions of a composition; the implied question is what is inter-assertional. It is quite another thing to speak of an explicit question as an assertion, to be related to another assertion by means of a conjunction. Still, insofar as explicit questions do occur in compositions, and insofar as they do function as some sort of continuation of the assertional presentation, we are obliged to analyze in some way their relationship with assertions that come before and after. The final step of our *grammatical* study, then, before embarking on the *rhetorical* study, is to analyze explicit questioning. Yet, so fine is the line between explicit and implicit questioning that we have designated this category of inter-'assertional' relationships "rhetorical". In our generative rhetoric a rhetorical question is an implicit one for the purpose of eliciting an explicit answer. Traditionally a rhetorical question is an explicit one not intended to elicit an explicit answer. Both are useful concepts; and for the present purpose, what the two have in common – meaning as question – is more important than the difference of implicit or explicit manifestations.

The following short paragraph provides a minimum context necessary for analyzing questions and answers. Unlike the inter-assertional relationships, which could all be exemplified within single sentences, questions require a larger context.

What has become of the doctrine of original sin? Undoubtedly, all men are sinners, but is this to be taken as proof of original sin? Some still claim that to assert the one and to deny the other is inconsistent. This is not my position or the position of most modern theologians. The current consensus is not in accord with the traditional doctrine. Can we assume, then, that this consensus indicates the eventual disappearance of this once widely held belief? Who can predict the future of religion?

Here are the individual assertions and questions:

What has become of the doctrine of original sin?

Undoubtedly, all men are sinners,
but
is this to be taken as proof of original sin?

Some still claim that { to assert the one / and / to deny the other } is inconsistent.

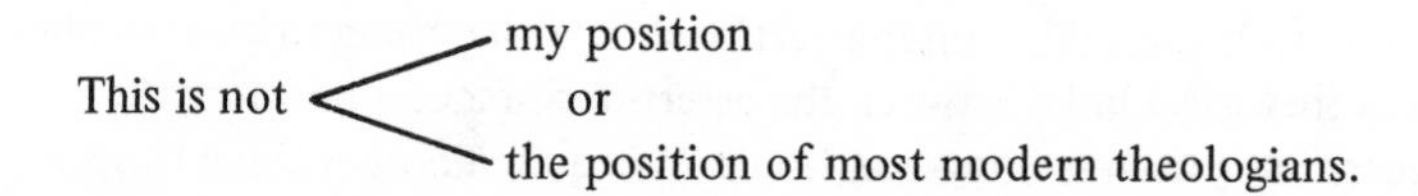

The current consensus is not in accord with the traditional doctrine.

Can we assume, then, that such theological consensus indicates the
eventual disappearance of this [once widely held] belief?

Who can predict the future of religion?

Admittedly this is extreme and probably unjustified use of rhetorical questions, but it is not conspicuously unidiomatic. And if we assume that there is nothing unidiomatic in the occurrence of individual questions here, we can infer several things about explicit questioning and answering. To begin at the beginning, we see that our previous assumption about questions arising out of previous assertions is not necessary. Although it is unusual, a question can introduce a composition; the answer or answers to the introductory question become the composition itself. Most of the assertions in this paragraph, either individually or collectively, answer this question. In brief, the answer is that the doctrine is fading but still alive among a minority.

Thus, a second point to make is that explicit answers are not simply the assertions that immediately follow. Indeed, in this case the assertion that follows the first question is one of the few in the paragraph that does not obviously provide an answer; it rather sets the stage for others that do. In contrast to this is the second question. The assertion that follows immediately upon "is this to be taken as proof of original sin? " may not be the complete answer, but it is a direct and obvious answer.

However, unlike both of these questions (which do elicit explicit answers in one place or another), the third and fourth questions are not answered. But even here there is a further distinction. Obviously, a composition that ends with a question is not providing any answer. Questions are sometimes left unanswered because the answer seems too obvious to mention. Thus in our discussion of implication we interpreted this question as all but expressing its own answer:

Why do you, the least qualified, claim the greatest reward? [2]

The clear, although not necessary, implication is that you should not claim the greatest reward. Similarly in our last question: we can assume that the answer is that no one can predict the future of religion. But this inference can only be made on the basis of what goes before, because nothing comes after.

However, with the question that precedes the final question there is a bit of a difference. No assertion follows it, so we cannot point to an explicit answer. The question "Can we assume, then, that such theological consensus indicates the eventual disappearance of this once widely held belief? " is quite an open and reasonable one. Nothing about it indicates that an answer could not reasonably go either way. In this respect it is unlike the question about reward and the question about religion. This would have been an unsatisfactory place to break off the composition – with a legitimate but unanswered question. But if we can infer from the next question that no one can predict the future of religion, then it would seem to follow that we *cannot* assume that such theological consensus indicates the eventual disappearance of this once widely held belief. The two concluding questions ask very much the same thing, but the one does so in a specific, qualified, business-

-like manner, while the other does so in a very general, off-hand, either/or manner. Surely one can make reasonable assumptions about historical trends, but just as surely one cannot predict the future of religion.

The final inference about questions to be made from this paragraph is that they can be introduced by conjunctions and even be linked in a sentence with assertions. "Undoubtedly, all men are sinners", is followed by a question that is linked to it by "but". This sentence ends with the question mark of the question rather than the period of the sentence – probably because question marks are thought to include periods. What we do not find as a matter of course is sentences that begin with questions and end with assertions. Question marks occur only rarely within a sentence, and when they do it is usually with a question that is inclosed in parentheses – as in a 'slash mark' compound sentence.

In addition to this compounding of question and assertion, we have seen two examples of questions that contain assertions in the form of additive modifiers. "once widely held" and "the least qualified" create internal assertions, but not within other assertions.

To give more attention than this to overt rhetorical questions would be to over-emphasize their importance and frequency. Indeed, we have already erred by focusing on the more unusual rather than the usual manifestations. If we decided to eliminate from our paragraph all questions but one, we would probably retain the penultimate one, because it is so obviously and reasonably elicited by the previous assertion. An assertion about a consensus is followed by a request for further analysis of it.

This is the very sort of question that we will be employing in our implied dialogs for the purpose of generating compositions. To show the standard relationship of assertion-question-answer at its most useful best, here is a modified version of the end of the paragraph:

The current consensus is not in accord with the traditional doctrine. Can we assume, then, that such theological consensus indicates the eventual disappearance of this once widely held belief? Probably not, because predicting the future of religion has proven to be a hopeless task.

And because any use of overt questioning in a composition is an unusual feature, we should be prepared to convert explicit dialog into more economical implicit dialog:

The current consensus is not in accord with the traditional doctrine. We cannot assume, however, that such theological consensus indicates the eventual disappearance of this once widely held belief, because predicting the future of religion has proven to be a hopeless task.

At this point, we are no longer even on the borderline between grammar and rhetoric. We have crossed the line.

NOTES

1 See p. 98.
2 See p. 181.

PART II

GENERATIVE RHETORIC

7. GENERATING A COMPOSITION

We have of necessity devoted six chapters to semantic grammar – to the elements of composition – but now we need to establish the generativeness and the rhetoricalness of our subject. Our claim is that generative rhetoric is considerably more generative, more helpful in the actual inventing or creating or composing of discourse, than any generative grammar has proven itself to be. There are many different systems of linguistic analysis, of breaking down into constituent elements already existing compositions. But it does not follow, and it has not followed, that these are necessarily a help in creating compositions from scratch. However, a system that is truly generative will of necessity also work in the opposite direction: it will be analytical and descriptive as well as generative.

There is also a philosophical or epistemological dimension to the argument for generative rhetoric. Dialog is not just a practical help, it is also a theoretical necessity when meaning is taken to be a matter of interpretation rather than reference. Positivistic conceptions of meaning emphasize agreement, the one-to-one correlation of linguistic symbol and referent. But rhetorical conceptions of meaning emphasize disagreement, the give and take between speakers as they attempt to clarify the differences that inevitably manifest themselves when people address each other. Like the Greek Sophist, the generative rhetorician remains sceptical that unequivocal truth and falsity are the basic criteria of linguistic meaning; he emphasizes instead matters of degree, and not so much degrees of truth and falsity as of meaningfulness.[1] This meaningfulness is always and necessarily a varying mixture of agreement and disagreement and thus never complete. What is essential to interpreting the meaning of an utterance is the disagreement that defines or delimits a statement.

Socrates was on firm ground in taking the actual dialog situation of oral communication to be the norm. The advantages gained by written discourse (great economy, accurate preservation, widespread dissemination, unrestricted length) are purchased by sacrifices in the possibility for step-by-step interruption and cross-examination. The possibilities for sustained nonsense are much greater in written discourse than in oral dialog. Dialog, whether actual or implied, is no answer to ultimate questions about the nature of language meaning, but it may very well be the *sine qua non* of language meaning because it is the "inter" that makes interpretation possible. Meaning is not constructed, not built up by adding one symbol or verbal unit to another; it is bargained for between two or more people who have enough in common to make discussion possible but who have enough disagreement to make progression inevitable. The interpretation of meaning is not like a trip down a paved highway from one city to the next; it is like an exploration expedition seeking a passage through only partially surveyed country.

Dialog is generative because questions are the probe that uncovers the inevitable weakness, incompleteness, inconsistency in what is stated. And no matter how successful is the answer to a question, the material of the answer creates new weakness, incompleteness, inconsistency – and on it goes. Once a beginning has been made, there is no unequivocal ending to a dialog. We cannot hope to determine precisely, ultimately, quintessentially what something is or what it means, but we can always do a more adequate, more accurate, job of delimiting what it is not and what it cannot mean. This is the epistemological theory behind generative rhetoric, and while it promises much less than some linguistic conceptions, it is more likely to make good on what it does promise than those that claim to be able to solve the mind-body problem or to invent a translation machine.

One of the fundamental promises that generative rhetoric makes is that implied dialog is really and truly generative, that it is a means of creating actual sustained compositions. Working with just the summary account given in the first chapter and with the simple one-paragraph composition analyzed there, we shall be able to do a bit of preliminary generating before analysing the grammatical foundations of a complete composition.

As with most discourse we must postulate here some kind of starting point or subject. In other times, when rhetorical exercises were more of a pedagogical staple than they have been in the twentieth century, we would have most likely settled on an abstract topic like "the nature of justice" or "the conflict between virtue and expedience". But let us be true to our times and pick a topic of current relevance and with something of a local setting. If nothing else, these factors will provide us with practice in marshalling specific information without preventing us from employing broad generalizations. Indeed, we might say that no topics are picked entirely out of thin air and that actual problems and disagreements are an important source of generativeness. The stimulus for this particular exercise then will be the growing realization that not even isolated Honolulu can ignore the growing problems of air pollution.

Air pollution in Honolulu will be our general subject, but for a specific starting point we need a full-fledged assertion. Let us envision a context in which a debate has grown up over different proposed scientific or technological solutions to the problem. Assuming this to be our context, we must ask ourselves what justifies our addressing an audience in the first place. What do we have to contribute? What question are we providing an answer to? Wherein do we disagree with something already put forward? Writing, at least of the sort worth studying because it constitutes an essential skill for a literate, democratic citizenry, is not mere self-expression but the addressing of an engaged intellect to a problem. Whether the need is to provide information, or to argue a position, or both, discourse arises out of the realization that all is not as it should be. To meet such a need with discourse is first and foremost to make an assertion. Whether we begin with a very general assertion, a very particular assertion, or something in between, our discourse has not gotten to the point where it can become self-generating until it has asserted something. Only then can the questioning begin. Here, then, is the first assertion:

a. Air pollution is now primarily a social rather than a scientific problem.

At a stroke, the author's almost unlimited options are greatly restricted. There is more than one reasonable question elicited by this assertion, but these are limited. On being confronted with this assertion, the imaginary interlocutor might reasonably ask, "What characterizes a social problem? " Or he might ask, "Why is it not a scientific problem? " Or perhaps he is troubled by "What exactly is meant by 'air pollution'? " Or the concept "primarily" may trouble him, and he would want to know "To what extent is it still a scientific problem? " The composition hangs together in the most elementary way by virtue of following one assertion by another that provides the answer to a particular implied question, and since there can usually be more than one question reasonably elicited, there can be different answers and thus different directions that the composition can go off in. A writer is obliged to decide after each assertion what question to acknowledge and what questions to ignore or defer. Indeed, the problem with implied dialog as the generating force in discourse is not that it sometimes fails to generate but that it usually over-generates: there is an embarrassment of riches, and as a result the writer is sometimes forced to make arbitrary choices as to which direction he will take when confronted by two or more equally reasonable or attractive possibilities.

Sometimes the writer can decide to answer one question and defer another until later, but this cannot be the usual course because his composition can very quickly become hydra-headed and devour itself in the futile attempt to incorporate everything in sight. However, let us begin ambitiously and decide that our opening assertion requires not only an answer to "*What characterizes a social problem?* " but also to "*Why is it not a scientific problem?* "[2] How the two answers will be integrated into a composition will not trouble us until later. What does trouble us now is the answers to provide. Having settled on a question, we usually find ourselves faced with alternative answers, or at least alternative forms of the same general answer. But at least our options are very much limited and thus more manageable than they were before we had a question to answer. In answer to the first question, let us say that:

b. At the heart of every social problem lies the question of responsibility.

and in answer to the second question, let us say that:

c. The facts are no longer at issue.

There is never one right question and usually no one right answer, so even if a dozen writers were to begin with the same opening assertion, they would hardly agree in their second assertions, and from then on would be writing significantly different compositions. A generative rhetoric does not provide the thinking on a topic; it merely provides the forms within which thinking can systematically occur. Implied dialog is a tool of thought and thus of discourse, but it is not the discourse itself. Consequently, one does not generate *the* composition but only *a* composition.

Having chosen to answer two questions, we are still obliged to decide which one to pursue and which one to defer – otherwise we would be committing ourselves to writing two parallel compositions. By saying that "the facts are no longer at issue" we are clearly drawing the line against pursuing a course of development by means of supplying detailed information as evidence to support our initial assertion. By no means all arguments are disputes over facts, and one of the initial responsibilities that a writer has is to indicate whether his argument is primarily about facts or primarily about values. The two are not mutually exclusive, but one ought to be predominant over the other, or at least the two be kept clearly separate. In characterizing a social problem, we must clearly distinguish problems of social value from scientific problems. If science is objective, disinterested, uncommitted, without social obligation, beyond good and evil, then we could say, at the risk of a certain amount of oversimplification, that responsibility is the *sine qua non* of social values. Whatever else may be involved in social problems (such as dispute over the facts) they always and fundamentally involve the need to trace responsibility, to apportion praise and blame.

Rightly or wrongly, then, our composition has chosen to view the problem of air pollution in Honolulu as an argument about social values and not as the presentation of information. It is possible that our contention about the facts could be challenged, but having taken our stand with the assertion that "the facts are no longer at issue", we have closed the line of development that marshals evidence to prove matters of fact.

At this point there should be more than the usual agreement as to the next question. And the asking of this question is likely to be a crucial point in this composition. "*Has responsibility for this problem been established yet?* " But whatever measure of agreement there is on the question, there is likely to be the widest diversity in the possible answers to provide. And it will not be surprising, then, that a single answer will not suffice in the composition. Just as an assertion can elicit two or more questions to which the writer feels obliged to provide answers, a question can elicit two or more answers. This will be especially true if answers to the question are to serve as the means of developing the composition. In answering our question about responsibility we might begin cautiously with a negative comment about one commonly alleged culprit:

d. The American automobile industry refuses to admit any responsibility for the smog that grips every major urban center.

But either here or further on in the composition we are likely to have more to say about this explicit denial of responsibility. For the moment, however, let us not concern ourselves with long-range developing of the composition and concentrate on the assertion-by-assertion generating.

Here again there are multiple lines of questioning that could arise. We can choose to raise more than one, as we did earlier, but only one can be pursued in any detail. The first question might be a call for some indication of what it is that makes air pollution such a danger in the first place. "*What is so serious about smog as to raise the issue of responsibility?* " A second line of inquiry might question the putting forth of the American automobile industry as a possible culprit because of the seeming disparity between a problem claimed to be so large and a culprit that is just a single industry. "*How could a single industry have such a large responsibility?* " A third question might ask why the industry's position is not as defensible a one as any on a matter open to so many different interpretations. "*Is the industry not entitled to its own opinion?* "

In answer to the first, let us say that:

e. The smog that grips every major urban center is strangling.

Obviously this calls for an answer to the question, "*What is meant by 'strangling'?* " But this question is likely to elicit the same sort of answer as to the question, "What are these facts that are no longer at issue? " And though we have disclaimed any intention to *marshal evidence*, we shall later be taking on the obligation to *provide examples* of that information now claimed to be common knowledge. So for the moment let us simply leave our metaphor to stand as a short-hand statement of the evils of smog.

In answer to the second question, let us say that:

f. The American automobile industry is the richest industry in the world.

And, to further emphasize the magnitude of its worldly position, let us add, in answer to the same question, that:

g. The American automobile industry is richer indeed than most countries.

Obviously these two assertions cry out for a less redundant form than two independent sentences. But while these will undoubtedly be combined by parallel structure in the finished composition, they must preserve their independent status with their own subjects and predicates as long as we are confining ourselves to the level of the assertion. Each assertion requires for formal and semantic completeness a separate subject and a separate predicate; otherwise it could not stand as a sentence. The fifty individual assertions that will eventually comprise this composition will prove to be reducible to approximately half that many sentences when integrated by means of complex sentence structure. Even in our simple paragraph on the problem of composition, four sentences with a total of 85 words yielded seven assertions with a total of 100 words.

In answer to the third question, asking why the industry is not entitled to its own opinion, let us return to our key point about the *facts* being no longer at issue and characterize the industry position as mere *opinion*:

c. The facts are no longer at issue.

In the final integrated composition we may or may not wish to repeat this point; we may wish to make it the third assertion or we may wish to make it the eighth one. Here we only note that it is the answer both to "Why is air pollution not a scientific problem? " and "Is the automobile industry not entitled to its own opinion? " Generative rhetoric is linear in theory, but in practice there is inevitable crisscrossing and backtracking. One reason for thinking that our assertion about the facts might well be postponed in the final composition is that it seems to require, if not all the facts themselves, at least some examples, some indication as to what sort of thing is being referred to. But before giving such an indication, let us continue a bit longer the line of discussion concerning the automobile industry's opinion about the matter.

If the facts are indeed no longer at issue, we would expect that the industry was alone in its opinion. Part of the proof that this denial of responsibility is just special pleading on the part of the culprits would be the absence of concurring opinion from other quarters. Thus a reasonable question to ask of an assertion that something is no longer at issue is the possible diversity of opinion. "*Does anyone share the industry's opinion?* " Here there is not much option in answering. To have claimed that there is no longer an issue is to claim that only obvious instances of special pleading mar the unanimity of informed opinion on the subject. We may incorporate more or less additional matter by way of complex modification, but the heart of our answer must be of this sort:

h. Only the culprits pretend that the internal combustion engine is not the prime producer of those toxic elements that have become a permanent part of our cities.

No more need be said after this unequivocal answer, although this is not to claim that the answer is unquestionably true but only that it has been clearly and unequivocally laid down as one of the givens in this composition. No composition, no matter how detailed, can escape the need to establish a starting point or series of postulates that make further discussion possible but are not themselves discussed.

Now for the facts, which are always infinite and thus reviewable only in summary form. We, however, will be doing even less than summary justice to them because our only motive is to indicate by a few examples what sort of things we are claiming as given beyond reasonable dispute. Here are seven assertions in answer to the question, "*What are these facts?* "

i. In the past decade, numerous scientific studies have demonstrated beyond any reasonable doubt that air pollution has increased in proportion to the number of automobiles on the road.
j. The number of automobiles on the road is growing.
k. In the past decade, numerous scientific studies have demonstrated beyond any reasonable doubt that air pollution has increased in proportion to the consumption of gasoline by their engines.
l. The consumption of gasoline by their engines is rising.
m. Their engines are increasingly powerful.
n. In the past decade, numerous scientific studies have demonstrated beyond any reasonable doubt that automobile exhaust has a toxic effect on the respiratory system.

What order these examples will appear in and how they will be related to each other in complex sentence structure is not our concern here, but from this list of information claimed to be no longer at issue reasonably arises the question, "*Why are these facts no longer at issue?* " Before answering this question, however, we should note that the last assertion has not only provided us with an example of facts no longer at issue but also with an answer to the earlier question, "What is meant by 'strangling'? " "Strangling" as used here means "has a toxic effect on the respiratory system". And now, in answer to why the facts are no longer at issue, let us say that:

o. The numerous studies that have demonstrated in the past decade beyond any reasonable doubt that air pollution has increased in proportion to the growing number of automobiles on the road and the rising consumption of gasoline by their increasingly powerful engines and that automobile exhaust has a toxic effect on the respiratory system were conducted by universities, industry, and government.

In short, the three major sources of large-scale research projects agree about the primary cause and effect of air pollution.

This summary of the current state of scientific research is of course not gospel simply because the author says it is, and the interlocutor can always deny the truth of an assertion, but his function in generating further assertions is not very well accomplished by simple denial. The point of creating an imaginary inquisitioner is not to create an impasse but to probe for weak spots, to search for supplementary explanation, to indicate seeming inconsistency. His function is to facilitate the presentation of additional material by pointing out the implications of what has already been said. He is neither the friend nor the enemy of the writer; rather, he is the interested but uncommitted audience that will not be put off with inconsistencies and glib generalizations. The next question, then, is not likely to be a disagreement with the assertion of unanimity in universities, industry, and government but an attempt to find out how the man-in-the-street can make sense out of these high-level demonstrations. Perhaps the interlocutor is not satisfied with the correlation of "strangling" on the one hand with "demonstrated . . . by universities, industry, and government" on the other. "*Is there actually sufficient exhaust in the air now to justify the label 'strangling' for what in the laboratory is termed 'toxic effect'?* "

There is not much option here but to answer "yes" in one form or another. The questioning, however, is not simply cross-examination, not content with "yes" and "no" answers. The audience wants an explanation, some kind of tangible correlation between the two very different sounding attempts to characterize the effects of air pollution. After all, everything from mosquito bites to radiation poisoning is explained by the concept of toxic effect. Is the toxic effect claimed to result from smog anything that the man-in-the-street can verify? And the answer is, yes:

p. This effect is now obvious to even the most insensitive eye.
q. This effect is now obvious to even the most insensitive nose.
r. This effect is now obvious to even the most insensitive throat.

The sentence structure most suitable for these three assertions is not difficult to determine, nor is it difficult to see the advantage of conciseness that would result from employing one sentence with parallel structure in place of these three independent assertions.

However, our interlocutor seeks more than conciseness and is still not satisfied with the summary of the evidence. After all, garbage piled up waiting to be hauled away is obvious to even the most insensitive eye, nose, and throat. "*Is there evidence for this effect being more than merely unpleasant?*" And the answer to this will, by its very nature, also provide another example of facts no longer at issue:

s. This effect is documented by a three-hundred percent increase in urban lung-cancer cases over the past twenty years.

Dozens of questions would properly challenge this very large generalization if it were offered as proof. But this is offered only by way of explanation and with the claim that all this is now beyond dispute. A generating challenge would not simply challenge the assertion but would look instead for inconsistencies. "*If the facts are so clear to everyone else, how can the industry pretend to be innocent?*"

The answer to this will of necessity reintroduce the basic notion of responsibility. When the question was first raised ("Has responsibility for this problem been established yet?"), it was answered by the assertion that "The American automobile industry refuses to admit any responsibility for the smog that grips every major urban center". But we inferred that this was not likely to be the only answer provided to this crucial question. Here is another one:

t. The fact that the automobile manufacturers themselves have devoted increased time and money to developing an electric vehicle is an implicit admission of guilt.

And even this is not likely to be the last answer to the question of responsibility – since the answers seem to be undergoing some modification as the composition develops. While assertion "d" is about an explicit denial, assertion "t" is about an implicit admission. But rather than pursue the notion of responsibility now, let us see what other lines of questioning are open.

The newly introduced subject of the electric vehicle as a possible solution to the smog problem is likely to elicit some kind of question, perhaps seeking a reassurance that all will be right now that the rich and resourceful automobile industry has devoted itself to the problem. "*Is it not just a matter of time then until the problem is solved by the industry itself with electric vehicles?* " It is not likely that the answer to this question will be in the affirmative if "air pollution is now primarily a social rather than a scientific problem". Indeed, so obvious is the answer likely to be, that the writer may have deliberately set himself to counter a question with a question to emphasize the questionable nature of the whole line of thought that looks to technology as the panacea for social ills. Though rhetorical questions play quite a minor role in most compositions and need play no role at all, they can, when used judiciously serve as a further generating force at a key point. To employ a rhetorical question is to break out of the *implied dialog* situation and to create *actual dialog*. The danger is that the explicit question will merely be following one unanswered question with another unanswered question and thereby leave the reader even more in the dark than when he began. If, however, the writer recognizes an obligation to provide eventual answers, and does not assume that because he knows the answer to his own question his reader does too, then a rhetorical question can be useful. In this case, the interlocutor has himself asked a rather rhetorical question by clearly implying what he thinks the answer should be. To counter this glib assumption, the writer asks his own question that clearly implies its answer – an answer that makes the opposite assumption about solving the smog problem:

> Is the public, however, to wait patiently for ten or fifteen years before General Motors makes as much money from the storage battery as it does now from gasoline?

This is not an assertion, although it does imply some assertions, and it can elicit further questions. Most probably further questions will pursue this new notion of the electric vehicle as a possible solution to the smog problem, but before developing this line of discussion, we should also note that another new element has been added – the public. "Will the public wait patiently? " "Should the public wait patiently? " "Is the thing waited for worth the waiting? " This sort of question is likely to be a factor as the composition develops, especially if the notion of responsibility continues to be pursued.

But for the moment, let us simply introduce this kind of consideration and then go back to the subject of electric vehicles. "*Is the public likely to wait patiently?* "

u. The public is docile.

Perhaps there is some connection between the public being docile and the kind of future solution promised by the electric vehicle. Several different questions could bring this out; as likely as any is a question inquiring into the writer's implied dislike of the automobile industry's attempt to solve the smog problem with an electric vehicle. "*Is there something wrong with the electric vehicle as a proposed solution?* " A possible answer, of the most cryptic, metaphoric sort, is that:

v. The electric vehicle is a red herring.

This assertion, whatever may be its precise meaning, is also an answer to the earlier question of whether it is not just a matter of time before the problem is solved by the industry itself with electric vehicles.

"Red herring" is a traditional, precise metaphor that in general needs no explaining. It is used of deliberate attempts to mislead, decoy, throw off the correct track. To drag a red (i. e. old and smelly) herring across the trail is to so confuse the bloodhounds with a new but irrelevant scent that the quarry escapes. But in particular cases this metaphor is by no means always self-explanatory. Thus, the next question is almost sure to be, "*How is it a red herring?* " The answer in this case will probably take more than one assertion because the metaphor of "red herring" is not so obviously related to electric vehicles as, for example, the metaphor of "strangling" was related to having a toxic effect on the respiratory system.

w. Its practical development is dependent on knowledge the automobile industry does not now possess.
x. While we wait, the problem grows steadily worse.

The accusation that something is a red herring imputes devious intentions, but it stops short of claiming complete wrong-headedness. There is usually something about a red herring that makes it seem plausible; this plausibility is just what makes it so effective as a distraction. The next question might well be an attempt to find that measure of plausibility in the electric vehicle. "*Is there any merit at all in this proposal?* "

y. Perhaps today's problem could be solved by electric vehicles.

"*Isn't the project worth pursuing, then?*"

z. If we allow it to go unchecked for another dozen years, far more drastic measures will be necessary.

This last assertion restates the point made just two assertions earlier and thereby indicates that one of the basic themes of the composition will be that time is running out. Still, every advocate urges that time is running out on the problem for which he has the solution. Quite a proper retort is to question whether ill-considered immediate action isn't likely to do more harm than good. "*Isn't it better to delay than to go off half-cocked?*" The answer can hardly be other than has already been repeatedly emphasized:

aa. There is no justification for delay.

"*What is there justification for?*"

bb. That which is a demonstrable and pervasive public menace is the proper subject for immediate legislative action.

"*Specifically what would be a proper subject for such action?*"

cc. Surely a health menace as serious as smog qualifies for such action.

Now we see that the composition has taken a new turn with the introduction of the notion of electric vehicles. What began as the discussion of a problem is now the discussion of possible solutions and kinds of solutions. Delayed technological solutions in general and electric vehicles in particular are being opposed, and immediate legislative solutions are advocated. Quite probably, then, the questioning will now pass on to consideration of the smog problem viewed in terms of restrictive legislation. And, since so much emphasis has been placed in general on the danger of delay, a question might well ask for an estimate of these dangers. "*What are the consequences of postponing legislative action?*"

dd. Unless legal restrictions are widely applied and rigorously enforced in the early stages of contamination, urban congestion becomes so great that the price of purifying the air is destruction of the city.

Some support for this claim, or at least an explanation of it, is clearly in order. It ought to be indicated, for instance, whether this is a prediction of a state of affairs not previously actualized or an inference drawn from already existing situations. "*What is the evidence for this?* "

ee. Los Angeles has been permanently contaminated.
ff. New York City has been permanently contaminated.

"*How was this allowed to happen?* "

gg. Legislative action was too little.
hh. Legislative action was too late.

If we were writing a book on the subject, or even an article, then all kinds of further questions would properly follow from this: "Are these the only cities? " "What is meant by 'permanently contaminated'? " "What sort of action was taken? " "How does one know what is enough action taken soon enough? " But since our editorial sized composition of fifty assertions is already more than half finished, we must push on to more pressing considerations that will lead us directly to our conclusion.

The questioning has led us from a consideration of the problem to a consideration of solutions – first in general, and now, very likely, in particular. Having argued in general for legislative solutions rather than technological, and pointing out that for some cities it is already too late for a solution short of destroying the cities, an obvious question is, "*Where is there still time to act?* " At this point we clarify whether the composition is primarily about the smog problem in general or the smog problem in particular:

ii. Here in Honolulu we must profit from their mistakes.

Now this answer seems to require a bit of explanation; after all, most people would think the differences between Honolulu and the giant mainland cities more significant than the similarities. "*What makes Honolulu comparable to Los Angeles and New York City?* " But equally called for is some indication of what the specific consequences are likely to be if immediate legislative action is not forthcoming. "*What will become of our problem if we do not act now?* " Answering the second question first, let us say that:

jj. If we continue to rely on the trade winds to ventilate our island, we will soon find the air as unpleasantly congested as the land.

Here is an assertion particularly conspicuous for containing a couple of very clearly implied assertions as part of the restrictive modification: "We have in the past relied on the trade winds to ventilate our island". "The land is already unpleasantly congested".

With this new notion of congestion, it is reasonable to expect some question raised about it. "*What accounts for such congestion?*" And the answer to this question can also serve as the answer to the question deferred above about what Honolulu has in common with Los Angeles and New York City:

kk. Our island is over-populated.

Here is another new notion, and one that could easily lead into a whole series of interesting and significant questions and answers. But more important even than the explanation of the problem in terms of over-population is following out the discussion that is clearly pointing to specific legislative remedies for Honolulu's smog problem. Given the very restrictive limits on the size of this composition, the next question will have to be some inquiry into the specific solution to be proposed as the means of keeping Honolulu from going the way of Los Angeles and New York City. "*What particular legislative action is needed to profit from their mistakes?*"

The answer, or answers, to this question will constitute the very heart of the composition, a composition that has increasingly revealed itself not as a disinterested presentation of a general problem, but as an argument for a specific course of action:

ll. We need laws, today, that will limit horsepower on all internal combustion vehicles.
mm. We need laws, today, that will discourage unnecessary driving by imposing increased ownership taxes.
nn. We need laws, today, that will discourage unnecessary driving by imposing increased use taxes.

There is hardly a statement of any significance that cannot be misconstrued in one way or another. If these three assertions are the focus of the composition, then we will do well to try and foresee the most likely misunderstanding of them. "*Isn't to advocate this to endanger the benefits of a mobile society?*" One of the most useful means of generating further elements in a composition, especially in an argument, is to raise and then dispose of possible misunderstandings of what one has already said:

oo. This is not to imply that we can do without the benefits of a mobile society.

pp. This is not to imply that we should do without the benefits of a mobile society.

"*What, then, is it to imply?*"

qq. This is simply to acknowledge that we have reached the point where we have more to lose than to gain unless we make a concerted effort to control the machine whose faulty design and indiscriminate use has resulted in a growing menace to urban America.

With the stating and explaining of the conclusion being argued for as the best solution to the problem, the composition, especially one as short as an editorial, could quite properly conclude. But implied as part of the complex restrictive modification in the last assertion is a very significant admission – so significant, in fact, as to reopen the entire question of responsibility. Our most alert and perspicuous interlocutor will hardly overlook this new factor. "*Is this to acknowledge, then, that the machine is only a partial cause of the problem?*" Having gone this far, the writer can hardly answer anything but "yes", although there is a variety of ways to say it. Since the previous assertion has been formulated in terms of a "point" having been reached, it is reasonable to formulate the answer also in terms of this point:

rr. When such a point is reached, a problem has two parts.

The next question can only be, "*What are these two parts?*"

ss. The two parts a problem has when such a point is reached are an initial condition and circumstances that allow that problem to flourish.

The interlocutor ruthlessly presses on – for obviously now a significant shift in emphasis is taking place in the closing stages of the composition. We already know what the initial condition is; what we want to learn is, "*What is it that allows this problem to flourish?*"

tt. The public is not just a victim.
uu. It is a victim that condones the victimizing.

The main point of the composition is probably the specific solution proposed for Honolulu's smog problem. But clearly an important subsidiary point is establishing the general question of responsibility. In the final assertions, after having concluded the discussion of solutions, the writer is now pressing home the need to act upon his proposal. And since the proposal is for legislative action, it is to the public rather than to the automobile industry that his exhortations are addressed. These exhortations are being based upon public responsibility, and thus the concluding assertions of the composition are attempting to establish this public responsibility – if not for the initial condition, at least for allowing the problem to flourish. Already the writer states that the victim has allowed himself to become a silent partner in his own persecution, and this admission is not likely to be the last one if the interlocutor presses the point. "*Is this to acknowledge, then, that the automobile industry is not the only culprit responsible for the problem?*"

vv. We have the means to oppose a great evil.

"*What follows from this?*"

ww. We have the responsibility to do so.

"*What will become of us if we do not act now?*"

xx. Either we act now or we become as culpable as the automobile industry itself.

Here concludes the composition – not necessarily, because the last word is never said on any subject, but reasonably, given the proportions of the different aspects of problem and solution and the editorial nature of the argument. Many more questions could of course be asked, but many have already been asked and answered. For example, the early question of responsibility, which was the first answered in terms of the automobile industry alone, is finally answered with the public (the perpetuator) sharing almost equal blame with the automobile industry (the perpetrator). And with this fuller analysis, and as a result of it, comes a call for action.

On more than one occasion we have conducted our analysis in terms of "problem" and "solution", and insofar as this is helpful or revealing we are going beyond an organization based simply on implied dialog. To say that the concept of implied dialog is fundamental is not to say that it is the exclusive principle of organizing discourse. Later on in putting the fifty assertions into integrated paragraphs we will have a better opportunity to discuss organization in other terms than question and answer. But for the present, we must take our newly generated assertions and apply the syntactic principles, the semantic grammar, by which these assertions may be formed into complex sentences.

NOTES

1 For a discussion of this concept of degrees of meaningfulness see "The Problem of Meaning in Linguistic Philosophy", *Logique et analyse*, 15 (1972), 609-29.
2 See p. 304 ff. for the complete dialog.

8. INTEGRATING A COMPOSITION

The fifty assertions about Honolulu's smog problem will be integrated here into less than half that many sentences, and the 800 words that comprised them will thereby be reduced to 550. The diagrams at the end of this chapter reveal how this economy is structurally possible. But conciseness is only one virtue of sentence complexity. When each assertion is written out as a separate sentence, all receive equal emphasis. Complex sentences enable the writer to say many different things that need to be said and yet to emphasize some things at the expense of others. Our integrated smog editorial should demonstrate that complex sentences, rather than leading to ambiguity, are more likely to be the means of gaining precision. Precision does not mean simply maximum detail and explicitness as expressed in an unlimited number of assertions; it also involves maximum attention to organization, to the relations among assertions. Sentences, unlike assertions, are capable of serving valuable organizational ends.

We assume as a matter of course that these assertions will not be left as simple sentences. Because the basic rule of thumb in constructing sentences is that these are organizational units made up of two or more subordinate units, we will usually not be debating whether or not an individual assertion should stand as a single sentence. The assumption is that it should be linked with at least one other assertion, and the debate will seek to determine which other assertion or assertions and with what sort of structure. Where we decide to leave an assertion to stand by itself, the burden of proof will be on us to present a special reason for doing so. But in debating the possibility of a simple sentence, as with all the other structural questions, the best that can be done is to provide *reasons* for the structure that is finally chosen; there will never be *proof* that the way chosen is the right one. Arbitrary choices are to be avoided, but there will always be reasonable competing alternatives.

In the semantical grammatical analysis that follows, much that could be said will have to be skimmed over and some even ignored if we are to cover all fifty assertions. But no matter how long it takes, what we must do is systematic justice to the crucial distinction between assertions and non-assertions and to the fundamental structural and semantic relationships between assertions.

a. Air pollution is now primarily a social rather than a scientific problem.

The conspicuous feature in this classifying assertion is the parallel construction: Air pollution is now primarily a social problem rather than a scientific problem. A consequence of this joint use of "problem" in the predicate is the potential for two assertions. A slight change in the assertion would indeed have resulted in two parallel assertions: Air pollution is now a social not a scientific problem. But this is not quite what the original assertion says. It does not claim that air pollution is *not* a scientific problem; it says only that as compared to its social nature, air-pollution is now less scientific. "Primarily" and "rather" are terms of comparison – not of opposition. A closer paraphrase of the assertion is: Air pollution is now more of a social than a scientific problem. But neither this version nor the original can be diagramed as it stands to give a separable parallel assertion. The writer is claiming only a relative relationship between social and scientific; he is not categorically denying anything. The parallel is thus necessarily unitary. The two separate assertion modifiers, "now" and "primarily", answer the two questions, "When is air pollution a social rather than a scientific problem? " and "To what extent is air pollution a social rather than a scientific problem? "

Having defined his subject, the writer continues his exposition by characterizing the larger area to which it belongs:

b. At the heart of every social problem lies the question of responsibility.

The conspicuous feature in this characteristic assertion is the inverted sentence structure – with the predicate ("lies at the heart of every social problem") coming before the subject ("the question of responsibility"). There is nothing wrong with this, but it is not usual and thus ought to have a reason for its departure from the norm. If we decide that the first two assertions ought to constitute a single sentence by virtue of some kind of semantic link, then we will not have to look far for either the common link or for the rationale behind the inverted structure of the second assertion. A fundamental concern of both the first predicate and the second predicate is "social problem". The transition from the attribute of the first assertion to the assertion modifier of the second is thus clear – especially in terms of the implied question, "*What characterizes a social problem?* " Our first sentence, then, is likely to be:

1. Air pollution is now primarily a social rather than a scientific problem, *and* at the heart of every social problem lies the question of responsibility.[1]

This is a compound sentence linked by the most common continuing conjunction. Parallel structure would have been a possibility here because of the common concern with "social problem". But parallel structure would require revising the form of the two assertions because the two attributes are still different; and in any case, this would lose the function of "social problem" as a link. Furthermore, this revising would be difficult because, although the two assertions have something in common, they are not really predicating "social problem" of two different things. A better possibility – which would, however, have required incorporating another assertion into the sentence – would have been an appositive non-restrictive modifier: Air pollution is now primarily a social rather than a scientific problem – a problem of responsibility rather than facts. A reason for not having recourse to this structure is that the assertion in the non-restrictive modifier is necessarily subordinated rather than emphasized, and it may well be that the composition calls for emphasizing both what it is that characterizes a social problem and also why smog is no longer primarily a scientific problem. Non-restrictive assertion structure is to be avoided if the assertion is an important one in the composition. A decision may be motivated primarily by what one wants to avoid or by what one wants to gain; the important point is to consider the alternatives and make a reasoned choice.

At this point we return to the old problem of deciding which of two implied questions to answer and thus which line of development to pursue. Either we answer the question, "*Why is it not a scientific problem?* " or, "*Has responsibility for this problem been established yet?* " Both would be continuing relationships, but the answer to the second question would be a more obvious continuation of the line of development already established by the previous inter-assertional relation, so let us be governed by that consideration.

d. The American automobile industry refuses to admit any responsibility for the smog that grips every major urban center.

And since the subject of this assertion is also the subject of two other assertions, let us assume that they will fit neatly into the same sentence.

f. The American automobile industry is the richest industry in the world.
g. The American automobile industry is richer indeed than most countries.

Almost as obvious is the relationship to "the smog that grips every major urban center" of the metaphoric characterizing of smog as "strangling".

e. The smog that grips every major urban center is strangling.

These three assertions share common elements with the fourth assertion, and thus readily lend themselves to parallel structure and non-restrictive modification:

2. The American automobile industry, the richest industry in the world, richer indeed than most countries, refuses to admit any responsibility for the strangling smog that grips every major urban center.

The subject of this function sentence is industry – not any and all industry, however, but only the automobile industry, and not every automobile industry either but only the American automobile industry. The steel industry, the petroleum industry, the European automobile industry, are unspecified but necessarily excluded industries. And further, the use of the definite, rather than indefinite, article makes clear that there is only one American automobile industry. There may be different American automobile companies, but the subject of this sentence is a single, undifferentiated industry. "The", "American", and "automobile" are thus restrictive modification of "industry". They exclude things that would be included by the headword if it were not so modified.

The attribute of this sentence is the function, "refuses". Unlike the subject, however, this attribute is not modified. It could have been (stubbornly refuses, consistently refuses, belligerently refuses), and this is our test for function, but in this case it is not. The statement of *what* is refused (as opposed to *how* it was refused) is a modification of the assertion as a whole.

The single long assertion modifier in this sentence, which has as its headword the infinitive "to admit", is, like most modification, primarily a means for restricting the meaning rather than for adding to it. The American automobile industry is not claimed to be refusing everything but only responsibility, and not responsibility for everything but only responsibility for smog. "Any" modifies "responsibility" inclusively; the industry not only refuses to admit *the* responsibility for smog, it refuses to acknowledge even partial responsibility for it.

"Smog" has two separate sets of modification, one non-restrictive and one restrictive. To continue our analysis of what is excluded from the assertion, let us begin with the restrictive relative clause – "that grips every major urban center". As was pointed out earlier, there need never be any ambiguity with a relative modifier. First and foremost, the punctuation convention is clearly established: Set off with punctuation additive relative clauses, and use no punctuation for limiting relative clauses. Also, there is the less adhered to practice, which has been recommended here, of using the relative pronoun *which* for additive clauses and *that* for restrictive clauses.

Thus, clearly implied by this limiting relative clause is the existence of different kinds of smog, only one of which is being blamed on the American automobile industry. For example, the smog created by non-urban mining, smelting, and refining industries would be included in this assertion about the automobile industry if this restriction had not been made. The headword "center" is further restricted by "urban" – to exclude, for example, cattle-raising centers and apple-growing centers. But not all urban centers are included either, only the major ones. To be sure, *major* and *minor* are not very precise modifiers, but they do serve to distinguish a city of say a hundred thousand from a metropolis of say a million. We would say, then, that any particular urban center of a hundred thousand may or may not be gripped by strangling smog but that "every" urban center of a million is gripped by strangling smog. "Urban" and "major" modify "center" by answering the question, "What kind? " "Every" modifies "center" inclusively by denying any exception.

"Strangling" is an additive modification of "smog", but unlike additive modification as a relative clause, this pre-positional form may be ambiguous. The only test for distinguishing pre-positional additive modification from pre-positional restrictive modification is the meaning of the modifier and the meaning of the thing modified. In this case, we must ask ourselves whether the writer is likely to be referring to different kinds of smog (that which strangles and that which does not strangle) or whether he is characterizing all smog as strangling. And our answer would probably be that smog is by its very nature strangling; air that does not induce respiratory irritation could not, by definition, qualify as smog. Thus we have an additional assertion, with "smog" as the subject and "[is] strangling" as the dependent attribute.

So far we have accounted for two of the four assertions in this sentence. The remaining two are both dependent additive modifications of the subject, but they differ in that one is also an alternate reference to the subject in an appositive parallel construction. There are three indications that the American automobile industry *is* the richest industry in the world: one, the absence of a conjunction between the two; two, the presence of commas around the second item; and three, the singular form of the attribute. (Notice the difference in, The American automobile industry and the American petroleum industry *refuse* to admit responsibility.) What makes the two parallel is that either one could serve without the other as the subject of this sentence. The writer is referring to exactly the same state of affairs whether he says "The American automobile industry refuses to admit responsibility" or "The richest industry in the world refuses to admit responsibility". The principle of restriction for the first "industry" (as to product and location) is, however, quite different from that for the second (as to financial stature); therefore, adding the second to the first does provide the reader with additional information. But the referent is the same: one and the same industry is included and all others are excluded.

It may, of course, be argued that the American automobile industry is not in fact the richest industry in the world – though for the purposes of this particular argument, it hardly matters whether it is the richest or only one of the richest – but grammatically there can be no doubt that such is being claimed. Truth and falsity are always basic elements in the interpretation of the complete meaning; they are not, however, necessary to determining grammatical meaning. Indeed, we could not determine truth or falsity without first having determined what was being claimed – i. e. grammatical or syntactical meaning.

The second additive modification of the subject is like the first in that it is a nature attribute, follows the subject, and is set off by commas. It is unlike the first in that it cannot serve as a subject – it is a characteristic and not a thing. Being richer is the characteristic, and this is modified, restrictively, by that which it is richer than. The subject is, as compared to industries, the richest industry; as compared to countries, it is richer. "Than most countries" answers the question, "Compared to what? " "The richest . . . . in the world" is a thing modifier; it answers the question, "Which one? "

Finally, we should note the emphatic or redundant modifier, "indeed", which draws attention to the word that precedes it. In speech, "richer" would receive additional stress, and the emphatic word would be unnecessary. In writing, stress can be indicated by an emphatic or by underlining. The writer of this sentence, having first played his king ("the richest industry in the world") now trumps with his ace ("richer indeed than most countries"), and he wants to make certain that the reader does not miss the extraordinary nature of what he has to say. Had the "indeed" occurred between two independent clauses, as it does in introducing the "implicit admission of guilt" sentence below, then we would have emphasized its function as a continuing conjunction rather than as an emphatic or redundant modifier. But in either position "indeed" is both. When it occurs past the point where it would be interassertional, we usually think of its function as being primarily emphatic.

c. The facts are no longer at issue.

This out-of-order assertion has been left this way to draw attention to what is revealed in several instances by the paragraph diagrams in Chapter 9: that, while an individual assertion appears in just one place in a composition, it may be functioning as the answer to more than one implied question or to an implied question raised earlier in the composition. The first assertion elicited the question, "*Why is air pollution not a scientific problem?* " However, the second assertion was not an answer to this but to another question raised by the first assertion, "*What characterizes a social problem?* " The decision to postpone the third assertion is governed by the consideration that this assertion provides an answer not only to "*Why is air pollution not a scientific problem?* " but also to a question raised by our sentence about the American automobile industry, "*Is the industry not entitled to its own opinion?* " It is this contrast between facts and opinion that gives us this assertion, and an obvious inter-assertional conjunction is "However".

"However" as an indication of contrast does not always serve primarily as an inter-assertional conjunction, as the introduction to a second assertion. Instead of saying "However. the facts are no longer at issue" we could have said, The facts, *however*, are no longer at issue. What would have been the difference, if any? In the second instance, "however" would, as in the case of "indeed" in the previous sentence, have been less obviously a conjunction and more obviously an emphatic – drawing attention to the word preceding it ("facts") in order to emphasize a contrast between facts and opinion. But whichever way "however" is used in this sentence, the contrast with "opinion" is only an implied one; it is dependent for its meaning on how we interrogate the previous sentence rather than on what the previous sentence explicitly states. What gives substance to this interpretation of the meaning of this sentence is the use of "however", in whatever position. Its use requires that we either discern precisely what two things are being contrasted or find serious fault with the assertion.

And, to face candidly the great amount of inferring that must be done in all compositions, no matter how explicit they may be, this implied contrast of fact and opinion is dependent upon other inferences that we must make about the previous sentence. We have moved from "air pollution" in the first sentence to "smog" in the second without explanation. Furthermore, we have not just implied existence by referring to air pollution/smog but have also gone on (in a restrictive modifier) to imply something very precise about its occurrence – "grips every major urban center".

Without taking the time to specify all this, we are moving in these opening sentences from generality to particularity: Smog is more specific than air pollution (excluding, for example, natural sources of air pollution such as volcanoes), and the smog of major urban centers is more specific than smog in general (excluding, for example, industrial sources outside of urban centers). Much that is potentially relevant of necessity never gets an explicit mention. What is required on the part of the writer is an ability to structure his material in such a way as to facilitate the reader's attempt to make reasonable inferences. What is demanded on the part of the reader is an ability to read between the lines – not just for ironies and innuendos but for the implied questions and the penumbra of meaning that illuminates those assertions that are explicitly stated.

Another instance of more or less required inference here is in the undifferentiated characteristic attribute, "are no longer at issue". "No longer" as an inseparable phrase does two things: it negates "at issue", and it answers the question, "When? " The assertion unequivocally states that the facts are not at issue, but there is more to this attribute than there would have been if it had simply said, are not at issue. "No longer" clearly implies that the facts were at one time at issue. But it is just an implication, not a discrete assertion modifier, because we cannot remove "no longer" from the attribute where it occurs without destroying the meaning of not being at issue.

h. Only the culprits pretend that the internal combustion engine is not the prime producer of those toxic elements that have become a permanent part of our cities.

The attempt to provide examples of these facts could very well follow immediately upon the claim that they are no longer at issue; however, equally reasonable is to continue a bit longer with the notion of opinion. We already know that the automobile industry does not admit the facts, so we need to ascertain whether anyone shares the industry opinion. Here is as good an example as any of the appropriate use of *and* to serve as an unobtrusive means of developing a line of exposition. Equally appropriate would have been the obtrusive conjunction *indeed*, which would have further emphasized the contrast between accepted facts and what the culprits pretend. But even the use of "pretend" alone is enough to clearly imply that more is involved than mere difference of opinion.

"Only" is a key word here. It modifies the subject exclusively. Just as important as who pretends is whether anyone else does so. But again, much is left to inference rather than stated outright. Not only do we infer who the culprits are, we infer that the long assertion modifier (answering the question, "Do what? ") implies the statement: The internal combustion engine is the prime producer of those toxic elements that have become a permanent part of our cities. And, furthermore, this assertion modifier taken as an assertion contains within itself further implications – e. g. , Toxic elements have become a permanent part of our cities. Implications may, of course, be a means of 'saying' things without having to take the responsibility for unequivocally asserting them, but just as likely they are a means of integrating and economizing. If, for example, the facts were still at issue, then a restrictive modifier would be no place for such crucial points as these. But as part of the background information in a composition designed to be other than an analysis of the facts, these are quite properly subordinated as restrictive implications.

Here, then, is our resulting compound sentence:

3. *However*, the facts are no longer at issue, *and* only the culprits pretend that the internal combustion engine is not the prime producer of those toxic elements that have become a permanent part of our cities.

The following assertions continue the exposition of the problem by providing answers to the deferred question, "*What are these facts?*"

i. In the past decade, numerous scientific studies have demonstrated beyond any reasonable doubt that air pollution has increased in proportion to the number of automobiles on the road.
j. The number of automobiles on the road is growing.
k. In the past decade, numerous scientific studies have demonstrated beyond any reasonable doubt that air pollution has increased in proportion to the consumption of gasoline by their engines.
l. The consumption of gasoline by their engines is rising.
m. Their engines are increasingly powerful.
n. In the past decade, numerous scientific studies have demonstrated beyond any reasonable doubt that automobile exhaust has a toxic effect on the respiratory system.
o. The numerous scientific studies that have demonstrated in the past decade beyond any reasonable doubt that air pollution has increased in proportion to the growing number of automobiles on the road and the rising consumption of gasoline by their increasingly powerful engines and that automobile exhaust has a toxic effect on the respiratory system were conducted by universities, industry, and government.

Three of these have an obvious and important common element: the same subject ("numerous scientific studies"), the same attribute ("have demonstrated"), and the same attribute modifier ("beyond any reasonable doubt"). Integrating these by means of parallel structure and the emphatic conjunctions, *not only . . . but also*, we have: In the past decade, numerous scientific studies have demonstrated beyond any reasonable doubt not only that air pollution has increased in proportion to the number of automobiles on the road and the consumption of gasoline by their engines but also that automobile exhaust has a toxic effect on the respiratory system. Although there are three legs of the parallel, two of the legs have a common element ("air pollution has increased in proportion to") not shared with the third leg – thus the justification for the two-part conjunction.

A particularly interesting aspect of the extensive assertion modifiers in this sentence is their necessarily implied character. One cannot say that numerous scientific studies have demonstrated something beyond any reasonable doubt and yet deny the truth of what has been so demonstrated. "That air pollution has increased in proportion to the number of automobiles on the road" is a restrictive assertion modifier that answers the question, "Have demonstrated what? " The incompleteness of "demonstrated" as a 'transitive verb' makes this relative clause especially obvious as a restrictive modifier. We cannot leave "scientific studies have demonstrated" as an idiomatic sentence. Yet we could leave "air pollution has increased in proportion to the number of automobiles on the road" as an independent assertion that is completely in accord with the meaning of the larger sentence. But we diagram this clause as restrictive (along with "air pollution has increased in proportion to the consumption of gasoline by their engines" and "automobile exhaust has a toxic effect on the respiratory system") because, like them, it cannot be divorced from the core of the assertion without destroying the basic meaning of that assertion. The core as a separate sentence plus the three modifiers as separate sentences would not add up to the inclusive sentence as we have it.

The two remaining modifiers in this sentence answer the same two questions that were raised in the opening assertion. We asked there "When? " and "To what extent or degree? " The answers were "now" and "primarily". Here the answers are "in the past decade" and "beyond any reasonable doubt".

This is certainly enough information for a single sentence, but we have by no means exhausted the possibilities for clearly integrating multiple assertions into a unified framework. Ordinarily there is more to lose (in comprehensibility) than to gain (in economy and unity) by attempting to integrate more than three or four assertions in one sentence, but sometimes there may be so much commonality in the assertions and so little importance attached to any one of them in itself that a single sentence is justified for half a dozen or more assertions. Our attempt to give a summary background account of the facts about urban smog is just such an occasion. With the addition of just ten words to our three-legged parallel sentence we can integrate four more assertions:

4. In the past decade, numerous scientific studies – conducted by universities, industry, and government – have demonstrated beyond any reasonable doubt *not only* that air pollution has increased in proportion to the growing number of automobiles on the road *and* the rising consumption of gasoline by their increasingly powerful engines *but also* that automobile exhaust has a toxic effect on the respiratory system.

The first of these four non-restrictive modifiers ("conducted by universities, industry, and government") is set off by dashes, but it is unlikely that the phrase would make very much sense as a restrictive modifier if the punctuation were dropped. It is not clear what more there is that could be eliminated. Who else conducts large-scale research projects except universities, industry, and government? Thus, rather than indicating that some, but not all, sources of such research concur in the results, the phrase indicates the totality of informed agreement on the subject. And because of this totality, it seems more accurate to say that the three sources taken together have demonstrated rather than that each one has done so. It would not be wrong, in the absence of clear indication one way or the other, to make this a separable parallel construction, but it seems more in accord with such an unequivocal claim to stop short of interpreting each of the three in and of itself as having done all that the sentence claims to have been accomplished beyond any reasonable doubt in the past decade. Thus we diagram the parallel as unitary. Finally, instead of answering the question, "*What are these facts?* " (as do the other six assertions in the sentence), this unitary assertion answers the question, "*Why are these facts no longer at issue?* "

The remaining three non-restrictive modifiers ("growing", "rising", and "increasingly powerful") are pre-positional and thus are not provided with punctuation as an aid to interpretation. Each one needs to be debated on semantic grounds to determine whether it makes more sense to interpret it as qualifying the phrase being modified or whether it makes more sense as an additional assertion. In our earlier example of "strangling smog" it seemed reasonable to interpret "strangling" as non-restrictive, because we usually think that air pollution must reach a certain level of respiratory toxicity before we are justified in referring to it as smog. But there is nothing logically necessary about this interpretation. People can and do use "smog" in slightly different senses without being thought of as being linguistically unique or irresponsible. With "growing", "rising", and "increasingly powerful", however, there is a question of logical necessity – not a serious one, to be sure, but sufficient to allow us to make a clear-cut decision about their non-restrictive, or more precisely, additive nature.

The number of automobiles on the road is a totality. We can refer to the number of automobiles on the road to Yosemite last night, and "to Yosemite" and "last night" will be limiting modifiers of the phrase as a whole. We can refer to the number of out-of-state automobiles on the road, and "out-of-state" will be a limiting modifier of "automobiles". If the phrase had read "the *total* number of automobiles", "total" would have been neither limiting nor additive but rather emphatic. Because the number of automobiles is by definition the total number of automobiles, "total" is, in the strict sense, redundant. Whatever we say, then, about the number of automobiles that is not redundant will necessarily add information but not restrict the scope of coverage. "Growing", "shrinking", "impressive", "frightening", etc. would all be non-restrictive modifiers.

The same argument from logical necessity applies to "rising" as a modifier of "consumption of gasoline". The consumption of gasoline is the totality, and thus, however we characterize it, we are making an additional assertion rather than restricting the scope of what is modified. And, granted the necessary knowledge about automobile engines, the same argument applies to "increasingly powerful" as a modifier of "engines". To know that an automobile has only one engine is to know that whatever is said about the engines of the totality of automobiles on the road must necessarily be non-restrictive. Such necessity would not, however, govern the interpretation of an assertion about vehicles that had a front and rear engine, or a left and right engine, or a gasoline and a diesel engine, or a main and an auxiliary engine. We can argue that as a matter of fact the totality of automobile engines on the road is not increasingly powerful, or that many individual engines are actually smaller than engines used to be. This may be true, but the nature of the claim is such that we are obliged to treat "increasingly powerful" as a non-restrictive modifier.

The continuing transition from this seven-assertion sentence summarizing the facts that are no longer at issue to the next sentence is the restrictive modification that constitutes the final leg of the parallel. As we noted above, "automobile exhaust has a toxic effect on the respiratory system" is both a restrictive modifier and a necessarily implied assertion. Furthermore, it is the link that gave rise to the implied question, "*Is there actually sufficient exhaust in the air now to justify the label 'strangling' for what in the laboratory is termed 'toxic effect'?* "

Obviously the three-part answer to this question will form a parallel sentence:

p. This effect is now obvious to even the most insensitive eye.
q. This effect is now obvious to even the most insensitive nose.
r. This effect is now obvious to even the most insensitive throat.

Less obvious, but equally reasonable, is the inclusion in the same sentence of an additional assertion that provides the laboratory counterpart of the man-in-the-street evidence and answers the additional question, "*Is there evidence for this effect being more than merely unpleasant?* " The answer to this question has the same subject as the previous three:

s. This effect is documented by a three-hundred percent increase in urban lung-cancer cases over the past twenty years.

Clearly, then, a four-part parallel structure is possible: This effect is now obvious to even the most insensitive eye, is now obvious to even the most insensitive nose, is now obvious to even the most insensitive throat, and is documented by a three-hundred percent increase in urban lung-cancer cases over the past twenty-years. But not only is this possibility unnecessarily repetitious, it fails to distinguish between the two parts of the sentence – answering the two different questions. A better possibility would be: This effect is now obvious to even the most insensitive eye, nose, and throat, and is documented by a three-hundred percent increase in urban lung-cancer cases over the past twenty years. This is more economical and, by virtue of the two main legs of the parallel, does distinguish between the two kinds of answers. But even so, it could be argued that the last answer is merely tacked on at the end rather than integrated into the sentence and that this tacked-on assertion is still just another leg of a pre-established parallel and thus not clearly distinguished in kind from what precedes it. To meet this objection, let us make the assertion about lung-cancer an additive modifier in what is otherwise a parallel sentence:

5. This effect, which is documented by a three-hundred percent increase in urban lung-cancer cases over the past twenty years, is now obvious to even the most insensitive eye, nose, *and* throat.

The use of commas to set off the relative clause clearly indicates the non-restrictive rather than restrictive nature of the modification, but even without the punctuation the use of "this" rather than "the" or "a" makes it unreasonable to consider the modifier restrictive. "This" provides the complete restriction, and anything else would be either redundant or additive. "Toxic" as a limiting modifier of "effect" would still leave room for further restriction, but "this" as a limiting modifier of "effect" is the final particularization. For emphasis we might say "this particular toxic effect", but "particular" would be neither limiting nor additive but redundant.

A redundant modifier that does occur in this sentence is "even". It emphasizes the completeness and unqualifiedness of the effect, but it contributes no meaning that is not already contained in "most". And if "most" were omitted from the sentence, "even" would still be redundant because it would contribute nothing that was not already contained in "insensitive". What important function "even" does perform, for all its lack of restrictive or non-restrictive meaning, is an impetus to the next question, *"If the facts are so clear to everyone else, how can the industry pretend to be innocent?* " "Even" emphasizes that no one is precluded from an awareness of smog by insensitivity; thus, the question arises as to how the automobile industry can avoid an admission of guilt. The answer is that behind the explicit denial is an implicit admission of guilt:

t. The fact that the automobile manufacturers themselves have devoted increased time and money to developing an electric vehicle is an implicit admission of guilt.

As it stands, this assertion clearly follows from the question, but it is less clearly linked to the preceding sentence. Looking again at "even", we can see that the emphasis in the previous sentences has been on the unequivocalness of the case against automobile smog. If we continue in this vein, in order to make the most of the 'admission' claimed to have been made by the culprits, we would find a made-to-order conjunction in *indeed*. So obvious is smog and the smog problem that the culprits *themselves* (another redundant-emphatic) cannot ignore it:

6. *Indeed*, the fact that the automobile manufacturers themselves have devoted increased time and money to developing an electric vehicle is an implicit admission of guilt.

"Themselves" as a redundant-emphatic modifier of "automobile manufacturers" functions in essentially the same way as "even" in the previous sentence. We could have said "the fact that even the automobile manufacturers have devoted . . . . ". And, had we wanted to pile on the emphasis with no regard for redundancy, we could have said "the fact that even the automobile manufacturers themselves . . . . ". If the automobile manufacturers can be found admitting the case, who could deny it? We already know that "only the culprits pretend that the internal combustion engine is not the prime producer of those toxic elements that have become a permanent part of our cities".

Having made this sentence a single assertion, we need to justify ourselves in the face of what looks to be a parallel structure – "time and money". The only way to account for this as a single assertion is to analyze it as a unitary parallel. And this will be more difficult to demonstrate than, for example, the unity of "Tom and his wife are a pleasant couple", where the logic of completeness left us no choice but to leave Tom and his wife as inseparable. There would be nothing illogical, or even unusual, about saying that the manufacturers had done two different things: devoted time and devoted money. Still, there are good reasons for thinking that a better interpretation of the sentence as a whole is to say that, although time and money are often properly thought of as two different things, they constitute one thing here. In the first place, what is being asserted here is not what the manufacturers *did* but what the fact of their doing it *constitutes*. Does devoting time in and of itself constitute an implicit admission of guilt? Does devoting money in and of itself constitute an implicit admission of guilt? Perhaps each alone does, but we have no clear indication of this apart from the minimum claim that the two together are "an admission" – not admissions. Since they are both in fact present here, it is of minor importance whether one or the other by itself would have been sufficient to constitute an implicit admission of guilt. But we are on safer ground, and at no real sacrifice in meaning, if we make time and money unitary parallel rather than separable parallel. This reasoning is reinforced by the nature of the two things – especially when in a business context one not only hears the maxim, "time is money", but also sees businessmen acting in terms of it. Thus, since the subject here is not the nature of time and money but how to interpret businessmen's devotion of increased time and money to a project, we are justified in taking its use here as unitary. In business, to devote time is necessarily to spend money.

The major question about this sentence, however, has yet to be raised: isn't there still more than one assertion here, and if there isn't, what justifies this single-assertion sentence? The first part of this question is obviously directed at the long relative clause, which constitutes more than half the sentence, "that the automobile manufacturers themselves have devoted increased time and money to developing an electric vehicle". The lack of punctuation indicates that it is restrictive, as does the nature of what is modified, "the fact". "The Eiffel Tower" takes no restrictive modification because it is *sui generis*; it is as particularized as it can get. But in the case of common nouns – like "man", "tree", "rock", "honesty", "fact" – the use of the definite article demands some indication of what particular man, tree, rock, honesty, fact is being referred to: the old man, the tree in my back yard, the projecting rock, the honesty of his admission, the fact that they devoted time and money to it. What it is that makes our long relative clause a special case is that it modifies a word that by its very nature makes a claim about the truth of the modifier. This clause is necessarily a restrictive modifier, but because it modifies "fact" it necessarily and unequivocally implies an additional assertion. In the strict or formal sense this sentence makes just one assertion, but in effect or semantically it makes two assertions.

For practical purposes, then, we do not have to defend this as a single-assertion sentence. But what does require some defense is the introduction of a new topic in such a subordinate way. In terms of what we have said earlier, this would seem to be the very place for a single-assertion sentence, thereby insuring that an important new and unprepared for idea will not be overlooked. This objection is not illegitimate, and all that can be done in answer is to indicate that the proper introduction of a new topic can be a complex consideration. In the first place, the whole tenor of the opening sentences of this composition is the emphasis on what is already known. The same reason justifying a giant seven-assertion sentence about the facts that are no longer at issue can justify this subordinate reference to developing an electric vehicle: it is assumed, rightly or wrongly, that the "facts" are already known and no longer at issue. It is not alleged that the automobile manufacturers' implicit admission of guilt is one such fact, but it seems to be alleged that their devotion of increased time and money to developing an electric vehicle is a known fact no longer at issue. The latter is part of the given upon which this composition is being constructed; the former is part of the argument that constitutes the heart of the composition. In the second place, as we see in continuing on to the succeeding sentences, the subject of the electric vehicle is not simply slipped in and then dropped; it is discussed at some length as an example of one of the major kinds of proposed solutions to the smog problem. Thus it is of less importance how the subject is first mentioned than how and to what extent it is developed. In relation to the subject of proving implicit guilt, the electric vehicle is indeed a subordinate part of the total composition. But in relation to the subject of what constitutes the most adequate kind of solution to the smog problem, the electric vehicle is a major part of the total composition. With regard to the different emphases of these two subjects, compare this sentence with "v" below: "The electric vehicle is a red herring". The question of emphasis vs. subordination is not determined by the topic of electric vehicles but by the different compositional functions for which the electric vehicle is being employed.

The implied question elicited by the first electric vehicle sentence ("*Is it not just a matter of time then before the problem is solved by the industry itself with electric vehicles?* ") is answered by the second electric vehicle sentence. But intervening between the two is an explicit or rhetorical question. And, while such a question does not qualify as a sentence in our sense of being a formally independent assertion, it may contain within itself a subordinate assertion in the form of an additive modifier. Here is the rhetorical question that is elicited by the first electric vehicle sentence:

Is the public, however, to wait patiently for ten or fifteen years before General Motors makes as much money from the storage battery as it does now from gasoline?

And here is an implicit question elicited by this explicit question: "*Is the public likely to wait patiently?* " Our answer to this question was that,

u. The public is docile.

The most economical way to dispose of this very simple assertion is to combine it with the rhetorical question:

7. Is the docile public, however, to wait patiently for ten or fifteen years before General Motors makes as much money from the storage battery as it does now from gasoline?

The potential problem with this structure is the possibility of interpreting "docile" as a restrictive rather than non-restrictive modifier. Usually we think of a collective noun like "public" as being the totality of people, but it is possible to add a restrictive modifier – e. g. the American public and the bicycle-riding public. Excluded by these modifiers are, for example, the French public and the automobile-driving public. The question then becomes, what would reasonably be excluded by "docile" if it were a restrictive modifier? It could only be the non-docile or aroused public. Is it then more in accord with the ordinary conception of the public (the citizenry as a whole) to think that it is by and large docile or that it consists of two parts, the docile and the non-docile? We can hardly claim that one or the other conception has very much semantic necessity behind it, and thus the difficulty of using this sort of pre-positional modification. But like our consideration of the nature of smog for the second sentence, this one does seem to lend itself to more and less likely interpretations: the nature of the public is to be docile rather than to be made up of docile and non-docile segments. Aroused individuals and groups within the public are not *the* public.

The use of explicit questions is especially conducive to the implying of assertions. Thus we have here not just the explicit assertion, "The public is docile", but such implicit assertions as: General Motors makes much money from gasoline, and if General Motors has anything to say about it, the public will have to wait until the storage battery is as profitable as gasoline. The first of these results directly from interpreting a restrictive modifier (answering the question, "For what goal or motive? ") as an independent assertion. The The second is a more involved extrapolation, which partly at least depends upon the common assumption that the answer to a rhetorical question is its ironic counterpart assertion. Since it hardly seems reasonable that anyone would think that the public should be under any obligation to accommodate General Motors on such a serious question of public policy, an implication might very well be that someone does think this.

The final consideration here is the parallel structure, "ten or fifteen years". From our earlier discussion of the various kinds of unitary parallel, it should be clear that this can make sense only as *between* ten and fifteen years. Ten years by itself and fifteen years by itself would not be in accord with the obviously intended concept here of between ten years and fifteen years.

The next sentence is not so much an answer to this explicit question as it is a continuation of the preceding assertion, providing the first characterization of what was only referred to there:

v/*8*. The electric vehicle is a red herring.

Grammatically it is so simple as to require no explanation – except, perhaps, for why "red" and "herring" are not either hyphenated or written as one word. The reason they are not is that the standard dictionaries treat the phrase as made up of two separate words, even as they define the phrase with no reference to either "red" or "herring". A red herring is neither a herring nor red. "Red" is not a limiting modifier that distinguishes one kind of herring from other kinds of herrings – as in old herring, young herring, big herring, small herring. Nor is it an additive modifier providing a characteristic of all herrings – as in the strong tasting herring or the nutritious herring. Rather, it is like the "green-" in "greenhorn". A greenhorn is neither a horn nor green, and thus the phrase is reasonably written as one word, and we do not consider "green" to be a limiting modifier. However, the illogical form of "red herring" obliges us to say, rather illogically, that "red" is a restrictive modifier. The principle of distinction is not among herrings on the basis of color but between all herrings in the literal sense and herrings as diversions in the metaphorical sense.

The concept of limiting modification is more trouble than it is worth here, but it does help us to formulate what must surely be the most likely sort of question to be raised by this – formally – simple sentence. "*How is it a red herring?* " Indeed, so important is an answer to this question that it might quite properly be incorporated into the electric vehicle sentence. However, our rationale for deciding against a sentence like "The electric vehicle is a red herring because . . . . " is that the basic nature of our objection to electric vehicles seems to require maximum emphasis. To provide a reason for the objection would result in sufficient complexity to dilute the simple initial impact. Further explanations and clarifications are always in order, but a concise statement of a basic point in an argument is no less important. The trick, of course, is to be certain enough of what is basic so as to use emphasis sparingly enough to be noticed.

Yet, how *is* it that the electric vehicle is a red herring? What support can be offered for this criticism? The electric vehicle is a red herring because

w. Its practical development is dependent on knowledge the automobile industry does not now possess.
x. While we wait, the problem grows steadily worse.

Each is equally important to the explanation: the one tells what is wrong with the proposed solution, and the other tells what is dangerous about it. A red herring is a means of confusing the pursuers, of occupying them with an irrelevant concern while the true quarry gets farther and farther afield. While the public is preoccupied with the electric vehicle, the true solution to the smog problem gets farther and farther from realization.

Thus, as good a sentence structure as any for this two-part answer is a compound structure connected by *and*:

9. Its practical development is dependent on knowledge the automobile industry does not now possess, *and* while we wait, the problem grows steadily worse.

"And" is appropriate here because it makes clear that the two assertions go together in their relation to the previous sentence.

The only further point of possible grammatical interest in this sentence is the restrictive adjective "steadily" to modify the function "grows worse". This is the only 'adverb', the only modifier of a function attribute, in the entire editorial. Partly this is explained by the kind of subject here: an argument is probably not as likely to employ function attributes in the first place, but certainly it is less likely to modify those that it does employ. No action is being described (as would be true in some journalism stories); no situations are being created (as in works of fiction). But partly this is explained by the fact that semantic grammar has redefined as assertion modifiers much that has traditionally been lumped together as being 'adverbial'. What remains, however, is a much more precisely conceived category – not just all attribute modifiers but specifically function attribute modifiers. When something *happens*, it can happen in a limited number of ways. In this case, the problem did not grow haltingly or spasmodically worse but steadily. Not everything that grows worse does so steadily. For example: the Roman Empire did not steadily decline but rather had periods of revival and rejuvenation interspersing the overall decline.

After the condemnation as a red herring and the reasons for labeling it such, there may be nothing to say in support of the electric vehicle. Still, our interlocutor is not so easily put off, and he seeks a qualification of this outright rejection. The next two assertions probably have to be taken as a pair, because the first

y. Perhaps today's problem could be solved by electric vehicles.

would seem to make a large concession unless accompanied by the second

z. If we allow it to go unchecked for another dozen years, far more drastic measures will be necessary.

The first one by itself seems to contrast with the previous condemnation, but the second contrasts with the first, so that the net result is only slightly different than before the concession was made. The conditional assertion modifier "perhaps" seems grudgingly offered and is easily retracted by a contrasting conjunction introducing the following assertion.

10. Perhaps today's problem could be solved by electric vehicles, *but* if we allow it to go unchecked for another dozen years, far more drastic measures will be necessary.

Both independent clauses are conspicuously introduced by conditional assertion modifiers, and the equivocalness of the sentence is further emphasized by "could" in the attribute of the first assertion. The best that can be said here in favor of the electric vehicle requires three conditionals. A further use of the assertion modifier in the second assertion is to imply another assertion. The difference between "if we allow it to go unchecked for another dozen years" and "if you allow it to go unchecked for the next dozen years" is the implied assertion: It has already gone unchecked for a dozen years. There is no way to get this subject-predicate assertion out of "another" except by implication. "Another" here functions restrictively just as, for example, "the next" – excluding the possibility of just any dozen years. "Another" provides a degree of precision that would be lacking without it, but its primary function is probably more to imply than to restrict.

A good candidate for a single-assertion sentence is the next assertion, which not only is a conclusion drawn from the previous sentence but also is an explicit answer to the question of whether the public is to wait:

aa/*11.* There is no justification for delay.

The very heart of the argument against the electric vehicle in particular and technological proposals in general is that time is running out. Thus, there is no better candidate for maximum emphasis in the composition than this cryptic, unequivocal statement. Even though the subject here is the semantically empty "there", no more cryptic formulation of the meaning is idiomatically possible. "No justification for delay exists" is a bit unidiomatic, and "Justification for delay does not exist" is not quite so cryptic. Furthermore, this second alternative, while it has a semantically significant subject, is a less obviously negative statement. A possible justification of the redundant "there" construction here is that it allows the subject to be preceded by the negative. A consequence of this introductory negative is that the entire subject is part of the core; all of the modification occurs within the core because, while "for delay" modifies "justification", "no" modifies the whole phrase. Insofar as the negative must be part of the core, then everything it modifies must also be part of the core.

However, there are two factors to consider in this sentence: the first is the semantic unity of a negative core, the second is the diagramatic unity of redundant *it* and *there* subjects. As can be seen in the diagram on page 314 below, we do not separate the headword or phrase from its modifiers. This reflects not a semantic unity but simply a limitation of our diagraming system. If we left unmarked the modifiers of a redundant subject, these would be indistinguishable from unmarked modifiers of the attribute. For example, if McNeill's sentence below had read "It is [quite] customary to distinguish a classical followed by a romantic tendency in European letters", then "quite" would have been an unmarked attribute modifier and "a classical followed by a romantic tendency in European letters" would have been an unmarked subject modifier.

At this point in our sentence-by-sentence analysis we might profitably pause and attempt a somewhat larger view. We are not yet ready to discuss paragraphing, but on the level of inter-assertional relationships we can already see certain patterns running from sentence to sentence. Beginning with the question about whether the public should wait patiently, we have been engaged in a dialog that is not just an interrogation but an argument. And with the last assertion ("There is no justification for delay".) we have an unequivocal answer. This interpretation is not simply a matter of analyzing the grammar of the assertions nor of spotting the inter-assertional conjunctions. It is the larger and more nebulous attempt to characterize the progress of the implied dialog. More often than not in a sustained argument explanatory conjunctions are absent because there are so many supporting and concluding relationships. To indicate every one with an appropriate conjunction would be so obtrusive as to complicate more than clarify. However, both reader and writer must be able to recognize the appropriate relationships in the absence of conjunctions.

Attempts to lay out arguments schematically are never more than partially successful, but the attempt must be made, if only to open up this crucial concern to analysis. The following chart – with appropriate conjunctions supplied in brackets – is one such attempt. That it is an over-simplification is readily admitted, but at least it should complement the implied dialog rather than conflict with it. Reasons for a succeeding conclusion are enclosed in a box; reasons for preceding reasons are indented.[2]

Similar to the previous sentence in having a redundant subject is the next assertion:

bb. That which is a demonstrable and pervasive public menace is the proper subject for immediate legislative action.

However, the redundancy here results from identity: the proper subject for immediate legislative action is that which is a demonstrable and pervasive public menace. In this case, there is just a single headword on each side of the equal sign, and all the rest of subject and attribute is restrictive modification of "that" and "subject". This is true even of the parallel structure in the subject. "Demonstrable and pervasive" are not necessarily unitary, but, as with "fill out the form and pay the fee", it makes little sense here to think that either one or the other in itself is sufficient to meet the condition. It could perhaps be argued that both "demonstrable" and "pervasive" are rather redundant, that a public menace is by its very nature demonstrable and pervasive. But it is reasonable to distinguish between a minor public menace (like my neighbor's overflowing cesspool) and a major public menace (like the fallout from atmospheric nuclear testing). The first is very demonstrable but not very pervasive; the second is very pervasive but the adverse effects are difficult to demonstrate. Rightly or wrongly, the writer here is claiming that both conditions are the necessary conditions for *immediate* legislative action. Lesser problems could be met by more leisurely legislation; immediate action requires extreme conditions.

Perhaps this assertion sufficiently implies that urban smog is a demonstrable and pervasive public menace, but the identification is too crucial to the argument to be merely implied, no matter how obvious the implication. Thus the following assertion is closely linked to the previous one:

cc. Surely a health menace as serious as smog qualifies for such action.

This characteristic assertion is a continuation of the previous one, differing only as particular to general. Thus "and" is a reasonable means of linking these two "menace" assertions:

Explicit question	7.	Is the public to wait patiently for ten or fifteen years before General Motors can make as much money from the storage battery as it does now from gasoline?
		[because]
Support for the answer	8.	The electric vehicle is a red herring.
		[because]
	9.	Its practical development is dependent on knowledge the automobile industry does not now possess, and while we wait, the problem grows steadily worse.
Support for the support	10.	Perhaps today's problem could be solved by electric vehicles, but if we allow it to go unchecked for another dozen years, far more drastic measures will be necessary.
		[therefore]
Answer	11.	There is no justification for delay.

12. That which is a demonstrable and pervasive public menace is the proper subject for immediate legislative action, *and* surely a health menace as serious as smog qualifies for such action.

The second assertion is introduced by an emphatic, which is semantically redundant because it neither restricts what it modifies nor makes an additional assertion. This by no means necessarily implies a criticism, because judicious use of emphasis (like the judicious use of conditions) can make one's primary and secondary points easier to follow. The "perhaps" used above to grudgingly admit that the electric vehicle might have some value if employed immediately is an indication that the argument being offered does not hinge on that particular point. The "surely" used here is an indication that the argument being offered does hinge on a health menace as serious as smog qualifying for immediate legislative action.

It is worth noting that the subject of the second assertion is "menace" not "smog". The second assertion is indeed more specific than the first, but it is not as specific as it could be – i. e. "Smog qualifies for such action". Here is an instance of information cast in the form of restrictive modification but in effect making multiple assertions. Instead of two assertions completing the syllogism,

And surely a health menace as serious as smog is a demonstrable and pervasive public menace.

Therefore, smog qualifies for immediate legislative action.

we have a single assertion with extensive restrictive modification that implies the additional assertions. "Surely" is thus not a mere intensifier but a means of drawing attention to the necessary conclusion in this abbreviated syllogism. We have already chosen to link the two assertions in this sentence with "and". This emphasizes the continuing relationship of major (general) and minor (particular) premises. But we could logically have used *therefore*, emphasizing the relationship of a conclusion to the reason that precedes it. The choice not to use *therefore* was based on the fact that not everything in the second assertion is the conclusion; part of it is the minor premise. The ubiquitous "and" seems more in accord with the abbreviated form of the syllogism.

"As serious as smog" is a restrictive modifier, because not all health menaces are being claimed to qualify for immediate legislative action. For instance, minor health menaces like my neighbor's over-flowing cesspool or the latest outbreak of influenza are not sufficiently serious. How serious does a health menace have to be before such action is warranted? The general standard is "demonstrable and pervasive". The specific standard is "as serious as smog". Has anything been gained by using this abbreviated, and thus possibly more difficult to follow, formulation? Yes. The gain in economy was such that our version required only sixty percent of the words required by the syllogism.

The next assertion is a candidate for a single-assertion sentence, not so much because of its special importance as because of its very extensive restrictive modification. And this decision is pretty much settled when we look ahead to the next assertions, which much more obviously go together with each other than with this assertion.

dd/*13*. Unless legal restrictions are widely applied and rigorously enforced in the early stages of contamination, urban congestion becomes so great that the price of purifying the air is destruction of the city.

This assertion is related to the previous assertion as support; it provides a negative reason for thinking that the problem of smog qualifies for immediate legislative action – not what good will be gained by such action but what evil will be avoided. In this respect, this general assertion functions in the same way as the much more specific negative assertions that follow. But what distinguishes this assertion from the four that follow is that they (sentence 14) provide evidence for the conclusion asserted *here* (sentence 13).

Sentence 13 is introduced by a long conditional assertion modifier that contains a unitary parallel. "Widely applied and rigorously enforced" (like "demonstrable and pervasive" in the previous sentence) provides a pair of criteria that do not necessarily go together. The Eighteenth Amendment (establishing national prohibition) was applied to the widest possible spectrum of people, situations, and beverages – but it was not rigorously enforced, and thus did not accomplish its avowed purpose. On the other hand, some municipal laws against trees infected with Dutch Elm disease have been rigorously enforced locally, but because they could not be widely applied have also failed. In the absence of any indication that the relation between "widely applied" and "rigorously enforced" is either/or, we assume that both criteria must be met. A way of making this unitary interpretation unequivocal in the two sentences would be to preface the parallel items with the redundant modifier "both". But to say "both a demonstrable and pervasive public menace" and "both widely applied and rigorously enforced in the early stages of contamination" is to be no more than redundant if the sentences are easily and reasonably interpreted as the same with or without the "both".

The subject of this sentence ("urban congestion") presents no problems, but the attribute needs some comment. Because the "becomes" gives no indication of the attribute meaning except undifferentiated function, we must incorporate additional words into the core. But how many? What is to be done with the "so" between "becomes" and "great"? Is "that the price of purifying the air is destruction of the city" an assertion modifier? If so, what question does it answer?

Granted that this is a function assertion, there are two kinds of possible modifiers for the attribute core: answering the questions, "Do in what manner? " (e. g. *quickly*) and "To what extent or degree? " (e. g. *very*):

quickly [becomes great.] [becomes very great]

Quickly modifiers are the usual sort of function modifiers; *very* modifiers are more associated with characteristic attributes. The second kind, however, is the kind represented in sentence 13, but with the difference that the modifier in sentence 13 answers the question of how great in two parts: "so . . . that the price of purifying the air is destruction of the city". This modifier is restrictive because it makes more precise what is meant by "great", by excluding for example such degrees of seriousness as "so great that people must carry independent sources of oxygen". Unlike the relative clause in "He said that the price of purifying the air is destruction of the city", the relative clause in our sentence does not have separate status as an assertion modifier because it is inseparably linked with "so" to answer the question, "How great? " or "To what extent or degree? " rather than "Do what? " Furthermore, because the answer modifies "great" alone and not "becomes great", it is not properly labeled as an attribute modifier. It is simply an indivisible part of the attribute core. The principle is the same one manifested in "She became a nuclear physicist". "Nuclear" is a restrictive modifier of "physicist", but it is not a modifier – in any way – of "became a physicist".

The next two assertions must surely be linked together in a parallel structure:

ee. Los Angeles has been permanently contaminated.
ff. New York City has been permanently contaminated.

And the two after these must surely follow suit:

gg. Legislative action was too little.
hh. Legislative action was too late.

But whether or not the two sets of parallels should be joined with each other depends on the semantic relationship between them, and this in turn depends on what the implied question is. If the question is "*Why?* " or "*How was this allowed to happen?* " then "gg" and "hh" follow "ee" and "ff" as support or reasons. The simplest way to handle this kind of relationship is with the conjunction *because*. And since we cannot begin a sentence with *because* if the conclusion has already been stated, the obvious choice is to make a single sentence out of the four assertions:

14. Los Angeles *and* New York City have been permanently contaminated, *because* legislative action was too little *and* too late.

The parallel structures are too obvious to need analysis, but, as in the previous sentence, some comment may be in order on the attribute modifiers: "permanently" and "too". The contrast between the two parallel sets is interesting. "Little" and "late" are clearly *characteristics*, and the appropriate kind of characteristic modifier answers the question, "To what extent or degree? " "Too" is not different in this respect from "very". "Permanently" also answers the same question, but it is diagramed as part of a *function* attribute. To be sure, "contaminated" can occur as a characteristic attribute in many contexts, and "permanently" can also be used as a characteristic modifier:

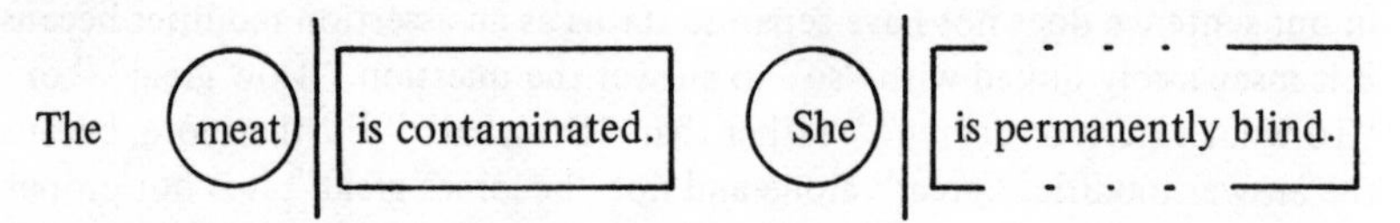

Why, then, is "have been permanently contaminated" diagramed as object/function rather than as characteristic?

Like "fastened", discussed in Chapter 2,[3] "contaminated" is either function or characteristic depending on its actual or potential modification in the context. Clearly implied by what precedes this sentence is that smog is the agent that has done the contaminating. Unlike "blind/blinded" there are no alternate forms of "contaminated" to distinguish characteristic from object/function; thus, in the absence of determining assertion modifiers, we have only the context on which to base an interpretation. The following sentences in and of themselves would present no such problems:

Los Angeles and New York City were contaminated for several generations before the citizens finally took action.

Los Angeles and New York City were contaminated by greedy people.

The first is characteristic; the assertion modifier answers the question, "How long a time? " The second is object/function; the assertion modifier answers the question, "By what agent? " A city, or most anything else, for that matter, can *become contaminated* (agent/function) without having an outside force causing the function. (Just as one grows old without having been 'oldened' by some outside agent). But such an interpretation would be completely at variance here with all that precedes our sentence 14. We could just as well have explicitly stated that Los Angeles and New York City have been permanently contaminated *by smog*, but this hardly seemed necessary under the circumstances.

The next assertion has some claim to autonomy because it introduces the final specification of the subject. For the first time we are told that the target of the argument is not urban smog in general or the American public in general. In the most precise sense, the problem is smog in Honolulu, and the audience is the citizens of Honolulu.

ii/*15.* Here in Honolulu we must profit from their mistakes.

A possibility does exist here, however, for multiple assertions. In one sense "here" and "in Honolulu" refer to exactly the same thing, and as such they would constitute an appositive parallel. The resulting assertions would be: "Here we must profit from their mistakes". "Here [is] in Honolulu". Superficially we could dismiss this possibility simply by reference to the lack of punctuation around "in Honolulu". But the crucial question is not whether the phrase has been punctuated as appositive but whether it *should be* punctuated as appositive.

On the one hand, we could reasonably treat "here" and "in Honolulu" as synonymous in this context and justify this redundant construction as a means both of specifying the place and of locating the speaker in that place. On the other hand, "in Honolulu" is very precise, and "here" is very general. Where the speaker is is not just in Honolulu but in Hawaii, and in the United States, and in the middle of the Pacific, and on Earth. The possible interpretations of "here" are infinite. Even if the audience knew exactly where the speaker was located when he uttered this sentence, they would still not know precisely what the "here" referred to. Insofar as "in Honolulu" makes more precise what is only generalized by "here", it is properly understood as a limiting modifier.

How we decide to diagram this particular sentence is quite a small concern, with no significant consequences either way. But the question is an interesting one to raise because this sentence provides us with one of the best examples of a very small class – those modifiers that are close to being unaffected by the fundamental distinction between restrictive and non-restrictive.

A good example of a much larger class – assertions making conspicuous use of implication – is this one:

jj. If we continue to rely on the trade winds to ventilate our island, we will soon find the air as unpleasantly congested as the land.

As we noted in the previous chapter, "We have in the past relied on the trade winds to ventilate our island" and "The land is already unpleasantly congested" are the next best thing to component assertions. What, of course, has been gained by this approximation, by this use of complex clauses as both restrictive modifiers and conspicuously implied assertions, is economy.

We have in the past relied on the trade winds to ventilate our island; however, it is becoming unpleasantly congested. Consequently, if we continue to rely on them, we will soon find the air as unpleasantly congested as the land.

Here are the three assertions all explicitly stated, and the total words have been increased from twenty-five to forty. The end of economy by no means always justifies the means of dual-purpose restrictive modification. This point will be emphasized in the next chapter when we analyze the syntactical problems in the prose of an economy-minded historian. But economy is always a relevant factor in constructing sentences. And other things being equal, it is to be sought rather than avoided, especially in written composition.

Other than the conspicuous implications, there are no grammatical points here in need of analysis. The introductory "if" clause, like the introductory "unless" clause in sentence 13, is a conditional assertion modifier: the core assertion is not necessarily true in and of itself. The two other assertion modifiers, "soon" and "the air as unpleasantly congested as the land" answer the questions, "When? " and "What? " They are not conditionals because the core assertion is necessarily true quite apart from their presence or absence.

A passing comment might be in order here on the possibility of recasting sentences into different semantic kinds. Why an agent/function sentence here ("we will soon find . . . ") rather than, say, a characteristic sentence ("the air will soon be . . . ")? Is our discovering the consequences more to the point than the state of affairs discovered? In the last analysis, this composition is an argument directed at a specific group of people (we citizens of Honolulu) to do a specific thing or else personally suffer the consequences. As the composition progresses, this reference to the victimizing victims becomes more and more emphasized. The previous sentence was "we must profit . . . ".

This sentence is "we will soon find . . . " The next one is "we need laws . . . . ". There is much more to deciding on the form of a sentence than meeting the minimum criterion of referential truth. And not only is this particular sentence more appropriately framed as agent/function, this appropriateness is reinforced by the introductory conditional modifier: "If *we* continue to rely on the trade winds to ventilate . . . . ". In this sentence even the conspicuous implication is agent/function – with the same subject as the core assertion.

The next assertion is not a major point in the argument, nor does it consist of many words, nor does it easily integrate with the assertions that follow it. Therefore, it is a reasonable candidate for inclusion in the above assertion – providing, of course, that we can find an appropriate slot for it.

kk. Our island is over-populated.

And, in fact, it seems made to order for an additive modifier of "our island" in the conditional assertion modifier:

16. If we continue to rely on the trade winds to ventilate our over-populated island, we will soon find the air as unpleasantly congested as the land.

Citizens of Honolulu have just one island, and once "island" has been restrictively modified by "our", the ultimate level of specification has been reached. Whatever additional modification there is must be non-restrictive rather than restrictive. We do not, for instance, have an under-populated as well as an over-populated island. The citizens of Hawaii, on the other hand, have many islands. Thus they can refer, for example, to "our under-populated islands" (e. g. Niihau) as distinguished from "our over-populated islands" (e. g. Oahu), and in this case, "under-populated" and "over-populated" are restrictive modifiers.

Unlike the several assertions before and after it, this one does not make a direct contribution to the line of argument leading up to the conclusion that "We need laws . . . . ". Its inter-assertional relationship to its context is simply continuation rather than support or conclude. As the dialog indicated, the assertion about over-population is by no means irrelevant, but it is subordinate. Therefore additive modification is an appropriate means of expressing it.

What is in the main line of development, and indeed constitutes one of the culmination points in the whole composition, is the next three assertions – the specification of the solution to Honolulu's smog problem:

ll. We need laws, today, that will limit the horsepower on all internal combustion vehicles.
mm. We need laws, today, that will discourage unnecessary driving by imposing increased ownership taxes.
nn. We need laws, today, that will discourage unnecessary driving by imposing increased use taxes.

No discussion is necessary to agree that these three assertions have a fundamental unity in their common subject and attribute and thus form a natural parallel sentence:

17. We need laws, today, that will limit the horsepower on all internal combustion vehicles *and* that will discourage unnecessary driving by imposing increased ownership *and* use taxes.

There are two unusual features of this sentence: the first is a question of the semantic kind of "need", and the second is the unorthodox position of the assertion modifier "today". *Need* is not a word with a variety of meanings, yet while the general sense is clear enough, it is possible to argue that this sense lies athwart our different semantic categories. To say, for example, that the house needs paint or needs painting is certainly to state a static characteristic of the house. The indivisible attribute core in this case would be "needs paint" or "needs painting". However, to say that I need a drink of water is approaching, at least, a function interpretation. When a person consciously and actively craves something, we can quite idiomatically say "I desperately need a drink of water". "Desperately" here looks very much like a function modifier. Even *suddenly* is not an impossibility: "I suddenly needed some fresh air". Moreover, there is a third possibility for *need*. In a few cases we can reasonably interpret it as a modal, as an imperative: "You need to follow instructions". This usage seems to differ in no significant respect from "You should/must/ought to/have to follow instructions". As imperatives, these would be diagramed as indivisible functions with "follow".

In deciding how to diagram "we need laws" we probably have to admit that this conscious and active craving is not quite as unequivocally functional as needing a drink of water. Yet, it is still quite possible to pass the 'adverb' test with a modification like "We desperately need laws". Thus, even while admitting that the entire phrase "need laws . . . that will limit the horsepower on all internal combustion vehicles and that will discourage unnecessary driving by imposing increased ownership and use taxes" could reasonably be interpreted as an indivisible characteristic attribute, we have opted for "need" as a function attribute. The two long relative clauses that remain are then taken to be assertion modifiers.

The second unusual grammatical feature here is the occurrence of an assertion modifier within an assertion modifier. "Laws that will . . . " answers the question, "We need what? " "Today" answers the question, "We need it when? " We have seen assertion modifiers coming at the beginning of an assertion, at the end of an assertion, and in various relationships with other assertion modifiers after the attribute. But this seems to be a new wrinkle. How do we know that "today" is a separate assertion modifier, and how do we account for this deviation from standard practice?

The conspicuous key to the problem is the punctuation around "today". In the most general sense parenthetical punctuation of this sort functions to make what it encompasses easily detached from its context. This, for example, is the rationale for punctuating post-positional additive modifiers. The punctuation here encourages us to temporarily set aside "today" and read what is left as a unit: "we need laws that will . . . . " Is the reference here to any and all laws? No, just to those laws that will limit the horsepower on all internal combustion engines and that will discourage unnecessary driving by imposing increased ownership and use taxes. Are there other kinds of laws? Of course. The great bulk of laws – from establishing salaries of public officials to establishing the penalties for murder, rape, and treason – are other than these. "Today" in this sentence has nothing to do with kinds of laws. It has to do with time of need. The usual order for multiple assertion modifiers of the *what* and *when* sort is to state the *what* first and the *when* second. There are two general reasons why this common order would be disturbed: to emphasize something or to avoid deemphasizing something. Both are relevant to the present sentence. Because of the two long parallel legs, the occurrence of "today" at the end of the sentence would place it very far from the subject and attribute ("We need") from which it derives its meaning. But more positively, "today" is quite an important part of the sentence – more so perhaps than even the kind of laws being advocated. The theme of "no justification for delay" is a central feature of this composition, and the use of "today" is a reminder that in this problem at least timing is as important as what is to be done. For emphasis, then, "today" is placed as close as possible to the subject/attribute core of the sentence – not out of its natural order before the *what* ("laws") but before any of the complex restrictive modification that specifies the kind of laws. Not only is "today" not deemphasized, it is actually emphasized by virtue of its altered position and the punctuation that sets it off in what would otherwise be an unpunctuated sentence.

But now, having been able to offer such a cogent explanation for the positioning of "today", based partly at least on the punctuation, what are we to say about "soon" in the previous sentence? It would seem that "find" and its future tense auxiliary are as much a unit as "laws" and its restrictive relative modifiers. And yet there is no punctuation around "soon" and not much likelihood that such would idiomatically occur. "Soon" could idiomatically occur in more than one place in this sentence, but where it is is as idiomatic as any. As with "today" we could offer a rationale of emphasis here, but "soon" is a rather mild sort of emphasis as compared to "today", and in any case, this would seem to require punctuation. We probably have to rest content with this construction as exemplifying idiomatic but only marginally explicable usage.

The only other point of possible disagreement is the secondary parallel of "ownership and use". Is there any possibility that it could be unitary? In diagraming them as a separable parallel, we have committed ourselves to the interpretation that there are two different kinds of automobile taxes, that one can be in effect without the other, and that both are being advocated here. But one needs to know about the different kinds of automobile taxes (e. g. personal property taxes and gasoline taxes) in order to distinguish this sentence from sentence 6, which was about "increased time and money". Nothing formal about "increased ownership and use taxes" is the basis of the distinction between it as separable and "increased time and money" as unitary. And, as we freely admitted with sentence 6, sentence 17 is amenable to the opposite interpretation – not as adequate an interpretation probably, but still a reasonable one.

At this point we come to the end of another division in the argument. Having previously asserted in no uncertain terms that there is no justification for delay, we have since been arguing for what there *is* justification for. And the answer to this question is sentence 17. We continue to rely more on implied inter-assertional relationships than on explicit conjunctions. But the meaning must be interpreted as essentially argumentative, as providing reasons for conclusions and reasons for the reasons, even though only one of the seven explanatory conjunctions in the following chart actually occurs in the text. If we do not, we are left without support for the claim that "we need laws, today". The absence of explicit conjunctions in these sentences that are obviously argumentative is primarily accounted for by the complexity of the argument. Only with the aid of boxes and indenting are we able to make clear precisely how our added conjunctions function. Explanatory conjunctions are most commonly used inter-assertionally – that is between one assertion and the next. Less commonly they link pairs of assertions (as in sentence 14). But beyond this, the relationships have to be explained, not just labeled. And this explanation is in large measure a matter of dialog – of moving back and forth between alternatives. Partly this dialog is an explicit part of the actual composition; partly it is implicit and is fully revealed only by means of hypothetic-

Implicit question		[What is there justification for?]
		[because]
Support for the answer	12.	That which is a demonstrable and pervasive public menace is the proper subject for immediate legislative action, and surely a health menace as serious as smog qualifies for such action.
		[because]
Support for the support	13.	Unless legal restrictions are widely applied and rigorously enforced in the early stages of contamination, urban congestion becomes so great that the price of purifying the air is destruction of the city.
		[because]
Support for the support for the support	14.	Los Angeles and New York City have been permanently contaminated, because legislative action was too little and too late.
		[therefore]
	15.	Here in Honolulu we must profit from their mistakes.
		[because]
	16.	If we continue to rely on the trade winds to ventilate our island, we will soon find the air as unpleasantly congested as the land.
		[therefore]
Answer	17.	We need laws, today, that will limit the horsepower on all internal combustion vehicles and that will discourage unnecessary driving by imposing increased ownership and use taxes.

al reconstructions.

Similar to "We need laws, today" in introducing the three related assertions of the previous sentence is "This is", which introduces these three:

oo. This is not to imply that we can do without the benefits of a mobile society.
pp. This is not to imply that we should do without the benefits of a mobile society.
qq. This is simply to acknowledge that we have reached the point where we have more to lose than to gain unless we make a concerted effort to control the machine whose faulty design and indiscriminate use has resulted in a growing menace to urban America.

Once again we are confronted by several parallel possibilities, treating some as unitary and some as separable even though they look pretty much alike. "Not to imply" and "simply to acknowledge" are separated, as are "can do without" and "should do without". But "faulty design and indiscriminate use" are treated as unitary.

18. This is not to imply that we can *or* should do without the benefits of a mobile society *but* simply to acknowledge that we have reached the point where we have more to lose than to gain unless we make a concerted effort to control the machine whose faulty design and indiscriminate use has resulted in a growing menace to urban America.

Before analyzing the parallel attributes, however, perhaps we ought to examine the subject. What precisely does "this" refer to, and, secondly, how is it interpretable as an instance of the class "to acknowledge"? A variation of this sentence might read:

I am not implying that we can or should do without the benefits of a mobile society but simply acknowledging that we have reached the point where . . . .

This would be agent/function. However, there are legitimate reasons for not wanting to inject personal reference into an argument. It is one thing to include one's nameless self in the total audience (e. g. we in Honolulu) for the sake of emphasizing that one is asking no more of others than he is of himself. But it is quite another to single himself out for special reference, because to do so can open the way to a charge of mere personal opinion. Most arguments, certainly this one, attempt to build a case for the reasonableness of something quite apart from the person who happens to be advocating it. Unless the writer has some special credentials for giving expert testimony, then he usually is better off letting the argument speak for itself.

What the "this" does, then, is to make it possible to comment on the previous sentence as part of an argument that can stand on its own merits. The referent for "this" is not a particular word or phrase preceding it, nor is it the whole sentence preceding it. Rather it is the *stating* of the previous sentence: *To state* the previous sentence is not *to imply* but simply *to acknowledge*. The casting of this sentence into the form of individual/class may require more effort than simply to let it emerge as agent/function, but the extra effort is semantically justified as a means of avoiding an irrelevant subject. Just as it was argued of sentence 16 that any additional effort needed to make "we" the subject was justified, so it is argued here that the effort to keep personal references from converting the general "we" to the individual "I" is justified. To argue for laws limiting horsepower and imposing increased taxes – no matter who argues it – is not to imply but simply to acknowledge.

Now, what makes this subject and these attributes an individual/class relationship? Whether 'verbals' are expressed in *-ing* form or in the 'infinitive' form by means of *to*, they cease to be functions and become things. They can function then as subjects, and their attributes can be of the same sort. The distinction, then, between identity, individual/class, and subclass/class will be only a matter of further discrimination among thing/thing assertions:

Identity. To levitate is to rise into the air and float in apparent defiance of gravity.

Individual. To leave now would be to lose all you have gained.

Subclass. To stand for hours on end is to risk serious back strain.

Our sentence is like the second one. A particular instance of doing something belongs to a class of functions.

Ours, however, is much more complex than this single-assertion sentence. It asserts two negative classification relationships prior to asserting the positive one. "Not to imply" includes of necessity the negative in the core attribute because negation is not merely a limitation but the very opposite meaning from what results without the negative. Although "not to imply" seems to be formally the very same sort of thing as "simply to acknowledge" there is an important semantic difference. "Simply" could be left out of its assertion, and what remained would be quite true in relation to the total sentence. But if "not" were left out of its assertion, then what remained would contradict the sentence as a whole. "Simply" is not, however, the usual restrictive modifier; it is not limiting but exclusive. Everything that follows "to acknowledge" is a limiting modifier: not everything is being acknowledged, only "that we have reached the point where . . . . ". But what precedes "to acknowledge" does not limit but rather indicates that nothing more is being acknowledged than the headword and its restrictive modification. Nothing more than this assertion is authorized by the writer as the interpretation of the previous sentence. To be sure, the writer may be quite unjustifiably denying clear implications of his proposal, but the meaning of "simply" in this assertion is clearly and unequivocally that of exclusive modification. The major parallel structure in this sentence, then, is the contrast (using the appropriate conjunction) between what is not meant and what is meant.

"Can" and "should" have already been exemplified in separable structures, and we noted that there can be a world of difference between what is possible (e. g. all-out nuclear warfare) and what is morally desirable. It is true that what we should do is contingent on what we can do, but unquestionably what we can do is not the criterion of what we should do.

The third parallel ("faulty design and indiscriminate use") could have presented a problem of interpretation if followed by the plural "have". But the use of the singular "has" is formal confirmation of what seems semantically quite reasonable – that two different factors have gone to create a menace not attributable to one or the other alone.

A final point to make about this sentence is the extensive use of restrictive modification for making implications. Going with "not to imply" is the relative clause "that we can or should do without the benefits of a mobile society". This clearly implies both that we can and should have the benefits of a mobile society even as we limit the horsepower on all internal combustion vehicles and impose increased ownership and use taxes. Perhaps this resort to implication is simply motivated by economy. Yet, this is a rather significant objection to proposals of this sort, and if the objection can be met, then this would constitute an important argument in favor of the proposal. But if it cannot be met, then we can understand why the writer chose to leave his counterclaim as strongly (but not necessarily) implied rather than asserted.

This implication is in contrast to the implication that derives from the restrictive modification of "to acknowledge". The nature of the headword here precludes the possibility of denying "that we have reached the point where we have more to lose than to gain unless we make a concerted effort to control the machine whose faulty design and indiscriminate use has resulted in a growing menace to urban America". To acknowledge is to claim the truth of something – something already asserted by others probably, but without any reservation as to the truth of it. However, this does not exhaust the obvious implications in this long and complex relative clause. If we were to diagram all subject-predicate clauses (which we do not because diagraming ceases to be useful when it ceases to be simple and fundamental), we would note "we" as a subject, "have reached" as an attribute, "point" as an assertion modifier, and everything after "point" as a restrictive modifier of it. But that modifier is itself another complex subject-predicate clause: "we have more to lose than to gain unless we make a concerted effort to control the machine whose faulty design and indiscriminate use has resulted in a growing menace to urban America". However, though we can say that the entire "we have reached" clause is necessarily implied by virtue of its direct modification of "acknowledge", we cannot say that the "we have more to lose" clause is necessarily implied. This modifies "point", and nothing about a point dictates necessary implication.

These clauses are by no means the extent of the not necessary implications here; indeed, the most important implication has still to be mentioned. Implied by "the machine whose faulty design and indiscriminate use has resulted in a growing menace to urban America" is that the machine referred to is the internal combustion vehicle and that both faulty design and indiscriminate use of it have caused the growing smog problem. Nowhere has it been explicitly stated that these vehicles are faultily designed and indiscriminately used, but the nature of the argument seems to require that this be inferred. The faulty design has been implied from the beginning of the composition, but the indiscriminate use was not a factor until the second half of the previous sentence. Yet what is introduced as an implication cannot be left that way if it is a crucial factor in the total composition. Thus the remaining four sentences in the composition clarify this implication about indiscriminate use.

The transition to this clarification is the continuing conjunction "and". What follows the conjunction is almost certain to be not just one assertion but a pair of them:

rr. When such a point is reached, a problem has two parts.
ss. The two parts a problem has when such a point is reached are an initial condition and circumstances that allow that problem to flourish.

The obvious common feature is the double use of the conditional "when such a point is reached". But there are even more shared elements if we relate the two assertions by means of an appositive parallel:

19. *And* when such a point is reached, a problem has two parts: an initial condition and circumstances that allow that condition to flourish.

The use of a colon as an equal sign equating the two legs of the parallel makes an appositive interpretation almost mandatory. It is possible to find as many as four component assertions in this sentence: three different parallels and an additive modifier. However, two of the parallels are logically incorporated into the two-part appositive.

The diagraming might present a bit of a problem here. Separable parallel marks, rather than unitary, are used throughout because there is no logical or semantic impediment to finding three parallel assertions. But to clearly indicate that both "an initial condition" and "circumstances that allow that condition to flourish" must be taken as a unitary additive modifier of "two parts", we use not two sets of additive brackets but only one. To do otherwise would be to allow for two separate assertions: The two parts a problem has when such a point is reached is an initial condition. The two parts a problem has when such a point is reached is circumstances that allow that condition to flourish.

A second possible diagraming problem is the extent of the "had" attribute. "Two" is clearly a restrictive modifier of "parts", "an initial" of "condition", "that allow that condition to flourish" of "circumstances". But these restrictive modifiers are not diagramed as attribute modifiers because they do not modify the entire "had" phrase. "Two" does not modify "has parts". It is an indivisible part of the core attribute. Where "had" is a part of the attribute beyond a mere tense auxiliary, what is had can be extensively modified, but these modifiers are part of what is had and are not modifiers of the having. However, with

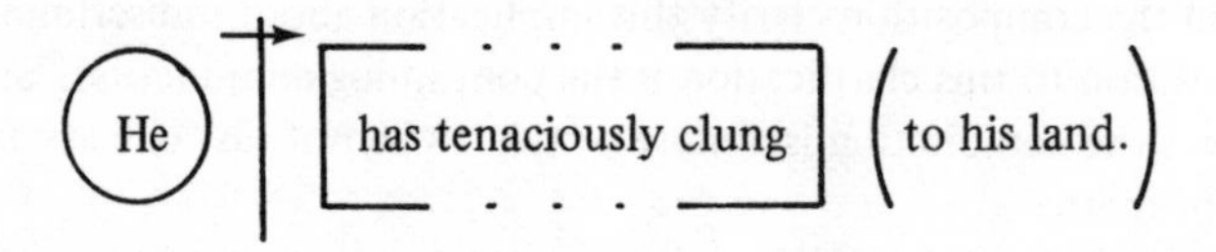

the function of "has" is merely auxiliary – to indicate past time continuing into the present. It has no semantic function beyond that. Thus "tenaciously" is a separable attribute modifier.

The next assertion presents us with a problem that combines the two kinds of pre-positional modifiers found in sentence 18 – negating and exclusive:

tt. The public is not just a victim.

Two questions have to be answered about this assertion: whether the public is an individual or a subclass, and how much of the attribute should be diagramed as part of the core. The argument for the first is a bit equivocal, so let us treat the second one first. In sentence 18 we reiterated the basic semantic principle that negatives must be part of the core; to grant this, however, is not to resolve the problem here. What precisely does the "not" negate? Does the assertion say that the public is not a victim? If we look to the next assertion, the answer is clear enough:

uu. It is a victim that condones the victimizing.

The public is, then, whatever else may be involved, a victim. Thus we cannot diagram as the attribute core "not . . . a victim". An exclusive modifier may modify the core (as in sentence 18), or it may be a part of the core (sentence 20). The reason that "just" must be part of the core here is because the negative must be part of the core and so must everything negated by the negative. "Just" goes with "victim", and "not" goes with the two together. The attribute core then is the indivisible phrase, "not just a victim".

Unlike this phrase is the attribute phrase in the assertion that follows it. "A victim that condones the victimizing" has "victim" as the core, and all the rest is limiting modification of it. There are different kinds of victims: those that condone the victimizing and those that do not condone the victimizing. The public belongs to the former, but whichever kind of victim one is, he is a victim. Thus there is no indivisible attribute core made up of an entire phrase. "That condones the victimizing" is limiting modification. "Not just" is not limiting modification, because it does not distinguish one kind of victim from other kinds of victims.

These two are clearly classification assertions. But what is classified – an individual or a subclass? Sentence 8 ("The electric vehicle is a red herring".) has been our only example in this composition of subclass/class. And this interpretation was not difficult to arrive at even though the subject was singular. "The dog is a mammal" is no less about a subclass than is "Dogs are mammals". "The electric vehicle" is a subclass of vehicles comprising all instances of electric vehicles. Such an understanding, however, does not automatically establish "the public" as a subclass, because the public is not obviously a class comprising all instances of publics. We might say that an instance of public is a person, yet person is more precisely referred to plurally as persons rather than as the public. We can refer in some contexts at least not just to all the people collectively as *the* public, we can also refer to subordinate publics by means of limiting modification: e. g. , the bicycle-riding public and the American public. But both of these attempts – to make persons the instances of the public or to make different publics the subclasses of the public – seem a bit forced as general interpretations of the common usage. Unless otherwise indicated, the public seems most commonly thought of as the indivisible body politic. And as such, it seems most adequately interpreted here as an instance of the class, victim.

The only remaining problem is the sort of sentence structure to employ for sentence 20. There is a possibility for parallel structure here but not without some rephrasing of the two assertions. It would be easy enough to make a contrasting parallel out of two unequivocally opposite assertions – e. g., The public is not a victim but a victimizer. However, the relation of our two assertions is more subtle; they are at the same time both continuation and contrast. Neither conjunctions nor parallel structure are very applicable to the pair as they are written. A better possibility is compound structure:

20. The public is not just a victim; it is a victim that condones the victimizing.

Here we keep the parallel form as conspicuous as possible to emphasize the comparison and contrast in the two attributes – and let the form substitute for a conjunction – while at the same time we repeat all that is necessary to create independent clauses. Independent clauses are the next best thing to single assertion sentences for emphasizing the significance of what is said. That the public is a victim that condones the victimizing is one of the half dozen or so key points in this composition. Some individual people will not be classifiable as such, but the citizenry as a whole, *das Volk*, society as an organic unit, will be.

No syntactical problems will confront us in the next assertion,

vv. We have the means to oppose a great evil.

because of its obvious relationship to an appropriate mate,

ww. We have the responsibility to do so.

Parallel structure is called for here as a means of linking reason to conclusion:

21. We have the means to oppose a great evil *and thus* the responsibility to do so.

At this stage in the composition the only grammatical feature that might require special comment is the "have" attribute. Does "to oppose a great evil" answer the question, "What kind of means?" If it does, then it should be diagramed as part of the attribute core. Similarly with "to do so": if it modifies "responsibility", then it cannot be an assertion modifier. As we have diagramed the sentence, however, "to oppose a great evil" and "to do so" are assertion modifiers answering the question, "For what goal or motive?" Insofar as different kinds of goals or motives result in different kinds of means, then diagraming is a toss up. Admittedly, neither of these two possibilities is unreasonable, but in the balance the assertion modifier looks more reasonable here than does the attribute modifier. If we are not careful, every modifier that occurs with a thing will be interpreted simply as limiting the scope of the reference of that thing. The result would be one ubiquitous grammatical category with no facility for making semantic distinctions.

Even more serious than overlooking the "For what goal or motive? " category in our sentence is the treatment of this commonly referred to pair by transformational grammarians:

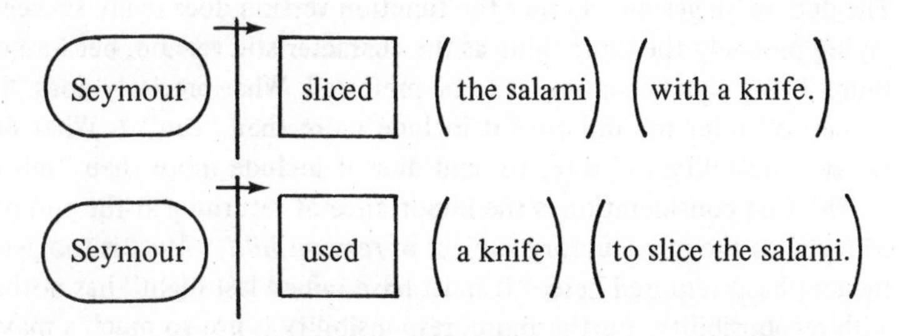

Though these grammarians disagree among themselves about the role of 'deep structure' in explaining the meaning, they agree that the sentences are synonymous. But do they really mean precisely the same thing? As our diagrams reveal, the first sentence has two assertion modifiers: answering the questions, "He sliced what? " and "He sliced it by what means? " The second sentence answers two different questions: "He used what? " and "He used it for what goal or motive? " The second sentence implies that the salami was in fact sliced, but it does not necessarily imply it, and it does not state it. To have a goal, motive, or intention is not necessarily to succeed. If the sentence had said

Seymour used a butter knife to slice the salami.

we would be much less ready to assume that he actually achieved his goal. And if the sentence had said

Seymour used a knife to slice the salami, but the blade was so dull that all he got for his effort was bits and pieces.

we would know that he did not achieve his goal. Only "Seymour sliced the salami with a knife" tells us unequivocally that the salami was actually sliced.

It is only a short step from this examination of two different agent/function sentences with two different meanings to a comment on the possibility of alternative semantic kinds of assertions with the same meanings. Isn't it rather arbitrary that sentence 21 is cast in characteristic form rather than, say, agent/function? Indeed, it could be argued that the meaning of this sentence is more appropriately function than characteristic, and the proof of this is that essentially the same meaning can be stated as function more economically than as characteristic:

We can oppose a great evil and thus must do so.

The debate hinges on whether the function version does really succeed in saying precisely the same thing as the characteristic version, because other things being equal economy is to be preferred. What precisely does "have the means to" refer to, and does it include more than "can" ? What does "have the responsibility to" refer to, and does it include more than "must" ?

The first consideration is the importance of returning at the end of the editorial to the introductory subject of *responsibility*. *Must* is too general for the emphasis required here. "It must have rained last night" has nothing to do with responsibility. Furthermore, responsibility is not so much a matter of doing something as it is a matter of a condition or aspect of one's existence. It is more like having blue eyes than it is like running: a person can choose not to run but he cannot choose not to have his blue eyes. On the one hand, we can have a responsibility without ever acting on it. On the other hand, we can attempt to oppose a great evil without really having the means to do it. And if one does not really have the means, he does not really have the responsibility. This sentence is not the end of the argument but rather the penultimate stage; it prepares the ground for the final sentence – which *is* about function rather than characteristic. There are two distinct stages to the argument here: (sentence 21) what we have whether we want it or not; (sentence 22) what we may or may not choose to do about it.

There is also more to the contention about economy than first meets the eye. While the proposed function sentence is a bit more economical than the characteristic sentence, the characteristic sentence is appreciably more economical than the argument that is actually implied by it:

To have the means to oppose a great evil is to have the responsibility to do so.

We have the means to oppose a great evil.

Thus, we have the responsibility to do so.

This syllogism is twice as long as sentence 21.

Further economy is always possible, and thus we always need to weigh the various factors of internal intelligibility and external requirements. The writer of this composition decided that little would be lost in reducing his syllogistic meaning to just the minor premise and the conclusion – that the major premise could be readily and unequivocally inferred. The incentive for this reduction was the great gain in economy. He might also have decided that the two stages of his concluding argument – the characteristic and the function – could reasonably be inferred from just the statement of function. But he decided to emphasize the two distinct stages rather than strive for maximum economy. Economy is not an end in itself; indeed, it is antithetical to generativeness. Therefore, to decide for economy in one place is to decide for development in another. The writer decided here that nothing was more important to his conclusion than laying out the separate stages of public responsibility. After all, to reduce an argument to its furthest extent is to eliminate all but the conclusion and thus to destroy its nature as an argument.

The last assertion must of necessity constitute a single sentence. In one sense there are two separate assertions left: "We act now". "We become as culpable as the automobile industry itself". But both of these cannot be true. Thus there is an either/or relationship, and thus in the strict sense they must occur together. They do not, however, constitute a unitary parallel because the complete subject and predicate of each is given. What we have instead is a unitary compound sentence:

xx/*22*. Either we act now or we become as culpable as the automobile industry itself.

There is no problem in analyzing "we act now". The subject, attribute, and assertion modifier follow a very familiar pattern. But the second attribute raises something of a problem because of the combination of "becoming" and a comparison. *Becoming* assertions necessarily include more than the *becoming* word in the core of the attribute. But how much more? Does this assertion say that either we act now or become culpable? For those of us who know how very culpable the automobile industry already is, the implication is clear that this is so. But the assertion only implies it; what is asserted here is only equality of culpability. If the auto industry is culpable, then so are we; if the auto industry is not culpable, then neither are we. "Becoming" goes with the entire predicate; nothing can be left out as a restrictive modifier without basically altering the meaning of what is left. The indivisible attribute core here is "become as culpable as the automobile industry itself". Even "itself" must be included, because its relationship is with something that must go with "become". It is a redundant modifier of "the automobile industry" but not of the attribute as a whole. Thus we do not diagram it separately.

A final clarification may be in order about the necessity of including the entire attribute in the core of a *becoming* function attribute. Is it possible for such an attribute to have a restrictive modifier? Yes. When the *becoming* function is modified in a distinctly functioning manner – "How done? " – then the *become* word is included as part of what is modified. In the examples below, "very" modifies only "rich" and "corporation" only "lawyer". But "steadily" modifies "became richer". One can not become very or become corporation, but one can become steadily.

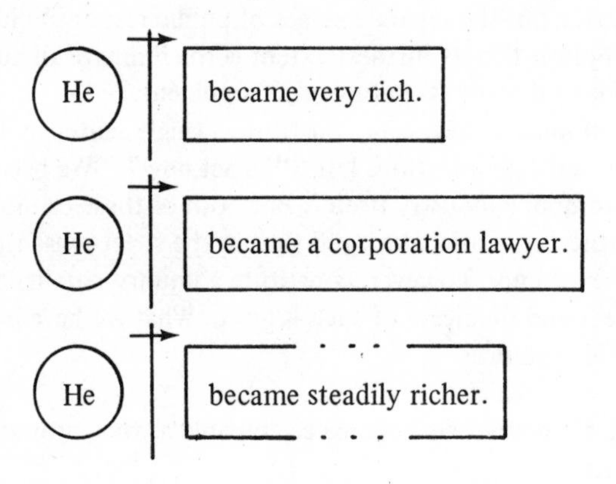

At this point we are able to lay out the final stage of the smog argument. Beginning with sentence 18 we have been providing support for the conclusion expressed in the last sentence. In answer to the implied question of what will become of us if we do not act now, we are given sentence 22. *Why* 22 is a proper answer is explained by 18, 19, 20, and 21. Lumping these four together does not do justice to the complexities of the reasoning, but we have done all the analyzing that can be done by means of inter-assertional conjunctions. Another attempt to discern the pattern of argument in the editorial – but one that requires extensive paraphrasing – occurs in the next chapter.[4]

By way of conclusion, we might note the different frequencies of occurrence of the six semantic kinds. At this point, no statistical data can be provided for definite conclusions. All we can do is assume that these fifty assertions constitute a fair sampling of the usage of semantic kinds and extrapolate from that. At best such an attempt to generalize from very limited data will be only suggestive, therefore, we will not even do any precise counting

Implicit question

[What will become of us if we do not act now?]

[because]

18. This is not to imply that we can or should do without the benefits of a mobile society but simply to acknowledge that we have reached the point where we have more to lose than to gain unless we make a concerted effort to control the machine whose faulty design and indiscriminate use has resulted in a growing menace to urban America.

Support for the answer

19. And when such a point is reached, a problem has two parts: an initial condition and circumstances that allow that condition to flourish.

20. The public is not just a victim; it is a victim that condones the victimizing.

21. We have the means to oppose a great evil and thus the responsibility to do so.

[therefore]

Answer

22. Either we act now or we become as culpable as the automobile industry itself.

– to do so would imply a degree of statistical validity that we cannot justifiably claim. But the very lopsidedness of the proportions *is* suggestive. Agent/function and characteristic assertions constitute more than half of the total. Object/function, identity, and subclass/class have little more than token representation. Somewhere in between these two extremes is the occurrence of individual/class.[5]

This much of a tentative conclusion might reasonably be drawn from these differences: agent/function and characteristic assertions are the two basic possibilities, and they are so most likely because they tend to be ubiquitous. There is no substitute for precision in the selection of semantic kinds of assertions; however, almost every meaning can be approximated with these two kinds.

The attempt to justify a fundamental realm of linguistic study called "stylistics" as the study of choice between synonyms has been one of the more conspicuous failures of language study.[6] The limits of such study are especially constricting when, as is usually the case, synonomy is taken to be primarily lexical, a matter of word meanings. To the extent that synonomy can provide the basis of a kind of productive linguistic study, this must include more than lexical atomism; there needs to be some sort of abstract semantic framework. Our six semantic kinds, for instance, would make possible a certain amount of legitimate search for synonomy. Primarily the classes reflect different kinds of meaning, but secondarily the flexibility of the six classes make possible the expression of some very similar, even identical, meanings in two different ways. No matter how we look at it, however, saying the same thing differently is and must be linguistically marginal. If it were not, communication would be seriously handicapped. The very nature of language is to say different things differently. But languages change; people change; things change. And as a result of both the development of the new and the breakdown of the old we sometimes find ourselves confronted with different statements that seem to be saying the same thing. Such occurrences are most conspicuous and most common when two different languages or dialects come into contact. However, since this contact is always unstable, synonymous formulations do not persevere for long.[7]

An appropriate analogy is to vehicles on a freeway. The many vehicles on the same stretch of road are all traveling in the same direction at approximately the same speed. But only very rarely do two vehicles in two different lanes happen to move for more than a minute or so side by side. Too many individual factors militate against coexistence, and there are no very compelling reasons for people to strive for it.

Even where the means for synonomy exist, organizational factors usually dictate the greater adequacy of one possibility. Integrating a composition is possible because there is a certain amount of lexical and grammatical flexibility in a language. But this flexibility exists *prior* to integration. An already integrated composition cannot in any semantically precise sense be expressed other than it is.

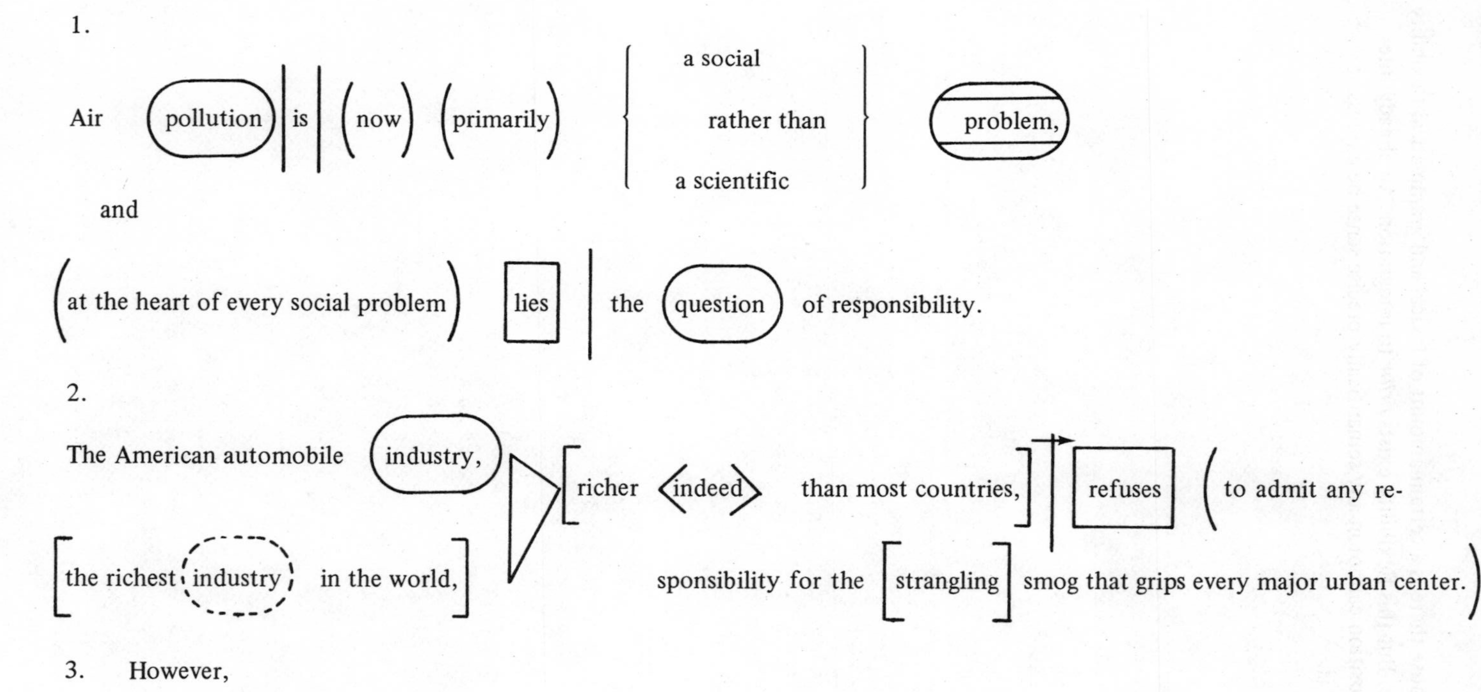
1.
Air pollution is now primarily
a social
rather than
a scientific
problem,
and
at the heart of every social problem lies the question of responsibility.
2.
The American automobile industry,
richer indeed than most countries,
the richest industry in the world,
refuses to admit any re-
sponsibility for the strangling smog that grips every major urban center.
3. However,
the facts are no longer at issue,
and

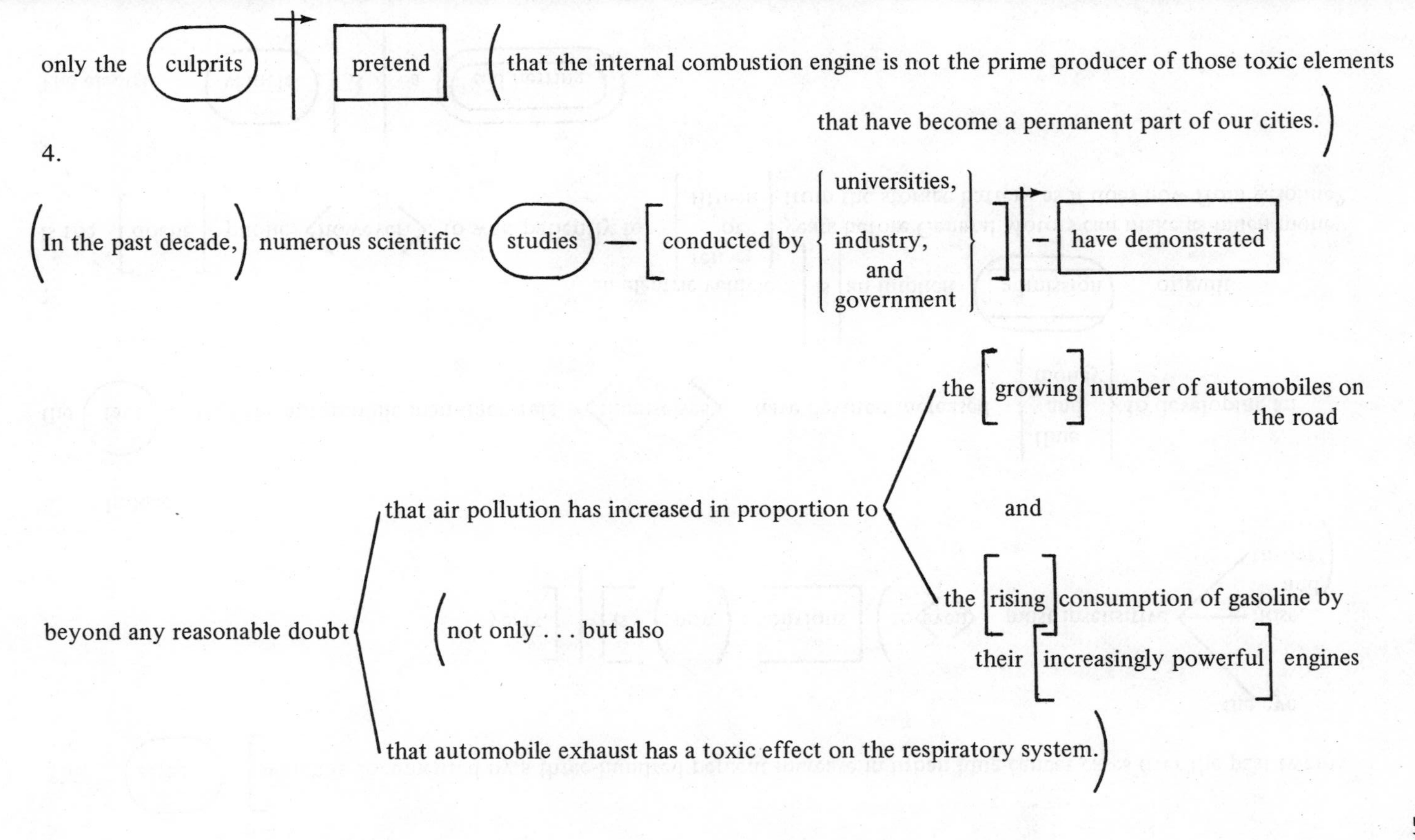

only the
culprits
pretend
that the internal combustion engine is not the prime producer of those toxic elements
that have become a permanent part of our cities.
4.
In the past decade,
numerous scientific
studies
conducted by
universities,
industry,
and
government
have demonstrated
beyond any reasonable doubt
that air pollution has increased in proportion to
the
growing
number of automobiles on the road
and
the
rising
consumption of gasoline by
their
increasingly powerful
engines
not only . . . but also
that automobile exhaust has a toxic effect on the respiratory system.

5.

This effect, which is documented by a three-hundred percent increase in urban lung-cancer cases over the past twenty

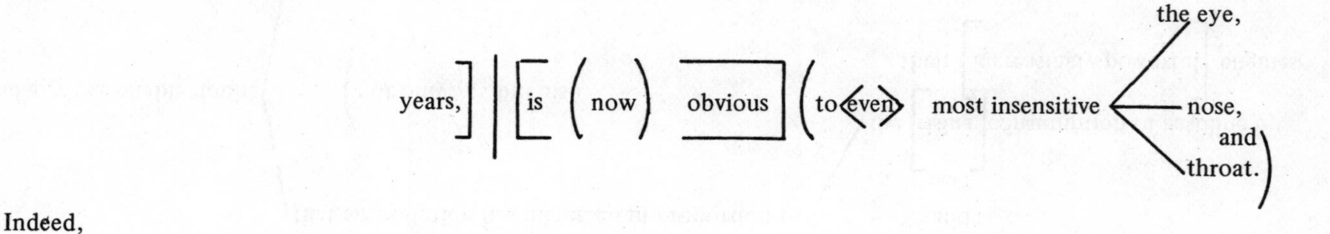

6. Indeed,

the fact that the automobile manufacturers themselves have devoted increased time and money to developing an electric vehicle is an implicit admission of guilt.

7.

Is the docile public, however, to wait patiently for ten or fifteen years before General Motors can make as much money from the storage battery as it does now from gasoline?

8.

The electric vehicle is a red herring.

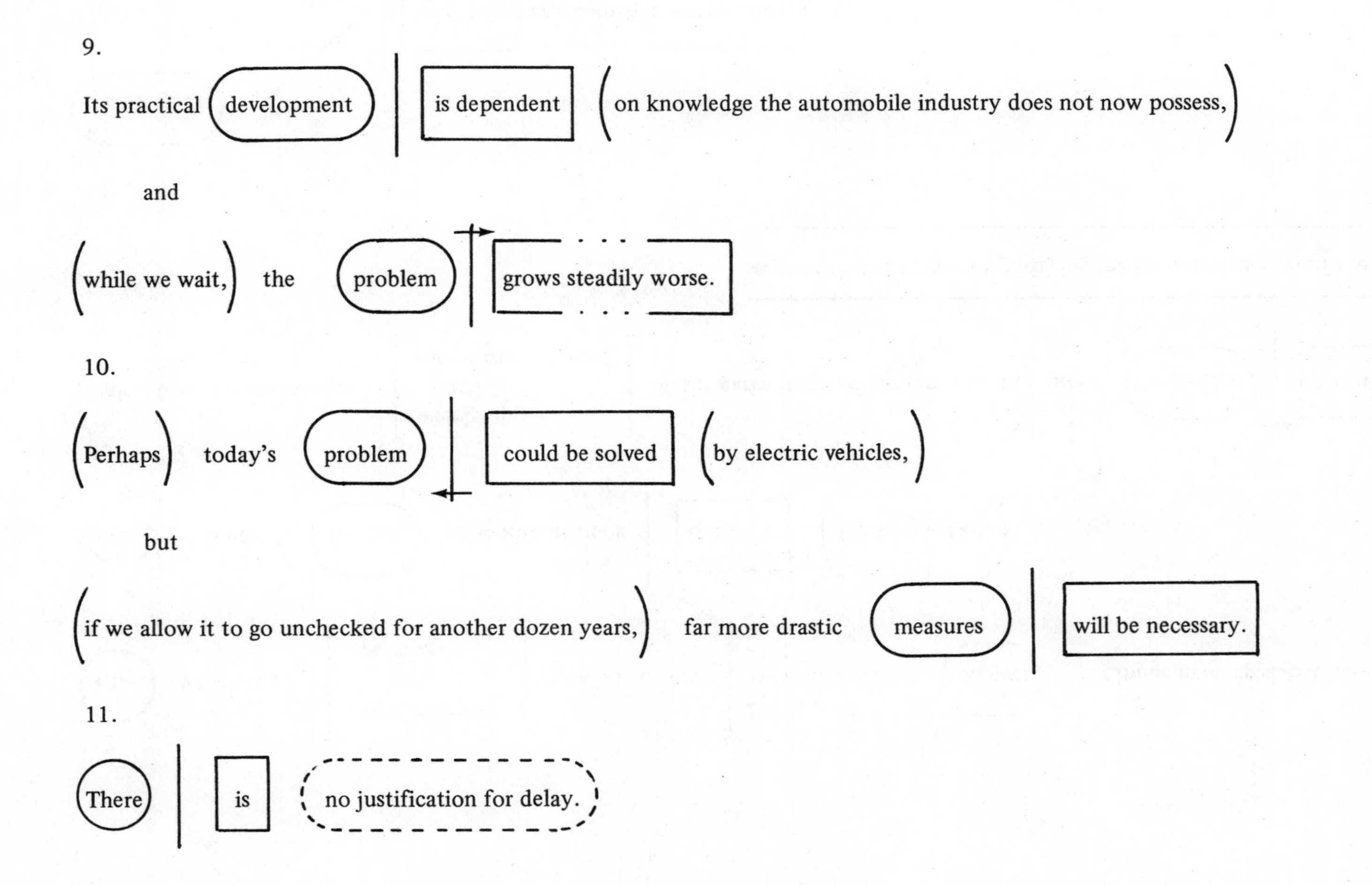
9.
Its practical
development
is dependent
on knowledge the automobile industry does not now possess,
and
while we wait,
the
problem
grows steadily worse.
10.
Perhaps
today's
problem
could be solved
by electric vehicles,
but
if we allow it to go unchecked for another dozen years,
far more drastic
measures
will be necessary.
11.
There
is
no justification for delay.

12.

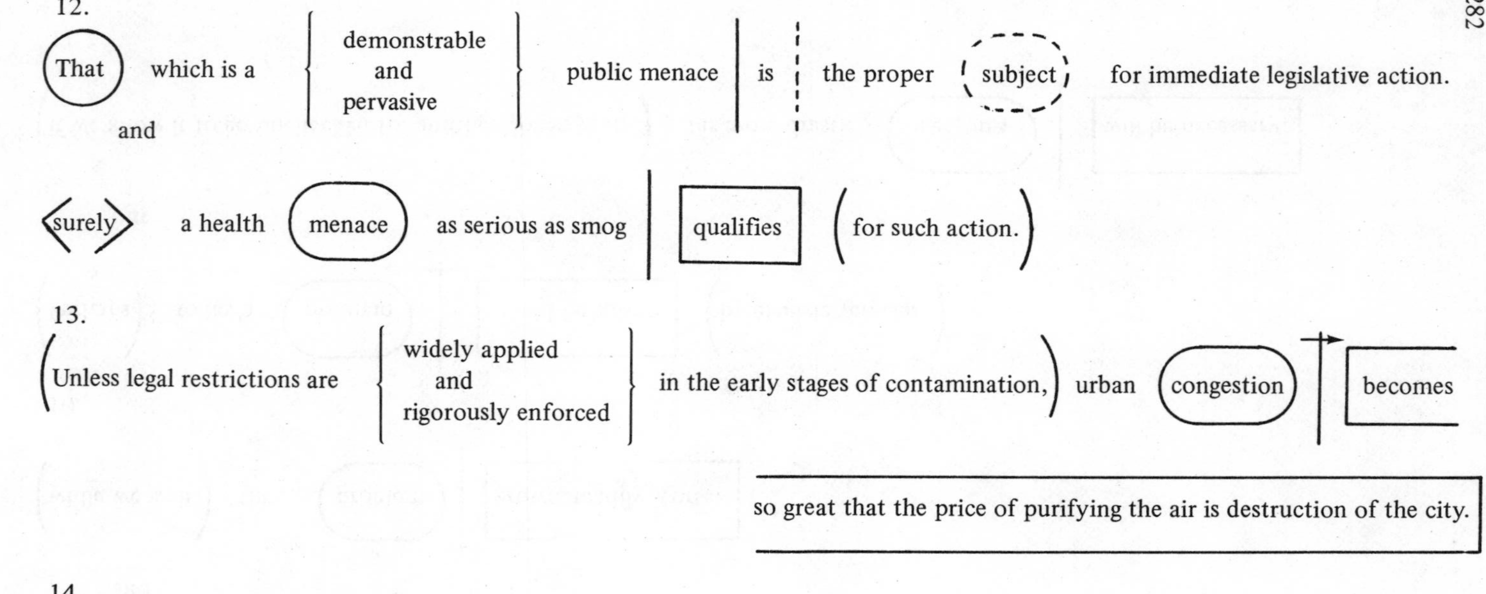
That
which is a
demonstrable
and
pervasive
public menace
is
the proper
subject
for immediate legislative action.
and
surely
a health
menace
as serious as smog
qualifies
for such action.
13.
Unless legal restrictions are
widely applied
and
rigorously enforced
in the early stages of contamination,
urban
congestion
becomes
so great that the price of purifying the air is destruction of the city.

14.

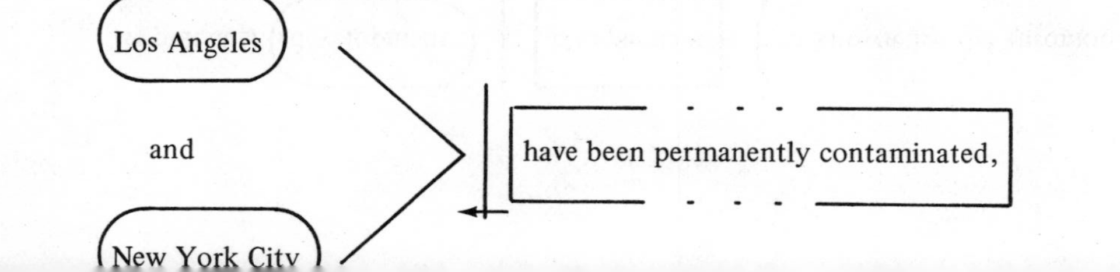
Los Angeles
and
New York City
have been permanently contaminated,

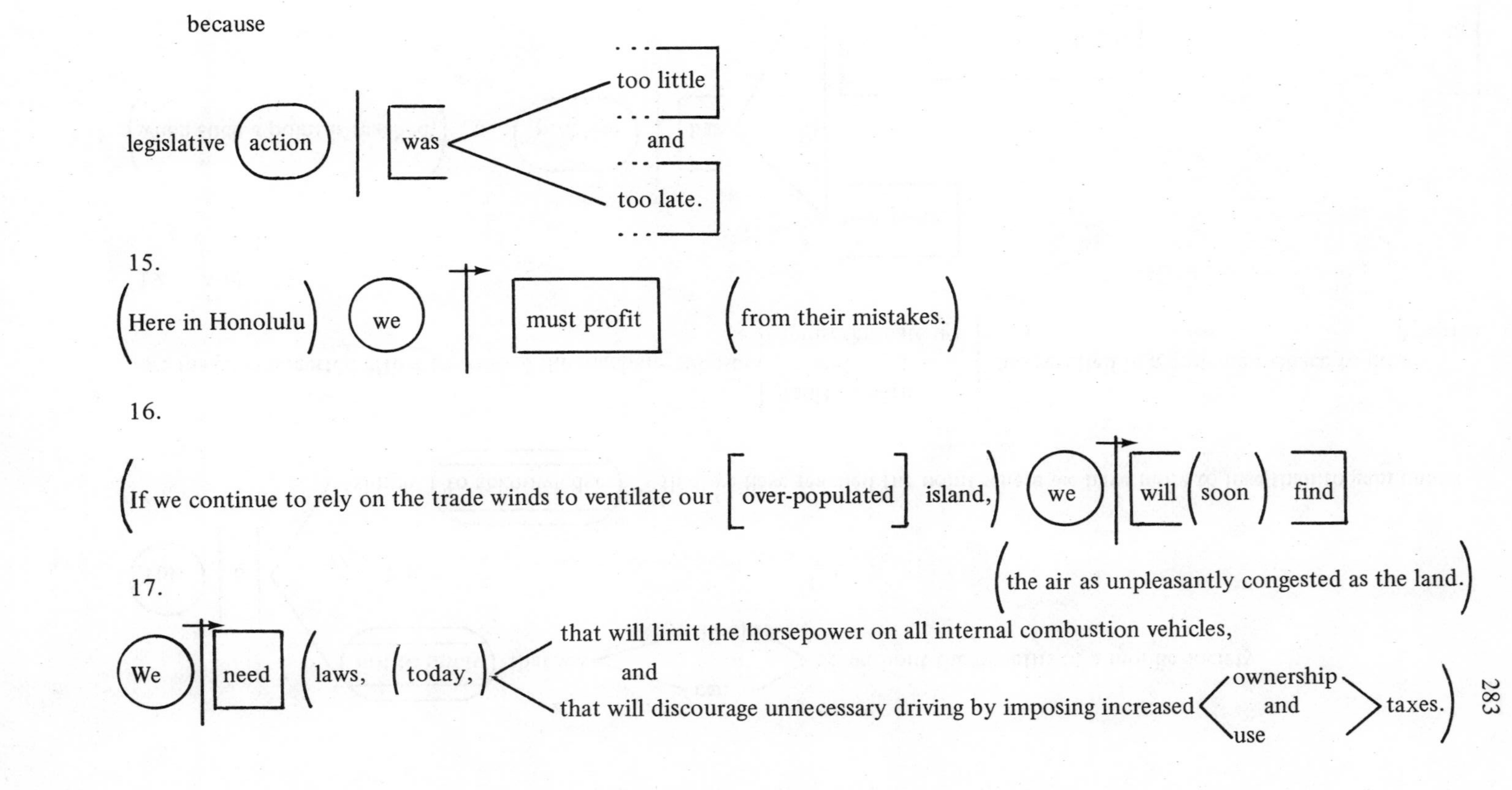
because
legislative
action
was
too little
and
too late.
15.
Here in Honolulu
we
must profit
from their mistakes.
16.
If we continue to rely on the trade winds to ventilate our
over-populated
island,
we
will
soon
find
the air as unpleasantly congested as the land.
17.
We
need
laws,
today,
that will limit the horsepower on all internal combustion vehicles,
and
that will discourage unnecessary driving by imposing increased
ownership
and
use
taxes.

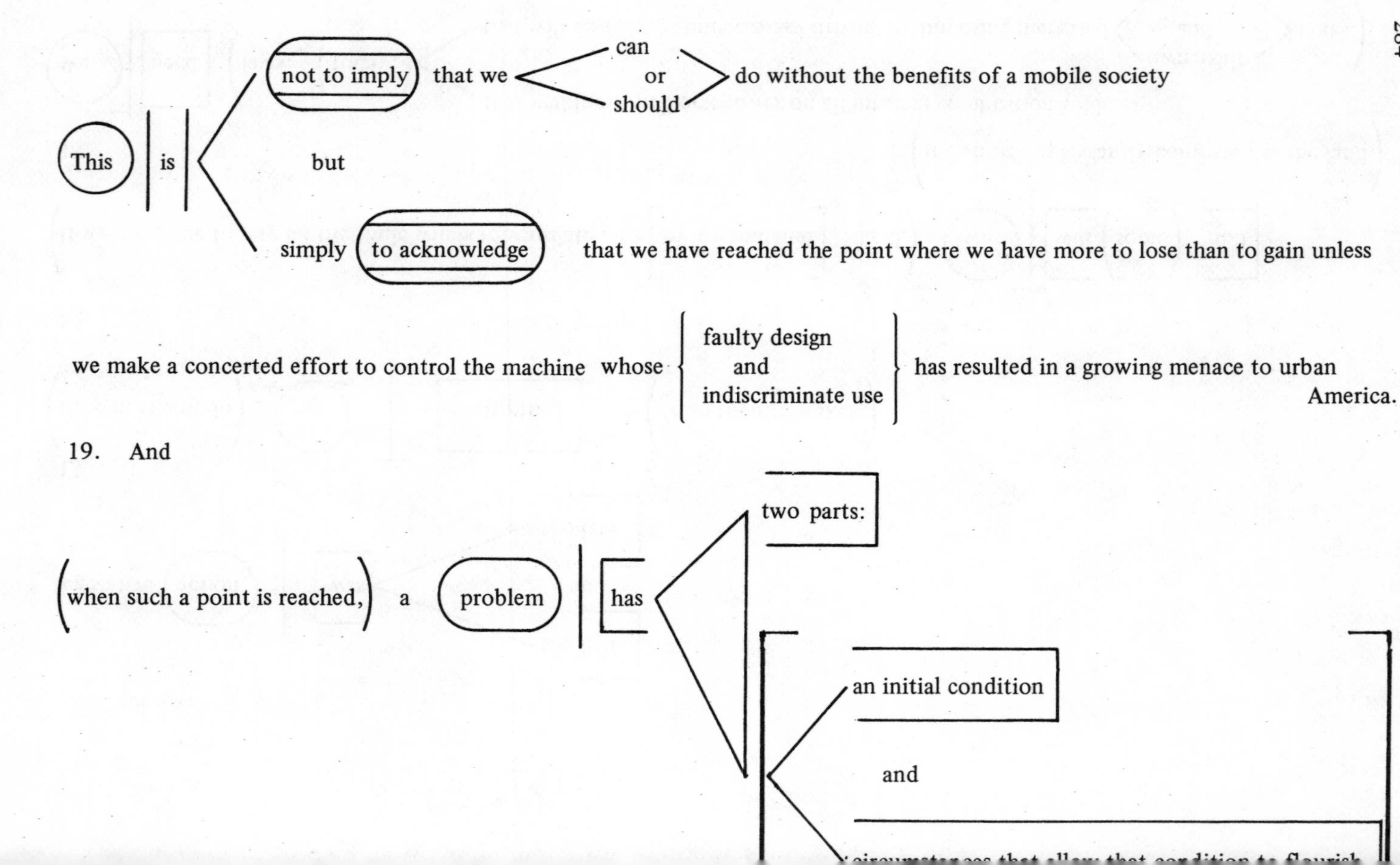
18.
This
is
not to imply
that we
can
or
should
do without the benefits of a mobile society
but
simply
to acknowledge
that we have reached the point where we have more to lose than to gain unless
we make a concerted effort to control the machine whose
faulty design
and
indiscriminate use
has resulted in a growing menace to urban America.
19. And
(when such a point is reached,) a
problem
has
two parts:
an initial condition
and

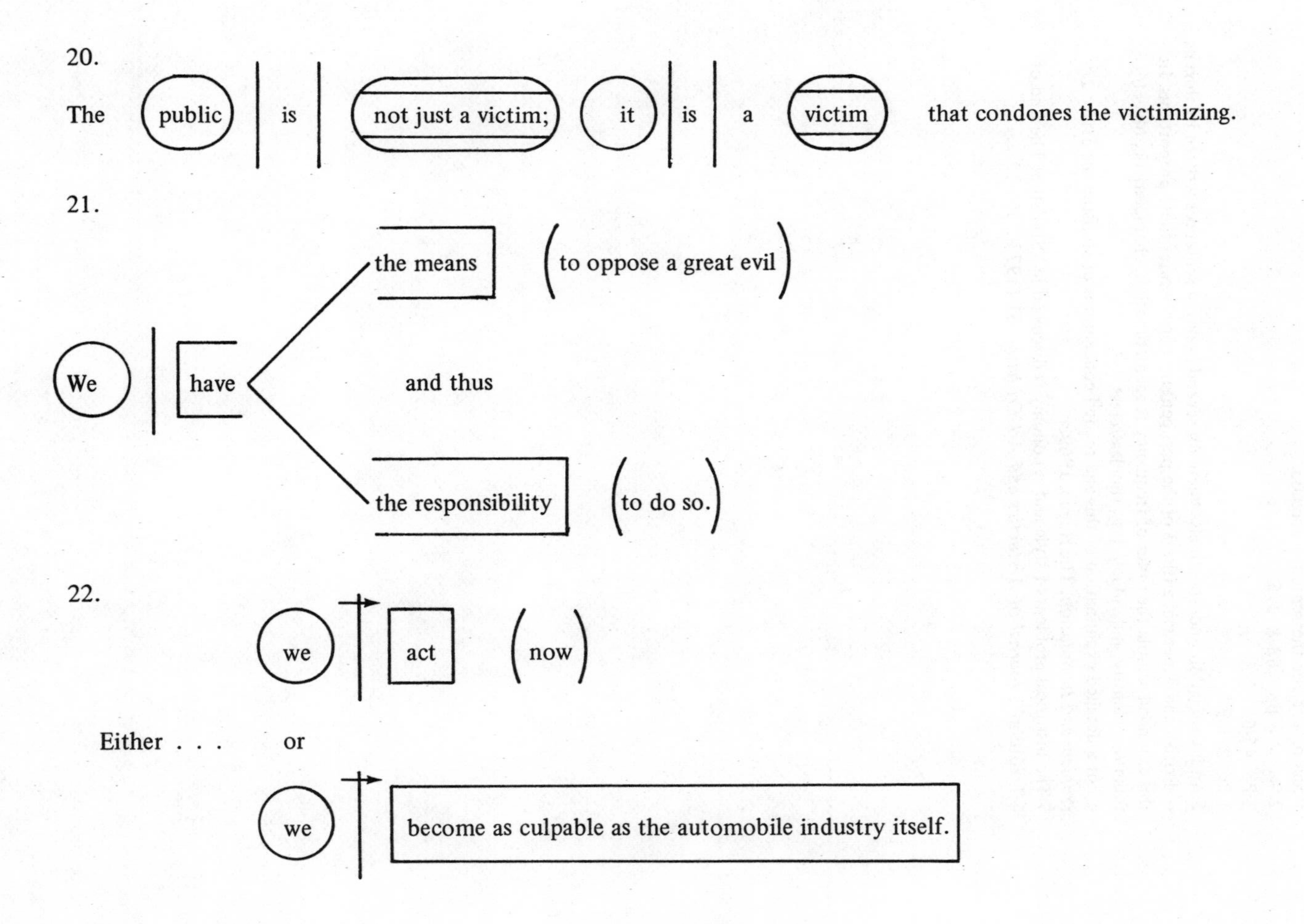
20.
The
public
is
not just a victim;
it
is
a
victim
that condones the victimizing.
21.
We
have
the means
to oppose a great evil
and thus
the responsibility
to do so.
22.
Either . . .
we
act
now
or
we
become as culpable as the automobile industry itself.

NOTES

1 See p. 278 for the sentence diagram.
2 See also pp. 263 & 275.
3 Pp. 45-6.
4 Pp. 296-97.
5 An investigation undertaken elsewhere on several hundred sentences written by dozens of British and American authors of the past century corroborates these proportions. In this extended sample the order of frequency is agent/function, characteristic, object/function, identity, individual/class, subclass/class.
6 For a detailed examination of this and related conceptions of stylistics see *Style: The Problem and Its Solution*, The Hague, 1969.
7 The historical problem of style and synonomy is discussed in "Stylistics: The End of a Tradition", *Journal of Aesthetics and Art Criticism*, 31 (1973), 501-12

9. THE FRAMEWORK OF DIALOG

The proof that there is more to composing integrated discourse than generating it assertion by assertion with implied dialog is to take the opening assertion of an already integrated composition and develop an alternate composition with no attention to a consistent line of questioning. Implied dialog is the generating principle, but without a framework for the dialog, the assertions generated will be like so many voices in a crowd. This problem of organization is a very real one in compositions and by no means confined to the work of the novice. In Barzun and Graff's lucid and widely used introduction to the researching and writing of history there is a paragraph quoted from one of the many books of an eminent literary historian. So diverse are the relationships between the assertions that Barzun and Graff's critique of it is almost charity: "The trouble with this passage, plainly, is that the facts and ideas have not been organized but rather thrown pell-mell at the reader. The result is that although the separate bits of information are all obviously there, the full meaning is not".[1] Each assertion is clearly related to some element in the previous assertion – some implied question is being answered – but the questions are quite unrelated to each other.

This kind of 'stream-of-consciousness' composition is common enough to merit some detailed attention – especially since it points up the limitations of the generativeness of generative rhetoric. Let us generate our own 'stream-of-consciousness' paragraph – a paragraph that not only will be unintegrated but unintegratable. And, to emphasize the contrast, let us take as our starting point the opening assertion of the smog editorial; but instead of following it with an inquiry about air pollution or social problems or scientific problems – inquiries designed to *clarify* what has already been said – the inquiry will *expand* the original assertion.

1. Air pollution is now primarily a social rather than a scientific problem.

   Is this the only kind of modern pollution problem?

2. Another modern pollution problem can be seen in the contaminated rivers, lakes, and oceans.

Doesn't contaminated water eventually cure itself with the aid of minute organisms?

3. The purification of water by micro-organisms is no longer possible.

Why is this impossible?

4. Much recent contamination is not bio-degradable.

Will the recent bio-degradable detergents solve the problem?

5. Some improvement would result from the widespread replacement of non-degradable with bio-degradable detergents.

Do bio-degradable detergents leave dishes and clothes as sparkling clean?

6. Of course, the housewife will have to make some sacrifices in her standards of wash-day brightness if we are to reestablish an ecologically balanced world.

Haven't housewives traditionally found washing the most disagreeable and time-consuming household task?

7. Admittedly, the introduction of technological aids to make washing easier and quicker has been one of the important means of liberating modern women.

Is this a criticism of Women's Liberation as unecological?

8. This is not to imply that Women's Liberation should be censured as unecological.

Isn't ecology relevant to analyzing this movement?

9. Enough opposition to this movement exists already without injecting ecology.

Will the back-lash from the Women's Liberation movement make it harder for women to secure equality of opportunity?

10. There is always a predictable back-lash when previously subordinated

groups seek to gain equality of opportunity.

Is equality of opportunity a feasible goal in a society made up of so many unequal people?

11. The standard fallacious argument is that God would have made people equal if it were best for them to be equal.

Does this mean that modern movements for equality are atheistic?

12. We need to recognize that equality of opportunity is now primarily a social rather than a theological problem.

Eliminating the questions and adding inter-assertional conjunctions where possible, we have the finished paragraph:

Air pollution is now primarily a social rather than a scientific problem, and another modern pollution problem can be seen in the contaminated rivers, lakes, and oceans. The purification of water by micro-organisms is no longer possible, because much recent contamination is not bio-degradable. Some improvement would result from the widespread replacement of non-degradable with bio-degradable detergents. But of course the housewife will have to make some sacrifice in her standards of wash-day brightness if we are to reestablish an ecologically balanced world. Admittedly, the introduction of technological aids to make washing easier and quicker has been one of the important means of liberating modern women. However, this is not to imply that Women's Liberation should be censured as unecological. Enough opposition to the movement exists already without injecting ecology. There is always a predictable back-lash when previously subordinated groups seek to gain equality of opportunity. A standard fallacious argument is that God would have made people equal if it were best for them to be equal. But we need to recognize that equality of opportunity is now primarily a social rather than a theological problem.

From air pollution to water pollution, from water pollution to micro-organisms, from micro-organisms to detergents, from detergents to women, from women to Women's Liberation, from Women's Liberation to movements for equal opportunities, from movements for equal opportunities to theology, from theology to social problems – all this in one paragraph. So diverse is the subject as to frustrate any rational attempt to provide a title for the composition. There is a rational link between every assertion, but there is no rationale to the dialog as a whole.

Compositions should be like an unrehearsed panel discussion on a prearranged topic with different participants representing different views or aspects of the topic: it is at any moment spontaneous, but the spontaneity occurs within a pre-determined framework.

A. THE SUBDIVISIONS OF A COMPOSITION

Our creating of the smog editorial was misleading because it implied that all there is to a composition is generating assertions by means of implied dialog and then integrating the assertions into complex sentences. But an unacknowledged factor that was operating all the time was a pre-established outline of subdivisions that guided the questioning. What this outline was is not difficult to discern on hindsight. Throughout our analysis we used the contrasting pair, problem and solution, to explain the different parts of the composition. More precisely, the composition began with the discussion of the problem and concluded with the discussion of the solution. This distinction provides the basis of the paragraphing in the composition.

With most paragraphs the organizing principle is simply linear, the chain of questions and answers. But one cannot juxtapose very many paragraphs before perceiving the need to have the individual paragraphs or groups of paragraphs organized according to some logical scheme. Here is the one used for the smog editorial:

Smog

I. The Problem (exposition).
   Smog is a serious social problem caused by automobile exhaust. (1st paragraph.)

II. A Solution (argument).
   A. In general
   Immediate legislative action is needed to prevent permanent urban contamination. (2nd paragraph.)
   B. In particular
   In Honolulu laws are needed to restrict horsepower and unnecessary driving. (3rd paragraph.)

Notice first that while each paragraph represents a logical division in the outline, the paragraphs bear different relations to each other by virtue of treating either a subdivision or a sub-subdivision. Paragraphing depends not just on logic but also on the degree of emphasis accorded to the different aspects of the subject. The smog editorial is primarily a matter of argument for a solution and only secondarily a matter of presenting information about the problem. The paragraph of exposition covers logically the same proportion of the outline as the two paragraphs of argument, but the emphasis is on the argument. All that paragraphing requires in this respect is that the paragraphs correlate in one way or another with changes of pace in the overall development. One could not tell in advance what the paragraphing of a problem/solution composition should be. But one could tell in advance what it should not be: it should not be three paragraphs split evenly between two main divisions. A paragraph and a half of problem and a paragraph and a half of solution would defeat the basic purpose of using paragraphs for organizational purposes.

Looking back at our integrated composition, we can perceive without too much difficulty where paragraph divisions would most reasonably occur. The main division in the composition must occur where the discussion of the problem leaves off and the discussion of the solution begins.[2] And we are partly helped in discerning this point by the organization of the questions and answers in the opening sentences. Notice that one of the first questions raised was about establishing responsibility. The first answer that was provided introduced the subject of the American automobile industry. This, however, was a rather equivocal answer, though it did lead us directly into a discussion of the central role of the automobile in the smog problem. The second answer was deferred until the discussion of the internal combustion automobile had been concluded. At this point – when the facts about the cause have been presented, and when the second, modified, answer to the question of automobile industry responsibility have been provided – is the place to look for a break in the logic of the composition. The second answer clearly links everything down through sentence 6 as going together in answer to the large question of what it is that constitutes the problem of urban smog.

Implied dialog is not just a means of getting from one assertion to another; it is also the means of getting from one paragraph to another and ultimately from one composition to another. As soon as we have finished paragraphing our smog editorial we will attempt to formulate a question that will expose what a reasonable reader might take to be the basic weakness of our position. Until a writer can foresee not merely the questions raised by each of his assertions but also the questions raised by his composition as a whole, he will be easily carried away by the music of his own words.

If the discussion of the automobile as the primary cause of urban smog had run to four hundred words rather than two hundred, we would not be likely to think of it as a single paragraph. But two hundred words is quite a proper size for a paragraph in mature, complex prose: long enough to treat a subject in detail, short enough to be comprehended in a single non-stop perusal. This is no criticism of paragraphs of one- and three-hundred words, but if our rule of thumb were three-hundred, we would not be able to say that a hundred words either way was still quite within the limits of standard paragraphing. And if we postulated the one hundred word paragraph, we would be even less able to give or take a hundred words.

There is no clearly logical subdivision in this introductory paragraph of six sentences, but it does have something of a capstone in the assertion that in devoting increased time and money to developing an electric vehicle the automobile manufacturers have made an implicit admission of guilt. This shows up clearly on the paragraph diagrams at the end of this chapter. Because it is a rare composition that raises only one question at a time and answers it completely at once, a composition is not just a single chain but a main chain supported to a greater or less degree by subordinate chains that take care of deferred answers and reintroduced questions. As the diagram shows, the question of responsibility is given an immediate but incomplete answer in the second sentence, another more complete answer in the sixth sentence, and a final answer in the last sentence. And just as sentence 22 concludes the second section, sentence 6 concludes the first section.

The transition from the first paragraph to the second is made in two ways. The first way is by means of the electric vehicle – the same subject treated in two different ways. It is first introduced in sentence 6, where it functions as evidence of the guilt of the automobile industry. Its function in the opening sentences of paragraph two is as the main competing solution to the smog problem. The second way is by means of the explicit question. Of course not every rhetorical question properly marks a new paragraph, but questions are always conspicuous. Thus, like short, single-assertion sentences, they tend to draw attention to themselves and should have some special rationale for being – like introducing a change of pace in the discourse. In a general sense a composition is broken after every assertion by an implied question. But more specifically an explicit question conspicuously breaks into a monolog consisting of all the previous assertions.

Having thus gotten into the second section, we must now decide about the paragraphing of it. Logically, it could be left as it is. But there are two reasons for not leaving it as a single paragraph. First, it contains about 350 words – not an impossible number for one paragraph but approaching the upper limit. Second, there are two different logical divisions represented in these 350 words. Except in journalism, paragraphing is not primarily a means of breaking up lines of print for easier reading. It is first and foremost a means of emphasizing changes of pace or logical divisions. Thus we have rather strong reasons for further paragraphing the second section and no particular reason for not doing it. And the place where the break would occur if we decided to make it is as obvious as it was for the first paragraph. Through sentence 14 we have said nothing about Honolulu; after sentence 14 the subject consistently includes Honolulu. Thus, we should have no qualms about beginning a third paragraph with "Here in Honolulu we must profit from their mistakes". The transition from the second paragraph to the third is cities: in the second paragraph, New York and Los Angeles as representative examples, in the third paragraph, Honolulu as the particular instance.

Here, then, are the three paragraphs, and we have only to supply our composition with a title to offer it to the world as a finished product. As we will demonstrate shortly, it is by no means beyond reasonable criticism. No finished composition is ever perfect; it is always just a subdivision of some larger potential discourse, a stage in an ongoing dialog that has no necessary terminus. But first the title. Titles may or may not be humorous, but they ought to be informative about the primary subject or theme of a composition. Furthermore there is the possibility of giving some indication of the kind of treatment accorded that subject. In the most general sense, our editorial would be entitled "Smog". For a short, single word, it would be hard to beat this. Yet this leaves much of the most important aspect of the composition obscure. Appending to it a short subtitle would render it much more precise: "The Problem and a Solution". This has the advantage of indicating not only the aspects of smog to be treated but also the order and organization to be employed. The title becomes more informative and provides a guide to the reading of the composition. However, it also fails to do some other things that are perhaps of equal importance. For example, nothing is said about the very important point of Honolulu being the primary focus. If the editorial were to appear in a Honolulu newspaper this objection would be somewhat mitigated but not entirely eliminated. Nor is any indication given as to the kind of solution being argued for. Still, a title can do only a very limited amount of informing. The important point is that the opportunity not be wasted to be informative and to provide some reliable guide to the reading of the composition. "Smog: The Problem and a Solution" is not an opportunity wasted.

Smog: The Problem and a Solution

Air pollution is now primarily a social rather than a scientific problem, and at the heart of every social problem lies the question of responsibility. The

American automobile industry, the richest industry in the world, richer indeed than most countries, refuses to admit any responsibility for the strangling smog that grips every major urban center. However, the facts are no longer at issue, and only the culprits pretend that the internal combustion engine is not the prime producer of those toxic elements that have become a permanent part of our cities. In the past decade, numerous scientific studies – conducted by universities, industry, and government – have demonstrated beyond any reasonable doubt not only that air pollution has increased in proportion to the growing number of automobiles on the road and the rising consumption of gasoline by their increasingly powerful engines but also that automobile exhaust has an toxic effect on the respiratory system. This toxic effect, which is documented by a three-hundred percent increase in urban lung-cancer cases over the past twenty years, is now obvious to even the most insensitive eye, nose, and throat. Indeed, the fact that the automobile manufacturers themselves have devoted increased time and money to developing an electric vehicle is an implicit admission of guilt.

Is the docile public, however, to wait patiently for ten or fifteen years before General Motors can make as much money from the storage battery as it does now from gasoline? The electric vehicle is a red herring. Its practical development is dependent on knowledge the automobile industry does not now possess, and while we wait, the problem grows steadily worse. Perhaps today's problem could be solved by electric vehicles, but if we allow it to go unchecked for another dozen years, far more drastic measures will be necessary. There is no justification for delay. That which is a demonstrable and pervasive public menace is the proper subject for immediate legislative action, and surely a health menace as serious as smog qualifies for such action. Unless legal restrictions are widely applied and rigorously enforced in the early stages of contamination, urban congestion becomes so great that the price of purifying the air is destruction of the city. Los Angeles and New York City have been permanently contaminated, because legislative action was too little and too late.

Here in Honolulu we must profit from their mistakes. If we continue to rely on the trade winds to ventilate our over-populated island, we will soon find the air as unpleasantly congested as the land. We need laws, today, that will limit the horsepower on all internal combustion vehicles and that will discourage unnecessary driving by imposing increased ownership and use taxes. This is not to imply that we can or should do without the benefits of a mobile society but simply to acknowledge that we are at the point where we have more to lose than to gain unless we make a concerted effort to control the machine whose faulty design and indiscriminate use has resulted in a growing menace to urban America. And when such a point is reached, a problem has two parts: an initial condition and circumstances that allow that condition to flourish. The public is not just a victim; it is a victim that condones the victimizing. We have the means to oppose a great evil and thus the responsibility to do so. Either we act now or we become as culpable as the automobile industry itself.

Perhaps the present stage in our overall project is an appropriate place to emphasize what *The Grammatical Foundations of Rhetoric* is not: it is not the principles of rhetoric. For instance, it only scratches the surface of different kinds of organization. All the complexities that exist between implied inter-assertional dialog on the one hand and logical subdividing on the other are simply ignored as being beyond the scope of an introduction to the grammatical foundations. Yet we are at least obliged to admit that there is much more to be said about rhetoric; indeed, there is much more to be said about the rhetoric of "Smog: The Problem and a Solution". We have not yet exhausted even the usefulness of dialog in analyzing our editorial. As a token gesture, then, to what a complete rhetoric would contain, especially the principles of organization that develop out of argument, let us add one final dimension to our analysis of the development of this one particular composition. The *logical* foundations of rhetoric would be a whole project in itself, but we can very briefly characterize the argument in "Smog: The Problem and a Solution".

There is an element of the Socratic dialog in our editorial. The Socratic method of constructing an argument is to begin with statements commonly and readily accepted as true. But the assent that is readily granted to these introductory points or premises will, by the end of the argument, be seen to require assent to conclusions very much disputed. The force of the argument is thus in the essential similarity between things not heretofore recognized as essentially similar – in this case between the auto industry and the public. The *sine qua non* of the Socratic method of organization is the introduction: the presentation of a point that is too obvious to need demonstration but that is accepted for reasons that cannot be consistently confined to just that particular point. The interlocutor in a Socratic dialog is not the disinterested inquisitor that we have posited in our generative rhetoric. Rather he is the person to be converted. Socrates' interlocutor follows very confidently and agreeably the presentation of the premises, but shortly he will be caught on the horns of the dilemma: either he must retract his initial assent or he must change his mind on a disputed conclusion. Here is the dialog between Socrates and J. Q. Public on the subject of Honolulu's smog problem:

SOC You would agree with me wouldn't you, J. Q. , and with the great majority of our fellow citizens (excluding, of course, those with a vested interest in the American automobile industry), that urban smog is a serious social problem and that, although it is caused primarily by automobile exhaust, the automobile industry refuses to admit any responsibility?

JQ Of course, Socrates; the facts are no longer at issue (as any fool can plainly see). But what is to be done about the problem if the culprits won't take responsibility?

SOC That is a good question, all right, but the situation is not hopeless. After all, the auto industry has implicitly admitted its guilt by devoting so much time and money to developing an electric vehicle.

JQ Well, implicit admission of guilt is better than no admission at all. If those responsible for social problems won't face up to the facts, I fail to see how problems like urban smog can ever be solved.

SOC Well spoken J. Q. You would admit, then, that those who contribute to social problems have an obligation to help solve them.

JQ Absolutely! The automobile industry has victimized the innocent public long enough.

SOC But is the public really so innocent?

JQ Now what do you mean by a crack like that? The public doesn't design those Detroit monsters.

SOC Quite right, but who buys and drives them?

JQ I fail to see your point, Socrates.

SOC Obviously the faulty design must be laid at the door of the auto industry, but a problem of this magnitude is more than just faulty design. After all, what sits with an empty gas tank in Detroit is not polluting Honolulu.

JQ True.

SOC Doesn't it follow, then, that the public is partly responsible for the problem?

JQ I guess so.

SOC And since you yourself said – and I believe I quote you here verbatim (correct me if I don't) – "If those responsible for social problems won't face up to the facts, I fail to see how problems like urban smog can ever be solved", aren't you obliged to face up to your share in the problem and to act to solve it?

JQ But, Socrates, I was talking about just the automobile industry.

SOC No, J. Q. , *we* were talking about those who contribute to social problems. I said, if you will recall, "You would admit, then, that those who contribute to social problems have an obligation to help solve them". And you responded "Absolutely! "

JQ That's not fair, Socrates, to lump together the public and the auto industry.

SOC Well, can you find a way to convincingly distinguish between your contribution to the problem and the auto industry's?

JQ That's an unfair question. After all, I'm no expert. Only more research can answer that.

SOC Now wait a minute, J. Q. We began by agreeing that the nature of the problem was already well established. In your own words, "The facts are no longer at issue". You have implicated yourself by your own admission. Short of retracting all that you previously said, you are obliged to act now or to become as culpable as the automobile industry itself.

The easy-to-accept condemnation of the auto industry has become the difficult-to-accept condemnation of oneself, to be avoided only by agreeing to act now to establish immediate legislative restrictions limiting horsepower on all internal combustion vehicles and imposing increased ownership and use taxes. The first is aimed at the auto industry and the faulty design of its products; the second is aimed at the indiscriminate use by the accessories to the 'crime'. Instead of dividing the argument for a solution into two levels, general and particular, as done in the outline, our Socratic dialog emphasizes the two targets of the argument.

In a nutshell, our Socratic dialog reflects this kind of organization:

I. Statement of shared premises (1st paragraph)

II. Argument for a not-yet shared position
  A. About what should be done
    (2nd and first half of 3rd paragraph)
  B. About ultimate responsibility for doing it
    (second half of 3rd paragraph)

Although this could be used to support the creation of a final, fourth, paragraph – by dividing the last paragraph in two – it is merely a variation of the problem and solution outline already discussed; they are not incompatible alternatives.

Outlining is primarily a matter of subdividing, and argument is not always very satisfactorily presented in outline form. But what is too complex for a simple, unified set of divisions and subdivisions is well handled in dialog – not the step-by-step inter-assertional dialog that has been the basis of our generative rhetoric but rather a hypothetical or fictional dialog as presented above. All this, however, takes us far afield and into a subject that requires a separate volume. We need to resume our concern with dialog as a generating force, this time not on the level of assertions but on the level of whole compositions.

B. A COMPOSITION AS A SUBDIVISION

What are the most reasonable questions that could be raised, not about parts of the composition, but about the composition as a whole? An important part of the writer's craft is the ability to step back and view his 'final draft' as simply a subdivision in his larger dialog with the world. He needs to foresee the likely response to his composition as a whole so as to be able either to modify his 'final draft' or to be prepared with the next statement when his turn comes round again.

It is neither here nor there to foresee the objection: "I personally disagree with you". If one is a movie star, the head of the Mafia, the President of the United States, perhaps his mere personal opinion will be of interest to the world. But this takes us quite beyond the concerns of rhetoric. On the grass-roots level, or even on the bush-league level, and sometimes on the level of competing forest giants, the world demands reasoned analysis, reasons that stand or fall quite apart from who may happen to be offering them at the moment. On questions of disputed facts we usually give precedence to the reasons of certified experts in the field (although this begs the whole crucial question of what constitutes a field and who does the certifying), but on questions of disputed evaluations (on social rather than scientific problems) there are no unequivocal experts. This is why rhetoric through the centuries has concentrated on compositions that emphasize value judgments and on questions where competing alternatives do not lend themselves to a single authoritative judgment.

We could say of "Smog: The Problem and a Solution" that "your facts are all wrong". But this would take the problem into a realm where scientific concerns would have to be resolved before the rhetorical problems could be analyzed. Besides, one can raise this question of any composition, without having even read it. We should not lose sight of the fact that generative rhetoric is not a matter of real debate between actual contending parties trying to defeat each other. What we have is implied dialog employed by the writer himself as a means of ascertaining what are the possibilities and limitations of his composition. He wins no points by bringing his train of thought to a grinding halt. His concern is rather to keep himself on his toes and his assertions, and his compositions, following easily and reasonably one upon the other.

One of the best kinds of questions that a writer of a composition can ask himself is whether or not it has been developed on a basic inconsistency. He can assume from the beginning that what he has written will fall short of the truth, the whole truth, and nothing but the truth. No one has ever succeeded in meeting this standard anyway. Far more serious is to find oneself confronted by a question that lays bare incompatible or inconsistent elements. This is the most effective form of debate because it begins by granting much of what the opposition claims. Then on the basis of things granted for the sake of argument, the interlocutor points to the self-defeating nature of what has been said: things asserted on the one hand and denied on the other. This is not a matter of proof in the narrow scientific sense of marshalling evidence but, equally strong, proof in the dialectical or philosophical sense of turning the very words of a speaker or writer against himself.

This is by no means to imply that the work of the world can go on day in and day out simply by means of dialectical argument. The notion, or hope, that it could has been often pointed out in some extreme forms of medieval or 'scholastic' thought. There is some legitimacy in the charge that medieval education was not very perceptive about the limitations on dialectical reasoning. Modern science had to fight a bitter war against an increasingly anti-intellectual rear-guard of decaying scholasticism, and the smug attitude of the victor is still very much with us. As a result, we have lost sight of the central role that dialectical reasoning plays in composing. The writer who gives little or no thought to the ever-present pitfall of inconsistency will surely be defeated by his own efforts. But this is only the negative side; on the positive side is the great aid to generating new material (as part of the same composition or as a new composition) that perceptive questioning provides. Not even the best of compositions is immune to a charge of inconsistency. To charge inconsistency is not to have established it, but it does awaken one to the possibility and suggest ways of further clarifying what has already been said.

Concern with inconsistency is just one aspect of the generating force of dialectical composing. Another aspect is the ability to perceive logical counterparts of a subject. In talking, for example, about men, a logical question is: What about women? In talking about technological aspects of a problem, a logical question is: What about the ecological aspects? In talking about the history of a subject, a logical question is: What about the contemporary state of the subject? In talking about high-rise housing, a logical question is: What about ground-level housing? In talking about the nature of a social institution, a logical question is: What about its function? In talking about the advantages to be gained from adopting a new proposal, a logical question is: What about the disadvantages? In talking about the common nature of all plants, a logical question is: What about the different kinds of plants? And, of course, in talking about a problem, a logical question is: What about a solution?

An obvious abuse of this sort of generating results from the scholastic addiction to dividing and subdividing as ends in themselves: where every subject has two or three or four subdivisions, and every subdivision has two or three or four sub-subdivisions, and every sub-subdivision has two or three or four further subordinate levels. But for all the obvious abuse of imposing a series of seemingly arbitrary distinctions on a subject, this kind of analysis just as obviously is generative – is a means of finding or inventing related things to say about a subject. A composition on the Women's Liberation movement, for example, might distinguish between the moderates and the extremists, then distinguish among the extremists between those committed to passive resistance and those committed to violence, then distinguish among those committed to violence between those whose goal is formulated primarily in political terms and those whose goal is formulated primarily in social and economic terms, then distinguish among those whose goal is formulated primarily in social and economic terms between those who advocate greater segregation of the sexes and those who advocate greater integration of the sexes, etc. etc.

This is as likely to end up as an exercise in computer programing as in a purposeful composition; but it *is* generative. And clearly some such effort to make orderly distinctions within a large subject is essential to getting it written up on the one hand and understood on the other. Not all programs for Women's Liberation are the same, and not all people who advocate them are the same. Distinctions within a unified framework are at the heart of composition, and distinctions systematically made are easier to explain than those unsystematically made. To discourse, for instance, on the subject of extremism in Women's Liberation will logically elicit a question about moderation in Women's Liberation. Whether the answer follows as part of the same composition or as a sequel to it, by the same author or another, the generating principle of dialectic is the same: finding things that correlate with or are counterparts of or are consistent with each other. And the standard dialectical criticism is that things have been lumped together that do not correlate, are not counterparts, are inconsistent.

As with the individual assertions that elicit more than one reasonable question, a composition as a whole is likely to elicit more than one reasonable question. We will, however, be satisfied with just one in the example below. After carefully studying the smog editorial with an eye to internal consistency, let us see if this question does not readily parlay itself into an answering composition: *In light of your final blanket condemnation of the public, have you really offered a practical and painless solution to the smog problem in calling merely for legal restrictions?* To generate a complete rejoinder assertion-by-assertion would be too ambitious a project here. Instead, let us simply intuit a finished product. We need to see this one-sentence question elaborated into a fully developed paragraph, a composition detailed enough to be helpful in pointing up a possible weakness in the original composition. We are not interested in demolishing a composition but in showing how further material could be generated on the same subject. This rejoinder is no more the last word on the subject than "Smog: The Problem and a Solution" was the last word. One may feel metaphysically shaky about this indeterminacy and infinity, but one is on very solid ground rhetorically when he has developed this ability to easily generate new material. Like the trained lawyer, who knows how to go about formulating the always possible case for a client, the trained writer knows how to formulate the always possible next step of a composition. Whether one is working on the level of assertion, paragraph, or book, there is always a reasonable next step.

A Rejoinder

In the recent editorial "Smog: The Problem and a Solution" urban smog is characterized as a problem so well documented as to be beyond legitimate argument. What is argued for is a proposed solution to the problem – immediate restrictive legislation to limit horsepower and impose increased ownership and use taxes. However, there is an inconsistency here. Either the smog problem has been much over-estimated or what is required to solve the problem has been much under-estimated. On the one hand, the editorial begins with the automobile industry as the culprit; and to the extent that this is true, specific limited remedies directed at specific limited sources of trouble are feasible. But if the problem can be solved so readily and so painlessly as to entail no sacrifice in the benefits of our mobile society, we are hardly on the verge of urban destruction. The only case against the electric vehicle is that our time will have run out while we wait the necessary few years. On the other hand, the editorial concludes with the entire public sharing culpability; but to the extent that this is true, nothing short of mass reformation will suffice. Our technological society may indeed be headed for disaster, but no disaster was ever averted by the mere passing of laws designed to allow the public to have its cake and eat it too. Limited horsepower and increased taxes would at best only delay the inevitable destruction. We must be prepared to sacrifice many of the benefits of our mobile society if we want to escape a disaster that is the direct result of that society.

Our interest in this paragraph is not exhausted by its function as a rejoinder. As the diagram of it at the end of this chapter reveals, there is not just a linear organization of assertion-question-answer. Here is an example of a logical paragraph structure, a paragraph consisting of clearly defined subdivisions. The rejoinder picks up the either/or conclusion of the editorial ("Either we act now or we become as culpable as the automobile industry itself.") and slightly changes the focus. The result is three sentences devoted to "Either the smog problem has been much over-estimated" and four sentences devoted to "or what is required to solve the problem has been much under-estimated". The reader will have missed the point of the paragraph if he thinks that sentence 8 follows sentence 7 as the answer to a question raised by it. Sentence 8 is like sentence 5 in following 4 as an answer to a question implied by 4. The only difference is that 5, 6, and 7 answer one question implied by 4 ("How is the problem over-estimated? "), and 8, 9, 10, and 11 answer a second question implied by 4 ("How is the required solution under-estimated? "). The guide posts provided by the writer are chiefly the two introductory phrases: "On the one hand" and "On the other hand".

At this point we might reasonably ask why the two subdivisions are left as a single paragraph and the two subdivisions in the second half of "Smog: The Problem and a Solution" are divided into two paragraphs. There is, first of all, a difference of length: 275 words in the one and 350 words in the other. But more important than length is the kind of subordination involved in the two compositions. The two subdivisions in the rejoinder are necessarily tied to the sentences that introduce them. These sentences tell us that we must accept one or the other but not both of the two alternatives that follow. The two parts that comprise the explanation of an inconsistency constitute more of a unity of exposition than the two parts of a two-part subject. In the smog editorial the second half ("A Solution") has no other introduction than the first half ("The Problem"), and the composition as a whole could reasonably have ended after the discussion of a solution in general. But once a writer has embarked on the explanation of an inconsistency, he is obliged to follow his "on the one hand" with an "on the other hand".

Of course, if this explanation had run to several hundred words, there would have been no choice but to find some way to break it up into paragraphs. As it stands, however, it makes quite a unified paragraph, more unified than would have been the first four sentences alone, or the first seven sentences alone, or the last seven sentences alone. Probably the best alternative to leaving the composition a single paragraph is to break it up into three paragraphs: An introduction to the inconsistency (1-4), the first alternative (5-7), the second alternative (8-11). Although this would make the individual paragraphs rather short, it would be following the subdivisions as represented in the dialog diagram.

The diagrams on the following pages reveal the framework of dialog in compositions carefully written for the occasion. In the next chapter we will provide a more difficult test for our system of analysis by applying it to the compositions of writers who have no vested interest in espousing the value of semantic grammar and generative rhetoric. However, all examples are subject to the limits imposed by page size. One comment may be helpful for following the dialog in the diagrams on pp. 304-9, 310-1, 320-3, and 333-4. Although the layout implies that all assertions follow directly from the immediately preceding assertions, this is not always true. Not only is there the matter of logical subdivisions (e. g. the paragraph subdivisions on pp. 310-1), but also additive modifiers must sometimes be interpreted parenthetically. An independent assertion listed after a dependent assertion often follows semantically the previous independent assertion. The ideal layout for our implied dialogs would perhaps be one or more degrees of indentation to distinguish the main line of questioning from subordinate and terminal ones:

The American automobile industry refuses to admit any responsibility for the smog that grips every major urban center.

How could a single industry have such a large responsibility?	*What is so serious about smog as to raise the issue of responsibility?*
The American automobile industry [is] the richest industry in the world.	The smog that grips every major urban center [is] strangling.
The American automobile industry [is] richer indeed than most countries.	

However, *Is the industry not entitled to its own opinion?*

The facts are no longer at issue.

NOTES

1 Jacques Barzun and Henry F. Graff. *The Modern Researcher*. N. Y. , 1957, p. 231. For the passage and a detailed analysis of it see p. 328 ff. below.
2 See p. 304 ff. for the diagrams.

PARAGRAPH 1.

1. Air pollution is now primarily a social rather than a scientific problem.
   and *What characterizes a social problem? Why is it not a scientific problem?*
   At the heart of every social problem lies the question of responsibility.

2. *Has responsibility for this problem been established yet?*
   The American automobile industry refuses to admit any responsibility for the smog that grips every major urban center.
   How could a single industry have such a large responsibility?
   The American automobile industry [is] the richest industry in the world.
   The American automobile industry [is] richer indeed than most countries.
   What is so serious about smog as to raise the issue of responsibility?
   The smog that grips every major urban center [is] strangling.

3. However, *Is the industry not entitled to its own opinion? How is it strangling?*
   The facts are no longer at issue.
   and *Does anyone share the industry's opinion? What are these facts?*
   Only the culprits pretend that the internal combustion engine is not the prime producer of those toxic elements that have become a permanent part of our cities.

4. In the past decade, numerous scientific studies have demonstrated beyond any reasonable doubt that air pollution has increased in proportion to the number of automobiles on the road.
   The number of automobiles on the road [is] growing.

and
In the past decade, numerous scientific studies have demonstrated beyond any reasonable doubt that air pollution has increased in proportion to the consumption of gasoline by their engines.
The consumption of gasoline by their engines [is] rising.
Their engines [are] increasingly powerful.
not only . . . but also
In the past decade, numerous scientific studies have demonstrated beyond any reasonable doubt that automobile exhaust has toxic effect on the respiratory system.

Why are these facts no longer at issue?

The numerous scientific studies that have demonstrated in the past decade beyond any reasonable doubt not only that air pollution has increased in proportion to the growing number of automobiles on the road and the rising consumption of gasoline by their increasingly powerful engines but also that automobile exhaust has a toxic effect on the respiratory system [were] conducted by universities, industry, and government.

5. *Is there actually sufficient exhaust in the air now to justify the label "strangling" for what in the laboratory is termed "toxic effect"?*

This effect is now obvious to even the most insensitive eye.
This effect is now obvious to even the most insensitive nose.
and
This effect is now obvious to even the most insensitive throat.

Is there evidence for this effect being more than merely unpleasant?

This effect is documented by a three-hundred percent increase in urban lung-cancer cases over the past twenty years.

6. Indeed, *If the facts are so clear to everyone else, how can the industry pretend to be innocent?*
The fact that the automobile manufacturers themselves have devoted increased time and money to developing an electric vehicle is an implicit admission of guilt.

PARAGRAPH 2.

7. *Is it not just a matter of time, then, before the problem is solved by the industry itself with electric vehicles?*
Is the public, however, to wait patiently for ten or fifteen years before General Motors makes as much money from the storage battery as it does now from gasoline?
Is the public likely to wait patiently?
The public [is] docile.

8. *Is there something wrong with the electric vehicle as a proposed solution?*
The electric vehicle is a red herring.

9. *How is it a red herring?*
Its practical development is dependent on knowledge the automobile industry does not now possess.
and
While we wait, the problem grows steadily worse.

10. *Is there any merit at all in this proposal?*
Perhaps today's problem could be solved by electric vehicles.
but *Isn't the project worth pursuing, then?*
If we allow it to go unchecked for another dozen years, far more drastic measures will be necessary.

11. *Isn't it better to delay than to go off half-cocked?*

There is no justification for delay.

12. *What is there justification for?*

That which is a demonstrable and pervasive public menace is the proper subject for immediate legislative action.

and *Specifically, what would be a proper subject for such action?*

Surely a health menace as serious as smog qualifies for such action?

13. *What are the consequences of postponing legislative action?*

Unless legal restrictions are widely applied and rigorously enforced in the early stages of contamination, urban congestion becomes so great that the price of purifying the air is destruction of the city.

14. *What is the evidence for this?*

Los Angeles has been permanently contaminated.

and

New York City has been permanently contaminated.

because *How was this allowed to happen?*

Legislative action was too little.

and because

Legislative action was too late.

PARAGRAPH 3.

15. *Where is there still time to act?*

Here in Honolulu we must profit from their mistakes.

16. *What will become of our problem if we do not act now?* *What makes Honolulu comparable to Los Angeles and New York City?*

If we continue to rely on the trade winds to ventilate our island, we will soon find the air as unpleasantly congested as the land.

What accounts for such congestion?

Our island [is] over-populated.

17. *What particular legislative action is needed to profit from their mistakes?*

We need laws, today, that will limit the horsepower on all internal combustion vehicles.
and
We need laws, today, that will discourage unnecessary driving by imposing increased ownership taxes.
We need laws, today, that will discourage unnecessary driving by imposing increased use taxes.

18. *Isn't to advocate this to endanger the benefits of a mobile society?*

This is not to imply that we can do without the benefits of a mobile society.
or
This is not to imply that we should do without the benefits of a mobile society.

What, then, is it implying?

This is simply to acknowledge that we have reached the point where we have more to lose than to gain unless we make a concerted effort to control the machine whose faulty design and indiscriminate use has resulted in a growing menace to urban America.

19. And *Is this to acknowledge, then, that the machine itself is only a partial cause of the problem?*

When such a point is reached, a problem has two parts.

What are these two parts?

The two parts a problem has when such a point is reached [are] an initial condition and circumstances that allow that condition to flourish.

20. *What is it that allows this condition to flourish?*

The public is not just a victim.

It is a victim that condones the victimizing

21. *Is this to acknowledge, then, that the automobile industry is not the only culprit responsible for the problem?*

We have the means to oppose a great evil.
and thus
We have the responsibility to do so.

22. *What will become of us if we do not act now?*

Either we act now or we become as culpable as the automobile industry itself.

1. In the recent editorial "Smog: The Problem and a Solution" urban smog is characterized as a problem so well documented as to be beyond legitimate argument.

2. *What is not beyond legitimate argument?*

What is argued for is a proposed solution to the problem.

What is this proposed solution?

The proposed solution to the problem [is] immediate restrictive legislation to limit horsepower and impose increased ownership and use taxes.

3. However, *Is the argument reasonable?*

There is an inconsistency here.

4. *What is the inconsistency?*

Either the smog problem has been much over-estimated or what is required to solve the problem has been much under-estimated.

5. *How is the problem over-estimated?* *How is the solution under-estimated?*

On the one hand, the editorial begins with the automobile industry as the culprit.

and

To the extent that this is true, specific limited remedies directed at specific limited sources of trouble are feasible.

6. But *How is this inconsistent?*

If the problem can be solved so readily and so painlessly as to entail no sacrifice in the benefits of our mobile society, we are hardly on the verge of urban destruction.

7. *Is the argument dependent on imminent urban destruction?*

The only case against the electric vehicle is that our time will have run out while we wait the necessary few years.

8. On the other hand, the editorial concludes with the entire public sharing culpability.

but *How is this inconsistent?*

To the extent that this is true, nothing short of mass reformation will suffice.

9. *Do you deny the seriousness of the problem?*

Our technological society may indeed be headed for disaster.

but *Isn't it possible to avert this disaster?*

No disaster was ever averted by the mere passing of laws designed to allow the public to have its cake and eat it too.

10. *Would these laws have no effect at all?*

Limited horsepower would at best only delay the inevitable destruction.

and

Increased taxes would at best only delay the inevitable destruction.

11. *What can be done to escape this destruction?*

We must be prepared to sacrifice many of the benefits of our mobile society if we want to escape a disaster that is the direct result of that society.

10. DIALOG AS A TOOL OF ANALYSIS

The emphasis heretofore has been on implied dialog as a means of generating assertions and compositions. But we should also emphasize that dialog is an equally useful tool for analyzing what has already been composed. One does not have to claim that a composition has actually been generated by means of dialog in order to claim that dialog is always an applicable device for discerning compositional strengths and weaknesses. Another emphasis that needs to be corrected is our concentration on argumentative prose, with the consequent neglect of expository. In some respects, as we have indicated, argument and rhetoric fit, and have always been recognized as fitting, hand in glove. If, however, the great bulk of informative prose were only marginally handled by generative rhetoric, then we would have failed to make good on our claim for its universal applicability.

Two extended examples will be analyzed in this chapter: of similar length, on similar subjects, written at similar times by reputable historians, and intended for similar educated audiences. The important difference is that one proves to be, in spite of minor problems, a successful composition by our standards; the other proves to be, in spite of some obvious achievements, a much less successful composition.

The first, successful, example is from William H. McNeill's *The Rise of the West: A History of the Human Community* (Chicago, 1963; pp. 687-89). The following two paragraphs begin the sub-subsection, "Compromises in the Arts", which occurs in this context:

Chapter XII. The Tottering World Balance: 1700-1850 A. D.
  B. The Old Regime of Europe, 1650-1789 A. D.
    3. The Compromises of the Old Regime in Europe

Compromises in the Arts. The pluralism of European society and thought under the Old Regime was also manifested in the arts. In England in the latter part of the seventeenth century, the high seriousness of John Milton's epic *Paradise Lost* (1667) and the bawdiness of Restoration comedy overlapped; while a century later, the elaborate urbanity of Samuel Johnson's prose (d. 1784) jostled the artful rusticity of Robert Burns (d. 1796). It is customary to distinguish a classical followed by a romantic tendency in European letters; and art historians recognize three successive styles in architecture and painting: baroque, rococo, and classical. These classifications are useful, so long as one does not press them too hard; but they scarcely fit such a writer as Daniel Defoe (d. 1731) or the Dutch school of painting, and we should always remember that shifting standards of fashion and taste never displaced literary classics like Shakespeare from the English stage or Luther's Bible from German homes.

On the surface, the late seventeenth and early eighteenth century showed a remarkable cohesion in art and letters, as the prestige of French culture spread "classicism" throughout Europe. The great classical dramatists of France, Pierre Corneille (d. 1684), Molière (d. 1673), and Jean Racine (d. 1699) took rules of correctness seriously, both in diction (following the *Dictionnaire* of the Académie Française) and in composition (the "three unities"). In subsequent decades, lesser men assiduously followed their example, both in France and abroad; and French became the language of belles-lettres throughout much of Europe. Only English literature remained fully independent, while sharing in the classical norms of restraint, elegance, precision, and wit with writers such as Joseph Addison (d. 1719) or Alexander Pope (d. 1744). Yet an enormous variety coexisted with this high, cosmopolitan, self-conscious literary culture – running the gamut from the hectic visions of George Fox (d. 1691), founder of Quakerism, to the ponderous learning of the German jurist Samuel Pufendorf (d. 1694).

1\. The pluralism of European society and thought under the Old Regime was also manifested (in the arts.)

2\. (In England) (in the latter part of the seventeenth century,) the high seriousness of John Milton's epic *Paradise Lost* [(1667)] and the bawdiness of Restoration comedy overlapped;

while (a century later,) the elaborate urbanity of Samuel Johnson's prose [(d. 1784)] jostled (the artful rusticity of Robert Burns [(d. 1796).])

3.

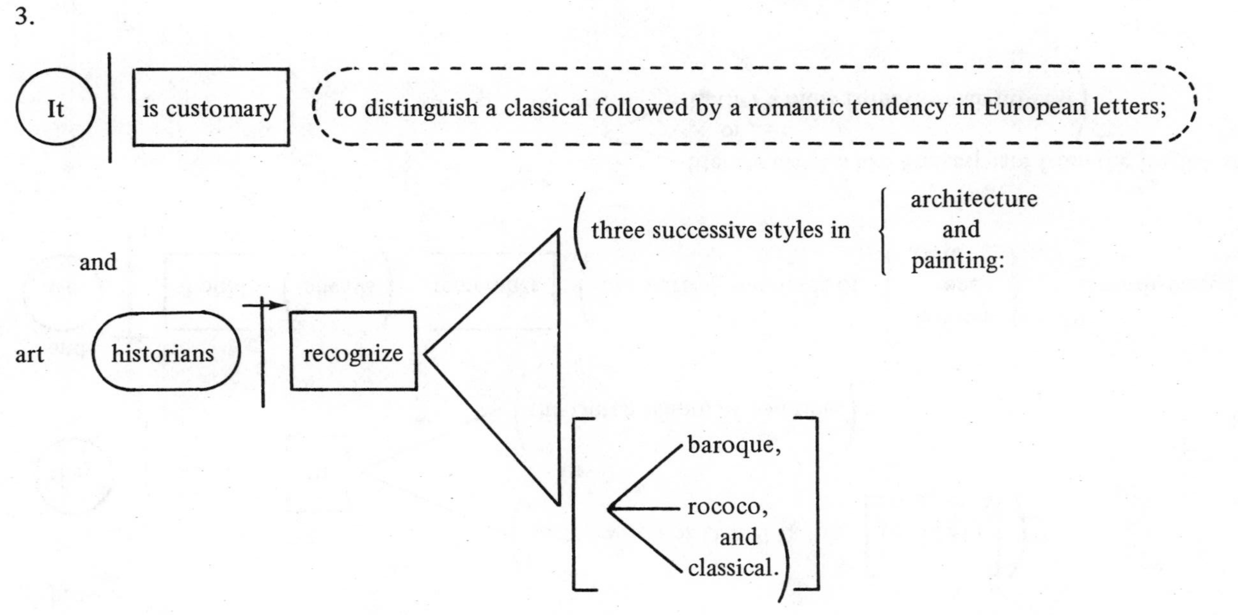
It
is customary
to distinguish a classical followed by a romantic tendency in European letters;
and
art
historians
recognize
three successive styles in
architecture
and
painting:
baroque,
rococo,
and
classical.

4.

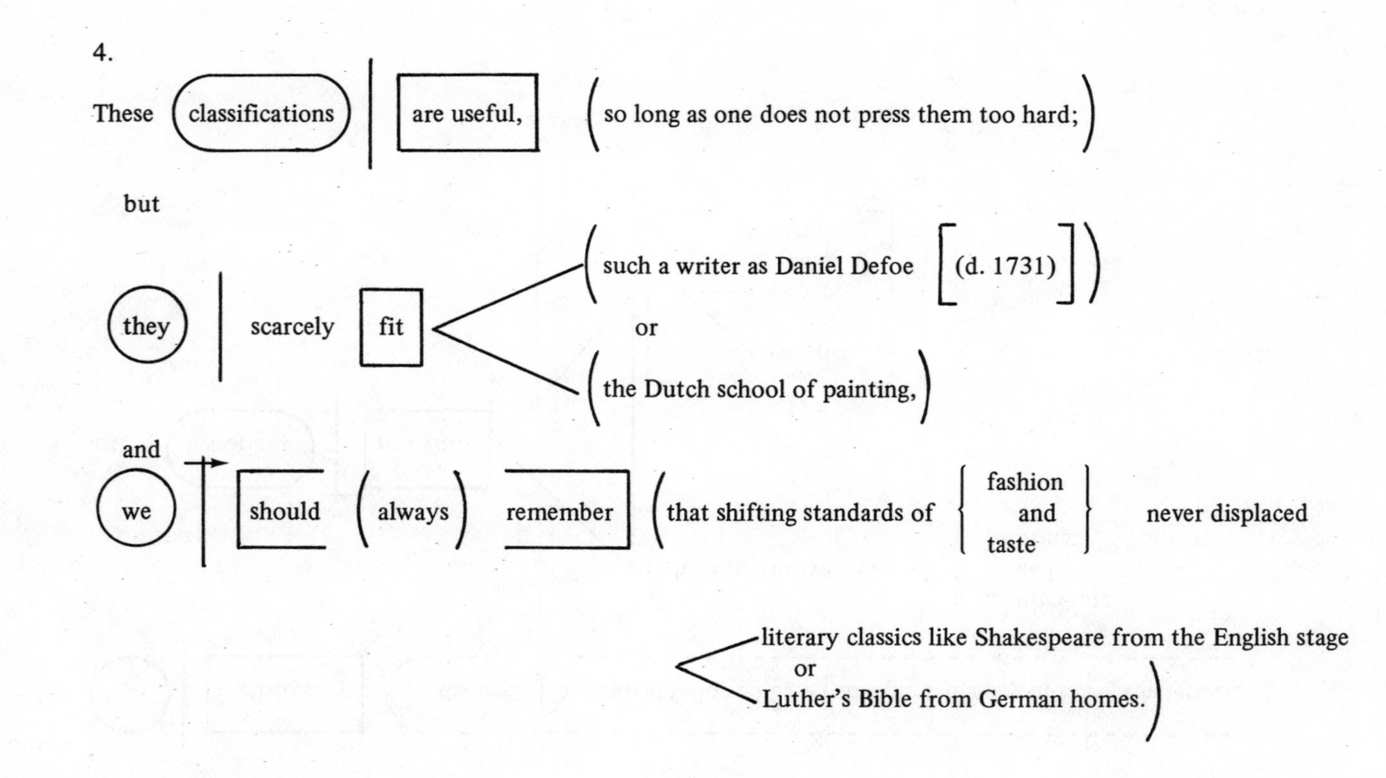
These
classifications
are useful,
so long as one does not press them too hard;
but
they
scarcely
fit
such a writer as Daniel Defoe
(d. 1731)
or
the Dutch school of painting,
and
we
should
always
remember
that shifting standards of
fashion
and
taste
never displaced
literary classics like Shakespeare from the English stage
or
Luther's Bible from German homes.

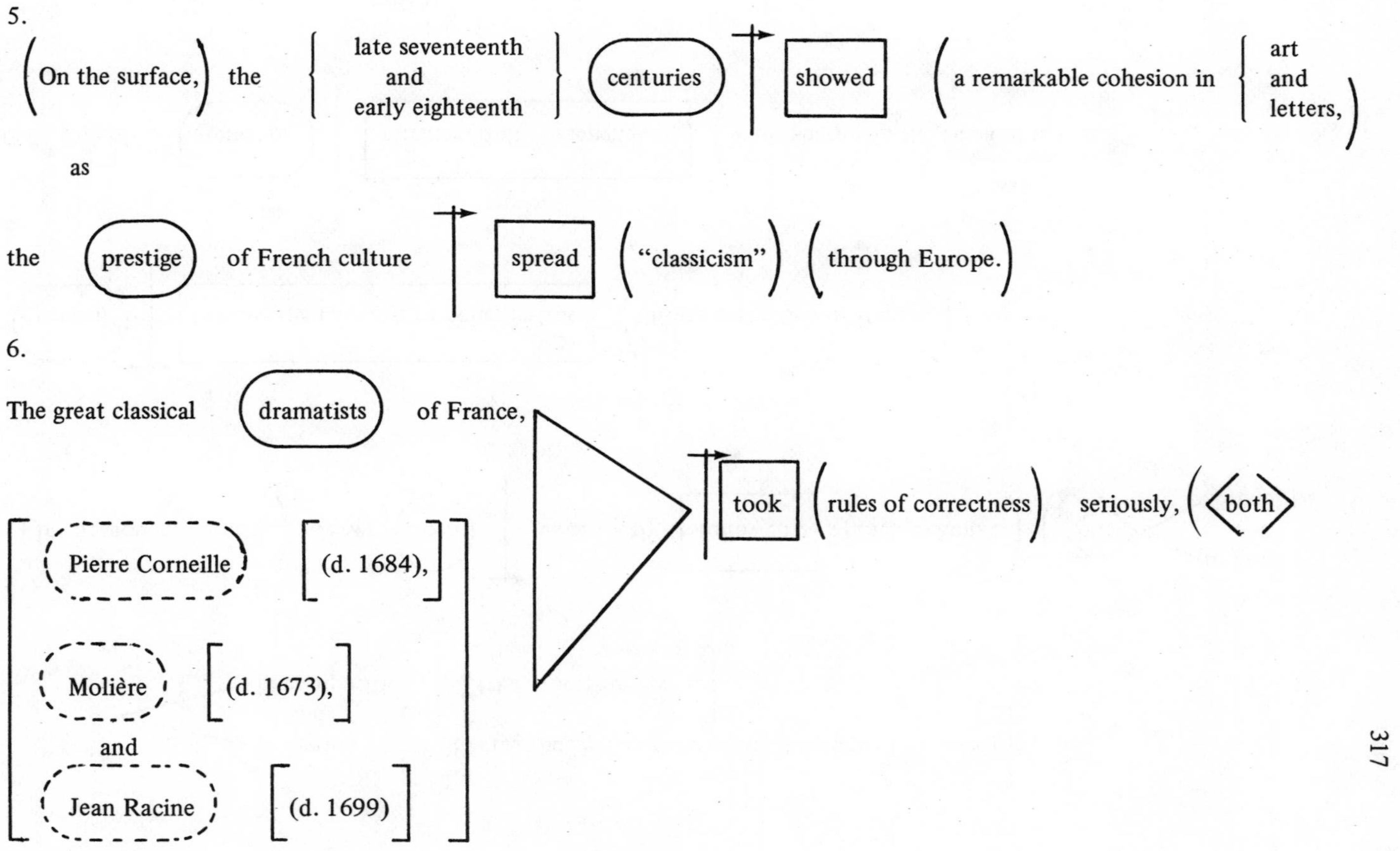
5.
On the surface,
the
late seventeenth
and
early eighteenth
centuries
showed
a remarkable cohesion in
art
and
letters,
as
the
prestige
of French culture
spread
"classicism"
through Europe.
6.
The great classical
dramatists
of France,
Pierre Corneille
(d. 1684),
Molière
(d. 1673),
and
Jean Racine
(d. 1699)
took
rules of correctness
seriously,
both

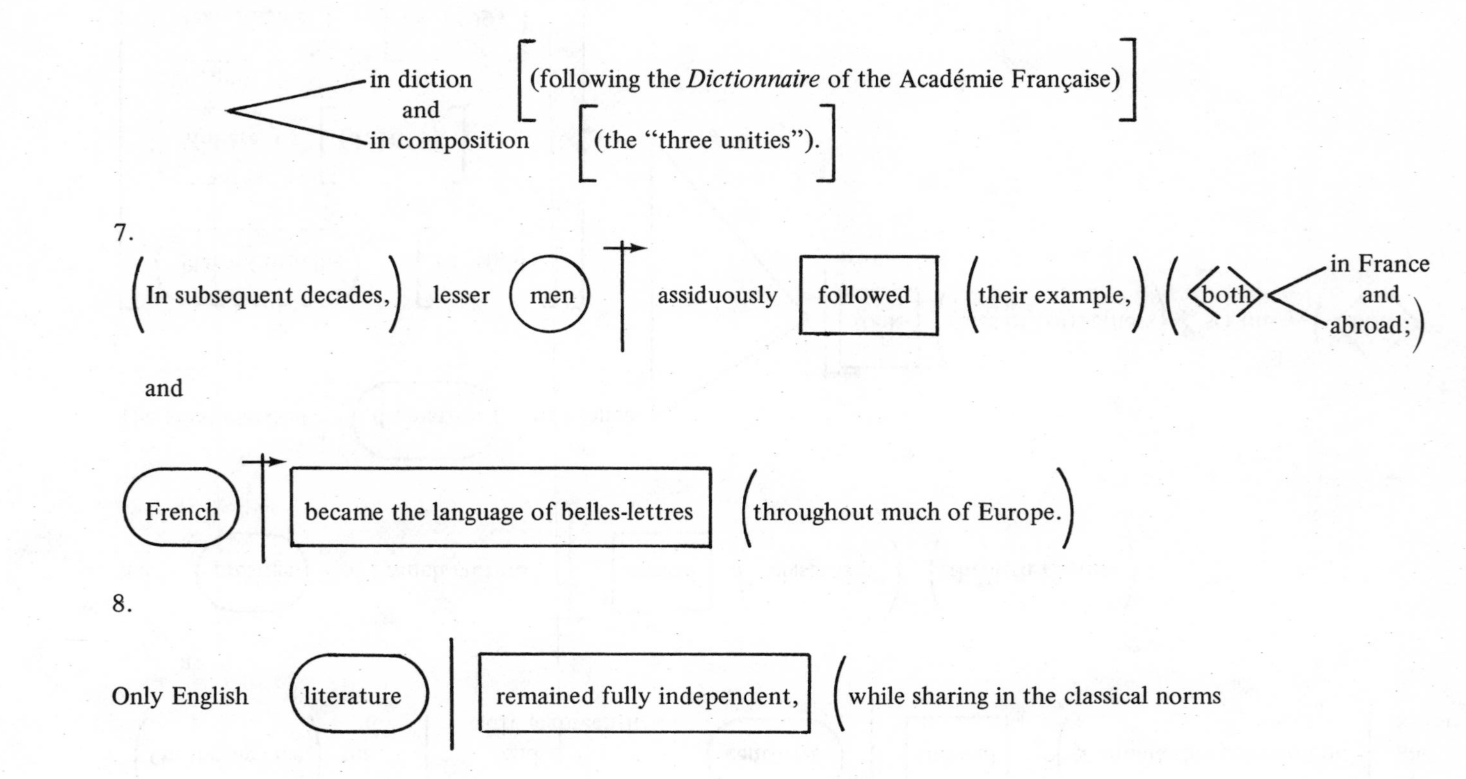
in diction
and
in composition
(following the Dictionnaire of the Académie Française)
(the "three unities").
7.
In subsequent decades,
lesser
men
assiduously
followed
their example,
both
in France
and
abroad;
and
French
became the language of belles-lettres
throughout much of Europe.
8.
Only English
literature
remained fully independent,
while sharing in the classical norms

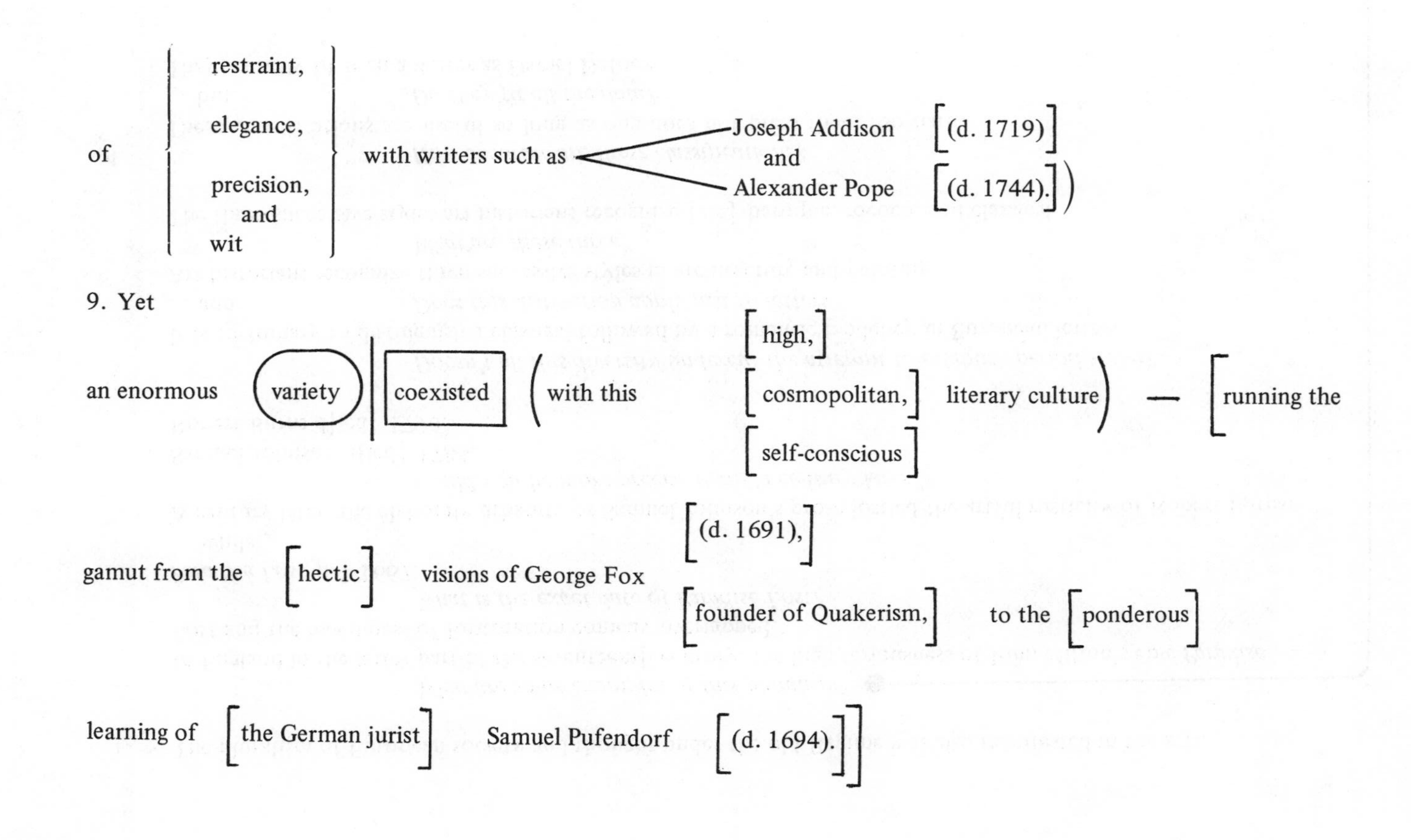
of
restraint,
elegance,
precision,
and
wit
with writers such as
Joseph Addison
(d. 1719)
and
Alexander Pope
(d. 1744).
9. Yet
an enormous
variety
coexisted
with this
high,
cosmopolitan,
self-conscious
literary culture
—
running the
gamut from the
hectic
visions of George Fox
(d. 1691),
founder of Quakerism,
to the
ponderous
learning of
the German jurist
Samuel Pufendorf
(d. 1694).

1. The pluralism of European society and thought under the old Regime was also manifested in the arts.

2. *What are some examples of this pluralism?*

In England in the latter part of the seventeenth century, the high seriousness of John Milton's epic *Paradise Lost* and the bawdiness of Restoration comedy overlapped.

What is the exact date of Paradise Lost?

Paradise Lost [is] 1667.

while

A century later, the elaborate urbanity of Samuel Johnson's prose jostled the artful rusticity of Robert Burns.

Could you be more precise than "a century later"?

Samuel Johnson d[ied] 1784.
Robert Burns d[ied] 1796.

3. *Doesn't all this diversity undercut the attempt to establish period styles?*

It is customary to distinguish a classical followed by a romantic tendency in European letters.

and *Does this distinction apply just to letters?*

Art historians recognize three successive styles in architecture and painting.

What are these three?

The three successive styles art historians recognize [are] baroque, rococo, and classical.

4. *How accurate are these classifications?*

These classifications are useful so long as one does not press them too hard.

but *Do they fit all the data?*

They scarcely fit such a writer as Daniel Defoe.

What is the date of Defoe?

Daniel Defoe d[ied] 1731.

or

They scarcely fit the Dutch school of painting.

and

We should always remember that shifting standards of fashion and taste never displaced literary classics like Shakespeare from the English stage.

or

We should always remember that shifting standards of fashion and taste never displaced Luther's Bible from German homes.

5. *Can it really be said, then, that there is a stylistic unity to the Old Regime?*

On the surface, the late seventeenth and early eighteenth centuries showed a remarkable cohesion in art and letters.

as *How is this explained?*

The prestige of French culture spread "classicism" throughout Europe.

6. *What are some examples of this classicism?*

The great classical dramatists of France took rules of correctness seriously in diction.

What was classical diction?

In diction the great classical dramatists of France followed the *Dictionnaire* of the Académie Française.

and

The great classical dramatists of France took rules of correctness seriously in composition.

What was classical composition?

Rules of correctness in composition [were] the "three unities".

Who were the great classical dramatists of France?

The great classical dramatists of France [were] Pierre Corneille, Molière, and Jean Racine.

What are their dates?

Pierre Corneille d[ied] 1684.
Molière d[ied] 1673.
Jean Racine d[ied] 1699.

7. *Doesn't it take more than a few great men to establish a period style?*

In subsequent decades, lesser men assiduously followed their example in France.

and *Was their influence restricted primarily to France?*

In subsequent decades, lesser men assiduously followed their example abroad.

and *Was this tradition restricted primarily to drama?*

French became the language of belles-lettres throughout much of Europe.

8. *Were there any national exceptions to this influence?*

Only English literature remained fully independent, while sharing in the classical norms of restraint, elegance, precision, and wit with writers such as Joseph Addison.

What is the date of Addison?

Joseph Addison d[ied] 1719.

or

Only English literature remained fully independent, while sharing in the classical norms of restraint, elegance, precision, and wit with writers such as Alexander Pope.

What is the date of Pope?

Alexander Pope d[ied] 1744.

9. Yet *Are we to conclude that except for this the literary culture was monolithic?*

An enormous variety coexisted with this literary culture.

What characterized this literary culture?

This literary culture [was] high.
This literary culture [was] cosmopolitan.
This literary culture [was] self-conscious.

What are examples of this variety?

The enormous variety that coexisted with this literary culture ran the gamut from the visions of George Fox to the learning of Samuel Pufendorf.

What are they noted for?

George Fox [was the] founder of Quakerism.
Samuel Pufendorf [was] the German jurist.

What are their dates?

George Fox d[ied] 1691.
Samuel Pufendorf d[ied] 1694.

What makes their difference so enormous?

The visions of George Fox [were] hectic.
The learning of Samuel Pufendorf [was] ponderous.

The conspicuous difference between McNeill's composition and the smog editorial analyzed in the previous chapters is the longer sentences with the much greater percentage of assertions per sentence and the fewer words per assertion in McNeill's prose.[1] This comes as no surprise, because we have deliberately sought out the kind of composition whose primary task is to convey the maximum amount of information in the minimum amount of space. The more concise the prose is the more assertions the writer is making in a limited space. And thus, we expect, and do find, that McNeill has made much greater use of additive modification than we did and less use of separable parallel structure. Such an all-out expository effort is not, of course, without its inevitable pitfalls; and we will have occasion to note where McNeill has over-reached himself. But before examining these, let us emphasize the dialogal success of McNeill's composition as compared to the dialogal failure of our paragraph on Women's Liberation and of Chambers' composition on Elizabethan spectacles.

What is the framework of dialog in McNeill's composition? What limits of subject matter keep it from wandering off into the swamps of marginalia? As indicated by the outline distinctions quoted from *The Rise of the West*, McNeill's topic in the large sense is the period of transition in European history when the Old Regime was increasingly obliged to make compromises with the emerging era of modern nationalism. Specifically, the subject at hand is "compromises in the arts". The questions that generate the composition are all about "compromises", "pluralism", "variety", as manifested in European culture of the late seventeenth and early eighteenth centuries. The first sentence speaks of "pluralism", the last sentence speaks of "variety". In between, the composition moves back and forth from unity to diversity in an attempt to ascertain the degree to which the alleged cohesion of French classicism actually provided the period with a basic unity. And while it is admitted that "*on the surface*", the late seventeenth and early eighteenth century showed a remarkable cohesion in art and letters", the conclusion is clear and consistent: "*Yet* an enormous variety coexisted with this high, cosmopolitan, self-conscious literary culture . . . " (italics added).

This example is a useful one for our purposes because McNeill's subject is one that readily lends itself to digressions. The subject of variety and pluralism is much easier to diversify than to unify. That McNeill has succeeded in achieving a substantial measure of unity is proven by the consistency of the questions we have been able to insert between the assertions. Even the seemingly marginal requests for dates that elicit the dozen parenthetical additive modifiers can be justified by the need to ascertain whether the diversity of examples is really drawn from the short period under discussion.

So much for the general success – what about the specific deficiencies?

Minor as these are, there is still a common explanation for them: the attempt to cram too much information into too small a space with too little attention to the precise semantic relationships pertaining. The first, and least serious, of these is the additive modifier "(d. 1784)" in the second sentence. This parenthetical information follows the phrase "the elaborate urbanity of Samuel Johnson's prose" and must be taken to modify the phrase as a whole or the subordinate phrase "Samuel Johnson's prose". Neither of these can in any rational sense be said to have "d[ied] 1784". What presumably was intended was to say that Samuel Johnson died in 1784. All the other parenthetical dates follow and clearly modify the names of specific people or works, and while this consistency helps us to reconstruct what McNeill must have *intended* here, what he actually *asserted* makes little sense. It is easy enough to account for this error. Parenthetical additive modifiers are a very economical means of inserting tangential information into a sentence constructed along other lines. But if these other lines do not correlate grammatically with the additive modifier – and McNeill wanted not just to refer to Samuel Johnson but to characterize his prose as elaborately urbane – then something has to be deferred to a later and more detailed statement. McNeill might have contrasted the elaborate urbanity of Samuel Johnson's *prose* with the artful rusticity of Robert Burns' *poetry* and eliminated the reference to dates, but this would have left out the precise clarification of "a century later". He might have contrasted *Samuel Johnson* and *Robert Burns* and appended the two death dates, but this would have left out the precise nature of the contrast between them. And of course he could have done one first and then followed that sentence with a second sentence doing the other. But this would have been less economical and given more attention to this one example than would have been warranted by the attention given to the other examples. The 'compromise' that McNeill settled for included everything but left part of the composing to the reader.

A second place where the urgency for economizing results in semantic difficulties is in the third sentence. The sentence consists of two independent clauses joined by a very noncommittal "and". There is nothing wrong with "and" as a conjunction unless the second assertion seems somehow inconsistent with the first. In such a case, "and" is no substitute for a detailed explanation. We have been able to link these two assertions with a reasonable question and to follow this sentence as a whole with another question that reasonably asks about the accuracy of such classifications as classical/romantic and baroque/rococo/classical. But the most obvious question has not been asked: "What is the relation between the classical/romantic distinction and the baroque/rococo/classical? " Are these different classifications offered by different scholars? Are these different classifications offered by the same scholars for different subjects? Are baroque and rococo subdivisions of romantic? Are baroque and rococo pre-classical, and is romantic post-classical? The author's desire to include as much relevant information as possible here has already taken precedence over the reader's need to understand the relationship between the different classes of information offered.

The problem in the sixth sentence takes us back again to McNeill's heavy reliance on parenthetical additive modifiers. It occurs in the parallel construction " . . . took rules of correctness seriously, both in diction (following the *Dictionnaire* of the Académie Française) and in composition (the 'three unities')". The assertion derived from the first can be constructed easily enough by changing the inflected participial form of "follow": "In diction the great classical dramatists of France followed the *Dictionnaire* of the Académie Française". But notice that the second parenthetical expression is not strictly parallel with the first. The first tells *how* the great classical dramatists took rules of correctness seriously: by *following* something. But the second does not tell *how*; it simply appends a noun phrase in quotation marks: "three unities". The problem is to decide the relationship of the three unities to taking rules of correctness seriously. If the sentence had read "*the* rules of correctness" the task of interpretation would be somewhat easier. We could say that "the rules of correctness in composition were the three unities". But historically this is not quite accurate, and understandably McNeill did not want to make such an unequivocal over-simplified assertion. And even so, the grammatical relationship here seems to require (as in the first parallel) an answer of *how done* to go with "took". As the sentence stands, we can only say: "Rules of correctness in composition [were] the 'three unities'." The meaning is perhaps that the unities are examples of such rules. But how these are actually rules and how they were in fact followed as a means of taking correctness seriously in composition is unclear. The reader does not need to know anything specific about the *Dictionnaire* of the Académie Française to understand that following it could be a means of taking rules of correctness seriously in diction. But even knowing something about the three unities does not eliminate the problem of determining precisely how they relate to the taking of rules of correctness seriously in composition. The necessary clarification would almost certainly require the addition of more words and complex syntax than a parenthetical expression tacked onto the end of the second leg of a long parallel structure could accommodate. At best "Rules of correctness in composition [were] the 'three unities' " is only an approximate answer to our quite justifiable question of "What was classical composition? " – which is the parallel of the previous question that elicited the first parenthetical additive modifier. The problem, in short, is that the second additive modifier could not be made strictly parallel with the first, and the author again settled for a compromise.

The most serious problem occurs in the eighth sentence. Here is the place where McNeill's skill at maintaining the unity of a diversified subject breaks down into inconsistency. As in the third sentence, the problem here can be traced to an over-reliance on a vague conjunction. We noted earlier that "while" is much too ubiquitous to specify a precise relationship in the presence of seeming inconsistency in the meanings of the two things joined. "While" can introduce both restrictive and non-restrictive elements, and thus the precise nature of the relationship must be obvious from interpreting the things conjoined. The first part of the sentence tells us unequivocally that only English literature remained fully independent of the classical tradition. The second part of the sentence tells us unequivocally that English literature shared in the classical norms of restraint, elegance, precision, and wit with writers such as Joseph Addison "or" (a rather unidiomatic conjunction where "and" seems to be called for) Alexander Pope. At best this is a paradox. But is the inconsistency merely in appearance? How is it possible to interpret "while" so as to leave English literature both fully independent of the classical tradition and sharing in the classical norms? To rephrase the question in grammatical terms: does "while" introduce restrictive or non-restrictive modification? The problem here is partly explained, as it was above, by the author's attempt to provide more cryptic information than the structure of his sentences can clearly handle. An additional sentence devoted to admitting and explaining this paradox might have been sufficient. But then again, it might not have been, for the simple reason that the first part of the sentence is probably much overstated. English literature would not be the only European literature that remained more or less independent of the classical tradition, and English literature remained only partly independent of the classical tradition.

The simplest way to solve the grammatical aspect of the problem would be to rewrite the sentence as a compound contrasting sentence: Only English literature remained fully independent, although it did share in the classical norms of . . . . The paradox still remains, however, and another sentence would still be required to explain it away. But at least we would have eliminated the great dangling restrictive modifier. We are obliged to call it restrictive because there is no way to interpret it as non-restrictive without rewriting the sentence to put the additive modifier next to its subject. The sentence would then have read: Only English literature, which did share in the classical norms of . . . , remained fully independent. Here again the grammatical problem would have been eliminated. But the semantic inconsistency would have become even more obvious than it was in the original, because the attribute would have been buried underneath a great layer of additive modification that had the opposite meaning.

The final problem to be noted is in the final sentence – a sentence that is something of a *tour de force* with its ten additive modifiers. The problem is not a serious structural one, resulting from an inability to keep these ten systematically coordinated. It is a minor problem resulting from a failure to envision the final, fully articulated, form of an additive modifier as it is joined to its subject. The two modifiers in question are "founder of Quakerism" and "the German jurist". Because George Fox is *the* founder of Quakerism, and Samuel Pufendorf is only *a* German jurist, we would have expected that the modifiers would have read "the founder of Quakerism" and "German jurist". But as the sentence stands, we have been obliged to provide the not quite authorized article for the Fox assertion and to retain the not quite explicable article for the Pufendorf assertion.

As compared, however, to the problems in E. K. Chambers' composition on Elizabethan liturgies, these blemishes are only devices for making McNeill seem human. The application of dialog to "Compromises in the Arts" proves the composition to be by and large a unified success. The application of dialog to Chambers' work proves it to be, if not an ununified failure, at least seriously flawed. The problem is not primarily in Chambers' sentence structure or in the information behind the prose; it is in the lack of a framework for the questions that elicit the individual assertions.

A study of the context of McNeill's nine sentences helped to substantiate the claim that his composition was a sustained, unified effort. But a study of the context of our excerpt from Chambers reveals his composition to be even less unified than the ten sentences appear to be. We might have decided that the analysis of McNeill's nine sentences revealed no very compelling reason for presenting them as two paragraphs rather than one. But this would have been a minor point as compared to what we are obliged to say about Chambers' non-paragraph. Ununified as these ten sentences are, they are much more unified than the *1200-word paragraph* of which they form the middle part. So, bearing in mind that the following composition looks more like a unified paragraph than in fact it is, let us turn to the great spectacles of Elizabeth's reign.

The great spectacles of [Elizabeth's] reign were liturgies, undertaken by her gallants, or by the nobles whose country houses she visited in the course of her annual progresses. The most famous of all, the "Princely Pleasures of Kenilworth" in 1575, was at the expense of Dudley, to whom the ancient royal castle had long been alienated. Gradually, no doubt, the financial stringency was relaxed. Camden notes a growing tendency toluxury about 1574; others trace the change to the coming of the Duke of Alençon in 1581. Elizabeth had found the way to evoke a national spirit, and at the same time to fill her coffers, by the encouragement of piratical enterprise, and the sumptuous entertainments prepared for the welcome of Monsieur were paid for out of the spoils brought back by Drake in the *Golden Hind*. The Alençon negotiations, whether seriously intended or not, represent Elizabeth's last dalliance with the idea of matrimony. They gave way to that historic pose of unapproachable virginity, whereby an elderly Cynthia, without complete loss of dignity, was enabled to the end to maintain a sentimental claim upon the attentions, and the purses, of her youthful servants. The strenuous years, which led up to the final triumph over the Armada in 1588, spared but little room for revels and for progresses. They left Elizabeth an old woman. But with the removal of the strain, the spirit of gaiety awoke.

The Elizabethan Stage
E. K. Chambers
Oxford, 1923, Vol. I, p. 5.

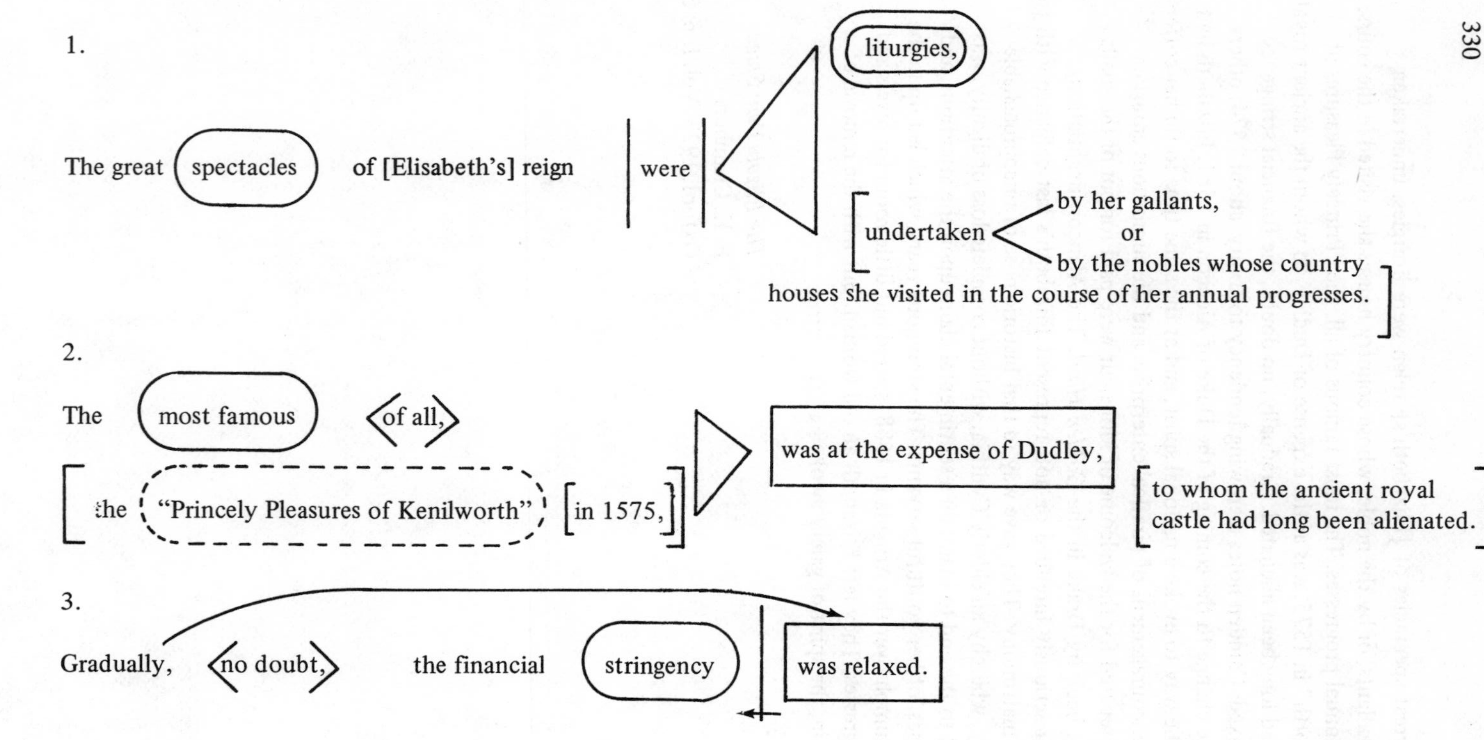
1.
The great
spectacles
of [Elisabeth's] reign
were
liturgies,
undertaken
by her gallants,
or
by the nobles whose country houses she visited in the course of her annual progresses.
2.
The
most famous
of all,
the
"Princely Pleasures of Kenilworth"
in 1575,
was at the expense of Dudley,
to whom the ancient royal castle had long been alienated.
3.
Gradually,
no doubt,
the financial
stringency
was relaxed.

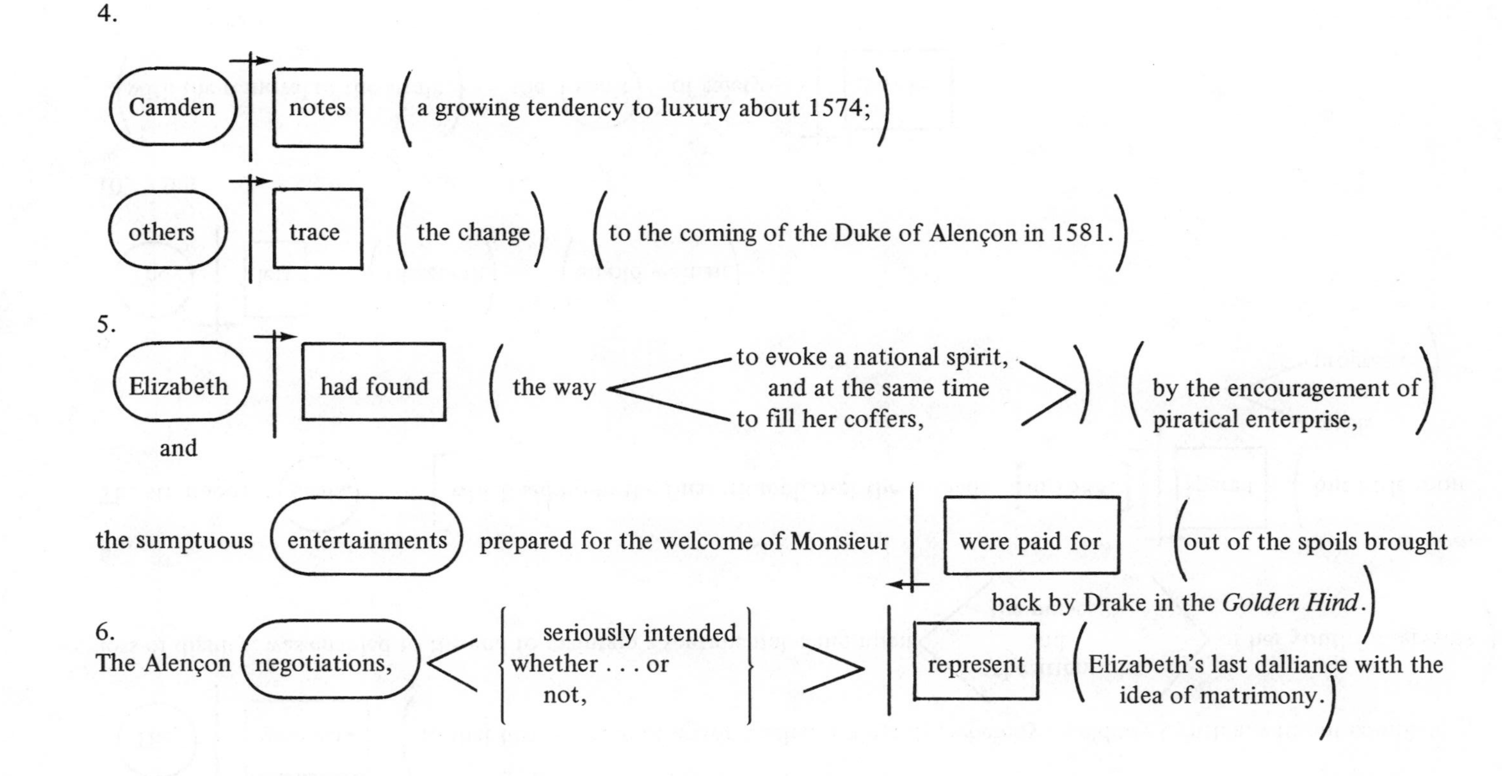
4.
Camden
notes
a growing tendency to luxury about 1574;
others
trace
the change
to the coming of the Duke of Alençon in 1581.
5.
Elizabeth
had found
the way
to evoke a national spirit,
and at the same time
to fill her coffers,
by the encouragement of
piratical enterprise,
and
the sumptuous
entertainments
prepared for the welcome of Monsieur
were paid for
out of the spoils brought
back by Drake in the Golden Hind.
6.
The Alençon
negotiations,
seriously intended
whether . . . or
not,
represent
Elizabeth's last dalliance with the
idea of matrimony.

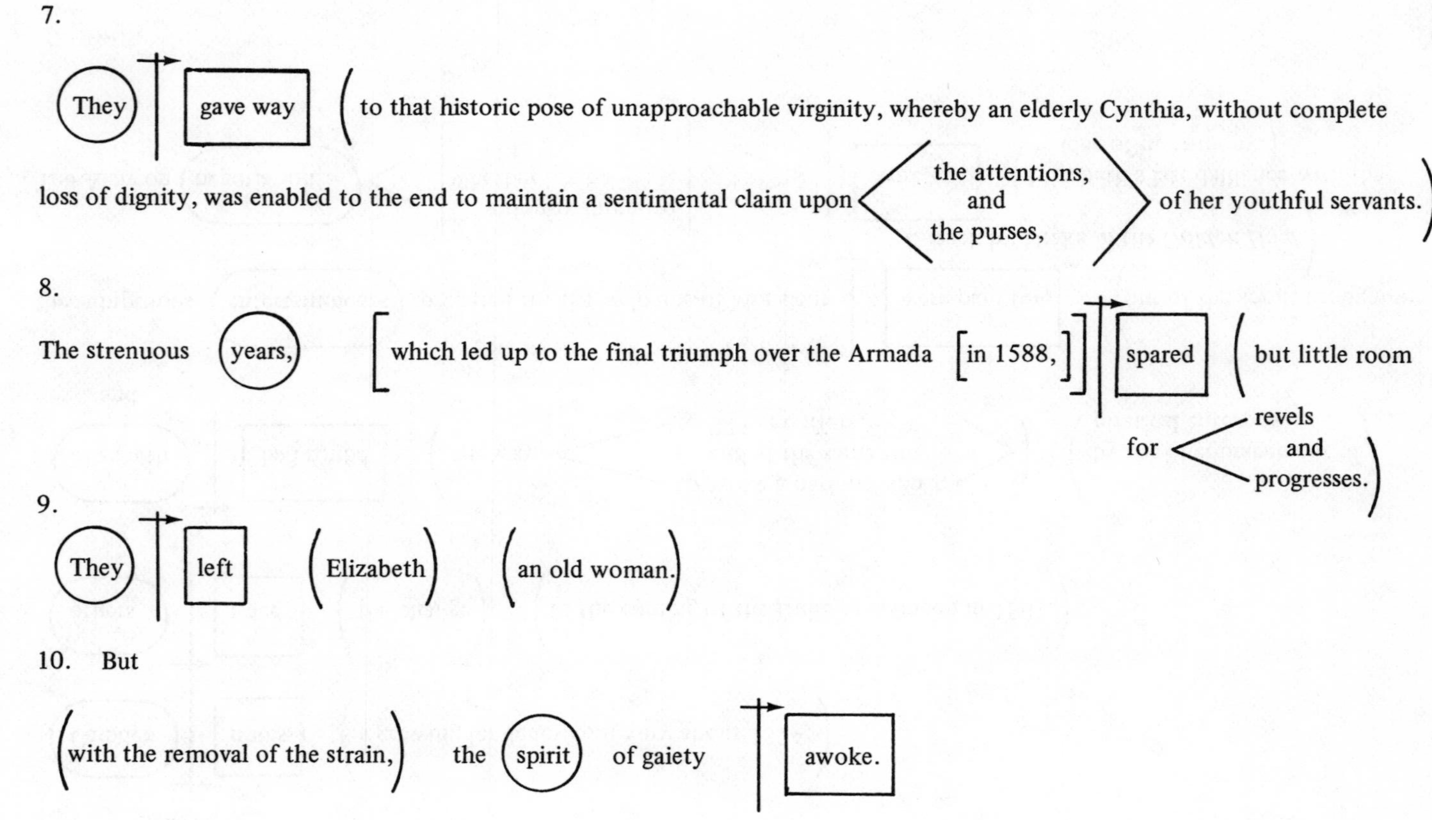
7.
They
gave way
to that historic pose of unapproachable virginity, whereby an elderly Cynthia, without complete
loss of dignity, was enabled to the end to maintain a sentimental claim upon
the attentions,
and
the purses,
of her youthful servants.
8.
The strenuous
years,
which led up to the final triumph over the Armada
in 1588,
spared
but little room
for
revels
and
progresses.
9.
They
left
Elizabeth
an old woman.
10. But
with the removal of the strain,
the
spirit
of gaiety
awoke.

1. The great spectacles of [Elizabeth's] reign were liturgies.

Who put on these liturgies?

Liturgies [were] undertaken by her gallants.

or

Liturgies [were] undertaken by the nobles whose country houses she visited in the course of her annual progresses.

2. *Can you give a specific example?*

The most famous of all was at the expense of Dudley.

What was the name of it?

The most famous of all [was] the "Princely Pleasures of Kenilworth".

What was the date of it?

The "Princely Pleasures of Kenilworth" [was] 1575.

What was Dudley's relation to Kenilworth?

The ancient royal castle had long been alienated to Dudley.

3. *Weren't these expenses heavy for such a small country?*

Gradually, no doubt, the financial stringency was relaxed.

4. *When did this relaxing begin?*

Camden notes a growing tendency to luxury about 1574.

Is this date generally accepted?

Others trace the change to the coming of the Duke of Alençon in 1581.

5 *What accounts for the financial significance of the Alençon date?*

Elizabeth had found the way to evoke a national spirit by the encouragement of piratical enterprise.

and at the same time

Elizabeth had found the way to fill her coffers by the encouragement of piratical enterprise.

and *But what do pirates have to do with Alençon?*

The sumptuous entertainments prepared for the welcome of Monsieur were paid for out of the spoils brought back by Drake in the *Golden Hind*.

6. *What was the purpose of this visit and these entertainments?*

The Alençon negotiations, whether seriously intended or not, represent Elizabeth's last dalliance with the idea of matrimony.

7. *Then what did she dally in?*

They gave way to that historic pose of unapproachable virginity, whereby an elderly Cynthia, without complete loss of dignity, was enabled to the end to maintain a sentimental claim upon the attentions of her youthful servants.

and *Was this just a case of vanity?*

They gave way to that historic pose of unapproachable virginity, whereby an elderly Cynthia, without complete loss of dignity, was enabled to the end to maintain a sentimental claim upon the purses of her youthful servants.

8. *Did the end of matrimonial negotiations mean the end of spectacles?*

The strenuous years spared but little room for revels.

and

The strenuous years spared but little room for progresses.

What were these strenuous years?

The strenuous years led up to the final triumph over the Armada.

When was the final triumph over the Armada?

The final triumph over the Armada [was] 1588.

9. *What was the effect of these years?*

They left Elizabeth an old woman.

10. But *What followed these years?*

With the removal of the strain, the spirit of gaiety awoke.

As the questions indicate, the problem here is to find a way to make something, like "the great spectacles of [Elizabeth's] reign", a unifying factor for these sentences. And the 1200-word paragraph as a whole is no more easily unified. The paragraph is the second one in the introductory chapter. Not only is the volume as a whole a prime example of information run rampant, the introductory paragraphs go the volume one better by attempting to summarize the entire period covered by the volume. The result is an almost complete breakdown in organization; each assertion can lead in a dozen different directions. The only framework provided for the 1200-word paragraph in question is the forty-five years of Elizabeth's reign. She ascends the throne in the second sentence and dies in the last sentence. Not only is the paragraph as a whole not confined to the subject of Elizabethan drama, the ten-sentence excerpt is not even confined to it.

Chambers had fewer problems with sentence structure and yielded less than McNeill did to the temptation to cram many assertions into single sentences. Indeed, as the statistics below indicate, Chambers was no more tempted by complex structure and cryptic additive modifiers than was the author of the "Smog" editorial:

McNeill	Smog	Chambers	
35.5	26.4	23.5	words per sentence
7.4	11.6	10.7	words per assertion
4.8	2.3	2.2	assertions per sentence

His basic problem is a lack of consistency in the questions that each assertion can be taken as answering. No prior theme of unity-and-diversity or problem-and-solution is operating here. A general subject like the reign of Elizabeth is not a theme or framework of dialog because it cannot guarantee consistent transitions from assertion to assertion. Thus, as we work our way through Chambers' composition, our emphasis will be on alternative questions that seem equally or more appropriate than the ones actually answered.

What questions most reasonably follow from the assertion that the great spectacles of Elizabeth's reign were liturgies? It is not unreasonable to ask "*Who put on these liturgies?* " But this is hardly the most obvious point of interest for an interlocutor. Very likely he would be confused about "liturgies", associating these with solemn church ceremonies rather than drama, theater, and spectacles. "What precisely are liturgies? " This question never does get answered and becomes increasingly perplexing as the composition goes on to speak of "sumptuous entertainments" and "revels". Less pressing than this question, but still more so than the one about who put on these liturgies, are questions like "Does this differ from other reigns? " and "What were the minor spectacles? " Unlike the question that is answered, these questions are elicited by specific elements in the assertion. It is never unreasonable to assume that restrictive modifiers are intended to offer specific contrasts. The reader could well assume that this assertion is leading into a contrast between the great spectacles and the minor spectacles or between Elizabeth's reign and the reigns before and after.

However, the implied question that is answered here results in the information that the liturgies were undertaken by her gallants *or* by the nobles whose country houses she visited in the course of her annual progresses. This two-part parallel answer, especially linked as it is by "or", seems to imply that there is a difference intended here. The most reasonable question would thus be "Was there a difference depending on which group did the undertaking? " However, nothing more of this distinction occurs in the composition. Instead we are provided with an answer to the question, "*Can you give a specific example?* " A request for an example is never out of order; the problem here is simply that the previous assertions seem to have been leading in other directions, specifically at this point in the direction of clarifying the nature and kinds of undertaking.

The next assertion, that the most famous of these great spectacles or liturgies was at the expense of Dudley, does, in addition to answering the question "*Can you give a specific example?* ", hint at an answer to a question about the nature and kinds of undertaking. Chambers seems to imply that "undertaken" means "paid for" or "at the expense of". Unfortunately, our knowledge of Elizabethan aristocratic spectacles – gained in large measure from Chambers' extensive scholarly efforts – indicates that much more was involved in undertaking a spectacle for the Queen than paying for it. Thus, we probably have to conclude that what the sentence seems to imply, Chambers did not intend. But certainly a reasonable question to follow the assertion about the expense of Dudley is "Does 'undertaken' mean just paid for? " Not unreasonable is an additional assertion providing, as a companion to the example of an undertaking, an example of the thing undertaken. We thus learn that the most famous of all was the "Princely Pleasures of Kenilworth". Yet here again we have to settle for related information instead of the most relevant transition. Wouldn't the interlocutor want to pursue the subject of great spectacles and liturgies? Wouldn't the most appropriate question to follow upon the specifying of the most famous liturgy be "What makes this a liturgy? " (considering the conspicuous occurrence of "pleasures" in the title) or "What accounts for this fame? " (considering the emphasis on "the most famous of all")? Not in Chambers' eyes. The questions he does answer are "*What was the date of it?* " and "*What was Dudley's relation to Kenilworth?* " The answer to the first – 1575 – is relevant enough, but in answer to the second we are provided with the quite gratuitous information that this royal castle had long been alienated to Dudley. So unprepared for is this assertion that the interlocutor would reasonably assume that the castle must have some important connection with the liturgy. He would thus ask "What was the relation of the castle to this liturgy? "

No answer is forthcoming because Chambers has moved on to a new sentence and a new subject. Picking up on the previous but unexplained use of "expense", Chambers now provides an answer to a rather forced question. "*Weren't these expenses heavy for such a small country?* " The question is forced because previous sentences have not been about heavy expenses for a small country. The question is thus much more the result of what follows it than of what precedes it. Admittedly, there is rarely a point in a composition where one and only one question is implied, and thus there is usually need to envision possible answers as a means of deciding on the question to ask. But the question ought clearly to arise out of what goes before or the composition loses its continuity. The third sentence ("Gradually, no doubt, the financial stringency was relaxed.") does not follow upon a discussion of a financial stringency. Thus, the most appropriate question to ask at this point is "What financial stringency was that? " A point introduced without preparation can always be at least partially redeemed by facing up to the lack of preparation and providing an explanation after the fact. But this is not Chamber's way. Instead he asks "*When did this relaxing begin?* " Admittedly, this does pick up on an element in the previous assertion, but even if we are to assume that no questions arise over the unexplained reference to financial stringency, we could still argue that more relevant than *when* the relaxing began is the question, "What caused this relaxing? " But like McNeill, Chambers is preoccupied with dates. If we know when events occurred, we have a solid narrative foundation for our composition. Like McNeill, Chambers unfolds his information in approximate chronological order; but unlike McNeill, he has no theme to aid him in deciding what few examples among the infinite number of occurrences within a given time span would be most cogently included. Not even the most detailed study outline of a subject is a miscellaneous collection of information.

Granted, however, that Chambers has a right to emphasize what he considers to be the important dates ("Camden notes a growing tendency to luxury about 1574."), we would reasonably expect the next question to be "What is the significance of this date? " But no such answer is forthcoming. (Nor, indeed, is it clear from the sentence alone whether 1574 is the date of the noting or the date of the growing tendency. We have diagramed the date as part of *what* Camden notes, but it might be another assertion modifier referring to *when* he did the noting.) The question that does seem to get asked ("*Is this date generally accepted?* ") is answered by a reference to what "others" think, and while this implies a contrast between Camden and these others, it is not pursued.

There can be little doubt that once reference has been made to the coming of the Duke of Alençon as a turning point in English history, the writer has an obligation to explain this new and quite unprepared for bit of information. Several questions spring to mind. "Who was the Duke of Alençon? " "Why did he come? " "Where did he come to? " "Where did he come from? " "Was 1581 his only visit? " But as usual, these are not the questions that spring to Chambers' mind. Instead, he asks "*What accounts for the financial significance of the Alençon date?* " The question, although not obviously primary, is still quite a reasonable one. But neither of the next two assertions seems to answer it: "Elizabeth had found the way to evoke a national spirit, and at the same time to fill her coffers, by the encouragement of piratical enterprise". The interlocutor must persevere: "*But what do pirates have to do with Alençon?* " "The sumptuous entertainments prepared for the welcome of Monsieur were paid for out of the spoils brought back by Drake in the *Golden Hind*."

Chambers' penchant for simply juxtaposing assertions raises not only problems of dialog but also problems of sentence diagraming. In this sentence, for example, "to evoke a national spirit" and "to fill her coffers" are obviously parallel, but the problem is to decide precisely what kind of parallel and precisely what the conjunction is. A somewhat similar problem, which we passed over without comment, occurs in the first sentence, with "liturgies" and "undertaken by her gallants or by the nobles whose country houses she visited in the course of her annual progresses."

In the first sentence we have diagramed the two legs as appositive parallel; this is consistent with the lack of conjunction and with the parenthetical punctuation. However, this construction is not entirely consistent with our description of appositive parallels as items referring to the same thing. The second leg of this parallel does not refer to a thing at all; rather it describes the first leg. The parallel assertions are thus of two different semantic kinds: the great spectacles were liturgies (subclass/class) and the great spectacles were undertaken (object/function). As long as it makes idiomatic sense to say that "liturgies [were] undertaken", then the minimum requirements have been met for an additive modifier and thus for an appositive parallel. But nothing of the usual appositive benefit has been gained here by repetitiously saying that liturgies were undertaken when this is also being said of their subclass, spectacles. Here is a rare instance of appositive parallel where the additive modification adds nothing to what the parallel structure does. And the explanation for this deficiency is that "undertaken . . . progresses" does not in any significant way follow from or clarify the classification of the great spectacles of Elizabeth's reign as liturgies.

In the fifth sentence there is more semantic rationale to the juxtaposing of the two legs; the confusion arises from juxtaposing "and" with "at the same time". "At the same time" can be considered part of the conjunction (as diagramed here); it can be considered part of the second assertion but not the first; it can be considered the sign of unitary parallel. Just as *while* is sometimes an assertion modifier answering the question "When? " and sometimes a conjunction (as in McNeill's second sentence), so *at the same time* can function in two ways. The problem with this sentence of Chambers' is that the relation of the two things in the parallel seems not so much a matter of time as of coextension; the encouragement of piratical enterprise was in and of itself both the evoking of a national spirit and the filling of her coffers. This is not, then, two different things happening at the same time but the same thing being interpreted in more than one way. Yet if this is what the sentence really means, why have we not diagramed "to evoke" and "to fill" as a unitary parallel? Probably because we are not entirely clear on what Chambers intends here and have chosen to compromise. Two clearly different things that happen to occur at the same time would constitute a separable parallel, and the "at the same time" would be an assertion modifier of the second assertion. Insofar as our diagram is a bit inconsistent, this reflects a bit of ambiguity in Chambers' meaning. We have kept the separable parallel; so to that extent, evoking and filling are interpreted as two different things that Elizabeth succeeded in doing. But we have interpreted "at the same time" as a second conjunction (analogous to "and furthermore") to reflect the emphasis that Chambers seems to place on the unified result of the piratical enterprise.

We still have not had Alençon's visit explained to us, but since Chambers insists on raising other points, let us follow where he leads. This reference to "sumptuous entertainments" cannot help but remind us that we are presumably still talking about liturgies and that we still have not been offered an explanation of them. It is thus reasonable to ask "Were these sumptuous entertainments liturgies? " As if sensing the growing impatience of his readers, Chambers does decide at this point to clear up one of the outstanding questions. To our confusion about Alençon and his visit, Chambers answers that the Alençon negotiations, whether seriously intended or not, represent Elizabeth's last dalliance with the idea of matrimony. This is not a bad beginning, but unfortunately it is also the end. "What was the outcome of these negotiations? " we want to know. No answer. "How could the negotiations have been serious and still have been a dalliance? " No answer.

Instead of continuing with Alençon and the entertainments for him, the questioning picks up on another new element – Elizabeth's dalliance. Having been informed that this was her last dalliance with the idea of matrimony, the interlocutor asks "*Then what did she dally in?* " The answer is that she adopted the pose of unapproachable virginity, whereby an elderly Cynthia, without complete loss of dignity, was enabled to maintain a sentimental claim upon the attentions of her youthful servants. This assertion elicits the question "*Was this just a case of vanity?* " And the answer is that she was also enabled to maintain a sentimental claim upon their purses. This sounds like no mean feat, and we would reasonably expect to hear something of how this was accomplished.

At this point, however, a digression in our analysis is in order. The difficulty of interpreting this sentence goes beyond the problems of dialog. We have been obliged to characterize the great bulk of the sentence as a restrictive modifier, yet the primary function of the major part of the "to" clause seems clearly to be the providing of additional information rather than the restricting of what has already been said. The whole clause is restrictive because the reference to "*that* historic pose" requires a completion of the relative clause begun with the pronoun "that". After all, we have only the author's prose to rely on; there must be a stated referent where there is no possibility of pointing to one. The assertion, "They gave way to that historic pose of unapproachable virginity", is not complete in itself. There must be either an antecedent for the pronoun to refer back to or a succeeding referent for it to introduce. In this case the second alternative is clearly operating. The question is, what possibilities are excluded by virtue of this restrictive modifier? And the answer is by no means clear. Indeed, it is also not clear what the evidently restrictive "historic" means and what it excludes.

Taking some liberty with the sentence, we might say that Chambers actually intends: They gave way to her pose of unapproachable virginity, one in which an elderly Cynthia, without complete loss of dignity, was enabled to the end to maintain a sentimental claim upon the attentions, and the purses, of her youthful servants. The three (instead of two) resulting assertions would then be:

They gave way to her pose of unapproachable virginity.

Her pose of unapproachable virginity [was] one in which an elderly Cynthia, without complete loss of dignity, was enabled to the end to maintain a sentimental claim upon the attentions of her youthful servants.

Her pose of unapproachable virginity [was] one in which an elderly Cynthia, without complete loss of dignity, was enabled to the end to maintain a sentimental claim upon the purses of her youthful servants.

Unless we can agree on some other historic pose that Elizabeth adopted and that would be included but for this restrictive modifier, we must conclude that Chambers has confused a non-restrictive modifier with a restrictive structure.

Returning now to the dialog, and to our desire to learn "How was she able to maintain this? ", we can only note that the questioning picks up instead on the subject of spectacles. "*Did the end of matrimonial negotiations mean the end of spectacles?* " The answer is, yes – but not for any reason connected with Alençon or the end of matrimonial negotiations. The reason is rather that the strenuous years spared but little room for revels and progresses.

And once again we are confronted with an entirely unprepared for new element. Chambers has certainly discerned the most appropriate question to follow these two assertions: "*What were these strenuous years?* " And his answer is clear enough: the strenuous years were those that led up to the final triumph over the Armada. (The further question eliciting the exact date – 1588 – is a relevant but minor addition.) The problem here is one of consistency. Cogent as the answer is in relation to the question that it answers and to the assertions that elicit the question, it seems quite out of keeping with the prior discussion of relaxation and luxury. The crucial question that arises at this point is "If at the beginning of the decade the financial stringency was relaxed and a tendency to luxury grew, how could the years that led up to 1588 be characterized as strenuous? " There is, of course, no answer to this. Instead, the interlocutor asks "*What was the effect of these years?* " And the answer, rather anticlimactically, tells us that they left Elizabeth an old woman. It does us no good to ask "How does her age affect the subject at hand? " All we are given is an answer to the question of "*What followed these years?* " Perhaps "With the removal of the strain, the spirit of gaiety awoke" provides us not only with an answer to this question, but also, if we are willing to interpret "the spirit of gaiety awoke" as referring to the revival of spectacles, a further answer to the earlier question about whether the spectacles came to an end. But this is at best a forced connection, because the earlier question is specifically about the relation of matrimonial negotiations to the fate of spectacles, and the final sentence informs us about the results of the end of the Armada, not about the results of the end of matrimonial negotiations. What precisely is meant by "the spirit of gaiety awoke" and how precisely this awakening relates to the end of matrimonial negotiations and to the defeat of the Armada, Chambers never says.

By way of conclusion let us return briefly to the explanation given by Barzun and Graff for the failure of Chambers' composition: "although the separate bits of information are all obviously there, the full meaning is not." On the basis of our analysis, we must have serious reservations about this explanation. In no useful sense can it be said of this passage that, chuck-full of information though it is, the separate bits of information are all obviously there. It is not true that *the* given amount of relevant information has been "thrown pell-mell at the reader." A generative rhetoric analysis of the passage demonstrates that much of the information present is irrelevant and that much relevant information is absent. The problem exemplified by Chambers' passage is more fundamental than how to present a given body of finite information. To say, with Barzun and Graff that the full meaning is not there is to miss the crucial point that no one knows what the full meaning would be. If Chambers had chosen to answer a more relevant question with his second assertion, then every step of the composition that followed after would have been significantly different. A semantic analysis can demonstrate what no formal analysis is capable of demonstrating – that every step of a sustained discourse is contingent upon prior contingencies.

Chambers has proven to be such a useful example for our purpose of exhibiting erratic dialog that we have almost certainly treated his composition to more uncompromising criticism than we treated McNeill's. But to admit a degree of unfairness to Chambers is not to retract any of our criticism of his organization. What we should do instead is to increase the rigor with which we analyze all compositions, our own and McNeill's included. Dialog as a tool of analysis makes possible a much more rigorous kind of semantic testing than has heretofore been possible. It is not objective, because it always involves matters of judgment, interpretation, and non-mathematically measurable degrees. But it can be systematic and consistent. It can make its judgments in the same terms as are understood by the actual users of the language. This cannot be done without some knowledge of the principles of semantic grammar, but such knowledge is no more important than the skill that only practice can bring.

NOTE

1 See p. 335 for the statistics.

APPENDIX

A. INFLECTION

CASE (OF PRONOUNS)

Person Number	Nominative	Objective	Possessive Adjective	Possessive Pronoun	
1st Singular	*I*	*me*	*my*	*mine*	
2nd Singular	you	you	your	yours	
3rd Singular	*he she* it	*him* her it	his her its	his *hers* its	
	M F N	*M F N*	*M F N*	*M F N*	*Gender*
1st Plural	*we*	*us*	*our*	*ours*	
2nd Plural	you	you	your	yours	
3rd Plural	*they*	*them*	*their*	*theirs*	

TENSE (OF "BE")

	Past	*Present*	*Future*	*Past Perfect*	*Present Perfect*	*Future Perfect*
1st Singular	was	*am*	will be	had been	have been	will have been
2nd Singular	were	are	will be	had been	have been	will have been
3rd Singular	was	*is*	will be	had been	*has been*	will have been
1st Plural	were	are	will be	had been	have been	will have been
2nd Plural	were	are	will be	had been	have been	will have been
3rd Plural	were	are	will be	had been	have been	will have been

Complicated though these two paradigms are, it is significant just how much of the inflectional rationale has been lost in these most inflected areas of English grammar. In the pronoun paradigm there are thirty-two slots but hardly thirty-two different forms. There are sixteen unique forms (italicized), and seven duplicate forms fill the other sixteen slots. Of the thirty-six slots in the "be" paradigm only three are filled by unique forms (italicized), and seven duplicate forms fill the other thirty-three slots. On the one hand, the traditional conception of inflections in English (represented in its least degenerate form by our two paradigms above) makes it easy to minimize inflectional considerations in a study of the grammatical foundations of rhetoric. Yet on the other hand, for a full grammar the concept of inflection can be expanded to include much more than the traditional categories of person, tense, gender, number, and case. A grammar of English can be written so as to include a significant discussion of inflections without attempting to convert English into Latin. For such an effort, see my *Introduction to Semantic Grammar*.

B. KEY TO THE DIAGRAMING SYMBOLS

Assertions

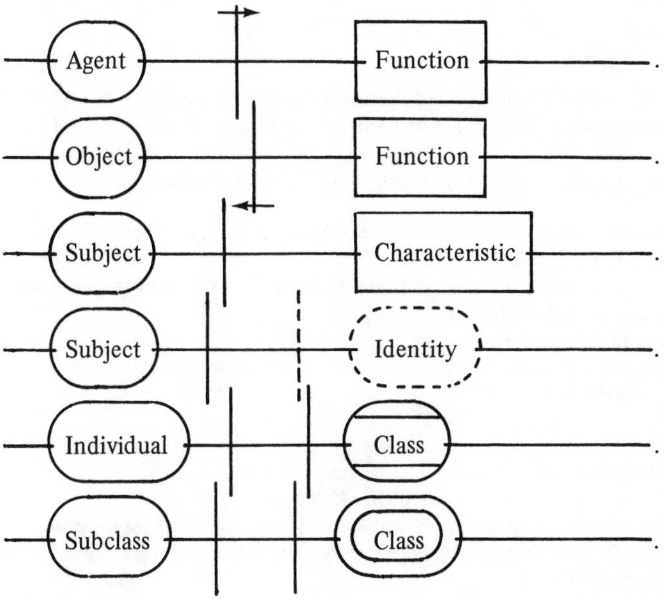

Agent — Function.

Object — Function.

Subject — Characteristic.

Subject — Identity.

Individual — Class.

Subclass — Class.

Modification

Restrictive Assertion

Additive

Redundant

Parallel Structure

Separable

Unitary

Appositive

Other Structure

Redundant Subject

Thing Function Attribute

Internal Compound

Displaced

Elliptical

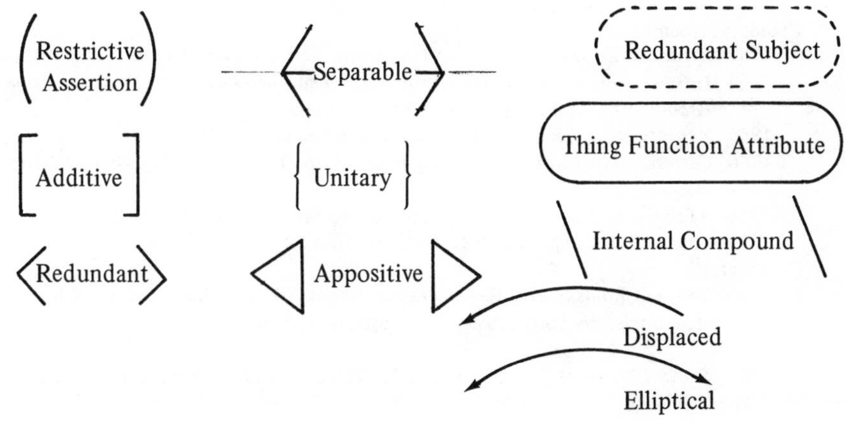

BIBLIOGRAPHY

Aarsleff, Hans

1970 "The History of Linguistics and Professor Chomsky", *Language* 46, 570-85.

1971 " 'Cartesian Linguistics': Fact or Fantasy? " *Language Sciences* 17, 1-12.

Algeo, John

1969 "Linguistics: Where Do We Go From Here? " *English Journal* 58, 102-12.

Alisjahbana, S. T.

1972 "Writing a Normative Grammar for Indonesian", *Language Sciences* 19, 11-14.

Arnauld, Antoine and Pierre Nicole

1964 *The Art of Thinking: Port Royal Logic*, tr. James Dickoff and Patricia James (Indianapolis: Bobbs-Merrill).

Bach, Emmon T. and Robert T. Harms, eds.

1968 *Universals in Linguistic Theory* (New York: Holt, Rinehart).

Barzun, Jacques and Henry L. Graff

1957 *The Modern Researcher* (New York: Harcourt Brace).

Bolinger, Dwight

1965 "The Atomization of Meaning", *Language* 41, 555-73.

Botha, Rudolf P. with the collaboration of Walter K. Winckler

1973 *The Justification of Linguistic Hypotheses: A Study of Nondemonstrative Inference in Transformational Grammar* (= *Janua Linguarum*, series maior 84) (The Hague: Mouton).

Chafe, Wallace L.

1970 *Meaning and the Structure of Language* (University of Chicago).

Chambers, E. K.

1923 *The Elizabethan Stage* Vol. I (Oxford: Clarendon).

Chomsky, Noam

1957 *Syntactic Structures* (= *Janua Linguarum*, series minor 4) (The Hague: Mouton).

1964 Introduction to *English Syntax: A Programed Introduction to Transformational Grammar* by Paul Roberts (New York: Harcourt Brace).

1965 *Aspects of the Theory of Syntax* (Cambridge, Mass. : MIT).

1966 *Cartesian Linguistics: A Chapter in the History of Rationalist Thought* (New York: Harper).

1966 "The Current Scene in Linguistics", *College English* 27, 587-95.

1972 *Language and Mind* 2d ed. (New York: Harper).

Collinder, B.

1970 "Noam Chomsky und die Generative Grammatik: Eine Kritische Betrachtung", *Acta Societatis Linguisticae Upsaliensis*, Nova Series 2: 1.

Coseriu, E.

1969 *Semantik, innere Sprachform und Tiefenstruktur* (Tübingen: Romanisches Seminar).

Danielsen, Niels
1973 "Plädoyer gegen die generativen Tiefenoperationen: Kritik einer Scheinlehre", *Archiv* 210, 241-62.
Derwing, Bruce L.
1973 *Transformational Grammar as a Theory of Language Acquisition: A Study in the Empirical, Conceptual and Methodological Foundations of Contemporary Linguistics* (Cambridge University).
Dik, Simon C.
1968 *Coordination: Its Implications for the Theory of General Linguistics* (Amsterdam: North-Holland).
Emery, Donald W.
1961 *Sentence Analysis* (New York: Holt, Rinehart).
Enkvist, Nils Erik
1971 "On the Place of Style in Some Linguistic Theories", *Literary Style: A Symposium*, ed. Seymour Chatman (London and New York: Oxford), 47-61.
Fillmore, Charles J.
1968 "The Case for Case", *Universals in Linguistic Theory*, ed. Bach and Harms, 1-88.
1971 "Types of Lexical Information", *Semantics*, ed. Steinberg and Jakobovits, 370-92.
Fillmore, Charles J. and D. Terence Langendoen, eds.
1971 *Studies in Linguistic Semantics* (New York: Holt, Rinehart).
Francis, W. Nelson
1954 "Revolution in Grammar", *Quarterly Journal of Speech* 40, 299-312.
1958 *The Structure of American English* (New York: Ronald).
Fries, Charles C.
1952 *The Structure of English: An Introduction to the Construction of English Sentences* (New York: Harcourt Brace).
1954 "Meaning and Linguistic Analysis", *Language* 30, 57-68.
Garvin, Paul L.
1970 "Moderation in Linguistic Theory", *Language Sciences* 9, 1-4.
Gleason, H. A. , Jr.
1965 *Linguistics and English Grammar* (New York: Holt, Rinehart).
Gleitman, Lila R.
1965 "Coordinating Conjunctions in English", *Language* 41, 260-93.
Grady, Michael
1967 "A Note on the Theory of the Primary IC Cut in English", *Glossa* 1, 68-74.
Gray, Bennison
1969 *Style: The Problem and Its Solution* (= *De Proprietatibus Litterarum*, series maior 3) (The Hague: Mouton).
1972 "The Problem of Meaning in Linguistic Philosophy", *Logique et analyse* 15, 609-29.
1973 "Stylistics: The End of a Tradition", *Journal of Aesthetics and Art Criticism* 31, 501-12.
1974 "Toward a Semi-Revolution in Grammar", *Language Sciences* 29, 1-12.
1975 "The Same Meaning with Different Forms", *Language Sciences* 38, 1-8.
1976 "Counter-Revolution in the Hierarchy", *Forum Linguisticum* 1, 38-50.
1977 "Semantic Taxonomy", *Lingua* [forthcoming].
1977 "From Discourse to Dialog", *Journal of Pragmatics* 1.

Greenberg, Joseph, ed.
1963 *Universals of Language* (Cambridge, Mass. : MIT).

Hall, Robert A. , Jr.
1969 "Some Recent Developments in American Linguistics", *Neuphilologische Mitteilungen* 70, 192-227.
1972 "Why a Structural Semantics is Impossible", *Language Sciences* 21, 1-6.

Halliday, M. A. K. , A. McIntosh, and P. D. Strevens
1964 *The Linguistic Sciences and Language Teaching* (London: Longmans).

Hammarström, Göran
1971 "The Problem of Nonsense Linguistics", *Acta Societatis Linguisticae Upsaliensis*, Nova Series 2: 4.
1973 "Generative Phonology: A Critical Appraisal", *Phonetica* 27, 157-84.
1976 *Linguistic Units and Items* (Berlin: Springer)

Harris, Roy
1973 *Synonomy and Linguistic Analysis* (University of Toronto).

Hasan, Ruqaiya
1968 *Grammatical Cohesion in Spoken and Written English I* (= Programme in Linguistics and English Teaching, Paper 7) (London: Longmans).

Hawkey, R. L.
1970 "A Critique of Certain Basic Theoretical Notions in Chomsky's Syntactic Structures", *Folia Linguistica* 4, 193-209.

Hill, Archibald A.
1966 *The Promises and Limitations of the Newest Type of Grammatical Analysis* (University of Cincinnati).

Hockett, Charles F.
1968 *The State of the Art* (= *Janua Linguarum*, series minor 73) (The Hague: Mouton).

Householder, Fred W.
1971 *Linguistic Speculations* (Cambridge University).

Jackendoff, Ray
1972 *Semantic Interpretation in Generative Grammar* (Cambridge, Mass. : MIT).

Jacobs, Roderick A. and P. S. Rosenbaum
1971 *Transformations, Style, and Meaning* (Waltham, Mass. : Xerox).

Karlsen, Rolf
1959 *Studies in the Connection of Clauses in Current English: Zero Ellipsis and Explicit Form* (Bergen: J. W. Eides).

Katz, J. J.
1967 "The Synonymy of Active and Passive", *Philosophical Review* 76, 476-91.

Katz, J. J. and J. Fodor
1963 "The Structure of a Semantic Theory", *Language* 39, 170-210.

Koerner, E. F. K. , ed.
1975 *The Transformational-Generative Paradigm and Modern Linguistic Theory* (Amsterdam: John Benjamins).

Labov, William
1969 "Contraction, Deletion, and Inherent Variability of the English Copula", *Language* 45, 715-62.
1970 "The Logic of Nonstandard English", *Report of the Twentieth Annual Round Table Meeting on Linguistics and Language Studies*, ed. James E. Alatis (Washington, D. C. : Georgetown University), 1-43.

1972 *Sociolinguistic Patterns* (Philadelphia: University of Pennsylvania).
Lakoff, George
1968 "Instrumental Adverbs and the Concept of Deep Structure", *Foundations of Language* 4, 4-29.
1970 *Irregularity in Syntax* (New York: Holt, Rinehart).
Lancelot, C. and A. Arnauld
1968 *A General and Rational Grammar*, tr. anon. (Menston, England: Scolar)
Langendoen, D. Terence
1969 *The Study of Syntax: The Generative-Transformational Approach to the Structure of American English* (New York: Holt, Rinehart).
1972 "The Problem of Grammaticality", *CEA Chap Book: Selected Papers from the 33d Annual Meeting of the College English Association*, 20-3.
Leech, G. N.
1969 *Towards a Semantic Description of English* (London: Longmans).
1974 *Semantics* (Harmondsworth, England: Penguin).
Lees, Robert B.
1963 "The Promise of Transformational Grammar", *English Journal* 52, 327-30, 345.
Lehrer, Adrienne
1971 "Semantics: An Overview", *The Linguistic Reporter* Supp. 27, 13-23.
Long, Ralph B.
1961 *The Sentence and Its Parts* (University of Chicago).
Long, Ralph B. and Dorothy R. Long
1971 *The System of English Grammar* (Glenview, Ill. : Scott Foresman).
Lyons, John
1968 *Introduction to Theoretical Linguistics* (Cambridge University).
1970 *Noam Chomsky* (New York: Viking).
Maclay, Howard
1971 "Overview" to "Part II: Linguistics", *Semantics*, ed. by Steinberg and Jakobovits, 157-82.
Makkai, Adam
1973 "A Pragmo-Ecological View of Linguistic Structure and Language Universals", *Language Sciences* 27, 9-22.
1974 " 'Take One' on *take*: Lexo-Ecology Illustrated", *Language Sciences* 31, 1-6.
Malmstrom, Jean and Constance Weaver
1973 *Transgrammar: English Structure, Style, and Dialects* (Glenview, Ill. : Scott Foresman).
Marckworth, Mary Lois
1972 Review of *Language and Rules* by Jon Wheatley, *Language Sciences* 20, 33-7.
McCawley, James D.
1968 "The Role of Semantics in a Grammar", *Universals in Linguistic Theory*, ed. Bach and Harms, 91-122.
1971 "Where Do Noun Phrases Come From? " *Semantics*, ed. Steinberg and Jakobovits, 217-31.
McNeill, William H.
1963 *The Rise of the West: A History of the Human Community* (University of Chicago).
Mehta, Ved
1971 *John Is Easy to Please: Encounters With the Written and the Spoken Word* (London: Secker and Warburg).

Nida, Eugene A.
1960 *A Synopsis of English Syntax* 2d ed. (= *Janua Linguarum*, series practica 19) (The Hague: Mouton).
1964 "Linguistic and Semantic Structure", *Studies in Languages and Linguistics in Honor of Charles C. Fries*, ed. Albert H. Marckwardt and Carol J. Kreidler et al. (Ann Arbor, Mich. : English Language Institute), 13-33.
Noss, Richard B.
1972 "The Ungrounded Transformer", *Language Sciences* 23, 8-14.
Pence, R. W. and D. W. Emery
1963 *A Grammar of Present-Day English* 2d ed. (New York: Macmillan).
Percival, K.
1972 "On the Non-existence of Cartesian Linguistics", *Cartesian Studies*, ed. R. J. Butler (Oxford: Basil Blackwell), 137-45.
Postal, P. M.
1964 *Constituent Structure: A Study of Contemporary Models of Syntactic Description* (Indiana University Publications in Folklore and Linguistics) (The Hague: Mouton).
Postman, N. and C. Weingartner
1966 *Linguistics: A Revolution in Teaching* (New York: Dell).
Ray, Punya Sloka
1961 "The Logic of Linguistics", *Methodos* 12, 239-254.
Reichling, Anton
1961 "Principles and Methods of Syntax: Cryptoanalytical Formalism", *Lingua* 10, 1-17.
Reichling, Anton and E. M. Uhlenbeck
1964 "Fundamentals of Syntax", *Proceedings of the Ninth International Congress of Linguists*, ed. H. Lunt (The Hague: Mouton), 166-71.
Robinson, Ian
1975 *The New Grammarians' Funeral: A Critique of Noam Chomsky's Linguistics* (Cambridge University).
Saussure, Ferdinand de
1960 *Cours de linguistique générale* 5th ed. (Paris: Payot).
Scott, Robert Ian
1972 *The Writer's Self-Starter* (Toronto: Collier-Macmillan).
Searle, John R.
1969 *Speech Acts: An Essay in the Philosophy of Language* (Cambridge University).
Sigurd, Bengt
1970 "The Phonemic Principle and Transformational Grammar", *Language Sciences* 11, 15-18.
Steinberg, Danny D. and Leon Jakobovits, eds.
1971 *Semantics: An Interdisciplinary Reader in Philosophy, Linguistics, and Psychology* (Cambridge University).
Stockwell, Robert, Paul Schachter, and Barbara Partee
1973 *The Major Syntactic Structures of English* (New York: Holt, Rinehart).
Teeter, K. V.
1964 "Descriptive Linguistics in America: Triviality vs. Irrelevance", *Word* 20, 197-206.
Thomas, Owen and Eugene R. Kintgen
1974 *Transformational Grammar and the Teacher of English: Theory and Practice*

(New York: Holt, Rinehart).
Uhlenbeck, E. M.
1973 *Critical Comments on Transformational-Generative Grammar 1962-1972* (The Hague: Smits).
Vallins, G. H.
1956 *The Pattern of English* (London: André Deutsch).
Weinreich, Uriel
1963 "On the Semantic Structure of Language", in *Universals of Language*, ed. by Greenberg, 114-71.
1966 "Explorations in Semantic Theory", in *Current Trends in Linguistics* Vol. III, ed. Thomas Sebeok (The Hague: Mouton), 395-477.
Yamada, Sae and Itsuko Igarashi
1967 "Co-ordination in Transformational Grammar", *Zeitschrift für Phonetik, Sprachwissenschaft und Kommunikationsforschung* 20, 143-56.
Yngve, V. H.
1969 "On Achieving Agreement in Linguistics", *Papers from the Fifth Regional Meeting of the Chicago Linguistic Society*, ed. R. I. Binnick, A. Davison, G. M. Green, and J. L. Morgan (University of Chicago), 445-62.
Ziff, Paul
1965 "What an Adequate Grammar Can't Do", *Foundations of Language* 1, 5-13.
1966 "The Nonsynonymy of Active and Passive Sentences", *Philosophical Review* 75, 226-32.

ADDENDA

Christensen, Francis
1967 *Notes Toward a New Rhetoric* (New York: Harper).
Gray, Bennison
Introduction to Semantic Grammar (The Hague: Mouton).
The Limits of Grammar: A Primer for Linguists (The Hague: Mouton).
1975 *The Phenomenon of Literature* (= *De Proprietatibus Litterarum*, series maior, 36) (The Hague: Mouton).
Green, Georgia M.
1974 *Semantics and Syntactic Regularity* (Bloomington: Indiana University Press).
Grimes, Joseph E.
1975 *The Thread of Discourse* (= *Janua Linguarum*, series minor, 207) (The Hague: Mouton).
Halliday, M. A. K. and Ruqaiya Hasan
1976 *Cohesion in English* (London: Longmans).
Harris, Zellig S.
1963 *Discourse Analysis Reprints* (= *Papers on Formal Linguistics*, 2) (The Hague: Mouton).
Keenan, Edward L.
1972 "On Semantically Based Grammar", *Linguistic Inquiry*.
Paillet, J.- P.
1972 "Some Aspects of a Semantic Taxonomy", *Cahiers Linguistiques d'Ottawa* 2, 39-55.

INDEX

additive modifiers (dependent & subordinate) 95, 109-14, 116, *123-35*, 184-8, 191, 198-9, 203, 206, 232-85, 324-8
adjective 52-6, 65-6, 345
adverb XII, 45-6, 54, 119-20, 140, 142, 146-50, 156, 248, 260, 274
ambiguity 131-3, 142-51, 185-9, 203-4, 233-4, 246, 325-7, 339-41
appositives 13-15, 104, *109-16*, 126-7, 194-5, 232-5, 257, 267, 278, 284, 338
articles (definite & indefinite) 87-8, 151-2, 233, 244, 328
assertion 4, 11-16, 17-91, 98, 123, 149-50, 324, 335
assertion modifier XII, 18, 23, 32-5, 44-9, 102-4, 118, 121, 123, 128, 140-2, *143-5*, 164-5, 179-80, 187, 202-4, 231-85
attribute XII, 7, 18, 20, 22, 26, 27, 33, 42, 53, 69-70, 101-2, 117-20, 123, 128, 146, 152, 154, 163

be 22, 30, 43, 115, 122, 125, *345-6*
become 30, 42-3, 77, 254-5, 273-4, 282, 285

case 71-2, 164-7, *345-6*
causal assertions 37-41, 203-5
causal implications 183-9, 199, 203-5, 250-75
command 7-8, 10, 12
comparison and contrast 23-4, 171-2, 178-81, 231, 278
compound or indivisible attribute core 54-69, 117, 119, 154, 235-6, 260, 268-9, 273-4, 278, 281-5
compound sentence
  internal 98, 198
  juxtaposed 13-15, 92-9, 185-8, 191, 197, 200, 202-6, 231-2, 248, 270, 273, 278, 280, 285
  participial 185-8
conditional modifiers 62-3, 138, *155-9*, 249, 254, 258, 281-2
conjunctions
  continue & contrast 112, 115, 192, *193-201*, 235-70, 278, 325, 327, 336, 338-9
  support & conclude 96-8, 192, *201-5*, 250, 256, 270, 282-3, 285
  subordinate 96-8, 201-5
cumulative sentence 142-51

demonstrative pronoun 75
diagraming
  rules & symbols 16*n*, 20-6, 30-3, 54-7, 95, 143-5, 152-4, 156-7, 163, 167*n*, 250, 260, 303, *347*
  of complex sentences
    "Smog" 278-85
    McNeill 314-19
    Chambers 330-2
dialogs
  Socratic 3-4, 14-16, 295-7
  frameless 287-9, 333-42
direct object XII, 23, 35, 44, 58-60, 140, 164-7
displaced or inverted structure 75, 116-20, 156, 161, 163, 231, 278
do 30, 64

elliptical structure 116, 120-1, 146, 148

gender 345-6
get 30, 42, 64-5

have 22, 27, 30, 55, 57, 61-4, 268, 270, 284-5
hermeneutics XII

immediate constituents XII, 133, 167
imperative 52, 62-5, 260
implication 11, 13, 25, 137, 155, *168-89*, 199-205, 207, 236-7, 239, 249

inclusive/exclusive modifiers 138, 159-62, 233, 237, 265-6, 268, 278-9, 285
indefinite pronoun subject 75-6
independent assertions (simple & complex) 92-3, *94-9*, 191
indirect object 23
infinitive 57, 265
inflectional languages XII-XIV, 17, 22, 30
inflections 22, 30, 71-2, 76, 106, 109, 121, 123, 163-7, 185, 188, 326, *345-6*
intra-assertional link (linking verb) 18, 20-2, 83, 119
lexicology XIV, 276
limiting modifiers 113-14, 116, 118, 131-3, *138-54*, 170-1, 174-8, 180, 182, 186-8, 231-85
literacy 3

modal auxiliaries 52, 55, 62-5, 156-7, 260
morphemes XVII, 5, 17-18

names 7, 132-3
negation 28-9, 50, 63, 109, 152-4, 160, 181, 250, 265, 268-9, 281, 284-5
non-restrictive modification 33, 93-4, 99, 109-14, 116, *122-37*, 151, 184-8, 232-85, 327
noun 7, 27, 55
number 22, 106-7, 167, 234, *345-6*
numerical characteristic 54, 65, 178-9

paradigms XIV, 30, *345-6*
paragraph diagrams
    "Smog" 303-9
    "Rejoinder" 310-11
    McNeill 320-3
    Chambers 333-4
paragraphing 17, *290-8*, 302-3, 328, 335
parallel
    separable 14-15, 92-4, *99-109*, 110, 112, 115, 147, 177, 184-5, 191, 197, 206, 231-85, 324, 326, 338
    unitary 73, *104-8*, 113, 116, 142, 146, 201, 206, 231-2, 240, 243-4, 247, 251, 264-6, 278-80, 282, 284
participle 53-7, 183-8, 198-9, 326
passive XVI, 34-5, 49
phenomenology XI
phonemes XVII, 5, 18
positional languages XIII-XIV, 17
post-positional modification 93, 114, 116, 123-7, 129-31, 175
pre-positional modification 13, 93, 114, 116, 128-29, 131, 175-8, 240-1, 246, 258, 279-80, 283
predicate XII, 6-7, 17-18, 20, 26, 174-5
preposition 54, 65-6, 117
punctuation 96-8, 106, 114, 116, 146, 197, 200, 208, 233-85

question
    explicit or rhetorical 8-16, 181-2, *205-8*, 222, 245, 280, 292
    implicit 11, 15-16, 23, 31, 34, 45-7, 58, 60, 69, 113, 121, *138-50*, 156, 164-5, 186-8, 202-5, *213-28*, 231-75, 298-301, 312, 320-3, 325-6, 335-42

redundant modifiers (emphatic, punctuational) *135-7*, 156, 159-60, 181, 194-7, 205, 235, 240-3, 253-4, 273, 278, 282, 285
redundant *there* & *it* subjects 74-6, 250, 281
Reed-Kellogg diagraming system XVII*n*
reflexive pronouns 137, 243, 273, 285
relative pronouns and clauses 123-7, 140, 164-5, 170-1, 233-4, 242, 251, 255, 260, 266-7, 279-80, 282, 284
restrictive modification 32-3, 63, 93-4, 113-14, 116, 118, 131-3, *138-67*, 170-1, 174-8, 180, 182, 186-8, 231-85, 327, 336, 340

semantic kinds
    agent-function 20-32, *34-44*, 45-8, 53, 56-65, 74-5, 77-8, 118-20, 129-30, 138, 142, 146, 150, 154, 156, 159-61, 164-5, 175-6, 179, 201-2, 258-60, 268, 271, 274-6, 278-9, 281-3, 285, 314-8, 331-2
    object/function 20-8, 34-5, 43, *44-50*, 60, 65, 130, 138, 159-62, 176, 274-6, 281-2, 330-1
    characteristic 20-8, 31, 33, 36, 40, 42-3, 45-50, *51-69*, 74-5, 78, 116-17, 120, 130, 138, 142, 147, 152, 154, 162-3, 170, 179, 198, 260, 274-6, 278, 280-5, 314-16, 318-19, 330-1
    identity 20-9, 33, 38-9, *69-77*, 130, 138, 162, 170-1, 265, 274-6, 282
    individual/class 20-9, 39, 52-3, 61, 77-80, *81-6*, 87-8, 119, 129-30, 139, 154, 179, 265, 269, 274-6, 278, 280, 284-5

subclass/class 20-9, 38, 40, 52, 57, 77-80, 85, *86-90*, 130, 139, 159, 265, 269, 274-6, 280, 330
sentence 4-16, 24, 324, 335
style XII, XV, 276
subject XII, 6-7, 17-18, 20, 27, 34-5, 42, 52, 57-8, 69-70, 99-100, 117-20, 123, 125-6, 128, 152, 154, 161-4

take 30
tense 22, 58, 61-3, *345-6*
thing function attribute 41-2
titles 293

transformational-generative grammar VIII-XVII, 5-6, 15, 18, 68-9, 163, 168, 176, 214, 271
transitive/intransitive 23, 34, 239

utterance 8-11

Venn diagrams 24, 25, 28-9, 79, 83, 85
verb 22, 7, 30-2, 41-2, 55-60, 106, 119-20, 142, 157, 166-7

word 5, 61, 67, 324, 335

TEXAS WOMAN'S UNIVERSITY LIBRARY